Roaring Texans

The History of North American T-6/SNJ/Harvard Closed Course Pylon Air Racing 1946–2023

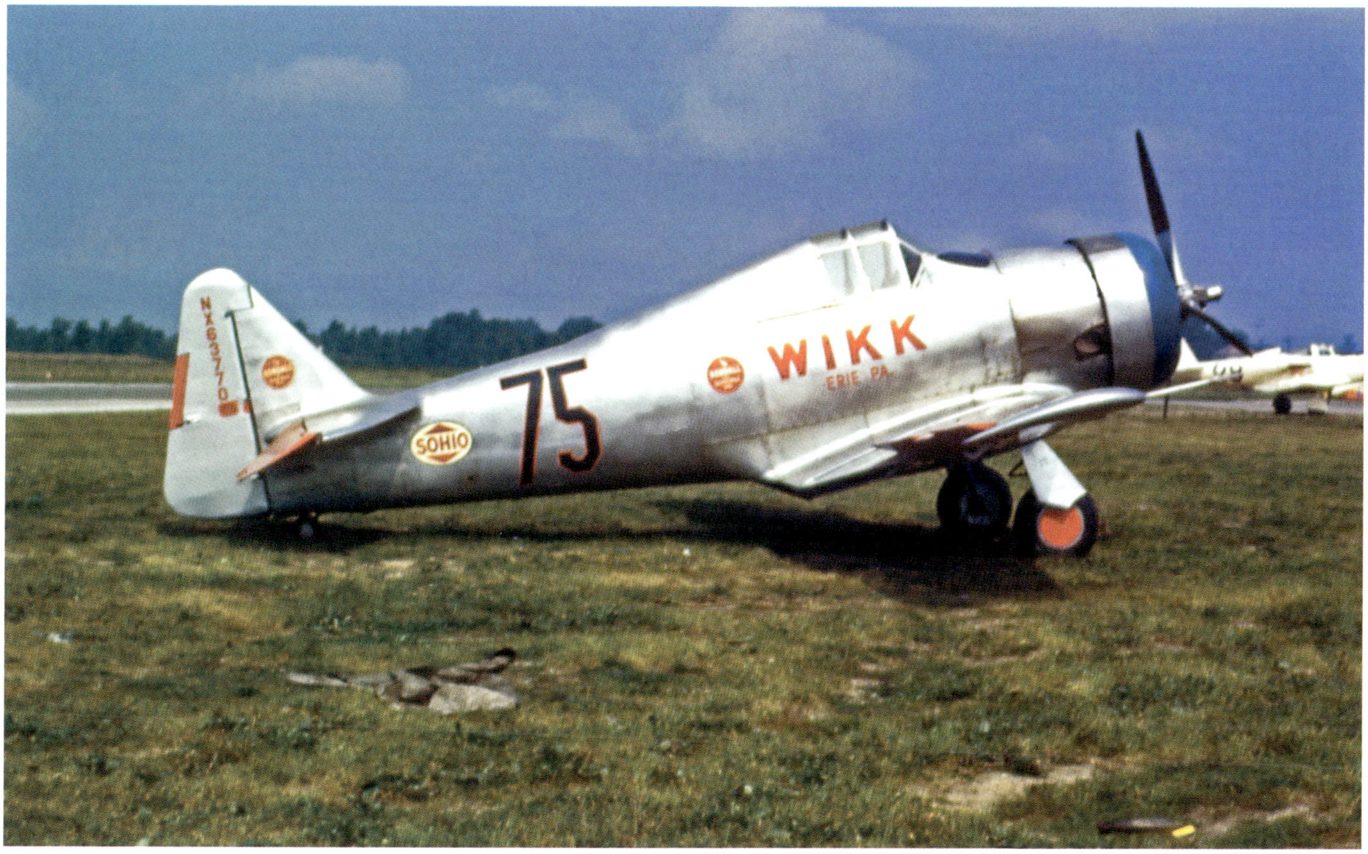

BOB KENNEDY

KEY Books

COVERS AND TITLE PAGE

Front cover image: #5 at Reno, Nevada (NV), in 2021. *Big Red* has raced in almost every event that has had Texan racing. (Kenneth Smith)

Title page image: Race #75 at Cleveland 1948. (via Tim Weinschenker)

Contents page image: (Mike Henniger)

Back cover image: A gaggle of Texans at the scatter pylon. (Jim Dunn)

Published by Key Books
An imprint of Key Publishing Ltd
PO Box 100
Stamford
Lincs PE9 1XQ

www.keypublishing.com

The rights of Bob Kennedy to be identified as the author of this book have been asserted in accordance with the Copyright, Designs and Patents Act 1988 Sections 77 and 78.

Copyright © Bob Kennedy, 2023

ISBN 978 1 80282 646 3

All rights reserved. Reproduction in whole or in part in any form whatsoever or by any means is strictly prohibited without the prior permission of the Publisher.

Cover design by Myriam Bell Designs

Typeset by SJmagic DESIGN SERVICES, India.

Dedication

This book is dedicated to some of the greatest aviation historians and photographers that ever lived. These seven men were my mentors, teachers, great oral libraries, and my friends. I had the good fortune to be a proud member of this prestigious West Coast clan. These men taught me everything I know about documenting and photographing aviation history. I was the last and youngest member to join the clan. They are William T. "Bill" Larkins, Emil Strasser, Al Hansen, Dustin "Dusty" Carter, Harry Gann, Russell Hiatt, and my closest friend Gerald "Jerry" Liang. Dan Hagedorn, who was not part of this group but should have been, also taught me a lot and is a great historian, and a true friend. The center of this group was William T. Larkins, who was a close friend for over 30 years. Bill and I discussed the idea of this book for years, but we never had time to do it. He loved North American's beautiful T-6 Texan as I do.

Acknowledgements

I would like to thank the following for their help, information, photographs, support, and words of encouragement:

Nick Veronico, Dan Hagedorn, Jim Dunn, Ron Olsen, Roger Cain, Mike Henniger, Geoffrey Goodall, Kenneth Smith, Ed Good, Doug Slowiak, Ed Maloney, Dennis and Tami Buehn, Nick Macy, Tom Dwelle, Jr., Eddie Van Fossen, Tim Weinschenker, Malcolm Gougon, the National Championship Air Races, the Ninety-Nines, the Women Airforce Service Pilots (WASP) Association, all of the pilots that raced, and my friend Jerry Liang. If I have failed to acknowledge anyone, I apologize. I attempted to ensure that all photographs are credited to the original photographer.

A very special thank you to my children, Courtney, Brian, and Jason, for putting up with their father's craziness all these years.

Contents

Introduction 6

Abbreviations 9

Chapter 1   A Brief History 10

Chapter 2   Something New, Air Racing 24

Chapter 3   Air Racing, A New Era 33

Chapter 4   Photo Gallery 141

Chapter 5   Accidents, Pace Planes, Pilots and Sponsors 344

Chapter 6   Tables 360

Further Reading 400

Introduction

Since the first air race was held in 1910, air racing has been a thrilling, dangerous, and noisy sport. The roar of raw horsepower, whether piston or jet, has a tremendous effect on those watching or participating. With the advancement of time and technology, the roar and speeds (48mph in 1910) have increased, as has the thrill of watching and participating.

Additionally, the danger has also increased. With the desire to produce more speed (156.5mph by 1920), more chances were taken with men and equipment. Every ounce of weight, every wire or thick wing decreases speed.

The two main ways of increasing speed are aerodynamics and horsepower. The first is reducing drag by lowering the profile of the aircraft, reducing the frontal area, finer wings cords, and cleaning up the fuselage by using flush riveting. The second is horsepower, using larger engines, in-line or round, thrust to weight ratios. Using all of this helped boost speeds to 201.9mph by 1930.

The Winner's Circle at the National Air Races (NAR), in Cleveland, Ohio (OH), September 1939. (via Emil Strasser Collection)

US Navy Curtiss F6C-6 BuNo. A-7144 raced at the 1929 NAR in the Free-For-All Race, during the period when the US military was allowed to compete, and racing speeds were starting to break 200mph. (via Emil Strasser Collection)

#77 Laird "Solution" NR10538 at 1931 NAR which won the 1930 Thompson Trophy Race and finished 3rd in 1931 with a speed of 211mph. (via Emil Strasser Collection)

Just before the start of World War Two, racing speeds were approaching 300mph. Engine manufacturers had refined their products by testing them on the racecourses. The results were more horsepower, speed, and reliability.

With war clouds approaching, most of the major aircraft manufacturers adopted some of the engineering and technology that produced the great racers of the 1920s and 1930s and applied it to the new fighters and bombers needed to fight a new kind of war, a global air war. To fly and fight with these new aircraft, the military needed pilots, navigators, bombardiers, and gunners. To produce these war fighters, the military needed training aircraft. Requests were made by both the United States Army Air Corps (USAAC) and US Navy (USN) for Primary (PT), Basic (BT) and Advanced (AT) training aircraft. Almost all of the major airframe manufacturers responded in all three categories.

Hawks-Miller HM-1 NR1313 at 1936 NAR had begun using retractable landing gear and, with the Pratt & Whitney (P&W) 1,150hp R-1830 Twin Wasp nine-cylinder engine, it would reach speeds around 380mph. (Emil Strasser)

#4 Marcoux-Bromberg R-3 **NX14215 racer at the 1939 NAR had 700hp P&W Twin Wasp Jr. engine and flew to 224mph. (via Emil Strasser Collection)**

Abbreviations

AAC	Army Air Corps	N/C	Non-Competing
AAC s/n	Army Air Corp serial number	NCAR	National Championship Air Races (Reno/Stead)
AAF	Army Air Force	NTSB	National Transportation Safety Board
AAHS	American Aviation Historical Society	P&W	Pratt & Whitney
AB	Air Base	PIC	Pilot In Command
A/C	Aircraft	PRPA	Professional Air Race Pilots Association
AF s/n	Air Force serial number	PRS	Pylon Racing Seminar (Training Program)
AGL	Above Ground Level	Prop	Propeller
ARM	Air Race Management (Mojave)	RAF	Royal Air Force
AT	Advanced Trainer	RARA	Reno Air Race Association
BC	Basic Combat Trainer (USAAC)	RCAF	Royal Canadian Air Force
BuNo.	US Navy Bureau of Aeronautics serial number	s/n	serial number
CAP	Civil Air Patrol	SNJ	Scout/Trainer/North American
CCF	Canadian Car and Foundry	TIC	Technical Inspection Committee (Engine and Airframe)
C/N	Construction Number		
CNARC	Cleveland National Air Race Committee	TT	Total Time (Engine or Airframe)
C/R	US Civilian Registration Number	QUL	Qualify
DBR	Damaged Beyond Repair (Written Off)	UNK	Unknown
DMG	Damaged (Repairable)	USARA	United States Air Racing Association
DEMO	Demonstration Race	USAAC	United States Army Air Corp
DNF	Did Not Finish	USAAF	United States Army Air Force
DNQ	Did Not Qualify	USAF	United States Air Force
DNR	Did Not Race	USAFB	United States Air Force Base
DNS	Did Not Start	USMC	United States Marine Corp
DQ	Disqualified	USN	United States Navy
ENT/LT	Entry List (does not mean A/C qualified or raced)	WAFS	Women's Auxiliary Ferrying Squadron
ENT	Entered	WASP	Women Airforce Service Pilots
FAA	Federal Aviation Administration	W/O	Written Off (Wrecked/Damaged Beyond Repair)
FAST	Formation And Safety Training		

Race Event Abbreviations

FE	Foreign Equipment	BL	Billings, Montana
GPH	Gallons Per Hour	CLV	Cleveland, Ohio
HP	Horsepower	CM	Cape May, New Jersey
HRV	Harvard (RAF/RCAF)	CY	Casper, Wyoming
MCAS	Marine Corp Air Station	FTL	Fort Lauderdale, Florida
MFG s/n	Manufacturer's serial number	GR	Graham, Texas
Mi/DT	Miles and Distance in Statute Miles	JK	Jacksonville, Florida
Mil s/n	Military serial number (as used by AAC, USAF, USN, RCAF, RAF)	LN	Lincoln, California
Mil/Spec	Military Specifications	MI	Miami, Florida
MINS	Minutes: Seconds: Tenths	MV	Mojave, California
Mk	Mark (Series Sequence)	PR	Paso Robles, California
Mn/Spec	Manufacturer's Specifications	PX	Phoenix, Arizona
MPH	Miles Per Hour	RD	Redmond, Oregon
NAA	North American Aviation	R	Reno/Stead, Nevada
NAC	Noorduyn Aircraft of Canada	RW	Richland, Washington
NAF	Naval Air Field	STL	St. Louis, Missouri
NAR	National Air Races	TU	Tunica, Mississippi
NARA	National Air Racing Association	WD	Wendover, Utah
NAS	Naval Air Station	WL	Wilson, North Carolina

Chapter 1
A Brief History

One of the aircraft manufacturers responding to that request was North American Aviation (NAA) of Southern California, which built the NA-16 (NAA design number 16) prototype in a bid for an AAC trainer contract. The prototype was constructed of wood, metal, and fabric, with room for a student and an instructor in an open tandem cockpit. It had a fixed gear and was powered by a 400hp Wright R-975 engine. The first flight was made on April 1, 1935. After minor changes, the most notable of which was enclosing the cockpit, NAA built 42 aircraft as the BT-9 (Basic Trainer-9) for the AAC and 40 as the NJ-1 for USN, (N for trainer, J for NAA and 1 for the first aircraft from NAA) with a 500hp Pratt & Whitney (P&W) R-1340 engine.

The granddad of the North American Texan, this BT-9 had a 500hp R-1340. Note the fixed gear, fabric-covered tube fuselage, enclosed canopy, and wide rudder. Bakersfield, California (CA), 1936. (Russ Hiatt)

Next stage in the development of the Texan: a BC-1 aac, s/n. 37-636. Note the retractable landing gear and large round antenna between gear. It is fabric covered. Bakersfield, 1938. It was damaged (DMG) in August 1943. (Russ Hiatt)

The NA-16/BT-9/NJ-1/BC-1s were the granddaddies of what would become the greatest series of training aircraft built, the NAA AT-6/SNJ/Harvard. The AAC designation of "AT-6" is for Advanced Trainer number six, the USN designation "SNJ" is for Scout/Trainer/NAA, as the USN envisioned using the aircraft in the dual role of scouting and training. Great Britain, Canada and the Commonwealth allies call their aircraft Harvards. However, the name and designation that the world has come to know these aircraft as is the Texan.

A star at last – the new AT-6. This one is s/n. 40-2143 at Akron, OH. The design would remain the same throughout production. (Emil Strasser)

US Navy SNJ-3 BuNo. 6906 from a training unit passing through Bakersfield en route to a storage yard in 1946. It would be sold to the civil market and registered as NC62689. (William T. Larkins)

Designed by NAA engineering team of Dutch Kindelberger, Harold Raynor, and John Atwood, the AT-6/SNJ series of training aircraft would be used by most of the US's allies during the World War Two and postwar periods. Under several US Military Assistance Programs/Mutual Defense Assistance Programs (MAPs/MDAPs), Texans were supplied postwar to many US-friendly nations.

Spain, Italy, Japan, Germany, South Africa, Great Britain, Portugal, and most Latin American countries received Texans, either through direct support or on the open surplus market. Canada continued to use its indigenous-built Harvards into the 1960s.

By the time AT-6/AT-6As and SNJ-1/-2s began rolling off the line in Inglewood, California (CA)(with the suffix of -NA), they had retractable landing gear, metal fuselages and a refined wing design. Later changes included swivel gun mounts in the rear cockpit, a .30-gun fuselage on top of the cowling and wing mounted .30-gun, light bomb racks, tail hooks for carrier-landing training, camera mounts, and some models had prop spinners.

The AAC would also buy over 280 NA-26 BC-1 (Basic Combat) trainers, which were similar to the SNJ-1s. With the production of the NA-88 models, Texans had become identical, AT-6A/SNJ-3, AT-6C/SNJ-4, AT-6D/SNJ-5, and Harvard IIA and III. The standard engine was the Pratt & Whitney R-1340-A-1 with a two-bladed Hamilton Standard propeller. NAA production ended with the NA-121 model (AT-6F/SNJ-5/-6) in 1945. NAA produced the majority of the Texans at its Dallas, Texas (TX), facility (with the suffix -NT).

Noorduyn Aircraft of Montreal, Canada, built Harvard Is, IIAs/Bs, and IIIs (along with NAA Dallas), while Canadian Car & Foundry (CCF) built new Harvard IVs at Fort Williams beginning in 1951, some of which were ordered by the United States Air Force (USAF) as T-6Js for foreign military sales. An estimated 3,000 Harvards/Texans were built in Canada. Harvards were supplied to most of the Commonwealth nations, including India, Australia, New Zealand, South Africa, Rhodesia, and Kenya. South Africa used its Texans until 1995.

A civil registered Royal Canadian Air Force (RCAF) Yale I, s/n. 3406. The predecessor of the Harvard, N3406 is just one of the many Yales that were sold postwar. April 1983. (Bill Slate)

Royal Air Force (RAF) Harvard II s/n. AJ583 was on the Canadian civil registry as C-FHWX. May 1990. (William "Bill" Jesse)

Postwar-marked RCAF Harvard IV s/n. 20213 was on the Canadian civil registry as C-FUUU. April 1989. (William "Bill" Jesse)

According to the NAA Contracts and Proposals Report "O" Airframe Contract Record, as of July 27, 1956, some 13,680 Texans of all models were built. NAA also produced the NA-168, NA-182, NA-186, NA-188, NA-195, and NA-197 beginning in 1949. These were complete remanufactures of earlier models into new T-6G (the "A" for "Advance" had been dropped when the AAC became the USAF in 1947), with upgraded systems, the back-folding rear canopy was replaced by a fixed blown unit and steerable tail wheels. The aircraft were given new construction numbers (c/n) and new military serial numbers (AF s/n).

Around 1,800 were remanufactured. This took place at NAA plants located in Downey, CA (-NI), Long Beach, CA (-NA), Fresno, CA (-NF), and Columbus, Ohio (OH) (-NH). Some Texans were repurchased from the civilian market for this program. It is worth noting this same report lists a USN contract (NoA) number for the construction of 240 NA-198/SNJ-8, however the column for "Customer Serial Numbers" states "Contract Terminated in its Entirety." The USN did remanufacture some older model SNJs into an "SNJ-7" at its overhaul and rework facilities.

In this book, the term T-6 and Texan will refer to all models of AT-6s, SNJs and Harvards, unless there is a specific need to identify a particular aircraft, then the exact nomenclature will be used.

A T-6G in Michigan Air National Guard 171st Fighter Bomber Squadron (FBS) markings. AF s/n. 52-8227 went to the French Air Force for service in Algeria. (Robert O'Dell Collection)

Surplus Navy SNJ-6 BuNo. 112137 from Naval Air Reserve Station (NARS) Dallas, Texas (TX), at Long Beach, CA, in 1963. It became N2859G. (Emil Strasser)

Postwar

Military use of Texans continued postwar, both for training and war fighting. They were used in both wars for and against independence, coups, border disputes, and bush wars. Postwar conflicts where Texans were used include the Korean War (US), Algeria (France), Indochina (France), Angola (Portugal), Congo (Belgium), Biafra (Nigeria), Sahara (Spain), Kenya (Great Britain), Malaysia (Great Britain), Israel, and all through Latin America and Africa into the 1970s.

The US military held a large number of newer models in reserve. Some were for spare parts and others for foreign military sales. There were also groups of older models offered for sale to the public. Historian William T. Larkins recorded that on January 1, 1946, the AAC listed 890 AT-6 aircraft for public sale starting at US$850, while the Navy listed none. By 1948, the Navy held around 300 SNJ types at Naval Air Field (NAF) Litchfield Park in Arizona (AZ) from the postwar drawdown.

Fresh from the storage yard is T-6G AF s/n. 49-3307 with national ensign painted out and new registration number in tail. N3307 is flying today. (William T. Larkins)

T-6G AF s/n. 49-3158 N444RB is in a typical civil paint scheme of red/white and black at Madera, CA, 1980. This Texan is currently racing as #73 *Miss Humbolt Hunny* N158JZ. (Bob Kennedy)

Civil Life

The first wave of civilian Texans began with the sale of early models postwar. By 1947, Larkins recorded the following types on the US Civil Registry (USCR): three AT-6s, 367 AT-6As, 104 AT-6Bs, 62 AT-6Cs, 20 SNJ-2s, 82 SNJ-3s, and 132 SNJ-4s. The second wave of civilian sales began in the mid-1950s as newer training types, such as the NAA T-28 and Beech T-34, entered the service. Both the USAF and USN had phased the Texan out of service by the end of 1958. A third wave of sales got underway in the 1970–80s when large numbers of former foreign military Texans came back to the US from Spain, Portugal, Japan, Italy, Latin America, and South Africa during the rise of the warbird movement.

Surplus Texans found many uses. SNJ-4 BuNo. 26912 was converted into a single-seat crop duster/sprayer. N9522C was at Rantoul, Kansas (KS), in 1983. It has been fully restored and is flying today as N16JG. (via Aviation Photo Services)

RCAF Harvard IV s/n. 20232 N2048 is one of 11 Harvards that were converted to resemble Japanese Zeros for the movie *Tora! Tora! Tora!* It is not currently registered. (Bob Kennedy)

A Brief History

It should not be forgotten that the US Civil Air Patrol (CAP) used Texans into the mid-1960s. This offered younger pilots their first exposure to this fabulous aircraft. As many as 500 Texans are flying worldwide today thanks in part to those that have flown them, loved them, and taken great care in keeping them flying.

When the Texans retired, the US military began looking for a replacement and it was agreed that tail-dragger aircraft were out and that tri-cycled gear was needed to match the newer jet fighters entering service. Several designs were produced, with the NAA T-28 and Beech T-34 selected. The current advance trainers are built by Beechcraft and named Texan II. Perhaps one day they will race in closed course pylon racing.

Civil Air Patrol squadrons used surplus Texans for search and rescue flights. SNJ-5 BuNo. 51903 is seen at Bakersfield in the late 1950s as N3605. It is flying today as N51903. (Russ Hiatt)

When the US Air Force (USAF) was looking for a tricycle-equipped trainer, the Bacon Corporation hoped to get a contract to remanufacture the large amounts of surplus Texans. The result was a one-off Super T-6 N66J aac, s/n. 44-82028. The USAF declined the project, and the sole example has been passed around for years but is not currently registered. Mojave, CA, 1982. (Bob Kennedy)

New Beech T-6A Texan II AF s/n. 06-3826 of 12 Flying Training Wing (FTW) is at the former Williams Air Force Base (AFB), Arizona (AZ), in 2010. Williams was the site of the 1994 Phoenix Air Races. Perhaps one day we will see the newer Texans racing around the pylons. (Jarrod Wilkening)

Beech T-6B Texan II (read SNJ) BuNo. 166064 in Navy training yellow markings to commemorate the 100th anniversary of US Naval Aviation. The plane was assigned to Training Air Wing Five (TAW-5) when seen at Naval Air Station (NAS) North Island in 2011. (Gerald "Jerry" Liang)

RCAF CT-156 Harvard II 156118 of the NATO Flying Training in Canada (NFTC), proving the respected heritage of the Harvard and Texan names for these new aircraft. Randolph AFB, TX, was home to hundreds of Texans during World War Two. (Keith Snyder)

Type Specifications, Dimensions, Engine

The contemporary control panel today with minor differences from the factory standard aircraft. This is N6427D at Race #8. (Max Haynes)

Above: Installation of a P&W R-1340-AN-1 engine and Hamilton-Standard prop. (Max Haynes)

Left: Side view of P&W R-1340-AN-1 engine. Rugged, dependable, easy to work on and fast when tuned right. (Max Haynes)

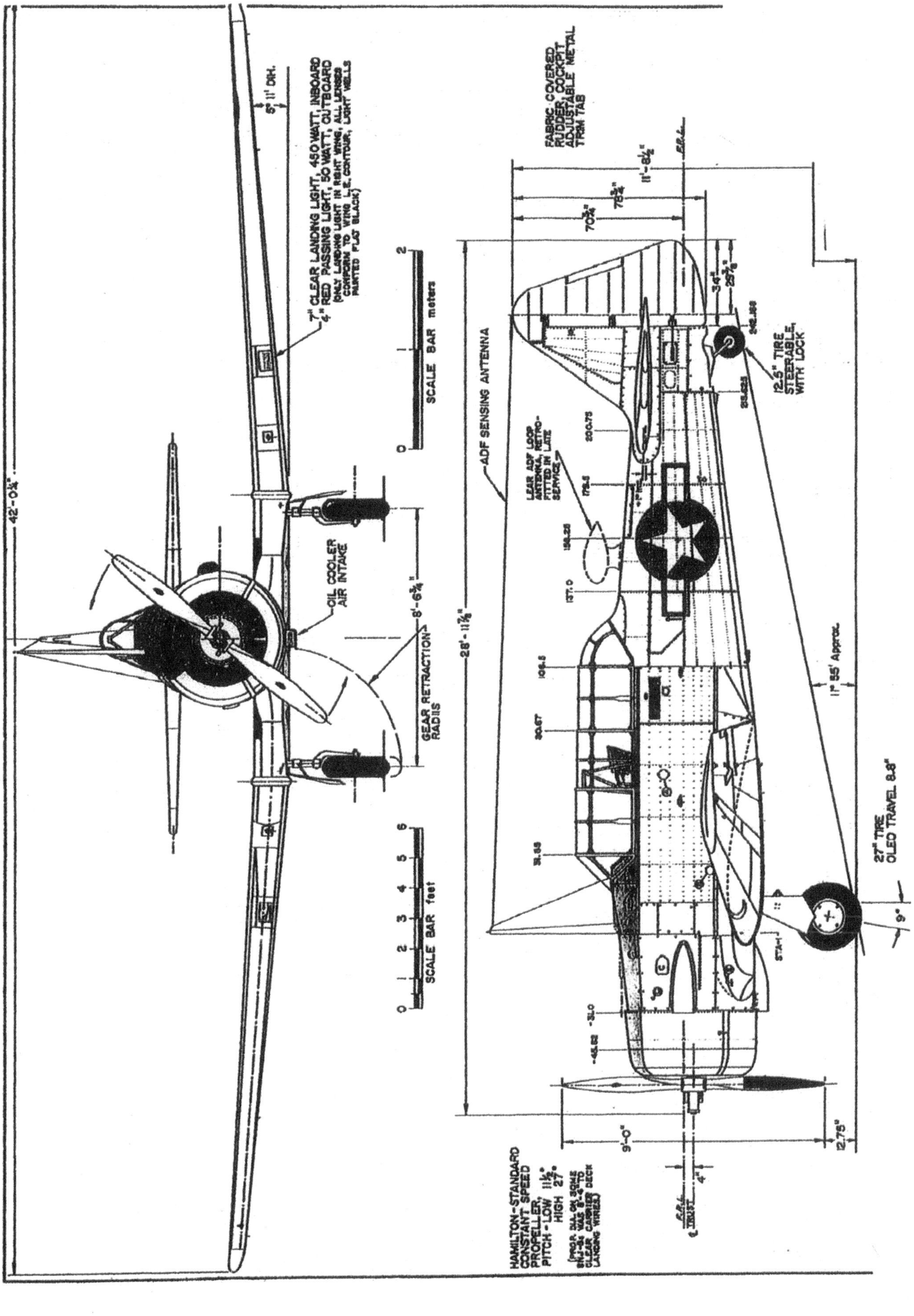

Side view drawing of North American Texan. (Dusty Carter)

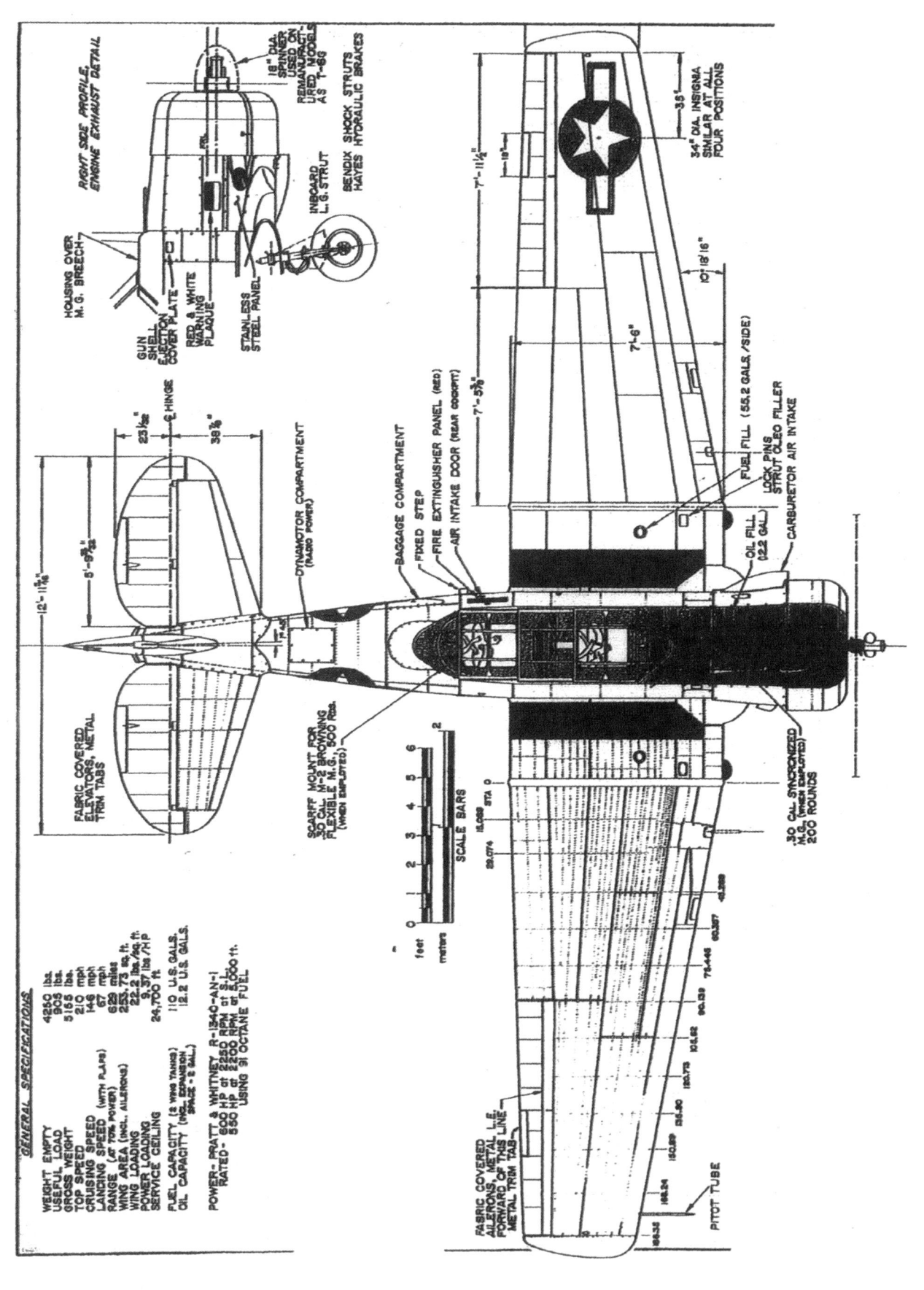

Top view drawing of North American Texan. (Dusty Carter)

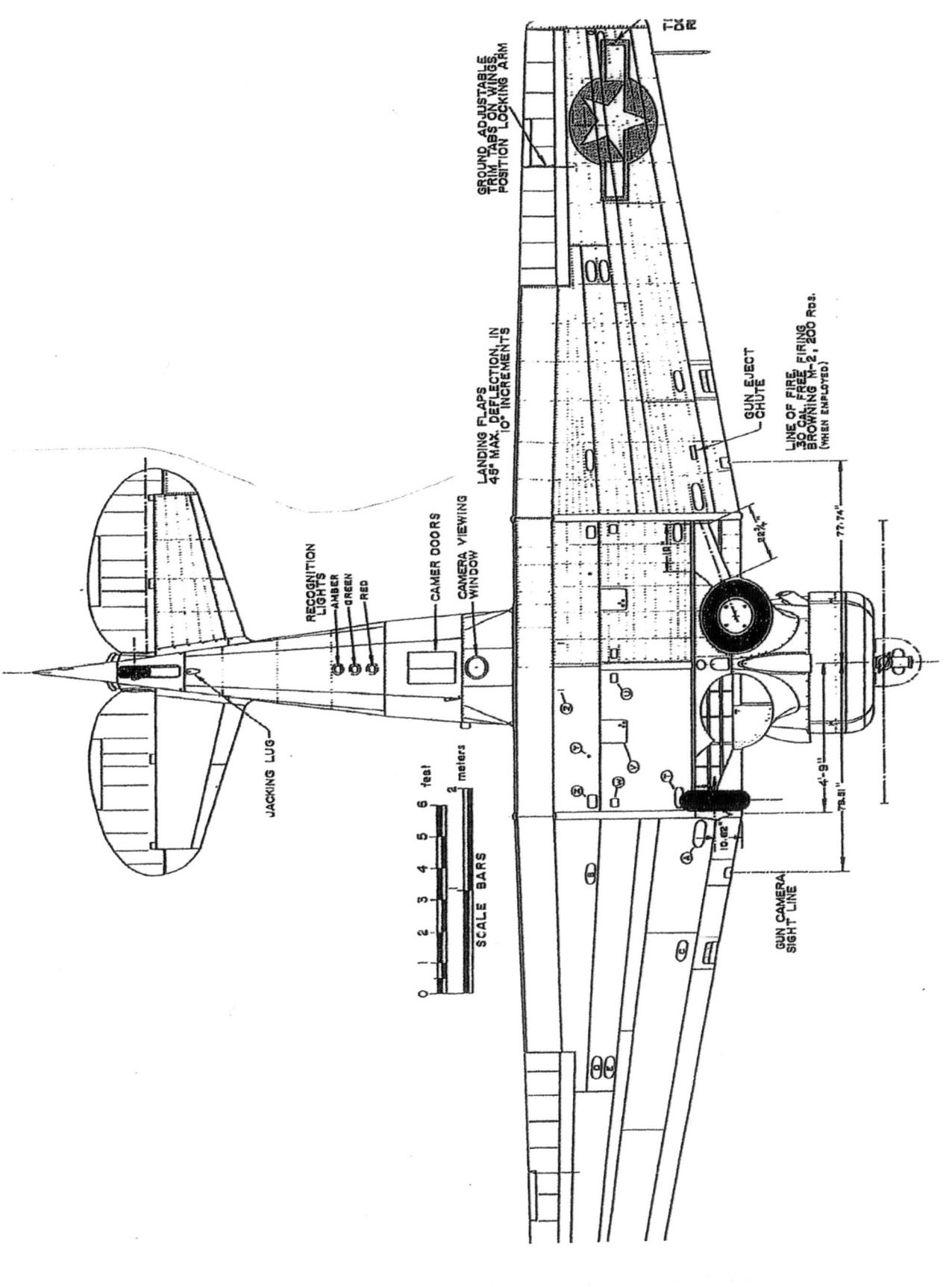

Underside view drawing of North American Texan. (Dusty Carter)

Chapter 2
Something New, Air Racing

Closed course pylon air racing returned postwar in 1946 at Cleveland, OH, and the American public loved it. Gone were the Lairds, Turners, and Crosby racers of the 1930s. They were replaced by Mustangs, Corsairs, Cobras, and Lightnings. All were military surplus fighters that produced dramatic increases in horsepower, speed, noise, and danger. Some attending the revived air races for the first time saw the fighter aircraft that had won the war. Former military service pilots were eager for the excitement, thrill, and money that air racing offered. Many pilots would race the same types of aircraft they had flown in combat.

Women had been participating in cross-country racing events since the 1920s, but not in closed course pylon events. This would change in 1946 when the Cleveland National Air Race Committee (CNARC) introduced a new class of pylon racers. This new class would be open only to women and utilized the NAA AT-6/SNJ series of aircraft. Since newer Texan models were still being used by the US military, the aircraft raced at Cleveland were early model AT-6/A/Bs and SNJ-2/-3s, plus one AT-6D and the only XAT-6E built. The XAT-6E was a one-off NAA-built Texan powered by a 575hp Ranger V-770-9 engine (compared to the 550hp R-1340-AN-1). Several other civil Texans were reengined with Rangers and one was raced at Cleveland. Performance differences between the two engines were not significant enough to warrant further production or conversions.

#63 Lockheed F-5G aac s/n. 44-53045 N21765 raced by Jane Page (Hlavacek) in the 1947 Bendix cross-country race from Van Nuys, CA, to Cleveland. She was one of two women who raced that year. Page had starting position one and finished ninth overall at 08:15.06 hours. Page made it in time to Cleveland to race in the Halle Trophy Race, where she finished fourth. There had been another pilot on standby to race if she did not arrive in time. (via Roger Besecker Collection)

In 1946, the women flew a one-lap qualifying lap and a five-lap final race, on a 15-mile racecourse (total of 75 miles) with slightly modified Texans in the Halle Trophy Race. The trophy was sponsored by the local Cleveland Halle Brothers department store. Race starts would be a racehorse standing start, like the Unlimited Class racers. The Texan was a stable aircraft to fly, and it was felt that women pilots could safely compete in closed course racing. The race program said this would be a race of "skill and beauty."

Flying straight and level or shooting touch-and-go landings is one thing, but racing is a bit different. "For closed course pylon racing, you fly about a hundred feet above the ground, there is turbulence from wind and heat, the other aircraft next to you or above you. You're monitoring your aircraft by listening to sounds of the engine, looking for your pylon turn point, keeping the other aircraft in sight, adjusting power settings and just plain charging ahead," said 1946 race entrant Ruth Johnson.

The women who raced were all experienced and qualified pilots. Some had backgrounds as flight instructors with the Civilian Pilot Training (CPT) programs and later with the War Training Service (WTS). Some had been Women Airforce Service Pilots (WASP) and had flown with the Women's Auxiliary Ferrying Squadron (WAFS), all with hundreds of flying hours. In a few cases, female pilots had more flight hours than the men racing the big fighters around the pylons. All entrants had to have at least 500 hours of flight time. Additionally, it was stated that "the National Air Races assumes no responsibility or liability in case of accident or damage to any participating pilot, mechanic, official, employee or airplane."

Race pilots had to pay their own expenses ("the NAR assume no responsibility and will not pay the hotel, transportation, storage, gas, and mechanical or living expenses of any contesting pilot, visiting pilot, passenger or airplane") and a $75 entry fee. Aviation gas (AVGAS) cost $0.27 per gallon in 1946, with a stock Texan burning an average of 30 gallons per hour (gph) at cruise and 50gph at high settings. An estimate of fuel/oil cost with engine runs, test flights, qualifying and main race, plus fuel to fly to and from the races, would be about $90.

Fuel for all the race classes was supplied by the Standard Oil Company of Ohio (SOHIO) with oil supplied by the Kendall Refining Company (Kendall), both major sponsors of the National Air Races (NAR). Both companies had races named after them.

The Races

There were five aircraft entered in the main 1946 Cleveland race with a $5,000 total purse. The total number of aircraft that applied for the 1946 races is not recorded nor are the qualifying times.

When the flag dropped for the racehorse start, the five were off quickly and headed for the first pylon of the five-lap, 75-mile race. They were #72 Dorothy (Dot) Lemon (professional pilot), #35 Arlene Davis (professional pilot/aerobatics), #54 Jane Page (working for a flying service), #41 Ruth Johnson (flight instructor), and #81 Marge Hurlburt (former schoolteacher/flight instructor).

#81 Hurlburt and #54 Page battled for first place all the way to the finish line. #41 Johnson and #35 Davis were in the middle, while #72 Lemon trailed them. As they finished lap 5, #81 Hurlburt was ahead. Confusion set in as #54 Page started another lap with Hurlburt right behind while the other three pulled up and out. Page was ahead at lap 6 completion and appeared to be the winner, but after landing the judges deemed it was lap 5 that mattered and Hurlburt was declared the winner. "The pylon turns count in a race like ours and that Hurlburt girl turns pylons," said Page.

Cover of the official program for the first postwar NAR at Cleveland in 1946, which featured the first running of the Halle Trophy Race. (Emil Strasser Collection)

Open air maintenance at Cleveland on #54 Betty Clark, likely before the start of the races in 1947. Since most of these racing aircraft had been modified to single-seaters, they had little use between race events and were usually parked at airports. Note sponsors and name. (via Nicholas A. Veronico Collection)

"I had the inside spot," replied Hurlburt. "If Jane had had my place, she'd have come in first." She continued, "Gosh, I was scared! I thought the sixth lap was the fifth, I saw Jane shoot ahead, and I was sure I'd miscounted."

"I flew that sixth lap just to be sure, I wasn't taking any chances," said Page. When Page was asked if she was sorry for not taking first place, she replied, "Not me. I'm pretty happy."

#81 Hurlburt had flown the 75 miles in 22:26.04mins with a speed of 200.588mph. She collected $2,500 for first place. Page was second with 22:28.89mins at 200.462mph and received $1,000. #75 Johnson won third with a time of 22:56mins at 196.221mph and earned $750. Fourth was #35 Davis with 23:33.89mins at 191.196mph and a win of $500. #72 Lemon finished fifth at 23:41mins flying 190.007mph and received $250.

When asked if she was disappointed in her finish, Ruth Johnson replied, "Sure I'm disappointed. But it was a good race." To which her husband added, "You did alright, your plane just didn't have the guts."

It was noted that when Hurlburt[1] went to the announcer's stand to receive the Halle Trophy and roses "she wore a grey dress with red trim and sandals." Page wore a khaki shirt, pants and "her lipstick was fresh."

It had been a great race and the start of a new class of air racing.

A dozen "Lady Birds" entered in the 1947 Halle Trophy Race, with a $5,000 total purse. The Halle Race was run as part of the opening program on the first day of the races. Only eight qualified to race. #61 Margrete McGrath was fastest at 223.3mph, flying the one-off Ranger-powered XAT-6E. Second was #75 Ruth Johnson at 215.1mph. Third was #44 Grace Harris at 213.4mph. Fourth was #54 Betty Clark at 212.9mph, flying one of only two turbocharged Texans conversions. Fifth was #42 Edna Gardner Whyte at 211.1mph. Sixth was #83 Jane Page at 210.7mph. Seventh was #65 Anna Logan at 206.4mph, and eighth was #49 Dori Marland in a Ranger-powered conversion. #23 Dot Lemon, #36 Bella Heineman, and #96 Jean Doherty did not qualify. #35 Arlene Davis was listed as first alternate to replace Jane Page[2] (who was racing in the Bendix race), if she was not able to start in the Halle Race.

---

1 Marge Hurlburt would unfortunately race only one time at Cleveland as she was fatally injured in an aerobatic T-6 accident in Iowa before the 1947 races.

2 Jane Page would finish ninth in the Bendix flying a Lockheed F-5G Lightning.

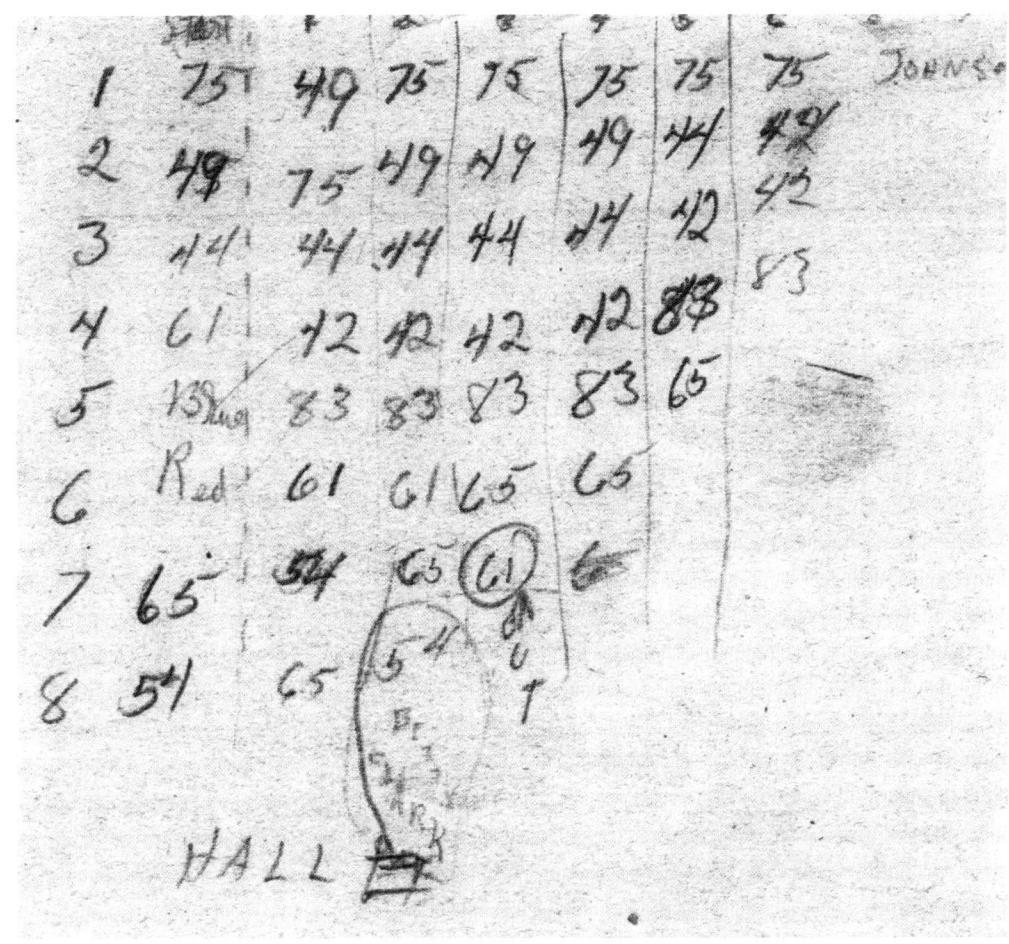

Ben Franklin's handwritten lap count for the 1947 Halle Trophy Race at Cleveland. Shows eight starters and their positions for each lap and #75 Ruth Johnson leading from lap 2 to the finish. (via Tim Weinschenker)

From the start, it was a Johnson and Marland fight, with Marland ahead by lap 2. They were followed by Harris, Whyte, Page, McGrath, and Logan. Clark was the first to drop out with a sour engine. Lap 3 saw Johnson take the lead from Marland and McGrath also dropping out with a sour engine. Johnson would stay out front until the end as Marland was forced out on lap 5 with engine problems and was listed as a did not finish (DNF). Marland had failed to switch fuel tanks and damaged her aircraft on landing but was unhurt.

#75 Ruth Johnson took first place in 20.09.19mins for the 75 miles at 223.290mph and won $2,500. #44 Grace Harris was second in 20.55.09mins and 215.090mph and received $1,000. #42 Edna Whyte[3] came third at 21.20.90mins and 210.789mph and earned $750. #83 Jane Page came in fourth and received $500 with a finish of 21.29.67mins at 209.356mph. #65 Anna Logan managed fifth in 24.05mins at 186.95mph and collected $250. It would seem Ruth Johnson's Texan had the guts this time.

Changes for the 1948 race began with a new sponsor and a change in the race name. Now sponsored by Kendall Oil Company, the five-lap race was called the Women's Kendall Trophy Race, so as not to confuse it with the previous men's race. Purse money was raised to $5,500 with rules changed to limiting airframe modifications (no clipped wings) and no more than 1,350 cubic inch engines. Kendall was proud to sponsor "these Ladies of the Air" and, as before, only the top eight qualifiers would race in the main event.

Contestants were #31 Kaddy Landry[4] in her first Cleveland race; #44 Grace Harris, #49 Betty Clark, flying the rebuilt Ranger-powered aircraft that Dori Marland had damaged in 1947, #65 Anna Logan, #23 Dot Lemon, #75 Ruth Johnson, #83 Nancy Corrigan; and #91 Helen McBride. It was both Corrigan's and McBride's first race. Jane Page was entered in the Bendix with a YP-47M, but did not start (DNS) and missed the Kendall race.

---

3 Edna Whyte would race again at Cleveland in 1968 and at Reno in 1968 in the Women's Stock Plane races.

4 Kaddy Landry had taken first place at the Miami, Florida (FL), races earlier in the year. She had placed second behind Marge Hurlburt at these same races in 1947. Miami was one of the many air events around the country that held air races during the postwar years for several classes of racers.

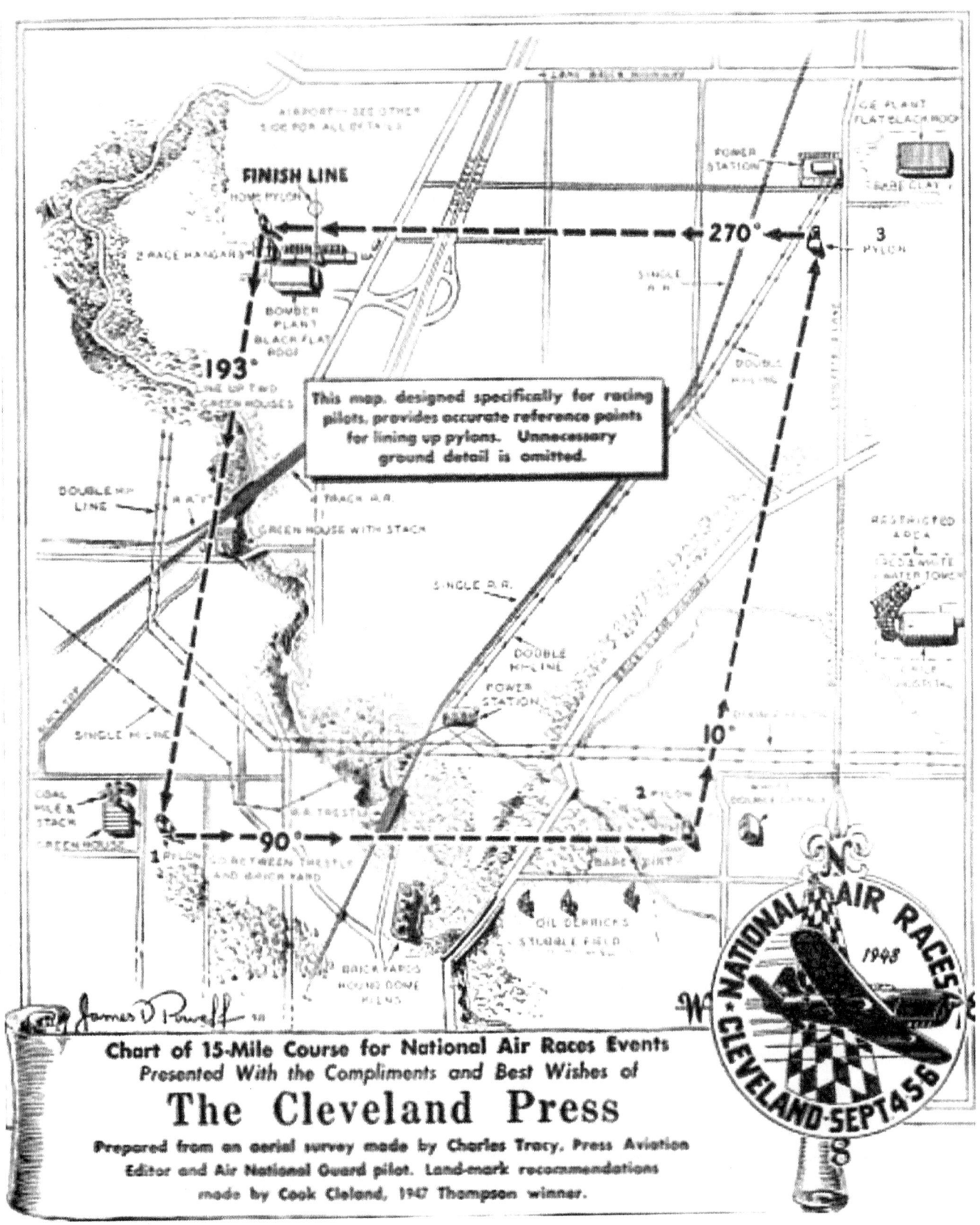

Map of the 1948 racecourse. Note that "Land-mark recommendations made by Cook Cleland, 1947 Thompson winner." (Emil Strasser Collection)

After holding back on the start with a balky engine, Harris jumped into the lead at the start pylon. It was almost a walkway race for Harris as there was little challenge, except for Landry who hung on from lap 3. Things became exciting when Clark and Corrigan scraped planes rounding pylon 3 as Clark passed under Corrigan. As quoted in the official press release "both girls saw their danger simultaneously, however, and veered off in opposite directions as Clark's plane shot toward the underside of Corrigan's."

#44 Grace Harris took first place at 234.9mph and $2,250. She flew one lap at 238.221mph and received an extra $500 for fastest lap and a silver tea set. Harris finished nine miles ahead of #31 Kaddy Landry, who finished in second place at 218.756mph and won $1,250. Following close behind in third was #23 Dot Lemon at 218.6mph, receiving $750. Fourth and $500 went to #49 Betty Clark at 215.5mph. "Irish Beauty" #83 Nancy Corrigan took fifth at 214.2mph and won $250.

```
(Subject to             1948 National Air Races
changes).
                        DAILY PROGRAM OF EVENTS

                             Sunday - Sept. 5


11:30 A.M.    KIM SCRIBNER - National Glider Aerobatics Champion.
              EXHIBITION - Civil Air Patrol.
11:50 A.M.    SOHIO BAND - The Standard Oil Company of Ohio.
12:00 NOON    BETTY SKELTON - Women's National Aerobatics Champion -
              The Steel Improvement & Forge Co.
12:10 P.M.    GOODYEAR TROPHY RACE - 1st heat semi-finals - 2 mile
              course - 10 laps.
12:30 P.M.    THRASHER TWIN ERCOUPE EXHIBITION - Nationwide Food
              Service, Inc.
12:40 P.M.    BEVO HOWARD - Aerobatics - flying a Buecker-
              Jungmeister - The Ohio Oil Company.
12:50 P.M.    SOHIO BAND - Demonstration of Fulton Airphibian.
 1:00 P.M.    OFFICIAL INAUGURAL CEREMONY - Aerial Salute to Star
              Spangled Banner - Parachute Jump by Dave Binns -
              The Standard Oil Company of Ohio.
 1:15 P.M.    ROYAL CANADIAN AIR FORCE - "Vampire" Jet Duo.
 1:25 P.M.    JIMMY GRANERE - Comedy Aerobatics.
 1:35 P.M.    DEMONSTRATION OF NAVY AND MARINE FLYING MIGHT.
 2:05 P.M.    WOODY EDMONDSON - National Aerobatics Champion -
              The Standard Oil Company of Ohio.
 2:15 P.M.    KENDALL TROPHY RACE for women pilots only - 75 miles -
              5 laps - 15 mile course.
 2:45 P.M.    INTERMISSION - SOHIO BAND - The Standard Oil Company
              of Ohio.
 3:00 P.M.    PRESENTATION - Kendall Trophy Race Winners.
 3:05 P.M.    ARRIVAL AND PRESENTATION - Allison Trophy Event Winners.
 3:10 P.M.    MARCEL DORET - International Aerobatics Champion.
              FRED NICOLE - French Aerobatic Star.
 3:30 P.M.    GOODYEAR TROPHY RACE - 2nd heat semi-finals - 2 mile
              course - 10 laps.
 3:50 P.M.    BENDIX AUTOMATIC PILOT DEMONSTRATION.
 4:00 P.M.    U. S. AIR FORCE - Flight Demonstrations.
 4:30 P.M.    DEMONSTRATION BY 155th FIGHTER SQUADRON - Tennessee
              Air Guard - The American Steel & Wire Co., Sub.
              U. S. Steel Corporation.
 4:50 P.M.    BEECHCRAFT DEMONSTRATION BY BEVO HOWARD.
 5:00 P.M.    SOHIO HANDICAP TROPHY RACE - 105 miles - 7 laps -
              15 mile course.
 5:30 P.M.    PRESENTATION - Sohio Handicap Trophy Race Winners.
 5:35 P.M.    DELAYED PARACHUTE JUMP - Jack Huber.
              SOHIO BAND
              GRAND PRIZE DRAWING


     Qualifying Trials Sponsored by      Downtown Press Hdqtrs: Carter
     The Industrial Rayon Corporation    Hotel - Firestone Tire and
                                         Rubber Company.

     Exclusive Radio and Broadcasting Rights
     Columbia Broadcasting System
```

Daily Program of Events, Sunday, September 5, 1948. "The Kendall Trophy Race for women pilots only – 75 miles – 5 laps – 15-mile course" was to be run at 2:15pm with the trophy presentation at 3:00pm. (Emil Strasser Collection)

Kendall Trophy Race data for 1948, showing information on the race and the prize money for the first five places. (Emil Strasser Collection)

Cover of the *Press and Radio Manual* for the 1949 NAR. Emil Strasser was an accredited member of the press corps covering the races for a number of years. The manual contained information on past winners, explanations of each race, race pilot information, schedules of events, details on military participation, as well as location where the press could file their stories. (Emil Strasser Collection)

#91 Helen McBride was sixth at 206.8mph, which placed her out of the prize money. #75 Ruth Johnson, the 1947 winner, dropped out on lap 3 with a sick engine. #65 Anna Logan was a DNS.

The 1949 races at Cleveland proved tragic for the air-racing community with the Bill Odom crash overshadowing all events. The women's event was now named the Women's Trophy Race and backed by the CNARC as Kendall had dropped its sponsorship. Rules changed for the event, and now both Ranger-powered Texans were excluded, as all racing aircraft were required to have "stock engines and two-bladed props." This was done to reduce the margin of speed between the racers, as #44 Grace Harris had finished almost 16mph faster than the second-place aircraft in 1948. Cropped canopies could continue to be used, but everything else was to be stock. Jane Page, who had finished fourth in 1947, entered a Curtiss SNC-1 trainer with a cropped canopy. Protest from the other racers prevented Page from racing. Only six Texans would qualify and with such a small field of contestants some thought was given to canceling the race.

The CNARC put up the $5,500 prize money to be shared by the six Texans that would start the main race. Records for total aircraft entered are not available. They would race around a new seven-sided 15-mile course making it safer for pilots, with no turn greater than 55 degrees. The new course allowed spectators in the grandstands to see more of the racers. #44 Grace Harris, the 1948 winner, predicted that the 1949 races would be slower. She proved to be correct as she crossed the finish line in first place at 216.7mph and collected $2,500. The other finishers were #31 Kaddy Landry in second at 214.8mph, #91 Helen McBride third at 210.0mph, with #45 Betty Skelton[5] hanging on to fourth after her engine developed an oil leak that covered her windshield. #75 Ruth Johnson was a DNF. It is unknown who the sixth pilot was.

By 1949, women's pylon racing had seemingly lost its glamor, as there are only two small paragraphs in the official press and radio manual. After four years of hard-fought racing, there is very little recorded to honor these pioneers.

T-6 pylon racing would return to Cleveland again for one race in 1969.

---

5 Both #45 Betty Skelton and #31 Kaddy Landry flew aerobatic/comedy routines during the three-day event.

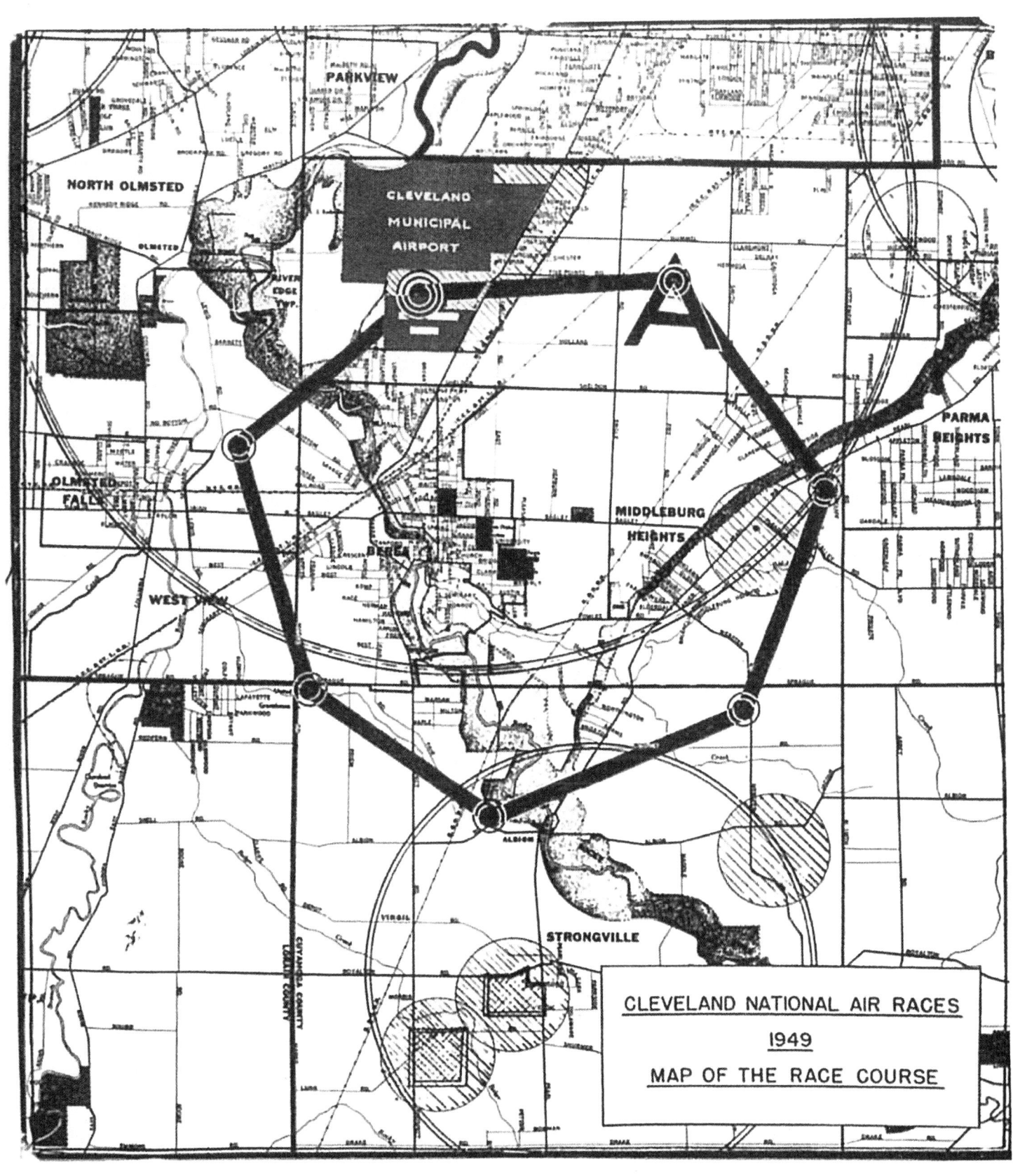

Map for the 1949 races after the course had been modified for safety and better viewing by the audience. (Emil Strasser Collection)

The last Texan races at Cleveland in 1949. Shown is #45 Betty Skelton taxiing out with #91 Helen McBride and #28 Jane Page's SNC-1 in the background. While the 1949 rules stated "stock," those Texans with modified canopies could race. (via Nicholas A. Veronico Collection)

#44 pushed off into the weeds post-race at Cleveland. After its last race in 1949, like so many others, it vanished into history. By 1950, North American had started a great "buy-back" from Texan owners for remanufacture of the aircraft for US military and foreign sales along with other airplane dealers wanting to cash in on foreign contracts. (via Nicholas A. Veronico Collection)

Chapter 3
Air Racing, A New Era

After a 15-year absence, Unlimited pylon racing returned to the United States. The 1949 Unlimited Cleveland Air Race tragedy and the start of the Korean War halted Unlimited and Texan closed course pylon racing. By the 1960s, the dust from both events had settled and a group of men in Reno, Nevada (NV), decided it was time to resurrect Unlimited close course and cross-country air racing as a way to draw people into the casinos and bring back the thrill and excitement of Unlimited racing. In 1964, this group of men led by William "Bill" Stead sponsored the first National Championship Air Races in Reno/Stead (NCAR Reno).

With the success of the NCAR races, other racing events like Reno were held around the US, but those did not feature T-6 races. As spectatorship increased, more races were added to the Reno race lineup, resulting in a T-6 demonstration race in 1967, which featured six Texans flown by members of the Southern California Condor Squadron.[1]

As in the 1949 NAR at Cleveland, all aircraft had to be stock Texans. Rules for the T-6 class were established in 1969 by the Professional Race Pilots Association (PRPA). These rules are in addition to the general rules of a given race under PRPA. T-6 Racing Association's 2021 general rules that differ from the 1969 rules are in bold print. The original rules were approved October 1969 by PRPA. Changes are as approved March 2021 by T-6 Racing Association. (Special thanks to William T. Larkins for providing a copy of 1969 rules.)

PILOT REQUIREMENTS
Pilots must be members of the PRPA in good standing for the current year. **All pilots must be members of the T-6 Racing Association**.

Pilots must have a minimum of 500 hours total Pilot in Command (PIC) time and a minimum PIC time of 25 hours in an AT-6/SNJ series aircraft, five hours of which must have been in the last 45 days. **Pilots must possess at least a Commercial Pilots Certificate, with at least a Class II medical issued within six months of a race. And have logged a minimum of 40 hours in an SNJ/T-/Harvard, within the last 24 months prior to any race.**

Pilots[2] must present proof of hours and demonstrate their ability to fly the AT-6 to the pilot qualification board in a demonstration flight over the race course. The board will pass or reject the applicants. **Must provide a current FAST (Formation and Safety Training) card and have successfully completed the RARA Pylon Racing Seminar (PRS) in a T-6 aircraft within the last two years, or have previously raced at Reno within the last three years.**

Only male pilots are eligible to enter and participate in the T-6 events.

All pilots must meet qualifications.

Pilots must complete at least five practice laps prior to qualification. **With the emphasis on safety and proficiency. All pilots must wear flame-retardant flight suits and flight gloves… must use a parachute with current repack sign-off when on the race course.**

---

1 The Condor Squadron pilots are members of the US CAP Squadron based at Van Nuys airport in Van Nuys, and fly a mixed collection of AT-6s, SNJs and Harvards on search and rescue duty when called upon. Their aircraft are painted in military color schemes (both USAAC and Luftwaffe) and are frequent performers at airshows across the country. Members of the squadron have been constant participants in air racing throughout the years.

2 Early PRPA member pilots were required to have a Federation Aeronautique Internationale (FAI) Sporting License for all National Aeronautic Association sanctioned races. In 1971, the licenses cost $5.

AIRCRAFT ELIGIBILITY
Any model T-6, AT-6, SNJ, BC-1, AT-16 or Harvard in current FAA license is eligible, if it is stock. Stock means that parts, engine, configuration, etc., must have been stock on some type of AT-6/SNJ/Harvard as assembled by North American. Stock parts from one model can be used on another model.

The following items must be installed: 42-foot minimum wingspan; stock wingtips; stock windshield; stock canopy; 12 ½′ span horizontal stabilizer; spacers at point rear of wing bolts to fuselage so wing angle-of-attack is stock; baggage compartment; electric starter; engine driven generator (35amp); AN3150 or D-6 battery (if smaller, additional weight must be carried in the baggage compartment); dual controls; tailwheel oleo assembly not tied up or secured in any way; 27″ main wheels and tires; 10:1 blower; two steps on left side. **If converted to an alternator—generator and associated equipment may be removed.**

The following equipment is optional: Nav lights; beacons; wing walk material; wax/polish, paint (but unsightly planes with peeling or sloppy paint destroy the AT-6 image and may be declared ineligible by the race committee); radio antennae; propeller spinner.

The following items are prohibited. Use of body putty, streamline fairings (not stock); streamline tape, 12:1 blowers and anything not stock that would improve speed or streamlining. **Taping of various areas completed in a professional and safe manner is permitted…except where specifically disallowed… filler may not be used to fill parts of the fuselage or panels. Only minor cosmetic enhancements will be allowed. All fairings and panels must be stock. No carbon or fiberglass panels will be allowed.**

ENGINE
Must be P&W R-1340-AN-1 (ungeared) or equivalent ungeared P&W R-1340, such as S3H-1 Canadian version.

Geared type P&W R-1340-AN-2, -45 or -47 equivalent engines are prohibited. **No helicopter or tank engine parts. The engine thrust line shall not be changed or altered.**

PROPELLER
Must be Hamilton Standard, two blade, hub model 12D40-. Propeller must have installed in the hub the following model blades; Hamilton Standard model 6101A(any). Diameter must not exceed 9′1″ (8′ 10⅜″ is legal minimum). **Diameter not less than 100″ and not more than 109″.**

There is no limit to the RPM setting, but be advised that FAA supervises the races and 2250 RPM is the legal maximum. Because of AT-6 prop noise, do not exceed 1800 RPM in the pit areas.

RADIOS
Two-way VHF radio capable of transmitting and receiving on primary tower frequency at the race site must be installed and **functioning properly** at the start of each race. **Two-way VHF transceiver of current technology is required.**

FUEL REQUIREMENTS
Shall have enough for race at full power plus 20 minute reserve. Running out of fuel causes an FAA violation (30 gals. minimum at start is recommended in the left tank). **Each aircraft will have a minimum of 50 gallons fuel to start each race. Engine shall be run on 100 low lead Avgas. No additives or injection permitted. All fuel must be dispensed from a common source at the race site.**

SPECIAL PROVISIONS
An "AT-6 Leader" shall be in charge at all races. He will be the AT-6 PRPA V.P. if present. If not present, an Active Race Pilot can be appointed by him or selected by the pilots present. Disputes will be settled by vote conducted by the AT-6 leader. (Note: if the AT-6 leader is a competitor, it is advisable to also have a class coordinator picked from PRPA ranks.) **No owner and/or pilot will attempt to enter an approved race course until the Technical Inspection Committee (TIC) has approved the aircraft.**

Immediately following the finish of a race, the aircraft finishing in the first three places will be subject to inspection by PRPA designated inspectors for the purpose of determining that all AT-6 class rules were complied with. Disputes as to whether any equipment or furnishings are stock will be settled by the Judge's North American Illustrated Parts Manual. **At the conclusion of a race all aircraft are subject to a TIC inspection and fuel may be tested.**

Race numbers must be at least 20 inches high and have a minimum leg of three inches. They must be located at least on both sides of the aircraft. It is also recommended, though not required, that numbers also be placed near the wing tip (top of the left wing, bottom of the right wing). **The number must be no less than 30″ high on both sides of the fuselage with a 2½″ wide stroke…**

Race numbers are officially assigned or approved, (at pilot's request), for a period of one year basis, thus they may not remain the same from year to year. Pilot has the right to keep it as long as it is used it. In 1971, it cost $10.

General racing guidelines/rules established by PARA are more or less the same as guidelines used today. They are summarized below:

Qualifying
All entries must qualify in order to establish eligibility and starting positions for their events. Qualifying will consist of two complete laps of the racecourse, starting from normal racing altitude. The first lap will be a warm-up lap with the speed of the second lap being used for qualification.

Starting Position
The selection of who races against who (called pairings) is determined by qualifying times/speeds and will determine starting positions for heat races, the fastest qualifier in the pole position and on down. The positions for the remaining races will be determined by the race speeds of these races. The fastest qualifiers (five or six) will be in the Championship Race, the next (five or six) will be in the Consolation Race. In some cases, slower qualifiers will be used as fill-ins. Later, these were changed to Gold, Silver, and Bronze races.

Bumping
Pilots can bump-up to the next higher race (except the top five qualifiers, who are locked into the Championship Race) by winning a Consolation Race (Bronze or Silver) or if any pilot drops out ahead of them for any reason or as an alternate to fill-in a position for a race. Pilots can also bump down if they feel they have a better chance of winning in a lower race.

Racehorse Start/Air Start
Racehorse starts were used during the classic air race era and postwar era. This type of start is where the racers are lined up abreast on a start line across the field and wait for the starter's flag to drop. Then it is a dash to the first pylon, sometimes bunched together. When there were fields not wide enough for line abreast takeoffs, the main runway and parallel taxiway were used. A few New Era races used this start. Some close calls were recorded using this method.

Air Starts are the current method used. This is where racers takeoff in pairs and then form up abreast on the backside of the course with a pace plane. Once everyone is aligned, the pace plane leads them down the chute towards the scatter pylon. If everyone is in line, they are released to race.

A Texan race pilot once said, "after over 30 years of airshow performing, a few years of crop dusting and all the other flying I have done, THAT dive in and the first pylon are the most dangerous flying I have ever done!"

Race Altitudes
The minimum race altitude on the course is pylon height. The maximum race altitude is 1,500ft above ground level (AGL).

Passing
All pylon turns must be made to the left and outside of the pylon. Any pilot being overtaken must not in any way impede the faster overtaking pilot. All pilots must keep all aircraft in sight at all times and only pass on the outside of the pylon and the passed aircraft, except where a wide pass can take place.

Mayday/Emergencies
A pilot can declare a mayday for any inflight problem. All pilots not involved in the emergency will pull up to a safe altitude and remain there until the emergency is cleared. A Yellow Flag will be displayed at the Home Pylon. The race may be continued based on the judges' determination for the safety of all pilots. If the race is to continue, the Green Flag will be displayed at the Home Pylon. If the race is to be terminated before all laps are completed, a Red Flag will be displayed at the Home Pylon.

Fines, Penalties and Pylon Cuts
If a pilot cuts a pylon, they could re-fly (circle back around) the pylon and not incur a penalty, if it is done before reaching the next pylon. This would cost them some overall time and perhaps a place but no placement penalty at the end of the race. This was a practice used in both prewar and postwar racing and some early New Era races. Pilots who cut pylons now in the New Era are attributed a time penalty for each cut. Claims of "forced cuts" will be determined by the pylon judges. Pilots who jump start are penalized one lap. Pilots can be fined cash or be disqualified for low or unsafe flying as determined by judges. Pilots can be disqualified for crossing the FAA established Dead-Line with no right to protest and forfeiture of any prize money. They could/can also be disqualified if found to be in violation of the technical or safety rules.

Winning
Finishing positions shall be taken from the pilot's position in the field at the time of race stoppage. To be considered the winner of any race, a pilot must have completed the required number of laps, or adjusted number caused by an emergency, at the Home Pylon in the fastest time (speeds) after any adjustments of time or penalties. [Author's note: When I calculated the number of wins for both pilots and aircraft, I only counted Bronze (Consolation), Silver (Medallion) and Gold Race wins.]

Seven-time Reno champion Eddie Van Fossen, when asked what it took to win at Reno, replied, "To win you need reliability, speed, skill, guts and luck!"

Cost
Currently, it costs about $750 to enter a Texan at the NCAR. Other costs to take into consideration are fuel/oil and accommodation for pilot and crew, which can run up to $1,500–2,500. All of these fees are covered by the pilot. A sponsor can help offset the cost of racing, as does winning.

Expansion and Contraction
The noise and the skills of close competition were a big hit, and led to other race venues including T-6 races. They began in 1969, with a total of four T-6 races. There were three in 1970 (strangely Reno did not have a T-6 race), four in 1971 (one was a demo), three in 1972 (one was a demo), three in 1973, two in 1974, three in 1975 (one was a demo race only), three in 1976, one in 1977, two in 1978, one in 1979, none in 1980, two in 1985 and 1986, two in 1988 (one was a demo), four in 1989 (three were demos), two in 1990, one in 1992, one in 1994, two in 2005, and, finally, just one that continues today at Reno every September. [See Chapter 6, Table #1 for events list.]

The narratives for each of the races are the most accurate that can be reconstructed from personal notes, conversations, direct observations, official press kits, race programs, newspapers, and other available publications. As the "Group," we were fortunate to have press/media credentials for the races and events.

A note must be included about the information used to determine the identities of the pilots and aircraft raced. Information was obtained from the official entry list, qualifying list, heat race results, consolation race results (medallion, bronze, silver) and championship race results (gold). Pilots could enter an event but not qualify or race. They could also qualify but not race. In some cases, they could race without qualifying due to the need to fill in a particular race field. So, to be classified as having raced, they had to have raced in at least one heat race, drag race or consolation/championship race. Pairing slips were only used to verify times and who would race in a particular race, as pilots could drop out for various reasons.

Throughout the years, pilots have swapped aircraft to either qualify or race for another pilot or for an owner or team. There have been several occasions when pilots have qualified two aircraft at the same event to determine which gives the best chance for winning. Some T-6 pilots also raced in other race classes at the same race event. With regard to identifying racing aircraft and pilots, the following pattern is used: race number and pilot's first and last name (#27 Eddie Van Fossen). Aircraft names are commonly not used in the narratives as these were not always painted on the aircraft or may change during a particular event. For a complete list of all Texan aircraft that have entered/raced, see Chapter 6, Table #2.

United States Air Racing Association (USARA), PRPA, and the T-6 Air Racing Association have organized and held several regional demonstration/exhibition races over the years with the same stated goals: "This type of race is held to test the drawing power of a Class of racing in an area which has never had racing. Speeds are kept down below normal racing speeds on two to three mile race courses. Little prize money is offered, the spectators enjoy the racing just the same." By 1988, demonstration races were described by the T-6 Air Racing Association as "taking off in close trail or sections of two, join up in a 270-degree climbing turn, cross over the audience above 1,000' in a trail formation into line abreast while accelerating toward the race start line. As the pace plane breaks away starting the race, the audience is treated to the noise of six to eight P&W 1340 engines. This demonstration of precision formation flying in a wingtip-to-wingtip 'gaggle' will never be forgotten by the audience."

When air racing resumed in 1968, and for several years after, the T-6 Class used the USARA National Points System, in which each participant received points per sanctioned race just as the Miget/Goodyear Class had done. Points were totaled at the end of the racing season and a class champion was named in each. After a time (the split between race sanctioning bodies and fewer races), this system fell away.

The Races

"If GOD had intended man to race behind a horizontally opposed engine,
Pratt & Whitney would have built them that way."
Sign at the entrance to the T-6 Class pits in Mojave 1979.

1967

Although Reno had hosted cross-country and closed course pylon races since 1964, the T-6 Class of racers was not included until 1968. This race pattern was used to hold all future T-6 races. With a few exceptions, T-6 races continue every September at this premier air race event.

Held at the former Stead Air Force Base (AFB) from September 21–24, 1967, an "AT-6 Special Race (Exhibition)" was included in the overall race program. The planes would race over a 2½-mile course and each race would be six laps with one race per day on September 23 and 24. The six entrants were #1 Walter Morrison, #3 Hank Otzen, #4 Dick Gregory, #5 Don Gulotta, #6 Victor Baker, and #7 Darryl Greenamyer (yes, that Darryl Greenamyer).

The first race was a bit subdued as shown by race times and speeds. First place was #3 Otzen taking 6:00.3mins to complete the race with an average speed of 149.875mph. Second place went to #7 Greenamyer with 6:04.7mins and 148.067mph. Third was #1 Morrison with 6:05.5mins and 147.945mph. Fourth-place winner was #4 Gregory with 6:17.9mins and 142.895mph. Fifth was #5 Gulotta with 6:19.5 mins and 142.292mph, and sixth was #6 Baker with 7:03.5mins and 127.509mph.

Reno 1967 with all six of the Condor Squadron getting ready to start one of the exhibition races. Lined up are #1 Walter Morrison, #5 Don Gulotta, #6 Victor Baker, #7 Darryl Greenamyer, #3 Hank Otzen, and #4 Dick Gregory, with his wingtip just showing. (Emil Strasser)

1967 NATIONAL CHAMPIONSHIP AIR RACE RESULTS

```
TRANSCONTINENTAL RACE -- Rockford, Ill. to Reno, Nev. -- 1620 miles
1    #87    Mike Carroll      Sea Fury      3:50:55        420
2    #14    Ed Weiner         Mustang       4:01:20        403
3    #13    Dick Kestle       Mustang       5:16:15        307
4    #18    Tom Kuchinsky     Mustang       5:50:00        278
5    #83    Jim Fugate        Mustang       started late
-    #17    Mickey Rupp       Mustang       failed to finish

UNLIMITED CLASS -- Final Race -- 10 laps of the 8.04-mile course
1    # 1    Darryl Greenamyer Bearcat       12:17.2        392.621
2    #49    Ed Weiner         Mustang       12:54.5        373.712
3    #64    Clay Lacy         Mustang       13:16.9        363.207
4    # 5    Chuck Hall        Mustang       13:17.2        363.071
5    # 2    Mike Loening      Mustang       13:24.3        359.866
6    # 8    Chuck Lyford      Mustang       failed to finish

SPORT BIPLANE CLASS -- Final Race -- 10 laps of the 2½-mile course
1    # 3    Bill Boland       Mong Sport    9:53.5         151.643
2    # 1    Sid White         Starduster    9:54.8         151.311
3    #17    Bruce McIntire    Pitts Special 9:54.9         151.286
4    #99    Dallas Christian  Mong Sport    10:09.4        147.686
5    # 8    Clem Fischer      Mong Sport    10:13.4        146.723
6    #26    Branch Smith      Mong Sport    10:45.2        139.462

FORMULA ONE -- Final Race -- 12 laps of the 2½-mile course
1    #92    Bill Falck        Rivets        8:52.8         202.703
2    #14    Bob Downey        Ole Tiger     8:56.8         201.192
3    #16    Ray Cote          Shoestring    8:58.5         200.557
4    #31    Smokey Stover     Scholl Special 9:25.2        191.083
5    #81    Marion Baker      Boo Ray       9:47.3         183.892
6    #34    Jim Wilson        Snoopy        no time recorded

AT-6 SPECIAL RACE (exhibition) -- Sept. 23 -- 6 laps of the 2½-mile course
1    # 3    Hank Otzen                      6:00.3         149.875
2    # 7    Darryl Greenamyer               6:04.7         148.067
3    # 1    Walter Morrison                 6:05.0         147.945
4    # 4    Dick Gregory                    6:17.9         142.895
5    # 5    Don Gulotta                     6:19.5         142.292
6    # 6    Vic Baker                       7:03.5         127.509

AT-6 SPECIAL RACE (exhibition) -- Sept. 24 -- 6 laps of the 2½-mile course
1    # 3    Hank Otzen                      5:17.9         169.865
2    # 5    Don Gulotta                     5:23.0         167.183
3    # 1    Walter Morrison                 5:23.9         166.718
4    # 7    Darryl Greenamyer               5:25.9         165.695
5    # 4    Dick Gregory                    5:42.8         157.526
6    # 6    Vic Baker                       5:45.5         156.295
```

The official result sheet from the 1967 National Championship Air Races at Reno, showing the two AT-6 Special Race (exhibition) for both days. They flew six laps of the 2½ mile course. First (unofficial) Texan Closed Course Pylon Races since 1949. (via Emil Strasser)

By the second race on September 24, the pilots had some experience on the course and speeds improved, as did the quality of the racing. Again #3 Otzen took first place with a time of 5:17.9mins at 169.865mph, which was almost 20mph faster than the previous day. Second was #5 Gulotta with 5:23.0mins and 167.183mph. Third was #1 Morrison with 5:23.9mins and 166.718mph. Fourth was #7 Greenamyer[3] with 5:25.9mins and 165.695mph. Fifth was #4 Gregory with 5:42.8mins and 157.526mph, and sixth was #6 Baker with 5:45.5mins and 156.295mph.

Based on the results and spectator response, T-6 races would be included in the schedule for the 1968 races.

---

3   Darryl Greenamyer won the 1967 Unlimited Championship Race with his #1 Bearcat at a speed of 392.621mph.

1968

September 15–22, 1968, saw 17 T-6 pilots pay the $30 entry fee to qualify for the first fully official Reno Texan races. Like the 1949 NAR Cleveland races, all aircraft had to be stock Texans. Pilots qualified by flying one fast lap around the three-mile course. Racers would race in heat races grouped (paired) by qualifying speeds. Each of the two heats would have six racers with the winners moving up (bumping up) to the next race set. Heat races were six laps of the three-mile course for a total distance of 18 miles. Heats were followed by an eight-lap Consolation Race (Medallion/Bronze/Silver) of 24 miles with the winner bumping up to the Championship Race (Gold), also eight laps. Bardahl Racing Products would be the main sponsor for the 1968 T-6 Class. Of note, except for inclusion in the main schedule of events, the T-6 Class was not promoted in the official race program. Total purse for the Bardahl Trophy Dash was $2,750.

Qualifying lap times were around one minute for the three-mile course while speeds saw a 30mph difference. The top qualifier was #6 Victor Baker taking :57.5secs for his lap, giving him a 187.83mph speed. He was followed by #3 Richard Sykes at: 59.9secs and 180.3mph. Sykes was the only other pilot to post a speed greater than 180mph. Third to 17th were: #11 Howard Keefe 179.7mph, #9 Phillip Livingston also 179.7mph, #2 W. S. Halfhill 179.1mph in his first and only race, #38 James Wirtz 178.81mph, #1 Hendrik Otzen, the 1967 Reno Demo Race winner, 178.2mph, #37 Richard Gregory also 178.2mph, #88 Bob Metcalfe 177.9mph in his Harvard IV (first Harvard IV to race closed course pylon), #5 James Williams 177.3mph, #0 Hugh Glassburn 177.05mph, #4 Don Phillippi 175.0mph, #7 Ben Hall 173.3 in a Harvard II (first Harvard II to race closed course pylon), #50 USN Commander Walt Ohlrich 171.98mph (also racing his #10 Bearcat), #74 Leroy Penhall 167.44mph, #13 Joseph Andrade 166.1mph, and the last qualifier was #77 Harold Jolliff at 1:05.6mins and 164.63mph. Jolliff did not race (DNR) in his only entry into T-6 racing.

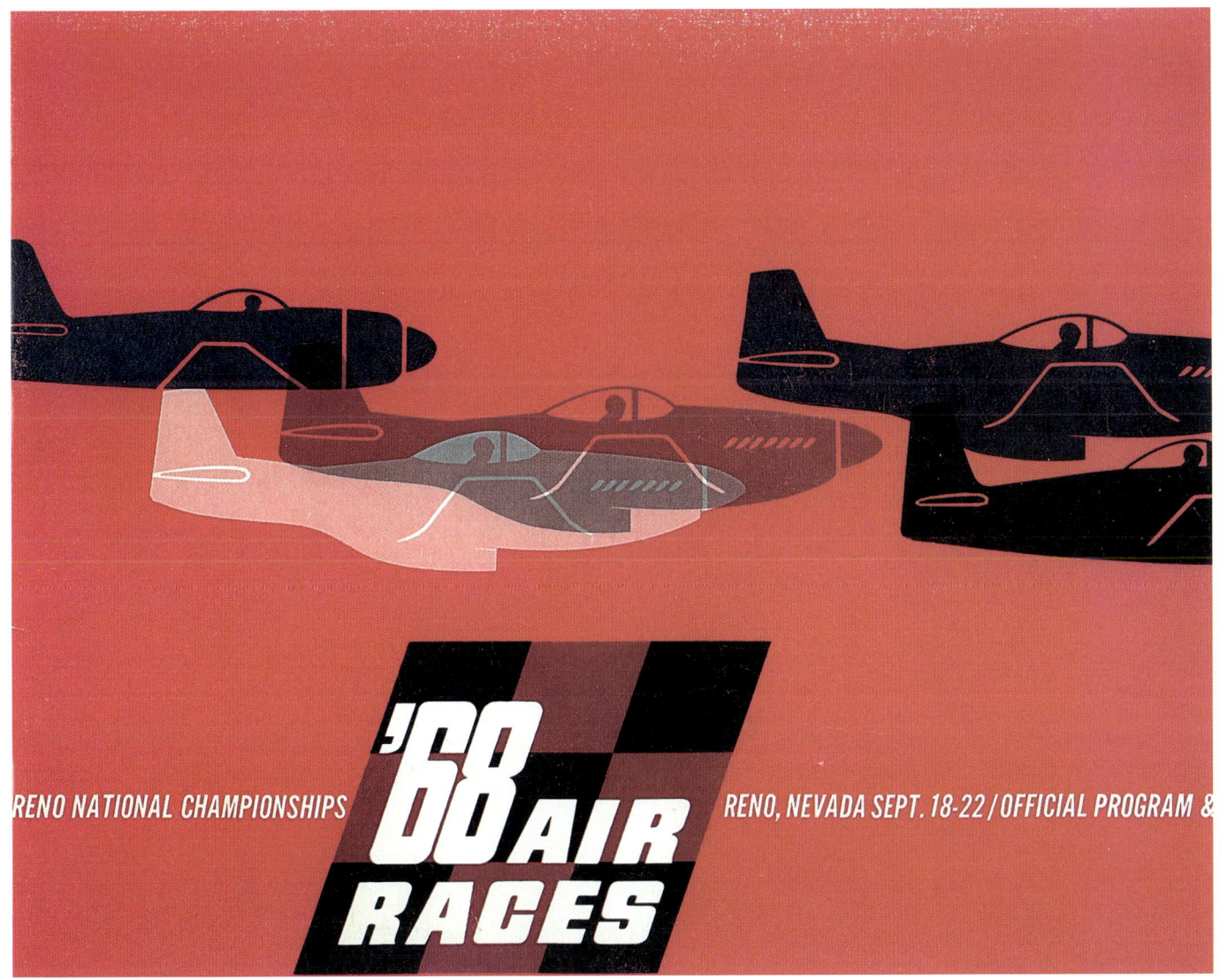

Program cover of the 1968 Reno National Championship Air Race that featured the first official Texan races. (via Emil Strasser Collection, Courtesy of the National Championship Air Races)

SCHEDULE OF EVENTS

WEDNESDAY, SEPT. 18, 1968

10:00 A.M.   Official Qualifications For All Classes of Pylon Racing Aircraft. 10:00 A.M. to 6:00 P.M. Each Day

SATURDAY, SEPT. 21, 1968

11:00 A.M.	Antique & experimental aircraft, balloon demonstration
12:00 Noon	Opening ceremonies — introductions
12:30 P.M.	Bardahl AT-6 Race, 6 laps, Heat 1-B
12:50 P.M.	Chuck Lyford, P-38 Lightning
1:05 P.M.	Aviation Services Inc., Sport Biplane Race, 6 laps, Heat 2-A
1:20 P.M.	Clyde Parsons
1:40 P.M.	Nugget Formula One Race, 6 laps, Heat 2-A
1:55 P.M.	Bud Fountain & Terry Holm, Wing riding exhibition
2:05 P.M.	Lucky Lager Woman's Stock Plane Race, 8 laps, Consolation
2:20 P.M.	Bob Hoover, North American Rockwell Shrike Commander
2:30 P.M.	INTERMISSION
3:00 P.M.	Bardahl AT-6 Race, 8 laps, Consolation
3:20 P.M.	Dean Engelhardt, Aeronca act
3:35 P.M.	Aviation Services, Inc., Sport Biplane Race, 6 laps, Heat 2-B
3:50 P.M.	Palace Club presents Art Scholl
4:05 P.M.	Nugget Formula One Race, 8 laps, Heat 2-B
4:20 P.M.	Bob Hoover, North American Rockwell P-51 Mustang
4:40 P.M.	Harrah's Unlimited Consolation Race, 10 laps

THURSDAY, SEPT. 19, 1968

10:00 A.M.   Official Qualifications For All Classes of Pylon Racing Aircraft. 10:00 A.M. to 6:00 P.M. Each Day

SUNDAY, SEPT. 22, 1968

11:00 A.M.	Antique & experimental aircraft, balloon demonstration
12:00 Noon	Opening ceremonies, United States Navy Band, 12th Naval District
12:30 P.M.	Chuck Lyford, P-38 Lightning
12:45 P.M.	Aviation Services, Inc. Sport Biplane Race, 8 laps Consolation
1:00 P.M.	Clyde Parsons, Aerobatic demonstration
1:10 P.M.	Nugget Formula One Consolation Race, 8 laps
1:25 P.M.	Bud Fountain & Terry Holm, Wing Riding Exhibition
1:35 P.M.	Bardahl AT-6 Trophy Dash, 8 laps, Final
1:55 P.M.	Bob Hoover, North American Rockwell, Shrike Commander
2:10 P.M.	Lucky Lager Woman's Stock Plane Final Race, 8 laps
2:30 P.M.	Palace Club presents Art Scholl
2:45 P.M.	Aviation Services, Inc. Sport Biplane Race, 10 laps Final
3:05 P.M.	Dean Engelhardt, Aeronca Act
3:15 P.M.	Nugget Formula One Race, 12 laps Final
3:35 P.M.	INTERMISSION
3:45 P.M.	United States Navy Blue Angels
4:15 P.M.	Bob Hoover, North American Rockwell P-51 Mustang
4:35 P.M.	Harrah's Unlimited Trophy Dash, 12 laps

Due to unforeseen circumstances, times are approximate. Schedule and events may be varied at the discretion of the Reno Air Racing Association, Inc.

Schedule of events for the 1968 Reno Races listing the three Texan races. (via Emil Strasser Collection)

Taxiing out for the start of the first Texan championship race at Reno 1968 are #5 James Williams, #9 Phil Livingston in a transitional paint scheme, and #3 Richard Sykes. Texan #9 last raced at Reno in 2018. (Ron Olsen)

Heat-1 winner #1 Otzen took 5:55.8mins to cover the 18 miles. #9 Livingston was second at :04.6secs behind, followed by #6 Baker, #0 Glassburn, #88 Metcalfe, and #2 Halfhill, who placed last after cutting pylon 3 twice.

Heat-2 was won by Condor Squadron member #3 Sykes at 179.9mph, just under his second place qualifying speed. Second place went to future P-51 *Miss America* pilot #11 Howard Keefe, #4 Phillippi was placed third, #5 Williams fourth, and fifth went to #38 Wirtz. #37 Gregory placed sixth for a rules infraction. The judges penalized him for improper number identification on his Texan. He had finish third at 173.68mph.

Reno's first eight-lap Consolation Race was won by #4 Phillippi in 8:04.2mins and 178.44mph in his only win. The next two, #0 Glassburn and #2 Halfhill, were bumped from second and third to fifth and sixth for pylon cuts. Both made safety laps around the pylons. This enabled fourth place #38 Wirtz to bump to second, fifth place #88 Metcalfe to third, and sixth place #37 Gregory to fourth. It is reported that #2 Halfhill cut a total of eight pylons during the race and made only one safety lap, bringing his 1968 Reno total to ten. He was ruled not a legal finisher. He never raced again.

The Bardahl AT-6 Trophy Dash Championship Race was a close fought race from the start, with the top three aircraft pulling ahead of the other three. At the finish line was #1 Otzen in first with 7:56.5mins at 181.32mph, collecting $400. Second was #3 Sykes at 7:56.7mins at 181.25mph, getting $300; he was followed by #9 Livingston 7:57.4mins at 180.98mph with $250. Further back in fourth was #5 Williams 8:15.2mins and 174.43mph and $200, fifth was #6 Baker 8:16.3mins 174.09mph with $190, and #11 Keefe in sixth 8:28.1mins and 169.71mph, collecting $160. Otzen's winning speed was 11.61mph faster than last place #11 Keefe. Otzen's only full race win was in 1968 and it was his last, as he never raced T-6s again. The class proved to be popular and would return in 1969.

Racehorse start of the 1968 Championship Race at Reno with #5 Williams, #1 Otzen, and #11 Keefe on the taxiway. #9 Livingston, #6 Baker, and #3 Sykes are on the runway. A perfect photo of a racehorse start. The race was won by #1 Hank Otzen, who had won the 1967 exhibition race. (Ron Olsen)

1969

The Fort Lauderdale, FL, National Air Races were held February 13–16, 1969. Weather caused low turnout and delays for the eight pilots who qualified to race around the three-mile course. #44 Howard Keefe took :58.3secs to qualify in first place at 185.2mph, #21 John Trainor :58.6secs for second place, #33 Leo Volkmer third, #22 B.F. McKinney fourth, #17 John Moriarty fifth, #96 Richard Minges sixth, #8 Bill Lumley seventh in his only race, and #99 Ed Snyder eighth taking 1:30.1min.

There were two heat races, a Consolation Race, and the six-lap Championship Race. There was some overlapping of aircraft in each of the four races due to the lower racer turnout. #96 Minges won the Consolation Race at 181.5mph with #22 McKinney second, #17 Moriarty third, #8 Lumley fourth, and #99 Snyder fifth. For the Championship Race, #21 Trainor took first and $750 at 175.9mph, #33 Volkmer second, #44 Keefe third, #22 McKinney fourth, and fifth place and $250 went to #17 Moriarty. Both McKinney and Moriarty were given penalties for pylon cuts. Some last-minute drama in the Championship Race was provided by #22 McKinney, who finished fourth. On landing, his gear collapsed, and he slid down the runway to a stop. He collected $300 in prize money.

Program cover for the first St. Louis National Air Races at Chesterfield, Missouri (MO), in August 1969. Fourteen Texans would qualify. The racing proved enjoyable, resulting in a second set of races in 1970. (Collection of Aviation Photo Services)

While the program announced the first St. Louis National Air Races, August 8–10, 1969, the location St. Louis, Missouri (MO), had a long history with air racing. The first races held there were the 1923 Nationals, so there were many years between events by the time the 1969 races rolled around. Races would be run with a racehorse start to a scatter pylon with six laps for the Consolation Race and eight laps for the Championship Race. The narrowness of the main starting runway only allowed five T-6s to start at a time, so three heats would be run, giving everyone a chance to race. Unfortunately, the starting line was back from the spectators' area, so it was not possible to see the starts.

The August 8 race began with one lap around the three-mile course for qualifying and 14 pilots qualified. This was unusual for air-racing events, as there were three pairs of tied qualifying speeds and a new fastest time set. #96 Richard Minges was first with a speed of 188.15mph. He was followed by #99 Ed Snyder also at 188.15mph. This pair was followed by #11 Howard Keefe in third at 186.21mph and #4 Don Phillippi in fourth place also at 186.21mph. These winners were followed by another pair with matching speeds – #22 B. F. McKinney earning fifth at 185.35mph and #33 Leo Volkmer coming in sixth at 185.35mph. This group was followed by #94 Bob Mitchem at 182.7mph in seventh, #21 John Trainor at 181.82mph in eighth, #6 Victor Baker at 181.2mph in ninth (Baker set the old fastest speed of 187.83mph the year before at Reno), #24 Gerald Swayze in tenth at 180.0mph, #44 John Mosby 11th at 176.7mph, #10 Don Barrett 12th at 172.8mph, #37 Dick Gregory 13th at 170.0mph, and #55 Len Tanner in 14th at 167.1mph.

The heat races were fast and close with Heat-1A being a runaway for #96 Minges, who took first at 185.04mph. He was followed by #4 Phillippi in second, #94 Mitchem in third place, and further back were #24 Swayze in fourth and #37 Gregory in fifth.

Heat-2A had #99 Snyder, #21 Trainor, and #22 McKinney bunched together most of the race and finishing first, second and third, respectively. They were trailed by #44 Mosby in fourth and #55 Tanner in last with a hung gear. Third-place finisher McKinney was fined for flying low but kept his third position.

Heat-3A began with some drama on the takeoffs with #11 Keefe applying too much power and nosing over, causing a prop strike putting him out at the start. The other four proceeded to race with #6 Baker taking first, #33 Volkmer second, #10 Barrett third, and #44 Mosby, who had flown as a fill-in so each heat could have five starters, placed fourth.

Diagram of the 1969 St. Louis Air Race course, showing the narrow taxiway and runway that necessitated the odd racing starts away from the spectators. In 1970, the races were moved across the Mississippi River to East Alton, Illinois (IL), but were still billed as the St. Louis Air Races. (Collection of Aviation Photo Services)

August 10 saw both the Consolation and Championship races run. At the start of the Consolation Race, low flyer #22 McKinney jumped to the lead and held on until passed by #94 Mitchem at the start of lap 4. Mitchem took first at 184.8mph, McKinney took second, followed by #33 Volkmer in third, and #24 Swayze in fourth. #10 Barrett in brought up the rear in fifth place.

Gear trouble would again affect the outcome of a race at St. Louis, with #6 Baker unable to fully retract his gear from the start of the Championship Race until he had flown one and one-half laps. #96 Minges led start to finish and set another speed record (187.7mph) in the process, his third for the weekend. The real fight was for second, third and fourth between Snyder, Phillippi and Trainor. Baker was well behind and finished fifth. At the start of lap 7, the middle three sorted themselves out to finish #99 Snyder second at 185.5mph, #21 Trainor third at 184.9mph, and fourth #4 Phillippi at 181.0mph. Prize payout for the Championship Race was $855 for Minges, $635 for Snyder, $500 for Trainor, $425 for Phillippi, and $385 for Baker.

Attendance was so high that extra prize money was paid to all pilots and plans were made for 1970.

Labor Day weekend, August 29–September 1, 1969, saw T-6 racing return to the Cleveland National Air Races for the first time since 1949. A two-and-a-half-mile course was set to see ten Texans qualify and race. Qualifying was done in pairs (one lap) and races were two heats (eight laps), a Consolation Race and a Championship Race, both with ten laps, a total distance of 25 miles.

#94 Bob Mitchem was the top qualifier at 187.3mph, followed by #99 Ed Snyder second, #44 Art Carlson third, #96 Richard Minges fourth, #11 Howard Keefe fifth, #22 B.F. McKinney sixth, #10 Don Barrett seventh, #41 Ralph Twombly eighth, #55 Len Tanner ninth, and rookie #71 Dick Foote tenth. #74 Fred Edison had engine problems and did not qualify (DNQ) or race.

The actual races went off without a hitch, with #94 Mitchem winning Heat 1A, #22 McKinney winning Heat 1B. McKinney #22 won the Consolation Race at 179.8mph, followed by #10 Barrett second, third #41 Twombly, fourth #71 Foote, and fifth #55 Tanner.

#94 Bob Mitchem won the Championship Race at 188.2mph, with #96 Minges second, #99 Snyder third, #44 Carlson fourth, and #11 Keefe fifth. Mitchem took home more than $800 in prize money for the weekend. Despite the success, Cleveland would host no future Texan races.

Texan racing returned to Cleveland in 1969 after the last race in 1949. Lining up for the racehorse start are #55 Len Tanner, #41 Ralph Twombly, and #22 B. F. McKinney. (Robert F. Pauley via Nicholas A. Veronico)

Walter Morrison rounding a pylon at Reno 1969 in #2, the KGIL Los Angeles radio station special N447CL. Morrison had raced #1 in the 1967 exhibition races. (Jerry Liang)

A double field of T-6s qualified for the September 1969 Reno races – 28 pilots qualified 27 aircraft out of 31 entered, the largest number ever for the class. The first five qualifiers set new class speed records for qualifying. It should be noted the old records had been set just the month before at St. Louis. Top qualifier #7 Ben Hall in his Harvard II posted a time of :53.9secs for lap 1 around the three-mile course for a speed of 200.37mph. The other record-setters were #99 Ed Snyder second at 191.15mph, #96 Richard Minges third also at 191.15mph. #14 Rudy Malaspina placed fourth at 190.48mph. This would be his only T-6 race. #22 Mac McKinney placed fifth at 189.61mph and :56.9secs. Sixth through 15th placed in the following order: #2 Walt Morrison in his last T-6 race :58.2secs and 185.5mph, #38 James Wirtz, #88 Bob Metcalfe, #3 Richard Sykes, #4 Don Phillippi, #70 Bill Turnbull, #0 Hugh Glassburn, #6 Victor Baker, #33 Leo Volkmer, and #94 Bob Mitchem. This group was followed by those under 180mph, including #35 Jay Quinn 1:00.7min and 177.92mph, #57 Walt Ohlrich, #50 George Sanders, #24 Gerald Swayze, #69 Bob Suacci, #5 James Williams, #38 Frank Ponke, who qualified in James Wirtz's aircraft and did not race, #11 Howie Keefe, #13 Joseph Andrade, #37 Richard Gregory, #44 John Mosby, #30 Hugh Alexander, and #9 Phil Livingston at 1:07.3mins and 160.48mph. This was 40mph slower than first-place qualifier #7 Ben Hall.

The four pilots who entered, but did not qualify or race, were #10 Don Barrett, #21 John Trainor, #66 Robert Drews, and #310 Jack Briggs. The Race Committee decided only 12 of the 28 aircraft that qualified could make the regular racing field and an additional six qualified for the Medallion Race only. #94 Bob Mitchem, who was qualified for the Medallion Race because of the speeds that were posted, filed a protest. This is what transpired quoted from the NCAR official records:

#94 Mitchem claimed that he had been improperly timed during his qualification run. This claim was supported by several of the other T-6 pilots, most notably #7 Hall, who had also had difficulty with his timing during qualifications. The protest was allowed and #94 Mitchem was moved up into the Consolation Race even though he did not run in either of the heat races. #2 Morrison, who had qualified in the top 12 and ran in the second Heat Race, had some mechanical problems and could not compete thereafter. Thus, the 19th qualifier #24 Swayze moved up and replaced #94 Mitchem in the Medallion Race. Consequently, when all was said and done, 19 of the 27 participating aircraft (one aircraft #38 was qualified by two pilots, thus the reasons for 28 qualifying positions) got to race. Qualifiers 20 through 28 did not make the field.

Note that #11 Keefe was cut from the T-6 races but would finish second in his #11 P-51 Mustang in the Unlimited Consolation Race.

#7 Hall easily won Heat-1 and set a new national speed record of 192.40mph breaking a record set just 18 days earlier at Cleveland by #94 Mitchem. Second place finisher #99 Snyder was 12 seconds behind at 186.1mph. Third was #22 McKinney at 178.51mph closely followed by #70 Turnbull fourth. #3 Sykes finished fifth and #88 Metcalfe finished almost a full minute behind at 6:27.6mins and 167.18mph.

Heat-2 was evenly paced at the start, but by lap 4 became a race between first and second places before #96 Minges pulled ahead. He finished first at 186.4mph with #4 Phillippi second at 183.4mph. Seven seconds back was #14 Malaspina in third, #38 Wirtz fourth, #2 Morrison was fifth, with #0 Glassburn :22.3secs behind the winner in sixth.

Those pilots racing in the six-lap Medallion Race found themselves again left behind between :05.0secs and :20.0secs by race winner #6 Baker, who finished at 182.13mph. #33 Volkmer was second at 177.97mph, and third was #35 Quinn. Fourth was #57 Ohlrich, who also raced his #10 Bearcat and took first in the Unlimited Consolation. Fifth place went to #50 Sanders at 6:20.2mins and 170.44mph, and in sixth was #24 Swayze 6:20.7mins and 170.21mph.

Having been placed into the Consolation Race after winning his protest, #94 Mitchem walked away with the win, setting a speed record in the process at 197.98mph, breaking the record set the day before by #7 Hall. Seventeen seconds back in second place was #3 Sykes, less than one second behind in third was #70 Turnbull, followed by #38 Wirtz in fourth, #0 Glassburn fifth, and in sixth, at :30secs back from first, was #88 Metcalfe.

Another runaway race by #7 Hall saw him winning the eight-lap Championship Race at 190.90mph and $850. It was not a record but still 8mph faster than second place finisher #96 Minges, who won $600. The other four finishers included third place #4 Phillippi with $500. Fourth place and $400 went to #99 Snyder, who was fined $25 for low flying. Fifth place finish went to #22 McKinney along with $350. He clipped a pylon at the start and then dragged the ground with his wingtip around a pylon. McKinney was also fined $25 for low flying. This was a pattern both he and Snyder would often repeat. Finally, in sixth and collecting $300 was #14 Malaspina, :42secs back from first place.

Hank Otzen's Texan cost an estimated $6,500 while the total Texan prize money for 1969 was $5,250.

Reno 1969 would set the style for speed[4] and action for all future races at Reno.

1970

April 16–19, 1970, provided better weather than the year before for the second Fort Lauderdale National Air Races. This resulted in a larger turnout of aircraft, with 19 total qualifiers. #44 John Mosby set the fastest time of 192.2mph around a slightly longer racecourse (3.189 miles) than the 1969 course. #24 Gerald Swayze posted the slowest at 183.6mph. The other qualifiers were second through 18th in order: #96 Richard Minges, #30 Hugh Alexander, #21 John Trainor, #99 Ed Snyder, #7 Ben Hall in his Harvard Mk II, #72 William Turnbull, #0 Hugh Glassburn, #10 Don Barrett, #6 Victor Baker, #33 John Moriarty,[5] #25 Tony Murgia, #12 Canadian Jim Strang in a Harvard 4, #11 Howard Keefe, #22 B. F. McKinney, #70 Charles Saunders, #8 Fred Edison, and #41 Ralph Twombly.

As in 1969, there were two heats of ten laps each, an eight-lap Consolation and an eight-lap Championship Race. Heat-1A was won by #72 Turnbull ($210), followed by #25 Murgia, #6 Baker, #10 Barrett, and #0 Glassburn. #33 Moriarty placed last for cutting pylon 2 on laps 1 and 8 and pylon 3 on laps 4 and 9, but he still received $115.

#7 Ben Hall won Heat-1B at a blistering 198.5mph and collected $770. He was followed by #96 Minges, #21 Trainor, #44 Mosby, and #30 Alexander. #99 Snyder dropped out on lap 1 with an oil leak, but still collected $280.

After repairing his oil leak, #99 Snyder won $210 for taking first in the Consolation Race at 189.088mph and bumped up to the Championship Race. #0 Glassburn placed second, #30 Alexander earned third, and #6 Bakers took $140 at 184.82mph for fourth. A Special Trophy Race of six laps was won by #11 Keefe at 179.61mph, #22 McKinney second, #8 Edison third, #41 Twombly fourth, and #12 Strang fifth. He received no time, having cut pylon 4 on laps 2 and 3.

#7 Hall jumped into the lead of the Championship Race and never looked back, taking first at 198.25mph and $770. This was a full 8mph faster than second place #96 Minges. #21 Trainor came third, #72 Turnbull fourth, #25 Murgia

---

4 With regards to speed records for T-6 racing, at this time the class was still evolving, and records would fall at almost every race as pilot skills and mechanical knowledge improved. Racecourse distances and elevations varied, which had an effect on speed.

5 John Moriarty would be fatally injured in the crash of this T-6 at Billings, New York (NY), in July 1970 at an airshow.

Fort Lauderdale, Florida (FL), April 1970. These are three of the 19 qualifiers: #72 William Turnbull, #25 Tony Murgia (which carried an overall white paint scheme with an orange box trimmed in black), and #7 Ben Hall (painted Indian Red), who would win the Championship Race. (Robert F. Pauley via Nicholas A. Veronico)

fifth, and #44 Mosby in sixth place won $280. #99 Snyder dropped out of the start of the Heat Race with a broken oil line trailing a large amount of smoke but landed safely. After holding races for two years, both producing low financial returns, Fort Lauderdale racing came to a halt.

Cape May, New Jersey (NJ), planned air races for June 2–6, 1970, but the races were cancelled three weeks before the planned event.

Wilson, North Carolina (NC), held air races featuring T-6 races for three years from 1970–72. The only change in the 2.43-mile course was the number of laps raced each year at the municipal airport.

Considered a regional air race by PRPA, the 1970 race would see low spectator turnout due to heavy rain in the days before the races held July 25 and 26. There were to be two heat races, a ten-lap consolation race and an eight-lap championship race. Seven aircraft showed up and all seven qualified. The top qualifier was #99 Ed Snyder at 194.0mph taking :45.1secs for the one lap. Next was #96 Richard Minges at 193.3mph. Third was #25 Tony Murgia at 184.8mph. #12 Jim Strang in his Harvard Mk 4 was fourth at 184.0mph. Fifth was #55 Jack Lowers at 181.7mph. Sixth was #41 Ralph Twombly at 179.0mph and seventh was #30 Hugh Alexander at 174.8mph.

With so few racers everyone was assured of racing for the weekend. Both heat races were just lapping the pylons and changing places while the consolation and championship races were a little more exciting.

The ten-lap Consolation Race was a mixed affair of two fast qualifiers and three fill-ins. #30 Alexander was first at 185.5mph with #55 Lowers second at 173.0mph. They were followed by the three fill ins: #25 Murgia, #12 Strang, and #41 Twombly. All posted speeds between 184mph and 176mph.

The eight-lap Championship Race was really a race between #99 Snyder and #96 Minges with both posting 192mph speeds. Snyder was .6mph faster and took first place. They were followed by Murgia, Strang, and Twombly, the latter DNF due to a broken prop spinner.

Total prize money was $1,000 and was split between the 19 T-6 and Formula 1 pilots. Humble beginnings, but plans were set for 1971.

Billed as the 1970 St. Louis Air Races and held from September 7, the all-T-6 event was relocated across the Mississippi River from St. Louis at the East Alton, Illinois (IL), airport over a 2½.5-mile course. This was four miles shorter than the 1969 course. Twelve pilots qualified to compete for the posted $5,000 in prize money for the regional races. There would be two eight-lap heat races with six racers on each and eight-lap consolation and championship races, also with six aircraft per race. The short course produced some good speeds and two new speed records.

Qualifiers were: #94 Bob Mitchem first at 213.270mph (a new record), #96 Richard Minges second 203.6mph, #99 Ed Snyder third 202.2mph, #6 Victor Baker fourth 200.8mph, #25 Tony Murgia fifth 198.2mph, #30 Hugh Alexander sixth 193.1mph, #10 Don Barrett seventh 192.7mph, #12 Jim Strang eighth 192.3mph in his Canadian-registered Harvard, #21 John Trainor ninth also at 192.3mph, #55 Art Carlson 189.4mph tenth, and 11th was #41 Ralph Twombly 181.4mph. #4 Don Reynolds was 12th at 175.0 in his first and only race flying Don Phillippi's Texan.

A new speed record was achieved during Heat-1A when #94 Mitchem completed the eight laps in 5:55mins, averaging 202.8mph, to take first. #99 Snyder was second at 199.5mph. He was followed by third #25 Murgia, fourth #21 Trainor, fifth #10 Barrett, and in sixth was #41 Twombly at 183.3mph. Twombly was :37.7secs behind first-place Mitchem.

Heat-1B was a scattered race from the start, with #30 Alexander out in front and taking the checkered flag in 6:18.2mins at 190.3mph. Further back, in second place, was #96 Minges at 188.5mph, possibly sandbagging to save his engine for the championship race the next day. Third went to #41 Twombly, fourth was #12 Strang in 7:15.7mins and a pylon cut penalty, #55 Carlson also had a pylon cut penalty and finished fifth in 7:52.0mins and 152.5mph. Baker in #6 dropped out with a bad prop seal and DNF.

The next day's Consolation Race was a bit faster, with the first three aircraft bunched almost to the end when #21 Trainor pulled a lead to take first at 195.2mph and a time of 6:09.2mins. #6 Baker was a scant :02.6secs behind in second. Third place #10 Barrett was a full :08secs behind first place. #41 Twombly in fourth place was just :00.03secs back from Barrett. Fifth went to #55 Carlson, :55secs behind first place. #4 Reynolds placed sixth, completing the eight laps in 7:52.0mins.

The afternoon Championship was again an all #94 Mitchem race, although a tad slower than his Heat-1A race. He finished first at 199.1mph. #96 Minges was second with 193.5mph. In third place was #99 Snyder at 193.4mph, however he was penalized one place for low flying. This moved #25 Murgia from fourth to third place. Fifth and sixth went to #30 Alexander and Canadian #12 Strang, who was :25.1 seconds back from first place.

During the two years of St. Louis T-6 racing, the sport had been enjoyable and fast with average attendance, but not enough to continue. There would be no more T-6 events in St. Louis.

Due to a disagreement between NCAR management and the T-6 Class management, there were no T-6 races at Reno in September 1970.

1971
A T-6 demonstration race was organized by T-6 racer Ed Snyder for April 25, 1971, at Herlong Field in Jacksonville, with five participants. Information recorded does not give the number of laps or course size. #25 Richard Murgia was first at 210mph. He was followed by #21 John Trainor, #12 Jim Strang, #41 Ralph Twombly, and #99 Ed Snyder, who DNF with an oil leak.

The Wilson 1971 regional races were again plagued by bad weather during the races. Held over the weekend of May 15 and 16, spectator attendance was low but 12 T-6s were entered and 11 qualified over the same course used in 1970. The T-6s would fly two heats and a 12-lap Consolation Race and a Championship Race, a total distance of 29.1miles. Qualifying was hampered by low visibility and rain. The race featured three rookies. They were #11 Ernest Opp in eighth with :46.65secs for his one lap, #17 Jozef Huysmans tenth with :46.7secs, and #89 John Silberman 11th with :51.05secs in his only T-6 race. #33 Richard Minges[6] was the fastest qualifier with :44.0secs (he had changed his race number from #96 to #33). #66 Jack Lowers was second, #30 Hugh Alexander third, #99 Ed Snyder fourth, #25 Tony Murgia fifth, #44 John Mosby sixth, #41 Ralph Twombly seventh, and #12 Jim Strang was ninth at :46.6secs.

---
6   Both #33 Minges and #99 Snyder would be fatally injured the following month at Cape May, NJ.

The program cover for the 1971 Cape May, New Jersey (NJ), Air Races. Organizers attempted to hold races the year before but were forced to cancel. (Collection of Aviation Photo Services)

Both heat races were flown in rain and drizzle, with the first being an air start for the six racers. #12 Jim Strang lapped most of the field to win Heat-1B at 190.1mph. The next race, Heat-1A, was won by #30 Alexander. Penalties were given to #44 Mosby for two pylon cuts and #66 Lowers for a jumped start. Photo evidence shows #99 Snyder was again low flying, as after the race, his left wingtip had scrape marks.

Five aircraft started the Consolation Race under overcast skies with #41 Twombly taking first place, well ahead of the others at 189.0mph.

#11 Opp served as the pace plane for the air start of the Championship Race. This was the first of Opp's two races. His second race entry was in the June Cape May races. It appears that while he qualified for both races, he did not race. The Championship Race was 12 laps with eight aircraft (two fill-ins), and #33 Minges took first with a time of 8:47.8mins. Minges was followed by #30 Alexander, #99 Snyder, #25 Murgia, and #66 Lowers in fifth. #12 Strang was given sixth with a pylon cut. The two fill-ins, #41 Twombly and #44 Mosby, placed seventh and eighth, respectively.

Results from 1971 prompted the organizers to plan for 1972.

Cape May held its one air race June 2–6, 1971, which was marred by the first fatal T-6 race accidents. There were 15 racers entered, 14 qualified, to race on the 2½-mile sea level racecourse and would use a flying start with a pace plane. Prize money was $8,000, put up by the beer company Schlitz Brewing. The top qualifier was awarded bonus money. Four heat races were scheduled followed by a Consolation Race and a Championship Race.

After one lap, qualifying in first place was #94 Bob Mitchem, who completed his lap in :43.0secs at 209.3mph and collected $250. He was followed in order of qualifying by #66 Jack Lowers, #30 Hugh Alexander, and #99 Ed Snyder, all flying over 200mph. Fifth #10 Don Barrett at 199.5mph was followed in order by: #33 Richard Minges, #35 Joe Quinn, #6 Victor Baker, #21 John Trainor, #41 Ralph Twombly, and #44 Art Carlson (this was John Mosby's regular Texan). #12 Jim Strang flew the only Harvard in the race. He was followed by #11 Ernest Opp and #18 Jim Flanagan, who placed 14th at 174.7mph and :51.5secs. #45 John Mosby was allowed to race even though he DNQ in a new Texan.

Saturday, June 5, 1971; the Cape May flightline before the start of racing. From right to left are #94 Mitchem, #6 Baker, #35 Quinn, #11 Opp, #12 Stang, #30 Alexander, #99 Snyder, #33 Minges, #66 Lowers, and #41 Twombly. (Kenneth Smith Collection)

#18 Jim Flanagan taxiing out at Cape May, possibly to qualify on Friday, June 4, with #35 Jay Quinn and #12 Jim Strang sitting in their aircraft. (Kenneth Smith Collection)

Art Scholl taxiing in front of the Texan line at Cape May, passing #6 Baker, #35 Quinn, #11 Opp, #12 Strang, and #30 Alexander. #66 Lowers was in the back and #41 Twombly was at the back far right. This would have been Saturday morning.
(Kenneth Smith Collection)

Heat-1A was won by #94 Mitchem and Heat-2A by #33 Minges. The next day, June 5, #94 Mitchem won Heat-1B. This race was followed by Heat-2B. At the first turn on lap 1, #33 Minges started his turn and struck #10 Barrett's rudder and canopy, causing #33 to lose the outer 10ft of its left wing. Minges' aircraft rolled over and crashed with an ensuing fire and was destroyed. Minges was fatally injured, while Barrett landed safety (see Chapter 5 for details).

A minute later at the start of lap 3, #6 Baker and #99 Snyder collided while passing each other, with Baker's aircraft losing its tail and both crashing fatally. Additionally, #35 Quinn crashed trying to avoid the debris from the collision (see Chapter 5 for details). The two remaining aircraft, #44 Carlson and #41 Twombly, were called off the course and the race was red flagged.

The Consolation Race on June 6 was canceled due to lack of sufficient aircraft to race.

The Championship Race was won by #94 Mitchem at 199.06mph and he earned $1,700. Second place and $1,050 went to #30 Alexander, third and $750 to #12 Strang, fourth and $600 to #66 Lowers, fifth and $480 to #41 Twombly, while the sixth-place finisher was #21 Trainor at 182.65mph and he won $375.

Rounding a pylon at Cape May in 1971 are #30 Alexander, #12 Strang, #33 Minges, and #66 Lowers. (via Dennis Buehn)

Start of the Heat-2B at Cape May with pace plane #11 Opp getting everyone formed up for the start. Of the six starters, four would fatally crash and one was damaged. (via Dennis Buehn)

Within a few minutes, T-6 closed course pylon racing had suffered its first fatal accidents, claiming the lives of four pilots. Unsurprisingly, with such a tragic start, Cape May held no more races.

On September 4–6, 1971, a Demonstration Race was held at the former USAAC/USAF training command air base at Bartow, FL. Bartow was a base for T-6s during the late 1940s and early 1950s. A reported $5,000 was offered in prize money for the T-6 Class. No further information is available.

With the T-6 Class returning to Reno from September 21–26, 1971, another large number of pilots qualified resulting in a field of 24. To accommodate this number, the NCAR decided, "The T-6 Racing Field at Reno 1971 was set up for 18 aircraft to fly six each in a Medallion, Consolation, and Championship Race. Since 24 aircraft actually showed up to qualify, an extra or 'Make-Up Race' will be held on Saturday before the formal opening of the show for the six lowest qualifiers. Thus, all 24 aircraft entered will get to race." There would be no heat races and pilots were placed "in this position by Contest Committee" as noted on an NCAR Qualifying Times sheet.

For the first time since the rebirth of Texan racing, both top national contenders were scheduled to race against each other. #7 Ben Hall and #94 Bob Mitchem both were speedsters, and the race fans held their breath.

#94 Bob Mitchem qualified first, taking :50.5secs to fly one lap around the three-mile course with a speed of 213.86mph. He set a new national and Reno qualifying record. Mitchem set the old national record the previous year at St. Louis (Alton). The seven pilots qualifying were all over 200mph: #4 Don Phillippi at 206.5mph, #3 Richard Sykes at 204.16mph, and #10 Don Barrett at 201.87mph, in a T-6 damaged during June's Cape May races. Rookie #47 Rod Kostelnik tied for fifth with #72 Bill Turnbull at 201.49mph. This pair was followed by #9 Pat Palmer and #69 Bob Suacci tied at 200.37mph. Ninth place rookie #80 Bud Collins qualified at 198.53mph but did not race due to mechanical issues. #70 Fred Saunders flew at 198.17mph. #7 Ben Hall, 1969 Championship Race winner, placed 11th at 197.08mph. #0 Hugh Glassburn and Reno newcomer #41 Ralph Twombly tied for 12th at :55.0secs and 196.36mph. Also qualifying were: #88 Bob Metcalfe at 194.95mph, #40 rookie Stan Gnesa at 194.25mph, #18 Jim Flanagan at 193.20, #30 Hugh Alexander at 192.86mph, rookie

Rookie #11 Jim Modes at Reno in 1971. Modes raced at Reno for four years and at Mojave for one. He also tried his hand at Unlimited Class racing. (Emil Strasser)

#42 Jim Mott at 192.17mph, rookie #11 Jim Modes at 190.81mph (Modes' aircraft #11 had been raced previously by other pilots), rookie #48 George Burdick at 189.14mph, #44 John Mosby was 21st at 188.81mph, and rookie #57 Marvin Quaid at 182.43mph. This aircraft had raced before with other pilots, and this was Quaid's only Texan race. Rookie #38 Don Hackett was 23rd at 175.90mph and 24th place went to rookie #87 Fred Kohler, who took 1:02.4min for one lap at 173.63mph. Nine rookies, plus Reno newcomer Twombly, and all but two with speeds greater than 180mph made for some interesting racing. With Hall qualifying 11th, he would not race in the Championship Race; the anticipated battle would have to wait.

On Friday, September 24, the six-lap racehorse start of the Medallion Race was like a runaway horse with #88 Metcalfe flying into the lead and staying there until the finish at 192.23mph. He was followed in second place by #30 Alexander, who had fumbled his start but caught up and overtook four others ahead of him. Alexander's time of 5:48.3mins was almost ten seconds slower than Metcalfe. The rest of the field was #42 Mott in third place, #40 Gnesa in fourth, #11 Modes in fifth at 179.7mph, and #18 Flanagan sixth at 174.85mph.

As promised, a six-lap Make-up Race was held the next day and featured the six lowest qualifiers, five were rookies. Veteran #44 Mosby had raced T-6s for two years but had difficulty qualifying and joined this group. The race was well flown and was quite close with the first three competitors almost together at the end. Rookie #48 Burdick took first at 188.76mph. In spite of his win, Burdick did not race T-6s again. In second place was rookie #11 Modes at 188.59mph and #44 Mosby was third at 186.1mph. He was followed :14.0secs later by rookie #57 Quaid in fourth. Quaid never raced T-6s again, although his aircraft did with another pilot. Fifth place went to rookie #87 Kohler with a 6:03.2mins time, just :00.5secs behind Quaid. Next was rookie #38 Hackett :00.4 back from Kohler. He also would not race T-6s again, but his aircraft would.

Engine problems would prevent #41 Twombly from racing the full eight-lap Consolation (Silver) Race. This reduced the field to five, as he pulled up and out before the start of the first lap. From the start, it was fast and a real ground-hugger, with mere tenths of seconds separating the five contestants led by #69 Suacci, #9 Palmer, and #7 Hall in front. At the finish line, the time between first and fifth was :11.8secs with #69 Bob Suacci first, #7 Ben Hall second, #9 Palmer third, #70 Fred Saunders fourth, and #0 Glassburn fifth at 188.28mph.

Drama opened the Championship (Gold) Race at the racehorse start when #3 Sykes stood his T-6 on its nose trying to adjust to the high winds. The race was stopped, but not before #4 Phillippi was airborne and headed for the first pylon. He realized he was alone and circled to land. The race was rescheduled, allowing #9 Palmer to race as he was the first alternate. Before the restarted race, it was found that #4 Phillippi did not have an operating radio. This is why he had not heard the call to stop the first race and Phillippi was not allowed to race. After the start, however, the wind increased, and it was deemed necessary to shorten the race from ten to six laps. This did not prevent race winner #94 Mitchem from setting a new speed record of 205.85mph (both national and Reno were held by Mitchem). Second was fill-in #9 Palmer a full 10mph slower, third was #72 Turnbull, fourth was #10 Barrett at 188.21mph, and rookie #47 Kostelnik[7] was fifth at 158.20mph, over 40mph slower than first place due to a sour engine.

Reno 1971 had been a great year with new records set, broken and re-set. The races in 1972 could only go up.

1972

The Wilson 1972 regional races held May 20–21 were billed as the "Richard Minges Memorial Air Races" after the late Minges, who had been fatally injured in the 1971 Cape May races. Minges was from Chamberland County, NC, and was flying his #33 T-6 at the time of his death. For the third year, rain kept spectator and contestant attendance low. Only six Texans were entered ensuring everyone would race around the 2.42-mile course.

Qualifiers were #30 Hugh Alexander[8] in first place at 204.08mph and :41.1secs. Second was #41 Ralph Twombly at 198.2mph. Third was #66 Jack Lowers at 196.9mph. Fourth was rookie #25 Roy McClain in Richard Murgia's former Texan. Fifth was #17 Jozef Huysmans, who was flying his second time at Wilson, and the last time he would race T-6s. Sixth place went to rookie #6 Art Bowles with 180.72mph in :46.8secs.

The two heat races were simply place-swapping with just six competitors. Both the Consolation and Championship races were eight laps of four aircraft each with #30 Alexander and #66 Lowers racing in both. The Consolation Race saw rookie #6 Bowles finish first at 181.9mph. Following in second was #17 Huysmans at 181.0mph. Top qualifier #30 Alexander was third at 180.7mph. Lowers in #66 DNF with mechanical problems but fixed them in time to race in the Championship Race.

The Championship Race was a runaway for first place finisher #30 Alexander. He was the only one to break 200mph. Second went to future RB-51 pilot #25 McClain at 191.8mph. Third was #41 Twombly and in fourth was fill-in #66 Lowers. Weather and low attendance for the third straight year put an end to the Wilson races. The quality of the racing was always high over its short course, but Mother Nature ultimately won.

The end of the Wilson air races also ended PRPA's attempt to bring about low-budget regional air races to raise awareness of the sport across the nation. It was a bold idea that never really caught on.

On June 23–25, 1972, Graham, TX, held a small PRPA Demonstration Race at the Rossner Ranch Airport, where five contestants participated. Racers took off from a grass strip and formed up before releasing themselves over the racecourse. Two heat races were run and a Championship Race on the last day. Those racing were #18 Jim Flanagan, #25 Roy McClain, #42 Jim Mott, #43 Dennis Buehn, and #48 Cliff Putman. Results for Heat-1 showed #25 McClain taking first at 8:25mins. Second was #18 Flanagan at 8:26.4mins. Third was #48 Putman at 8:52.0mins. Fourth was #42 Mott at 8:55.1mins. Fifth was #43 Buehn with 9:05.1mins. #43 Buehn took second in the finals at 194.5mph. With a positive outcome, plans were made for 1973.

Reno 1972 opened with 22 pilots qualifying out of 26 entered, eight were rookies, and the first ten qualifiers reached more than 200mph. One lap qualifying times were (in order): #44 John Mosby :51.3secs (210.53mph), #69 Bob Suacci :51.4secs, #25 Roy McClain :51.9secs, #72 Bill Turnbull :52.0secs, rookie #70 Calvin Early :52.7secs, #3 Richard Sykes :52.8secs, #4 Don Phillippi :53.0secs, #41 Ralph Twombly :53.4secs, #7 Ben Hall in his Harvard II :53.4secs, #88 Bob Metcalfe in his Harvard IV :53.7secs (201.12mph), #9 Pat Palmer :54.1secs, Reno rookie #24 Gerald Swayze :54.4secs, rookie #38 Donald Gaylen in his first and only T-6 race (this T-6 had raced in 1971 with Don Hackett as pilot) :54.5secs, #18 Jim Flanagan :54.7secs, #42 Jim Mott :55.7secs,

---

7 A post-race accident claimed the life of #47 Rod Kostelnik and a passenger on their way back to Seattle, Washington (WA), when they flew into a mountain in bad weather.

8 #30 Hugh Alexander was fatally injured almost a week later in the crash of an F-1 racer at the TRANSPO 1972 races after a mid-air collision.

A/C #	PILOT NAME	LAPS	TIME	RESULTS
25	Ray MacLean	1ST HEAT	8:25	1st
18	Jim Flanagan		8:26.4	2nd
48	Cliff Putman		8:52.0	3rd
42	Jim Mott		8:55.1	4th
43	Dennis Buehn		9:05.1	5th

Scoreboard at the 1972 Graham, TX, races. A small demo race was held at the Rosser Ranch airport. There were only five contestants for the race and the scoreboard shows the results of the first heat race. (Wings Publishing via Dennis Buehn)

#6 Art Bowles :55.9secs, rookie #65 D. J. Weinberger in his first and only T-6 race :56.4secs (he qualified but decided not to race), rookie #2 Bruce Payne :56.6secs, rookie #74 Don DeWalt :56.7secs, rookie #11 Calvin Conroy :56.9secs (this Harvard II had raced before with several other pilots), #43 Dennis Buehn :57.7secs (in a new #43 Texan), and rookie #37 Eugene Stover :58.2secs and 185.57mph. This T-6 had been raced before by several other pilots, but this was Stover's only entry.

The NCAR race committee cut the field to 18 slots so #11 Conroy, #43 Buehn and #37 Stover did not race. When #65 Weinberger dropped out of the race #74 DeWalt moved into 18th. The four pilots that were entered but did not qualify were #10 Don Barrett, #40 Stan Gnesa, #80 Bud Collins, and #11 Jim Modes. RARA announced that slots for the Championship Race would now be selected according to their finishing times in the heat races. Spirits were dampened for all the classes when it was announced that there would be no prize money for the heat races. In the end, the T-6 Class would collect just under $9,000.

When the flag was dropped for the six-lap Heat-1A racehorse start, not all pilots were lined up in starting position and confusion ensued. #7 Hall and #44 Mosby were off late. #9 Palmer had a minor gear problem that he sorted out on the first lap. Some of the pylon judges were not in place. As the race progressed, #25 McClain, #44 Mosby and #9 Palmer were tied in the lead position and, by lap 6, #9 Palmer was at the front. However, the judges decided to make it an eight-lap race to compensate for the bad start. #9 Palmer may not have heard the change and pulled back on the power thinking he had won. By the time Palmer realized his mistake, #44 Mosby was first, followed by #25 McClain second, and #4 Phillippi third. Palmer was awarded fourth after #7 Hall, who had crossed the line in fourth, was dropped to sixth for a pylon cut. In last place was rookie #70 Early at 189.47mph.

Heat-1B quickly became an all #69 Suacci event as he pulled into the lead and remained there until the end, finishing first at 200.25mph. #3 Sykes was second at 197.98, but was bumped to sixth for cutting a pylon on the first lap and not taking a safety lap. #72 Turnbull was moved from third into second, which bumped everyone up a place. #88 Metcalfe moved to third, #41 Twombly to fourth, and #24 Swayze one-half lap back from first was fifth at 162.20mph.

Next day's Consolation (Silver) Race was also a mixed-up race. At the start, #7 Hall and #70 Early fought for the lead, with Early just ahead of Hall. By lap 4, it had become a threesome with #9 Palmer seconds behind in third place.

#88 Bob Metcalfe at Reno in 1972. Metcalfe would race at Reno, Mojave, and Graham in 1973 before retiring after Reno 1974. (Emil Strasser)

They finished with #70 Early at 200.37mph. He was followed by #3 Sykes in fourth, #41 Twombly fifth, #24 Swayze sixth at 183.00mph. Then, #70 Early was bumped to fifth for cutting a pylon on the pace lap. Sykes was bumped to sixth for also cutting a pylon on the pace lap moving everyone up and giving #7 Hall the win.

Things became more confused during Sunday's Medallion Race for the six slowest qualifiers. Four aircraft were lined up for the racehorse start heading east on the main runway and three on the adjacent runway heading north. Rookie #74 DeWalt, as the alternate, was on the east-facing runway with rookie #2 Payne and rookie #65 Weinberger on each side of him when the starter raised the flag. Weinberger mistook this as the signal to takeoff and jumped the start. He realized what he had done and pulled the power back and turned off the main runway instead of going straight ahead as briefed, while the starter dropped the flag and everyone else began taking off. In this group was #2 Payne and #74 DeWalt. Payne had a moment of hesitation after smoke filled his cockpit and thought he might have to abort. He realized it was engine exhaust as his engine belched smoke when power was applied. During this moment, he and #74 DeWalt had to swerve to avoid #65 Weinberger, who was turning, causing #2 Payne to scrape a wingtip and nick his prop. DeWalt had leaned his engine too much, which caused a longer takeoff run. He continued to the first pylon, but cut pylon 2 while trying to adjust his engine. Rookie #38 Gaylen took off without problems, followed by #42 Mott, #18 Flanagan and #6 Bowles and headed for the first pylon. Payne and DeWalt were well behind trying to sort themselves out. Things appeared to settle down and #38 Gaylen and #42 Mott battled for the lead, but it was #38 Gaylen in first place at 193.26mph. #42 Mott came in second at 193.15mph, #18 Flanagan third, #6 Bowles fourth, #2 Payne fifth, and #74 DeWalt sixth. However, it was determined that first place finisher #38 Gaylen cut a pylon on the pace lap, and he was bumped to fifth moving everyone up. First place went to #42 Mott with #74 DeWalt remaining in sixth due to the pace lap pylon cut. DeWalt pulled back on the power and crossed the line at only 155.36mph. The Championship Race that followed was no less dramatic.

A Sport Biplane (#7 Herman Thomas) had crashed fatally during the previous race and the crash/recovery crews were still on the course when the eight-lap T-6 Championship (Gold) Race was flagged off to start. NCAR officials ordered all racers to maintain a 100ft minimum during the race. All six contestants took off without any problems. Soon after the pace lap, competitors bunched up, with the exception of #88 Metcalfe, who was at the back. The other five jockeyed back and forth flying wide, low and high trying to pass. By lap 5 they settled into a direct speed chase to the finish except

#88 Metcalfe who was a one-half lap back from the others. In first place was #25 McClain at 201.59mph ($1,500 prize), followed in second by #44 Mosby at 201.31mph ($1,000), third was #69 Suacci at 200.33mph, #4 Phillippi was fourth at 197.58mph, #72 Turnbull at 197.04mph was fifth, and #88 Metcalfe was sixth at 188.85mph. The judges disqualified both #69 Suacci and #4 Phillippi for low flying, which moved Turnbull ($900) and Metcalfe ($775) up. It was anyone's guess what 1973 would bring.

1973

T-6 racing returned to Florida three years after the last race at Fort Lauderdale. On January 16–21, 1973, Miami hosted the Great Miami Air Races at the new Tamiami Airport. The new racecourse was a three-mile course at sea level. The racing schedule showed a one-lap qualifier, six laps for four heat races, and eight laps each for the consolation and championship races. There were 12 qualifiers with John Mosby #44 being first at 204.1mph and receiving $500 for fastest time. #99 John Card was last at 183.6mph in :58.8secs. The other ten were: second #10 Calvin Early :53.5secs for his one lap, #7 Jack Lowers :54.2secs (in Ben Hall's Harvard), #25 Roy McClain :54.2secs (this had been Tony Murgia's Texan), #72 William Turnbull :55.3secs, #41 Ralph Twombly :55.4secs, #18 Jim Flanagan :56.1secs, #2 Bruce Payne :56.4secs, #11 Calvin Conroy in another Mk. II Harvard at :56.5secs, #6 Art Bowles :56.6secs, and #74 Don DeWalt at :56.7secs.

Heat-1B was easily won by #74 DeWalt, who was the 11th-place qualifier at 193.2mph. Twelfth place qualifier #99 Card finished last being unable to retract his landing gear. Payne's Texan ended up on its nose after a brake locked up and a tire blew on landing, putting him out of competition. After consultation of the judges, #99 Card was disqualified from further racing for extremely low flying.

The Heat-1A race was uneventful with #44 Mosby taking first place with a new class record of 208.49mph. Heat-2B held the next day was pretty much the same, with #11 Conroy scoring first place at the end of six laps at 196.3mph.

Heat-2A was fast and furious from the start with both first and second place aircraft charging ahead. #44 Mosby passed #25 McClain to win with another record speed of 210.53mph. This exceeded Mosby's record set the day before by a full 2mph with #25 McClain second at 206.9mph. Heat-2A was #74 DeWalt's turn to have gear retraction problems. He was able to get the landing gear up halfway through the race, but by then, DeWalt had been lapped by the leaders and finished sixth at 171.7mph.

Winds proved to be a problem for the Consolation Race as all the aircraft had to take off in the opposite direction towards the first pylon (the Unlimited scatter pylon). #41 Twombly made an error at the start of lap 1 by flying around the first Unlimited pylon instead of the T-6 pylon, which cost him several places. #18 Flanagan lost his prop governor and pulled out on lap 1. #74 DeWalt led the race until the end

Handbill for the 1973 Great Miami Air Race, giving the line up of races and airshow acts. The races were held at the new Tamiami airport where there was plenty of open space to race, which is not possible today. (Collection of Aviation Photo Services)

with #6 Bowles second and, having caught up with the others, #41 Twombly finished third. Race fill ins #10 Early and #7 Lowers finished last.

The Championship Race started with the two fastest racers #44 Mosby and #25 McClain and was sure to be a good race. The two did not disappoint as they battled wingtip-to-wingtip all the way to the end. Mosby overtook McClain to cross the finish line first at 207.69mph with McClain second at 206.5mph. #72 Turnbull was third at 203.3mph. Mosby collected $1,750, McClain received $1,100, and third place #72 Turnbull earned $700. Fourth place #10 Early won $550, fifth spot #11 Conroy won $500, while sixth place #7 Lowers received $450. The year 1973 would be the only T-6 race held at Miami.

Reno 1973 opened with 25 pilots (26 aircraft) qualifying for the 18 race slots, 15 at or over 200mph. Those qualifying in order were: #42 Jim Mott :51.2secs at 210.94mph, #70 Cal Early, #3 Richard Sykes, #72 Bill Turnbull, #69 Bob Suacci, #44 Jack Lowers (flying John Mosby aircraft as Mosby could not make the races) at 205.71mph, and #80 Bud Collins at 204.55mph. Collins had qualified in 1971 but did not race. Tied in eighth place were three pilots all at 203.77mph, rookie #10 Jim Wilson (this T-6 had raced before at Reno with another pilot), #9 Pat Palmer, and #11 Jim Modes. #88 Bob Metcalfe qualified at 203.39mph, while rookie #73 Ralph Rina was at 201.49mph, #43 Dennis Buehn at 201.12mph, and #25 Roy McClain at 200.37mph. He was the winner of the 1972 Championship Race. In 15th place was #41 Ralph Twombly. He was the last of the 200mph group. #24 Gerald Swayze flew a :55.0secs lap for 16th place. #6 Art Bowles at 194.95 tied with #74 Don DeWalt for 17th. #40 Stan Gnesa came in at 194.6mph, while rookie #14 Fred Sebby was 20th. #37 Bob Metcalfe earned 21st place, qualifying a second T-6 for owner Richard Gregory. #2 Bruce Payne was 22nd, rookie #97 Gordon Richardson in his only attempt at T-6 racing was 23rd, and #46 rookie Charles Beck at 24th and 187.18mph. #57 James Wirtz finished at 185.57mph in an aircraft that previously raced at Reno. Rookie #75 Barrie Simonson finished 26th at 183.67mph. Pilots and aircraft cut were #40, #14, #37, #2, #97, #46, #57, and #75.

Racehorse start for the Medallion Race at Reno 1973. Left to right are Don DeWalt in his original #74, #43 Dennis Buehn, and #6 Art Bowles. (Wings Publishing via Dennis Buehn)

Gusty winds greeted both Heat-1 and Heat-2, both close races with lots of back-and-forth flying. Heat-1 was won by #9 Palmer at 203.26mph followed by #42 Mott, #69 Suacci, #3 Sykes, #80 Collins, and #88 Metcalfe at 193.95mph.

Heat-2 was also a fast race with #72 Turnbull taking first at 200.19mph followed by #70 Early, and rookie #10 Wilson. #44 Lowers was fourth having caught up after missing the #2 scatter pylon at the start. Rookie #73 Rina was fifth and #11 Modes finished sixth at 192.00mph.

Seven aircraft were lined up for the Medallion Race, three on the main north-facing runway and four on the east-facing runway. #74 DeWalt was again the alternate. When #40 Gnesa had a mechanical issue and could not start, #74 took his place. All aircraft except #24 Swayze got off quickly and grouped on the backside during the pace lap, with #25 McClain in the lead. At the finish of lap 1, #25 McClain hit turbulence and pulled high, allowing #41 Twombly, #43 Buehn, and #74 DeWalt to pass. As the race progressed, #25 McClain retook the lead, leaving #41 Twombly and #43 Buehn to fight for second, followed by #74 DeWalt, #24 Swayze, and 6 Bowles who was a mile behind in sixth. They finished in this order. Later #74 DeWalt was bumped to sixth for cutting a pylon on lap one.

It could only be called a runaway for the six-lap Consolation Race as #44 Lowers had his T-6 in the lead from the start and, by the first pylon, had left the others behind. #3 Sykes flew an unchallenged second. In the middle of the pack, #88 Metcalfe and #80 Collins repeated their Heat-1 race while #11 Modes and rookie #73 Rina brought up the rear. When #44 Lowers crossed the finish line in first, he had set a Reno and national speed record of 212.39mph, breaking one set in Miami earlier in the year by the absent John Mosby in the same T-6. Thirteen seconds back in second was #3 Sykes at 203.26mph. The rest of the field finished with #88 Metcalfe in third, #80 Collins in fourth, #11 Modes placed fifth with #73 Rina sixth at 195.53mph.

From the first pylon of the eight-lap Championship (Gold) Race, it was #42 Mott, #69 Suacci and #72 Turnbull. This group was followed by #9 Palmer, #70 Early and #10 Wilson. By lap 5, the finishing order was set after #72 Turnbull passed under #42 Mott to take the lead. Turnbull took only 6:58.2mins to fly the 24 miles at 206.60mph to win the $1,700 first prize in a borrowed aircraft. Mott received $1,200 for second, #9 Palmer collected $1,000 for third, #69 Suacci got $800 for fourth, rookie #10 Wilson picked up $700 for fifth, and sixth place #70 Early got $600. The year 1973 was another good racing year for all.

Wind-swept Mojave, CA, is a small desert community northeast of Los Angeles. It hosted six air races featuring T-6s. This former desert Marine Corps Air Station (MCAS) near Edwards AFB would be the second longest running venue for Texan racing after Reno. It had the longest racecourse of any of the post-1940s races at 3.763 miles, for a total of 30 miles distance for its 1973 Championship Race. Mojave was also the first to hold one-lap Drag Races for T-6s. High winds, heat and cold, low prize money, and lack of accommodation were always against the promoters, but the racing never disappointed.[9]

Promoted as the 1973 California Air Classic races at Mojave, the races took place through the efforts of Unlimited Race pilots LeRoy Penhall, Howie Keefe, Clay Lacy, Lyle Shelton, and T-6 race pilot Dick Sykes as the Air Race Management Corp of Van Nuys. Sixteen T-6s qualified for the first event held October 18–21, 1973.

Qualifying first was #9 Pat Palmer at 216.455mph taking 1:03.2mins for his one lap with everyone else qualifying over 200mph, with the exception of #46 Charles Beck at 199.7mph and 1:08.5mins in 16th. The longer racecourse enabled the pilots to achieve good speeds. Also qualifying were: #25 Roy McClain second at 215.772mph, third #42 Jim Mott at 213.750mph, fourth #2 Calvin Conroy at 213.084mph, #41 Ralph Twombly fifth at 212.422mph, sixth #3 Dick Sykes at 211.111mph, seventh #43 Dennis Buehn at 211.111mph, eighth #69 Bob Suacci at 211.111mph, #73 Ralph Rina ninth at 209.815mph, tenth #88 Bob Metcalfe at 208.219mph, #11 Jim Modes was 11th at 207.272mph, #74 Don DeWalt was 12th at 207.272mph, #97 Gordon Richardson was 13th at 201.176mph, 14th #2A Bruce Payne at 200.586mph, and #14 Fred Sebby was 15th at 200.586mph. The former MCAS's narrow runways and winds required air starts with a pace plane for all races.

#9 Palmer started things off by taking first place in a closely raced Heat-1A, taking 6:26mins to fly the race with a speed of 212.642mph. Following was #43 Buehn in second at 207.482mph, third #3 Sykes at 207.063mph, fourth #74 DeWalt at 205.302mph, fifth #88 Metcalfe at 204.688mph, sixth #42 Mott at 7:56.7mins and 172.183mph and a penalty for cutting pylon 5.

Heat-1B was won by #25 McClain taking first at 216.913mph. In second place was #69 Suacci at 212.863mph. #11 Modes was third at 212.697mph. He was followed by #73 Rina in fourth at 210.785mph. Fifth was the other Ralph, #41 Twombly, at 208.324mph. In sixth place and one-half lap behind was #97 Richardson at 201.423mph.

---

9   Mojave had hosted the 1970 Unlimited-only 1,000-mile closed course races and the 1971 Unlimited-only 1,000km closed course races.

Program cover for the first California Air Classic in Mojave that featured Texan racing in October 1973. The races were promoted and organized by race pilots of both Unlimited and Texan classes. In addition to the pylon races, there were the first time one-lap drags. (Collection of Aviation Photo Services)

Rosser Ranch, Graham, in November 1973. These races were held after the California Classics at Mojave. Although a poor quality photo, it does show the grass airport and the Texan line starting with Jack Lowers flying Ben Hall's #7 and #72 Bill Turnbull. Also seen are #42 Mott, #41 Twombly, and possibly #73 Rina at the far end. (Don Fairbanks via Tim Weinschenker)

The Bronze Race was a confused and somber affair[10] with many pylon cuts and changes. #73 Rina was declared the winner at 200.9mph, followed by #46 Beck at 199.3mph. #2 Conroy was third at 200.9mph with cuts on pylon 5 and pylon 3 three times. In fourth place was #97 Richardson at 197.307mph with one cut on pylon 5 and pylon 3. Fifth place went to #2A Payne at 197.023mph with a cut on pylon 5 and two on pylon 2. The sixth finisher was #14 Sebby at 189.120mph with three cuts on pylon 5.

It was determined that pylon judges at pylon 5 were located too far from the pylon to properly observe the turns, so some of the infractions were removed but had little effect on some finishes. The pilots said that pylon 5 was practically impossible to see and race officials agreed.

While the Silver Race (Consolation) was a windy event, it provided some great racing. At the first pylon, #41 Twombly, #73 Rina and #74 DeWalt appeared to round the pylon as one aircraft and remained close almost to the end. It took #88 Metcalfe to come from behind to separate them and take first place at 206.9mph in 8:48.8mins. Metcalfe was followed by #41 Twombly at 206.902mph and 8:48.9mins. Coming in third was #73 Rina at 206.685mph in 8:49.5mins. Then came #42 Mott in fourth at 206.324mph. He was followed by #74 DeWalt fifth at 202.292mph and #97 Richardson sixth at 196.199 and 9:17.8mins. Metcalfe won $273.

The eight-lap Gold (Championship) Race was a strung-out affair with #9 Palmer leading all the way to finish first at 219.8mph and taking 8:17.7mins. For the eight laps flown, he collected $893. His winning time was a new record for Texans. In order of finish were: #25 McClain second at 218.880mph, third #43 Buehn at 218.051mph, fourth #69 Suacci at 213.125mph, fifth #3 Sykes at 212.175mph, and in sixth with three cuts of pylon 5 was #11 Modes at 212.381mph, who received $315.

While not a huge financial success plans were being made for 1974.

For the second year in a row, a regional race was held November 2–4, 1973, at the private Rosser Ranch airport in Graham. The sign at the entrance of the airport greeted everyone with "Welcome to Air Racing, King of the Motorsports." There were 12 qualifiers, and they would race over the 3½-mile, six-pylon course with six T-6s per race. Contestants took off from the grass strip. Qualifiers were: #7 Jack Lowers (in Ben Hall's Harvard), #42 Jim Mott, #41 Ralph Twombly, #72 Bill Turnbull, #88 Bob Metcalf, #6 Art Bowles,[11] #5 Roy McClain, #10 Jim Wilson, #73 Ralph Rina, #21 John Trainor, #24 Gerald Swayze, and #18 Jim Flanagan. Results are not recorded, and this was the last race held here.

---

10 #24 Bud Fountain had crashed his F8F Bearcat fatally during the Unlimited Heat-1A the day before.

11 #6 Art Bowles was fatally injured on his way home from these races after encountering bad weather.

Race Control at Graham 1973, showing the course layout. A portable control tower parked next to the grass runway was used. The main racing classes were Texans (12 raced) and sports biplanes. Don Fairbanks, who took these photos, raced his biplane #5 *White Knight Twister* at these races. (Don Fairbanks via Tim Weinschenker)

Backside view of the Texan line at Graham 1973 includes #41 Twombly, #72 Turnbull, #6 Bowles, #5 McClain, #73 Rina, #88 Metcalf, and #42 Mott. Those not shown are #10 Wilson, #21 Trainor, #24 Swayze, #7 Lowers, and #18 Flanagan. (Don Fairbanks via Tim Weinschenker)

1974

Reno 1974 was called lack luster by one writer, mundane by another, and a third said same-ol'-same-ol' when it came to all of the class races. Twenty T-6s qualified of the 21 entered, 14 were at or above 200mph. There were four new rookies who put on some fine racing.

#5 Roy McClain qualified first at 211.77mph, taking only :51.0secs for his one lap. This T-6 had formally been raced as #25. The second to qualify was #10 Jim Wilson at 209.30mph. #10 was previously flown by Don Barrett. #73 Ralph Rina in his second year at Reno came in at 208.09mph. #11 Calvin Conroy reached 206.9mph. #9 Pat Palmer and #24 Gerald Swayze tied at 206.50mph. #42 Jim Mott was seventh at 204.93mph. Mott was followed by #43 Dennis Buehn at 203.77mph and #74 Don DeWalt at 203.39 in his newly garishly painted T-6. #88 Bob Metcalfe at 201.87mph qualified next and rookie #12 M. D. Washburn followed with a respectable 201.49. #41 Ralph Twombly qualified at 200.74mph. #72 Bill Turnbull and #70 Fred Saunders tied for 13th at 200.00mph. #75 Barrie Simonson was in 15th place and managed 196.01mph in his Harvard II. #69 Bob Suacci at 194.95mph was just ahead of rookie #7 Colene Giglio in 17th at 192.86mph. Giglio was the first woman to race T-6s since 1949. Rookie #97 Gary Meermans finished at 192.17mph. The Harvard II flown by Meermans was entered and qualified before at Reno but had not raced. The slowest of the group were #46 Charles Beck at 186.85mph and rookie #33 Marshall Wells with 20th place at 184.30mph.

Heat-1 was a swap meet from the start between the three fastest contestants all at 200mph. They were #42 Mott, #9 Palmer, and #5 McClain. After lap 4, all three finished with Mott at 5:22.6mins, Palmer 5:22.8mins, and McClain 5:23.8mins. These were followed by #73 Rina in fourth, #74 DeWalt in fifth, and #12 Washburn in sixth at 5:42.2mins.

Heat-2 was a one-horse race with #10 Wilson out front from start to finish. There was a brief fight between #43 Buehn and #88 Metcalfe until the last lap. #41 Twombly pulled up and out on lap 1 with engine troubles and DNF. No one broke 200mph the entire race. Final results were #10 Wilson at 198.90mph, #88 Metcalfe, #43 Buehn, #11 Conroy, #24 Swayze fifth 14mph slower than first place.

#72 Turnbull controlled the Medallion Race from start to finish and the only action was a slight scuffle between rookies #97 Meermans and #7 Giglio mid-race. #69 Suacci finished second one-half mile behind Turnbull. Third place went to #70 Saunders. In fourth was #97 Meermans at 188.54mph. #7 Giglio placed fifth at 187.94mph, not bad for her first race. Coming in sixth was #75 Simonson with his Harvard II.

#24 Gerald Swayze qualified sixth for the 1974 Reno races. He would go on to finish sixth in the Consolation Race that year. (Emil Strasser)

The Consolation Race saw the first real skirmish of what would be called "The Battle of the Two Ralphs," #73 Ralph Rina and #41 Ralph Twombly. This friendly battle continued for years and always provided great racing between the two. They put on a fierce fight all the way to the end, and it seemed no one paid much attention to whoever was flying behind. There was an audible cheer from the crowd when #73 Rina slipped by to take first and speed away. Rina finished first at 205.98mph with Twombly second at 197.32mph. Rookie #12 Washburn was third, #74 DeWalt fourth, #11 Conroy fifth, and #24 Swayze sixth 15mph slower than first.

From flag drop to finish, #9 Palmer led the record-breaking eight-lap Championship Race taking only 6:48.8mins for the 24 miles. He was followed by #5 McClain, #42 Mott, #43 Buehn, #10 Wilson, and #88 Metcalfe. What made this race a record setter was that all racers finished at or above 200mph. Palmer received $2,731 for his 211.35mph win, McClain $1,706 for 207.84mph, Mott $1,226 for 206.01mph, Buehn $963 for 202.91mph, Wilson $785 for 202.53mph (Wilson and #10 would not race again), and Metcalfe $667 for 200.00mph in his aptly named Harvard *Super Slug*.

Far from "mundane," Reno 1974 saw two significant events – the return of a woman pilot to T-6 closed course pylon racing and an all 200mph race.

Pilots entered in the October 9–13, 1974, Mojave races were greeted with a number of changes. The first was a change in name to "The California National Air Races." Other changes included a slightly shorter course of 3.7 miles, a reduction in the number of laps from eight to six, and T-6 racers would fly counterclockwise. The race would be air started with a pace plane. Eighteen aircraft entered and 17 qualified. #33 Marshall Wells did not qualify or race. The race field was cut to 12, leaving the other five to race only in the standing start one-lap drag races.

Start of a one-lap drag race at Mojave 1974 with #43 Dennis Buehn vs #42 Jim Mott. From the starting flag, pilots applied full power, took off, cycled the landing gear, and made one lap around the course. (via Dennis Buehn)

#5 Roy McClain qualified first at 212.6mph taking 1:02.39mins for his one lap. The first woman to race in closed course pylon racing since 1949, #7 Colene Giglio, made the cut in 12th place at 202.8mph and 1:05.39mins. This was her second time racing; her first was at Reno in September. The other ten were #9 Pat Palmer 1:02.55mins second, #72 Calvin Early third 1:03.42mins, fourth #42 Jim Mott, fifth #3 Charles Beck for Dick Sykes, #74 Don DeWalt sixth, #41 Ralph Twombly seventh, #43 Dennis Buehn eighth, #12 Marlin Washburn ninth, #73 Ralph Rina tenth, and #69 Robert Suacci was 11th in 1:05.09mins and 203.810mph. Those regulated to the drags only were #11 Jim Modes, #97 Gary Meermans, #46 Charles Beck, #35 Fred Sebby, and #87 Fred Kohler, the latter with a time of 1:17.71mins and speed of 170.712mph, placing him 17th.

Heat-1A saw all racers posting speeds above 200mph for the six-lap race. #5 McClain took first place at 212.5mph with #72 Early second. #12 Washburn was third at 205.3mph. In fourth place was #3 Sykes 205.1mph, but he was moved to sixth with a pylon cut. #41 Twombly was fifth, and #69 Suacci placed sixth but moved up after Sykes' pylon cut.

Heat-2B had first place #42 Mott and second place #9 Palmer fractions of seconds apart, Mott at 210.571mph and Palmer at 210.566mph. They were followed by #74 DeWalt, #73 Rina, #7 Giglio bumped to sixth for a pylon cut, and #43 Buehn.

Mojave's drag-racing event was exciting as the paired racers roared off the line. The last place qualifier, #87 Kohler, had brake problems at the start of the race and stood his T-6 on its nose damaging the prop and engine. Kohler applied full power but failed to release his brakes.

The 1974 six-lap Silver (Consolation) and Gold (Championship) races were fast paced with almost everyone over 200mph. #69 Suacci was first at 207.130mph and 6:24.28mins in the Silver followed by #3 Sykes at 204.238mph, #41 Twombly third at 203.336mph, fourth #74 DeWalt at 200.904mph, fifth #7 Giglio at 198.405mph, and #43 Buehn. He finished second at 206.298 and 6:25.83mins but was placed sixth after cutting pylon 2 on laps 2 and 4.

First place qualifier #5 McClain led the Gold Race for the first three laps, posting a 216.2mph lap before pulling up and out on lap 4 with a sick engine. This left #42 Mott and #9 Palmer to battle for first. Mott got a lead on Palmer and stayed to take first place only seconds ahead of Palmer. Mott's winning speed was 213.0mph with #9 Palmer second at 212.772mph. They were followed by #72 Early third at 211.635mph, fourth #73 Rina at 206.031mph, fifth #12 Washburn at 206.015mph, with #5 McClain awarded sixth. Mojave 1974 had provided some great action and made "a little bread to spare" for its promoters. Even better things were promised for 1975.

1975

On May 15–16, 1975, at Lincoln, CA, USARA and Northwestern Area Group (NAG) held small demonstration races on a three-mile racecourse. No prize money was available, and the results of the races are unknown.

The 1975 California National Air Races at Mojave were held June 18–20 and saw the return of high winds and hot temperatures, but this did not prevent great racing. Seventeen Texans qualified, most with speeds over 200mph. Marshall Wells raced #9, the former Pat Palmer T-6, to a new T-6 Class qualifying speed of 232.2mph (:57.13secs) over the new shorter course of 3.685 miles. Wells was almost 10mph faster than #5 Roy McClain, who posted a 223.5mph lap for second fastest. #99 Pat Palmer in a new Texan was third at 216.76mph. Fourth went to #2 Dennis Buehn at 215.01mph in a borrowed Harvard. In fifth place was #3 Richard Sykes at 213.14mph followed by sixth place #11 Cal Conroy at 211.55mph. Seventh was #12 Marlin Washburn at 211.55mph and eighth was #69 Bob Suacci at 209.91mph. In ninth was #15 Fred Sebby at 208.74mph followed by tenth place #73 Ralph Rina at 206.96mph and #44 John Mosby was 11th at 206.31mph. #42 Jim Mott placed 12th at 205.04mph and 13th #41 Ralph Twombly at 203.81mph. The last qualifier above 200mph was #8 Chan Stokes at 200.39 in 14th. Those under 200mph were #46 Charles Beck/Jim Stirwalt 15th at 197.02mph, 16th #96 Mike Sukosky at 192.12mph, and 17th #7 Colene Giglio at 189.79mph and 1:09.90mins for her one lap. It has been rumored that some pilots used some exotic fuels to boost power instead of the regular 100 octane to obtain these speeds.[12]

Races were air started now with a pace lap before being released by the pace plane. At the release for Heat-1A, #99 Palmer jumped into the lead with #9 Wells in Palmer's former mount right behind. The other racers changed positions until the end when #99 Palmer crossed the finish line at 221.66mph, followed by #9 Wells, #12 Washburn, #44 Mosby, #3 Sykes, and #15 Sebby at 203.37mph. After a review, it was deemed that #9 Wells cut a pylon, placing him last, and moving everyone else up one position.

---

12 These rumors led to the T-6 Racing Class members establishing that all members would use only 100 octane fuel, as the other exotic fuels were seen to give unfair advantages.

Handbill advertising the 1975 California National Air Races and Air Show at Mojave. The Mojave races were held in June before the Reno races in September. Races were run in windy and hot weather but made a profit. (Collection of Aviation Photo Services)

Heat-1B started with #5 McClain in the lead all the way to the end (211.67mph) one-half lap ahead of second place #2 Buehn. Following were #69 Suacci, #73 Rina, #42 Mott, and #11 Conroy all close together. A second Heat-1A was run to allow the five slower qualifiers a chance to race with #11 Conroy as a fill in. As these six racers were all equally matched, speeds were in the 190mph range. This second Heat-1A was won by #11 Conroy at 191.3mph. In second place was #96 Sukosky at 191.21mph. Third was #7 Giglio at 190.75mph. Taking fourth was #8 Stokes. In fifth was #46 Stirwell at 186.83, while #41 Twombly DNF having dropped out with a sour engine.

The Medallion Race was again run for the five slower qualifiers plus #41 Twombly as fill in. It became a close race between Twombly and #8 Stokes from the start with Twombly getting the upper hand to take first at 210.65mph, and Stokes in second place at 210.15mph. #7 Giglio was third, #96 Sukosky fourth, and #46 Beck[13] fifth at 199.6mph. #12 Washburn had dropped out on lap 5 with a hung gear but was able to land without damage.

The year 1975 saw the return of the very popular one-lap Drag Races with the following results: #15 Sebby (winner) vs #12 Washburn, #11 Conroy (w) vs #3 Sykes, #44 Mosby (w) vs #2 Buehn, #73 Rina (w) vs #9 Wells in the first round. Round two was #73 (w) vs #2 Buehn, and #11 Conroy (w) vs #15 Sebby. All the race pilots had great fun in these races along with the spectators.

The Silver Race in 1975 was another strung out and confused race after #3 Sykes dashed into the lead and stayed there to finish first at 211.2mph. Further back was #73 Rina second at 208.65mph and #9 Wells at 208.65mph in third. These three were followed by #11 Conroy fourth at 200.05mph and #15 Sebby fifth at 194.2mph. #42 Jim Mott was sixth and a DNF again after having engine issues and cutting pylon 3. However, it was judged that first-place finisher #3 Sykes had cut pylon 3 and pylon 4 on lap 4 and he was bumped to last place moving everyone up. Rina was declared the Silver Race winner.

Desert heat greeted the six Gold racers when their eight-lap race started. #99 Palmer blasted to the lead and stayed there until the finish taking home $2,985 in prize money. The real racer was #44 Mosby, who started fifth on the opening lap and by the closing lap was second. #99 Palmer finished at 215.07mph and 6:10.10mins, while #44 Mosby was 211.31mph. In third place was #12 Washburn at 209.89mph. Fourth went to #69 Suacci at 205.48. Fifth went to #5 McClain, who was having carburetor problems. #2 Buehn was sixth at 202.46mph.

Things looked better for T-6 racing at Mojave and 1976 had promise for even better races.

Reno 1975 saw a rule change for T-6 race starts. Now all races would be air started with a pace plane. The racers would form up on the backside of the course to sort themselves out on the pace lap before heading around to the first pylons. Nineteen pilots qualified of the 21 entered for the 18 race slots with 13 reaching speeds of more than 200mph and three rookies.

Top qualifier was #99 Pat Palmer at 213.02mph and taking :50.7secs for his one lap. Next was #73 Ralph Rina at 208.90mph. They were followed by: #43 Dennis Buehn, #9 Marshall Wells at 206.90mph, Reno rookie #8 Chan Stokes, #72 Bill Turnbull, #98 Ben Hall in his new aircraft at 205.32mph, #42 Jim Mott and #5 Roy McClain tied at 204.55mph for eighth, #12 M. D. Washburn, #75 Barrie Simonson, #7 Colene Giglio at 202.25mph, #3 Richard Sykes, #15 Fred Sebby flying a new T-6 at 199.63mph, #97 Gary Meermans, #41 Ralph Twombly, rookie #76 John Gerber in an aircraft formerly raced as #18, #11 Jim Modes, and, at 188.81mph, rookie #46 Jim Stirwalt. This aircraft had raced at Reno before with another pilot. Stirwalt was the 19th qualifier and not scheduled to race.

Heat-1, consisting of the odd number qualifiers (in order of qualifying race number), lined up with the pace plane. As they came around the first pylon, #5 McClain was in the lead with #99 Palmer back behind #43 Buehn. By lap 3, Palmer had passed both and had the finish line in sight. Palmer placed first at 212.04mph, #43 Buehn in second had passed #5 McClain who was third at the end, #98 Hall was fourth at 200.43mph, #8 Stokes fifth, and #75 Simonson sixth at 195.83mph.

Heat-2 is described as follows from the official NCAR report (see Chapter 5 for details):

#12 Washburn leapt into the lead on the back straight at the "Air Start" and led still as they came down the front straight past the Home Pylon to begin the first official lap. In his eagerness to maintain and/or stretch that lead, he cut the #1 pylon a little too closely and hit the top of it with his left wing. A large section of the wing was instantly torn away and the airplane went straight in. Washburn died instantly.

The race continued under a yellow flag with greater separation between the racers. #73 Rina was first at 205.32mph, second was #9 Wells, third #72 Turnbull, fourth #42 Mott, and fifth #7 Giglio.

---

13   Of note is that Beck and Stirwalt shared the racing of #46, as Beck was also racing the #7 P-51 Mustang.

Marlin D. "M. D." Washburn goes around the pylons at Mojave 1975 during his second year of racing there. He would be fatally injured during the 1975 Reno races. (Emil Strasser)

Texan flightline at Mojave 1976 showing seven of the 16 qualifiers. Left to right are #76 Gerber, #74 DeWalt in his yet to be painted new Texan, #44 Twombly in John Mosby's Texan, #43 Buehn in his new Texan, #42 Mott, #7 Giglio, and #11 Modes. (Bob Kennedy)

Less than 20 minutes later, stunt flyer Gordon McCollom was fatally injured during an inverted ribbon pick-up.

#46 Stirwalt, the 19th qualifier, moved up to the Medallion Race for the six slowest qualifiers after the fatal accident. At the start on the back course was #15 Sebby, #41 Twombly and rookie #76 Gerber at the front. By lap 3, Gerber had passed both and taken the lead. There he stayed to take his first win in his first race at 206.11mph. The others finished as #15 Sebby second, #97 Meermans third, #41 Twombly fourth, #11 Conroy fifth, and rookie #46 Stirwalt sixth at 185.89mph.

A chance of rain hung over the Consolation (Silver) Race at the start as #8 Stokes and #42 Mott came around the front pylon, Stokes just in front of Mott. Both were focused and had a good lead over the others who were still mixing it up at the back. #98 Hall and #7 Giglio pushed each other until Hall came out ahead while #3 Sykes and #75 were strung out behind. All finished pretty much in order as #8 Stokes was first at 206.44mph and #42 Mott was .002secs behind at 206.30mph in second place. In third was #98 Hall at 200.56mph. #7 Giglio was .003secs behind Hall and placed fourth at 200.37mph. #3 Sykes caught up for fifth at 200.00mph. At the back was #75 Simonson in sixth at 189.81mph. This would be his last T-6 race.

From start to finish, #99 Palmer took the lead of the eight-lap Championship (Gold) Race, showing what preparation and skill can do as he stayed there for the win. Palmer took just 6:57.0mins to cover the 24 miles, netting him $2,985. #9 Wells, in Palmer's old aircraft, and #43 Buehn fought for second place. Buehn stayed ahead of Wells taking second and $1,856. Wells came in third and earned $1,340. #73 Rina flew his race alone, coming in fourth. The real action was at the back with #5 McClain and #72 Turnbull both pushing back and forth for fifth.

The two tragic events of Reno 1975 overshadowed some good racing.

1976

Organized by the new Pylon Air Racing Corp., a two-day regional air race was held in Lincoln on May 15–16, 1976, with the T-6 races fully sanctioned by PRPA. Lincoln had hosted a Demo Race in 1975 under the sponsorship of USARA and NAG over the same three-mile course that was used in 1976. Only five Texans participated. With such a small number, all were able to race around the pylons with four (two each) in four sets of one-lap drag races, three heats, and a Championship Race. Those racing were #8 Chan Stokes, #42 Jim Mott, #9 Marshall Wells, #96 Mike Sukosky, and #76 John Gerber.

Heat-1 was won by #9 Wells at 184.3mph. Heat-2 was won by #8 Stokes at 193.0mph. The Heat-3 winner was #96 Sukosky, with no speed listed. Each race was six laps for 18 miles total. The Sunday, May 16, final would be eight laps totaling 24 miles. The Championship Race finish was a bit confusing as #8 Stokes crossed the line first followed by #9 Wells, #42 Mott third, #76 Gerber fourth, and #96 Sukosky fifth. However, the pylon judges penalized #8 Stokes for cutting five pylons moving him back to fifth. Mott had three cuts, placing him in fourth. The results were #9 Wells in first, #76 Gerber second, and #96 Sukosky third. Although everyone had a good time, Lincoln hosted no more races.

"Welcome to the Fourth Annual California National Air Races" was the sign that greeted everyone as they arrived at Mojave on June 19–20, 1976. The fatal pre-race crash of Ken Burnstine's #33 Mustang put a somber tone to the start of racing. The mood did not improve when Lyle Shelton landed his #77 Bearcat wheels up after an engine failure on a test flight.

T-6 qualifying had 15 flying over 200mph. #5 Roy McClain at 225.9mph was the fastest, while 16th and last qualifier #46 Jim Stirwalt was 199.9mph over the 3½-mile course. Between these two were #9 Marshall Wells placing second at 224.2mph followed by #3 Sykes, #73 Rina, #99 Palmer at 218.0mph in fifth, #7 Colene Giglio, #42 Jim Mott, #44 Ralph Twombly using John Mosby's aircraft, #11 Jim Modes, #8 Chan Stokes, #76 John Gerber, and #96 Mike Sukosky. #74 Don DeWalt in a new Texan flew 202.6mph with the same wild paint job as his old #74. Last was Dennis Buehn in a new #43. #15 Fred Sebby DNQ. As before, there were heat races, drags and finals.

Three sets of one-lap standing start drag races were run with the first pairing being #11 Modes vs #46 Stirwalt, followed by #43 Buehn vs #96 Sukosky, and the last pair #8 Stokes vs #7 Giglio. The Drag final pitted #11 Modes against #43 Buehn with Buehn winning the one-lap race at 131.9mph taking 1:40.53min to Modes' 130mph at 1:41.84min. It is during the drag races that the T-6 produces its greatest amount of noise with the application of high revolutions per minute (RPMs) and the prop in flat pitch. It is truly a unique sound loved by all Texan fans.

As they came down the slot to start Heat-1A, #5 McClain accelerated and headed for the lead where he stayed to the end finishing at 212.5mph. McClain was followed by #99 Palmer, #3 Sykes, #74 DeWalt, #11 Modes and finally Gerber in his bicentennial-painted #76 collecting $44. #42 Mott was scheduled to race but had a prop strike while landing after the drag race. This allowed #74 to bump up. When asked later, Mott stated he realized his gear was up when the prop started throwing bits of the runway against his windshield, so he pulled on the power, flew the pattern, and landed.

#7 Colene Giglio winging her way to win the 1976 Mojave Silver Race. In 1974 at Reno, Giglio became the first woman to race a Texan in closed course pylon races since 1949. (Emil Strasser)

Heat-1B was slightly faster with #44 Twombly taking 6:04.8mins to win the six-lap race and collect $183. In second was #73 Rina 6:08.6mins and $114, third #9 Wells 6:16.11mins and $82, fourth #7 Giglio 6:19.23mins and $64, fifth #8 Stokes 6:30.37mins and $52, and sixth #96 Sukosky 6:35.97mins and $44.

At the start of the Silver Race, #7 Giglio and #11 Modes battled briefly, with Giglio taking the advantage and passing Modes to win at 206.9mph. This was Giglio's first win, and she collected $232. They were followed by #74 DeWalt, #76 Gerber, #8 Stokes, and finally #96 Sukosky, who had cut a pylon, but still collected $138.

Six pilots came down the slot to start the six-lap Gold Race with #44 Twombly and #99 Palmer already pulling ahead of the others as they crossed the starting line. Both pilots were consummate race professionals and stayed close together until the end, when #44 Twombly edged into the lead and first place at 1.12secs ahead. For first place, Twombly received $1,101, second was #99 Palmer with $687, and third was #5 McClain[14] and $494. Following were #73 Rina $388, #9 Wells $316, and #3 Sykes in sixth. Sykes was the only one not to exceed 200mph. He collected $268. While plans were under way for Mojave 1977, there were grumblings by the pilots about the rules and money.

Toward the end of the 1976 racing season, the grumbling grew worse, causing a split in USARA with several classes leaving and forming a new management group called the National Air Racing Association (NARA). The T-6 Class was one that spilt. See Reno 1977 for further details.

A release from NCAR committee at 1976 Reno announced:

Only 15 aircraft qualified out of the 19 entered. Thus, only three were eligible for the Medallion Race which would necessitate three other aircraft filling-in in that race. The field was cut down somewhat from what would have been a full field by the fact of Kirk McKee parking his own airplane #4 and racing Walt Nitowski's #76 who did not meet the pilot requirements for the class, plus the fact #8 Chan Stokes failed the medical, and rookie, #55 Bob Dodson, could not race because of engine trouble.

---

14 After finishing third at 207.7mph in the T-6 Gold Race, McClain jumped into the RB-51 *Red Baron* Mustang and won the Unlimited Gold Race at 406.7mph and collected $4,202. The big money would always be in the Unlimited Class.

The 1978 Reno race was the last year of the two-year agreement between the Texan Class and Reno Air Racing Association (RARA) after the troubles of 1976 and 1977. There would be no T-6 Class races in 1979 and 1980 at Reno. (Collection of Aviation Photo Services)

The 15 qualifiers were: #73 Ralph Rina :51.4secs and 210.12mph, #74 Don DeWalt at 209.71mph, #3 Richard Sykes at 208.9mph, #44 John Mosby and #99 Pat Palmer tied for fourth with 207.69mph, rookie #98 Jim Landry was fifth (in Ben Hall's T-6) at 206.5mph, #11 Cal Conroy at 204.93mph, #9 Marshall Wells and #42 Jim Mott tied for eighth at 203.01mph, #41 Ralph Twombly at 201.49mph, #46 Charles Beck 11th at :53.9secs with #7 Colene Giglio at :54.0secs. #43 Dennis Buehn was the first under 200mph at 198.90mph, with #96 Mike Sukosky at 197.44mph and rookie #76 Kirk McKee at 195.65mph for the 15th slot.

Both Heats 1 and 2 were straight forward, with each being won as they had started. Heat-1 saw #99 Palmer first, followed by #73 Rina, and #3 Sykes, all over 200mph. This group was followed by #42 Mott, #46 Beck and #11 Conroy, all in the 190s. Palmer picked up $225. Heat-2 was about the same, with the front four all over 200mph. First was #98 Landry, followed by #74 DeWalt, #44 Mosby, and #9 Wells. #41 Twombly and #7 Giglio placed fifth and sixth :0.02secs apart at the finish.

Only the front three starters were scheduled to race in the Medallion (Bronze) Race while the other three flew as fill-ins and had already been locked into the Consolation Race. At the start, it was #43 Buehn in the lead, flying a new T-6 fresh out of rebuild. Buehn finished first at 202.06mph ($350), second was #96 Sukosky 7mph slower with rookie #76 McKee in third. The last three were in fourth #46 Beck, fifth #42 Mott and #41 Twombly sixth. All flew at 193mph, saving their engines for the next race.

#9 Wells showed that there was some speed left in Pat Palmer's old T-6 as he jumped to the lead after coming around the home pylon. He passed #7 Giglio, who was in the lead at the scatter pylon, and stayed ahead to the finish of the Consolation (Silver) Race at 202.63mph, collecting $635. Second was #11 Conroy, winning $558. Coming in third was #42 Mott for $500. In fourth place was #46 Beck, who was dropped to fifth for a pylon cut on the first lap. This moved #7 Giglio to fourth and $446. #41 Twombly pulled out on lap one with a prop problem, but still collected $376, while Beck in last place received $411.

All six of the racers for the Championship (Gold) Race had qualified over 200mph and the front two were fractions of a second apart. As they came around to the front straight, it was #99 Palmer and #73 Rina almost flying as one aircraft with #74 DeWalt and #3 Sykes only a few yards back. As the race progressed, #99 and #73 were still up front, but #44 Mosby and #98 Laundry were now second and third. By lap 6, #99 Palmer had the edge ahead of #73 Rina and crossed the finish line first, having taken 6:50.1mins for the eight laps ($2,985). Rina placed second ($1,856) in 6:53.5mins. Third went to #44 Mosby ($1,340), and fourth to #98 Landry ($1,051). Sykes passed #74 DeWalt and placed fifth ($857) with DeWalt in sixth ($735). Both pilots took over seven minutes. This win gave #99 Pat Palmer a three-peat at Reno (1974, 1975, and 1976). This would be his last win.

1977
Troubles

In 1975, the PRPA changed its name to USARA. PRPA had been the governing and sanctioning body for air racing in the United States since before World War Two but felt the name change was necessary to better cover all aspects of air racing and not just a pilots' group. At the time, there were five classes of racers: Unlimited, T-6, Formula One, Sports Biplane, and Stock Planes. USARA would remain the governing body, but by Reno 1976, there was dissention in the classes over rules, sanctioning of races, points awards, and money. In 1977, negations broke down with the Unlimiteds, T-6s and a faction of the Formula Ones (called the International Experimental Limited Class [IXL]). They separated from USARA and formed their own governing body called NARA. NARA developed its own set of rules and specifications regarding how races would be run and the payout of prize money. USARA kept the Sports Biplane, Stock Planes, a group called Stock T-6s, and most of the F-1s. USARA announced that any pilot who raced in a non-sanctioned race would not score national points or have any new race records recorded as national records. This situation put race event organizers in the middle.

For T-6 racing, this only affected Mojave and Reno. The Air Race Management (ARM) at Mojave elected to cancel its races for 1977 and see what 1978 would bring. The Reno Air Race Association (RARA) elected to negotiate with the individual class organizations to race in 1977 and 1978, with the exception of the Stock Planes and the Sports Biplane classes along with some of the new IXL class. Reno 1977 would host just three classes: Unlimited, T-6 and F-1. This practice is still used by RARA.

Both USARA and NARA lasted for a few more years, but finally faded away leaving air racing without an overall governing body. It would seem for the better as racing continues, even though at a limited venue. The Sport Biplane Class returned to Reno in 1980 and a Jet Class was added later.

Eighteen T-6s were entered at Reno in September 1977 for a chance to win part of the class $20,000 prize money. Seventeen qualified with 14 reaching speeds over 200mph. Before qualifying, #4 Kirk McKee had engine problems in a new T-6 and did not qualify or race and did not return to T-6 racing.

#99 Pat Palmer, the 1976 winner, qualified first, taking :51.2secs for his one lap giving him a speed of 210.94mph. Second was #9 Marshall Wells at 210.12mph. Before qualifying his T-6, Wells had crashed an F-1 racer attempting to qualify it. Other qualifiers were #73 Ralph Rina at 209.30mph and tied for fourth were #74 Don DeWalt and Reno rookie #49 John Allcorn at 206.90mph. Next was #41 Ralph Twombly at 206.50mph. He was also in a new aircraft, the former #98 Hall/Landry racer. #3 Sykes placed at 205.71mph, #11 Jim Modes at 204.93mph, and #42 Jim Mott at 204.55mph. #2 Charles Beck at 204.16mph was also a new T-6. #96 Dennis Buehn at 203.77mph. This was a new T-6 for Buehn, but it had raced before. #7 Colene Giglio flew at 203.39mph. The last of the over 200mph group was #97 Gary Meermans at 203.01. Fourteenth place went to #44 John Mosby with :55.0secs for his lap. He was followed by rookie #8 Ron Hevle at 191.15mph in his only T-6 race. Helve would return as an Unlimited pilot and win a gold race. Returning after a year away from racing was #40 Stan Gnesa in 16th at 187.82mph. In last place was rookie #64 Ben Harrison at 183.99. Harrison entered the 1976 Mojave race but did not qualify or race and this would be his only T-6 race. "With only 17 aircraft qualifying for the field, only five were eligible for the Medallion Race, thus, one fill-in aircraft would be necessary."

Heat-1 was a simple race between #99 Palmer and #42 Mott at the front with everyone else behind. #73 Rina and #3 Sykes challenged each other for third and fourth place while #96 Buehn and rookie #49 Allcorn flew their own solitary laps. At the finish, #42 Mott (209.78mph) edged past #99 Palmer (209.71mph) for the win. They were followed by #73 Rina, #3 Sykes, #96 Buehn and #49 Allcorn, who was the only one below 200mph at 193.09mph.

With foul weather approaching, Heat-2 was moved up after an F-1 race was rescheduled due to winds. What follows is from the NCAR committee:

By qualifications, #97 Meermans should not have been in this heat, having qualified in the 13th position which would have normally made him eligible only for the Medallion Race. However, #7 Giglio who qualified in the 12th position, was unable to race (engine problems and this would be her last Reno appearance), thus moving #97 Meermans up a slot into the Silver competition. #44 John Mosby, who qualified in the 14th position, was also only eligible for the Medallion Race. He, too, could not race (mechanical issues), thus, when all was said and done, only three pilots were eligible for the Medallion Race, all rookies #8 Hevle, #40 Gnesa and #64 Harrison. Thus, they were joined by the designated fill-in pilots #96 Buehn, #97 Meermans and #11 Modes. Both these last two were permitted to race in the Medallion and the Silver!

So, the race progressed, with #41 Twombly jumping into the lead in his new mount and staying there to finish first at 211.01mph. This T-6 as #98 had finished third in the 1976 Championship Race. #74 DeWalt and #2 Beck (in his new racer) fought for second flying 201.81mph and 201.68mph, respectively. DeWalt finished second and Beck third. #9 Wells came in fourth only :00.10secs behind DeWalt and Beck. Fill-ins #97 Meermans and #11 Modes (both Harvards) held back to fifth and sixth places to save their engines for the next race.

There was no real competition in the Medallion (Bronze) Race as both #97 Meermans and #11 Modes pulled away from the three rookies to take first and second. They were followed by #8 Hevle in third at 186.69mph, #40 Gnesa fourth at 195.09mph, #64 Harrison fifth at 183.83mph, and #96 Buehn, who was the fill-in, was sixth at 183.47mph. When the race was over, #40 Gnesa was dropped to fifth for a pylon cut and this moved #64 Harrison to fourth.

When the pace plane released the six racers for the Consolation (Silver) Race, #97 Meermans was ready. The weather had cleared, and it was a beautiful day for a fast race, and by the end of lap 1, Meermans was ahead by at least eight seconds. By lap 3, it was Meermans alone out front with #3 Sykes and #9 Wells fighting for second place. Rookie #49 Allcorn and #96 Buehn did the same for fourth. #11 Modes was one-half lap back in sixth. At the finish line was #97 Meermans, who took first at 210.87mph, which was back-to-back wins for a bump-up pilot. #3 Sykes passed #9 Wells for second. They were followed by rookie #49 Allcorn in fourth, #96 Buehn fifth, and #11 Modes sixth :18.0secs behind first place.

As expected, #99 Palmer took the lead from the start of the Championship (Gold) Race. It looked like a runaway race for him, but it was not to be as Twombly gained on him every lap in his new #41. With these two at the front, #73 Rina flew into third as the other three were grouped together at the back. As the front two came around to the front stretch at the end of eight laps, it was #41 Twombly in the lead by tenths of a second. Twombly took first place at 209.66mph (6:52.1mins) and #99 Palmer at 209.51mph (6:52.4mins). In third at 206.16mph (6:59.1mins) was #73 Rina. In fourth, fifth and sixth places were #42 Mott, #2 Beck, #74 DeWalt all over seven minutes, but still over 200mph. This was #41 Twombly's first Reno win and second overall (Mojave 1976).

Reno 1977 had not disappointed and, with the new racing agreements between RARA and the race classes, things look bright for 1978.

1978

Weather for Reno 1978 caused issues the entire week of racing. Nineteen T-6s entered but only 18 qualified, seven were rookies and 11 qualified at or above 200mph. Setting a new Reno qualifying record of 218.18mph was #73 Ralph Rina taking :49.5secs for one lap. He was followed in order by #74 Don DeWalt at 215.14mph, #41 Ralph Twombly at 214.29mph, and #44 John Mosby at 213.44mph. Surprisingly in fifth was #99 Pat Palmer at 213.02mph, followed by #49 John Allcorn at 208.49, #3 Richard Sykes at 208.09mph, and #2 Charles Beck at 206.50mph. In ninth place

Rookie #8 Dimitry Prian qualified 11th at Reno 1978 at 202.25mph. While this was his first and only try at pylon racing, his Texan had been raced before as #38 and #43. (Jerry Liang)

was rookie #5 Cliff Branch at 204.93mph. He had entered before but had not raced. #42 Jim Mott reached 203.39mph and in 11th was rookie #8 Dimitry Prian 202.25mph. This T-6 had been entered and raced twice before with different race numbers and pilots. #11 Calvin Conroy qualified at 200.37mph. Rookie #39 Robert Nottke came in at 197.80mph in his first and only T-6 race. #90 Larry Havens[15] (his first T-6) was in 14th at 195.65mph and rookie #6 Charles Gilbert at 192.17mph. This was his only T-6 race, but his T-6 had raced under another number. Rookie #77 Jack Francis flew 191.15mph in his first and only Reno race. His T-6 was a former Twombly racer. At the back were rookie #71 James Fox at 190.48mph and 18th #96 Mike Sukosky at 189.47mph, returned after a year off. #7 Colene Giglio had to withdraw and did not attempt to qualify.

In an effort to speed things up, RARA announced "all of the T-6 races were to be reduced to five laps to make the program move more quickly. It is intended to keep the Championship race to a normal six- to eight-lap race."

As Heat-1 got under way, it started as another battle of the Ralphs with #73 Rina and #41 Twombly leading after the scatter pylon. They were followed closely by #99 Palmer and #3 Sykes, then #5 Branch and #8 Prian last. As the race progressed, Palmer caught Twombly and then Sykes caught Twombly and, by lap 3, Palmer passed Rina for the lead. The race ended with #99 Palmer first, #73 Rina second, #3 Sykes third, #41 Twombly fourth, and #5 Branch fifth. All were over 200mph except #8 Prian in sixth at 199.70mph.

Handbill for the 1978 California Nationals at Mojave. Returning after the 1977 troubles, only 11 Texans qualified. (Collection of Aviation Photo Services)

Heat-2 was hot and fast in the cold air with #11 Conroy leading from the start. By mid-race, #49 Allcorn passed #74 DeWalt and was moving up on Conroy, while #44 Mosby hung in last with #42 Mott and #2 Beck in the middle. Suddenly, #44 Mosby, flying high and wide, passed everyone and was gaining on Allcorn when the race ended. Allcorn placed first. Mosby came in second, #42 Mott third, #11 Conroy fourth, #74 DeWalt fifth, and sixth was #2 Beck. All had flown the race over 200mph. Allcorn won his first Reno race but was disqualified after the race for "failing to allow a technical inspection of his aircraft."

If Heat-2 had been fast, the Medallion (Bronze) Race slid backwards into a pretty sedate race with everyone almost in a line start to finish. Rookie #39 Nottke was first at 199.12mph and was bumped up to the Consolation Race. He was followed by #90 Havens, #96 Sukosky, rookie #6 Gilbert, #71 Fox, and #77 Francis last at 166.77mph. All flew under 200mph.

Saturday, September 16, started with weather delays and the crash of a banner-towing Stearman, which blocked a runway. Its pilot mushed into the ground while trying to pick up a banner. It was necessary to start the shortened Consolation (Silver) Race from the front of the course instead of on the backside due to winds. This caused everyone to bunch up as they came around to the front straight towards pylon 5. According to the official Reno report, "during the very first lap of this race, a mid-air collision occurred off the number 5 pylon which involved Dimitry Prian #8 and Don DeWalt #74. Both aircraft were completely destroyed, with Prian being fatally injured and DeWalt being pulled from the wreckage alive and rushed to the hospital, but he was dead upon arrival. The other participating aircraft, which included #39 Nottke, #11 Conroy, #2 Beck and #5 Branch, were immediately flagged off the course and landed safely." No official results were posted for this race.

---

15 He raced before at Reno in the Unlimited Class in 1971 in his Bell P-63C Kingcobra and qualified at 359.39mph.

Course & Timing Chart

Timing Chart The speed of a racer can be determined by the length of time needed for the plane to fly one complete circuit of the course. The spectator can use the second hand of his watch to get a rough idea of the qualifying speed of an aircraft by using these tables. Given below are representative speeds and times.

Formula IXL 3.685 Mile Course				Unlimiteds 8.5 Mile Course			
Seconds	Speed	Seconds	Speed	Seconds	Speed	Seconds	Speed
94.5	140	66.0	200	96.0	320	78.5	390
88.0	150	63.0	210	93.0	330	76.5	400
82.5	160	60.0	220	90.0	340	74.5	410
77.5	170	57.5	230	87.5	350	72.8	420
73.5	180	55.0	240	85.0	360	71.2	430
69.5	190	53.0	250	82.8	370	69.5	440
				80.5	380	67.9	450

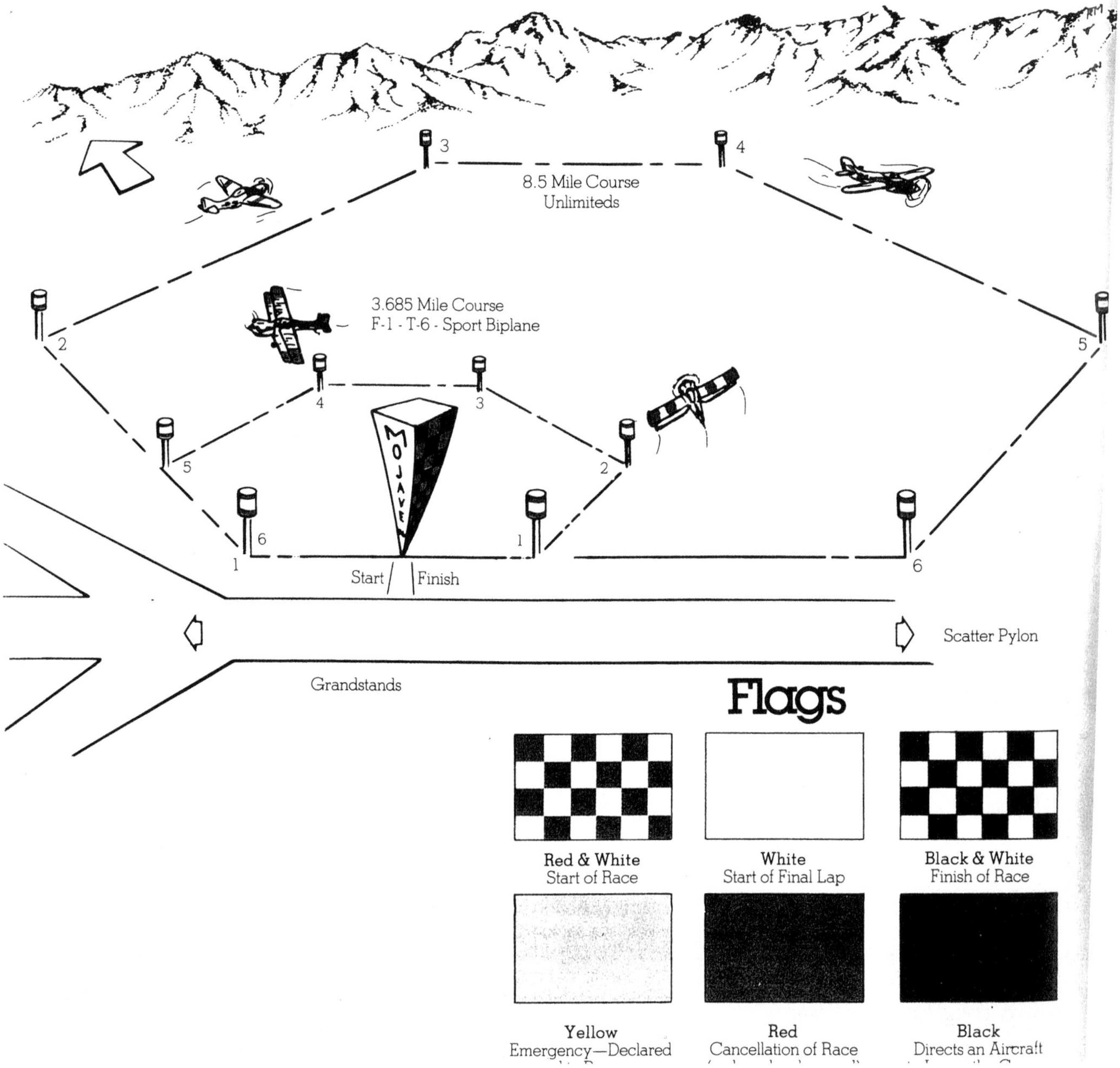

8.5 Mile Course
Unlimiteds
3.685 Mile Course
F-1 - T-6 - Sport Biplane
MOJAVE
Start
Finish
Scatter Pylon
Grandstands
Flags
Red & White
Start of Race
White
Start of Final Lap
Black & White
Finish of Race
Yellow
Emergency—Declared
Red
Cancellation of Race
Black
Directs an Aircraft

Course and timing chart for the 1978 California Nationals at Mojave. (Collection of Aviation Photo Services)

This was only #8 Prian's second race; he had 250 hours in T-6s. DeWalt had 600 hours in T-6s and over 30 T-6 races. His first Reno race was in 1972. According to the NTSB the probable cause was "Pilot(s) misjudged clearance" (see Chapter 5 for details). The bad times were not over. Less than two hours later, Bill Whittington had a prop failure in his P-51H during the Unlimited Consolation Race and ground-looped on landing.

#51 Jerry McDonald rounding a pylon at Mojave in 1978. This Texan had been raced as #25 by Tony Murgia and as #25 and #5 by Roy McClain. The Texan is currently racing as #5 by Joey Sanders. (Bob Kennedy)

Championship (Gold) Race day started out with weather delays. When the six Texans came around for the now shortened (five laps) race start, it was another battle of the Ralphs with #73 Rina just ahead of #41 Twombly. By lap 2, #3 Sykes was trying to challenge Twombly for second. #42 Mott passed #44 Mosby. #99 Palmer was at the back. As lap 5 started, #44 Mosby pulled up and out with a sick engine. At the finish, it was #73 Rina at 205.71mph in first, #41 Twombly second at 203.39mph, #3 Sykes was in third 201.79mph, #42 Mott fourth at 198.75 leaving #99 Palmer fifth at 190.54mph. Mosby was given a DNF. It had been a somber race.

The last year of the two-year T-6 Class racing agreement with RARA was in 1978. RARA made the decision not to re-sign. It was speculated this was due to the 1978 accident in the class.

According to the official press releases #78-07-RA and #78-23-JT:

> All eyes in the aviation world will be turned towards Mojave, California this coming weekend where on the 28th through the 29th of October the fifth renewal of the California National Air Races will be taking place… some of the country's finest pilots and aircraft will be competing in closed course pylon and drag races… pilots competing during this two day air racing classic will be competing for more than $50,000 in cash prizes.

The T-6 Class raced in "The Aircraft Cylinder T-6 Trophy Races" in 1978. This company was a major engine overhaul facility in Van Nuys, specializing in radial engines including the P&W R-1340.

Twelve pilots paid the $15 entry fee and ten qualified, nine were over 200mph, with #41 Ralph Twombly first at 218.01mph on the 3.685-mile course in a new #41, which previously had been #98, raced by Hall and Landry. In order of qualifying were #2 Charles Beck at 214.35mph second, #3 Richard Sykes at 214.94mph third, #73 Ralph Rina at 211.41mph fourth, #7 Colene Giglio 206.70mph fifth, and #90 Larry Havens at 204.31mph in sixth. #77 Jack Francis at 203.65mph flew Twombly's old #41 to seventh. #51 Jerry McDonald at 203.90mph placed eighth in the Texan that had formerly raced as #25 and #5. #11 Jim Modes took ninth at 201.92mph. In tenth was #5 Cliff Branch at 197.03mph in a Texan that had raced as #14. Rookie #1 Jim Furlong did not qualify but raced. #49 John Allcorn was entered but did not qualify or race. Three regular racers sat out Mojave but raced at Reno; it is unknown if this had to do with the management dispute. They were #99 Pat Palmer, #44 John Mosby, and #96 Mike Sukosky. Palmer was entered but was a no-show. Jim Mott had other commitments, but Dennis Buehn flew his aircraft in the Drag Race. Fred Sebby raced a Mustang in the Unlimited Class so did not race in the Texan Class.

Aircraft Cylinders Heat-1A five-lap race was all #41 Twombly, winning from the pole at 215.8mph. #2 Beck was further back in second. These two were followed by #7 Giglio third, #11 Modes fourth, #51 McDonald fifth, and rookie #1 Furlong as a DNS. Heat-1B, the Jefferson Air Force event, was the same sort of affair with #3 Sykes easily winning at 214.7mph. The rest of the field finished with #73 Rina second, #5 Branch third, #90 Havens fourth, and #77 Francis fifth.

The next day's Coors Beer-sponsored Drag Races were met by gusty high winds, but that did not stop the racing. The competitors were #77 Francis (w) vs #51 McDonald and #1 Furlong (w) vs #42 Buehn. Winds were calmer for the five-lap Aircraft Cylinders Silver Race, with only five contestants and a close race. #51 McDonald and #11 Modes flew a great race with McDonald slipping passed to take first at 195.73mph. Modes scored second at 195.33mph. Both times were the same at 6:46.65mins. In third place was #77 Francis 188.37mph. Fourth went to #1 Furlong at 183.37mph and #90 Havens was a DNS.

Sunday's Jefferson Air Force six-lap Gold Race was a runaway start to finish race right out of the slot by #41 Twombly. He set a new T-6 Class speed record at 231.07mph. #3 Sykes chased Twombly for two laps but pulled out with mechanical issues. At the end, it was #2 Beck taking second at 205.96mph, almost 25mph slower, #73 Rina third at 205.96mph, fourth #5 Branch at 200.93mph, and fifth #7 Giglio at 199.20mph. #3 Sykes was a DNF at sixth. In spite of the low number of race entrants, the 1978 races were a success, so ARM planned for 1979.

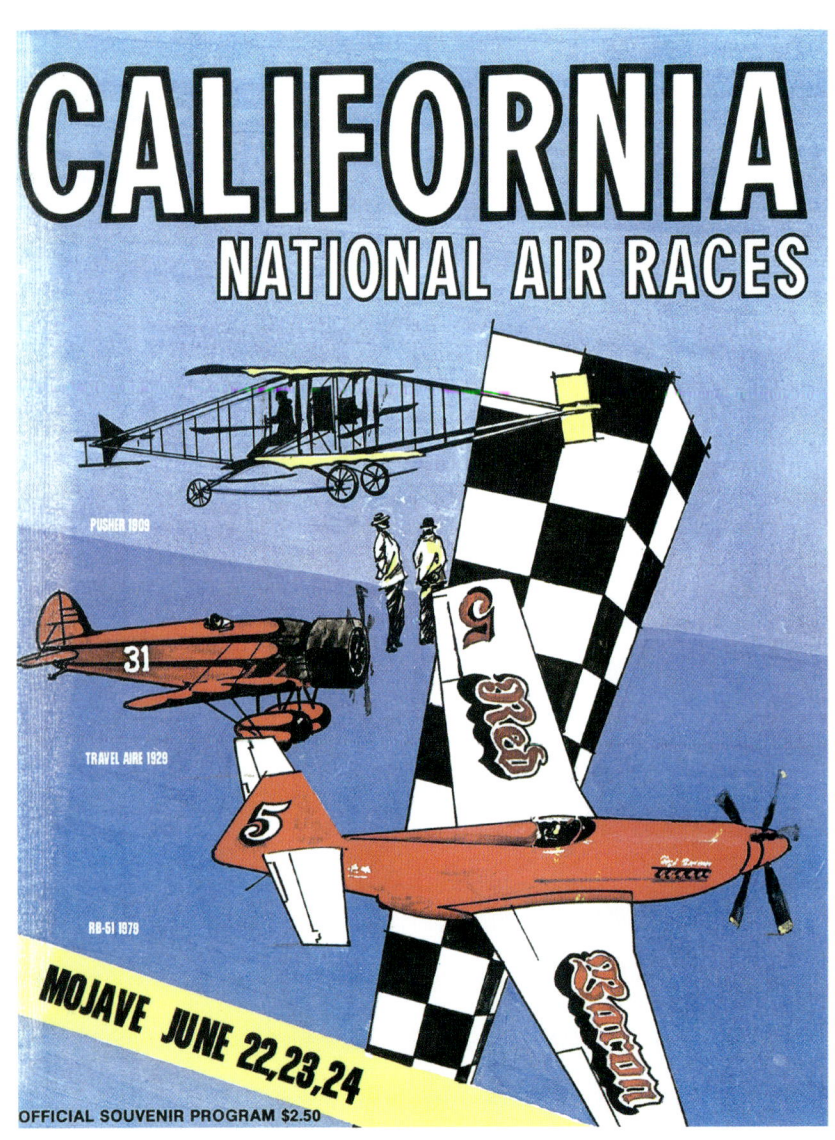

Program cover for the last California National Air Races held in June 1979. Inflation and high gasoline prices kept the racer entrants low at only nine, and fear of not finding gasoline to get to and from the race kept spectator attendance low. (Collection of Aviation Photo Services)

#39 Dennis Buehn cutting it close to a pylon at Reno 1982. (Bob Kennedy)

1979
Press release #79-06 GF, dated June 4, 1979:

> This year's California National Air Races will be extra special because they mark the 70th anniversary of air racing… bigger and more exciting than ever… including the stock cars of air racing-the T-6s, or SNJs as they were known in the Navy. These "round-engine" machines have been around for years… It's every pilot for his or herself because the competition is close and hard fought… the field of competitors is so evenly matched that T-6 races are traditionally the closest and most unpredictable in air racing… the difference between the fastest and slowest qualifiers can be as little as 10 miles per hour… jockeying for position wingtip to wingtip, 70 feet above the ground… and the dramatic intensity of the noise is literally breathtaking. California National Air Races June 23 and 24 at the Mojave airport. Don't worry about gasoline getting home… stations will be open![16]

Nine aircraft were entered, ten qualified and 12 raced. Rookie #49 John Kirkland qualified at 218.8mph for pole position followed by #99 Pat Palmer at 213.8mph. Third was #3 Sykes at 212.6mph followed by fourth #41 Ralph Twombly at 211.4mph. Twombly was the 1978 Gold winner. In fifth was #73 Ralph Rina at 210.4mph, sixth #2 Charles Beck at 208.1mph, seventh #7 Colene Giglio at 205.2mph, eighth #5 Cliff Branch at 204.6mph, ninth #51 Jerry McDonald at 201.5mph, and tenth rookie #39 Robert Nottke at 193.83mph flying the former #45 that had been raced by John Mosby. The other pilots who entered, but did not qualify, were #1 Jim Furlong, #9 Marshall Wells, #11 Calvin Conroy, #77 Jack Francis and #97 Gary Meermans. Furlong raced in the Coors Beer-sponsored Drag Races. #39 Nottke did not race for unknown reasons.

---

16 This was during the gas crisis.

The first set of 1979 Drag Races saw John Allcorn in #49 vs #73 Rina (w) both cutting pylon 3, Giglio #7 vs #5 Branch (w) both with pylon cuts, #1 Furlong vs #51 McDonald (w) with #1 cutting pylon 2. The second Drag set saw #5 Branch vs #73 Rina (w). The second pairing was #51 McDonald vs #99 Palmer (w). The third pairing was #1 Furlong vs #7 Buehn (w), who was racing Giglio's aircraft. These standing start one-lap races were always exciting to watch.

The heat races were just as exciting. Heat-1A had a good three-way at the start between #49 Kirkland, #3 Sykes and #73 Rina, with #51 McDonald and #7 Giglio challenging each other. At the finish it was Kirkland first at 212.880mph. Rina at 210.218mph was second having flown around Sykes, who was third at 208.957mph. Giglio got around McDonald for fourth at 203.946mph and McDonald placed fifth with 202.875mph. Heat-1B had just four contestants and was a fight between Palmer and Twombly. #99 Palmer took first at 215.713mph and #41 Twombly second 213.531mph. They were followed by #2 Beck in third and #5 Branch in fourth.

Sunday's final races were a windy and drawn-out affair. The Silver Race would see #7 Giglio take her second win at 210.5mph. This was fitting as it was her last Texan race. Giglio was followed by #51 McDonald at 208.3mph, third was #5 Branch at 204.5mph, fourth went to #2 Rina in Beck's aircraft at 199.7mph, and #11 Sykes in fifth at 199.5mph. He cut pylon 1 on lap 3.

Six pilots raced in the Gold Race with all finishing over 200mph. Veteran #99 Palmer took first at 215.7mph and was challenged the entire race by #41 Twombly, who was in second place fractions of a second back. Third was rookie Krikland at 212.8mph, then #73 Rina fourth, #3 Sykes at 208.9mph fifth, and sixth went to #2 Beck at 204.6mph. It had been quite a race and it would be the last.

Mojave provided some great racing over its eight-year run (years 1970–71 were Unlimited Class-only races), however, the rising cost and location would see racing end at Mojave in 1979, along with most other events, leaving only Reno to carry on T-6 closed course pylon racing.

There were no races in the T-6 Class at Reno in September 1979.

1980
There were no races in the T-6 Class at Reno in September 1980.

1981
The T-6 Class was back to racing at Reno in 1981 after a new agreement between RARA and T-6 Race Group. Fourteen entered and 13 qualified around a new 5.207-mile course. Each of the four races had only four laps for a total distance of 20.8 miles. There would be only two heats and the Consolation and Championship races.

Before qualifying began, rookie #49 John Hunt applied the brakes too quickly and flipped his racer over on its back during a trial run. He was unhurt but the tail, canopy, and engine were a write-off. This left 13 contestants to qualify with six of them rookies. The top qualifier was veteran racer #44 John Mosby. His one lap around the new course was 1:26.2mins with a speed of 217.51mph. He was followed by #73 Ralph Rina at 215.56mph, third was #3 Richard Sykes, and #5 Jerry McDonald was fourth at 214.18mph (in a T-6 that had raced as #25, #5, #51 and was now back to #5). Fifth was #2 Charles Beck at 213.40mph. Jim Mott's #42 reached 212.43mph but was raced by veteran Ralph Twombly for Mott. In seventh place was rookie #77 Mike Wright at 208.93mph. Eighth place was earned by rookie #8 Robert Jones at 205.70mph. This T-6 had raced before as #80. In ninth was rookie #68 Jimmy Gist at 205.70mph. Another rookie, #75 Al Goss, was in tenth place at 203.84mph. #72 James Fox was just 0.10secs back at 203.24mph. Twelfth was rookie #57 Edmond Colbert. He was the first under 200mph at 193.59mph. This was his first and only T-6 race. Last was rookie #4 Chuck Neeley at 189.60mph and 1:38.9mins in his first and only T-6 race. This T-6 was a rebuild of the Hall Racer #47.

Heat-1 was an all over 200mph race with #3 Sykes and #2 Beck at each other from the pace lap. They were followed by #44 Mosby and #77 Wright side-by-side, then #68 Gist by himself. #72 Fox was alone at the tail end. By lap 2, Beck moved past Sykes on the backside and stayed there to the end. It was #2 Beck in first at 216.91mph, #3 Sykes at 215.39mph, #44 Mosby at 215.15mph, #77 Wright at 210.45mph, #68 Gist at 208.09mph, and sixth #72 Fox at 201.43mph.

Heat-2 began from the pace lap as if it would produce some real action with #5 McDonald, #73 Rina and rookie #75 Goss tied together with #42 Twombly between this bunch. Rookies #8 Jones and Colbert brought up the rear. At lap 2, #73 Rina caught McDonald and everyone remained in place to the end. Rina won first at 210.14 (5:56.8mins), #5 McDonald was second at 206.28mph, followed by rookie #75 Goss at 205.54mph. #42 Twombly at 197.89mph was taking it easy in a borrowed aircraft. Rookie #8 Jones at 194.21mph was fifth. Last was rookie #57 Colbert at 186.03mph in 6:43.1mins.

The four-lap Consolation (Silver) Race was a straight up train start to finish, with #42 Twombly pushing the limits of Mott's Texan and blasting to the finish in 5:46.7mins with a speed of 216.25mph. Twombly was about 4mph faster than Mott's qualification speed. Second through sixth were #77 Wright at 206.92mph, #68 Gist at 205.02mph, #72 Fox at 198.36mph, #8 Jones at 195.52mph, and #57 Colbert at 188.32mph and 6:38.1mins.

If the previous race was a little lackluster, the Championship (Gold) Race was just the opposite from the start. #73 Rina had the lead at the start with #2 Beck, #3 Sykes and #44 Mosby bunched up behind. #5 McDonald and #75 Goss were flying their own race at the back. With the longer distance to fly around the course, but shorter number of laps, everyone had to make their moves quickly. Mosby flew wide and moved passed Beck and Sykes to chase Rina. As Rina and Mosby came around to the front straight on the final lap, both were high and dove for the checkered flag with Mosby 0.3secs faster taking first place. It was #44 Mosby at 222.78mph and 5:36.6mins in first and #73 Rina at 222.49mph and 5:37.0mins. They were followed by #2 Beck in third at 220.27mph, #3 Sykes at 219.35mph, #5 McDonald at 217.94mph, and #75 Goss at 214.65mph. Less than 0:13secs separated first and sixth with Mosby setting a new Reno record. Second through fifth also set new Reno race records. As RARA reported, "This is not surprising since this is the first time that this Class raced on the new 5.207 mile course."

Veteran #44 John Mosby's[17] last win was in 1981 and his last T-6 race. He was a true competitor and great pilot.

1982

Reno 1982 again held changes for the 15 contestants entered, including a new five-mile course, a return to five-lap Consolation and Championship races and seven participants in each race. On top of this, the weather was not the best during race week.

All 15 entrants qualified and 13 were over 200mph. Since there were only 14 racing slots, rookie #7 William Meier, who placed 15th at 193.18mph was cut. This was Meier's only T-6 race attempt. The fastest was #44 Ralph Twombly (flying John Mosby's T-6) at 219.25mph. Second was #73 Ralph Rina at 217.63mph and another battle of the Ralphs was shaping up. Rina was also racing Mustang #102. Not far behind in third was #3 Richard Sykes at 217.42mph. He was followed in order by: #5 Jerry McDonald at 214.31mph, #2 Charles Beck at 213.98mph, #68 Jimmy Gist at 212.79mph, #75 Al Goss at 211.57mph, and #39 Dennis Buehn at 211.52mph. This was a new T-6 for Buehn, however the Texan had raced before. #77 Mike Wright was ninth at 211.07mph and rookie #49 Phillip Gist was tenth at 208.58mph. Phillip Gist is the brother of Jimmy and this T-6 had been repaired since flipping on its back the year before when flown by John Hunt. During a pre-qualifying test, Gist suffered a partial gear collapse requiring an all-out effort by the T-6 camp to find the parts and repair it in time to qualify. Rookie #11 Ray Schutte qualified 11th at 205.25mph. This Texan had raced many times before with other pilots. In 12th was #72 James Fox at 204.62mph, followed by #8 Robert Jones at 201.50mph, and rookie #6 James Brennan at 198.76mph. This was his only T-6 race and he was 14th in the last slot.

Heat-1 was the first four-lap seven contestant race. The pace plane released them down chute. At the start Twombly, Sykes and Beck were bunched before stringing out around lap 2. All seven were over 200mph, including Schutte at the back. There was a brief tussle between Jones and Wright before the race ended with #44 Twombly first at 218.26mph, #3 Sykes second at 216.21mph, #2 Beck at 213.63mph, #75 Goss at 209.78mph, #11 Schutte at 202.32mph, #8 Jones at 202.07mph, and #77 Wright, having slipped back, was seventh at 201.40mph.

Heat-2 was #73 Rina's turn, as he led from the start with the only exciting moment being when #39 Buehn passed under #68 Gist to take second place on the last lap. So, it was #73 Rina at 218.47. He was just 0.2secs off Heat-1 winner Twombly. #39 Buehn was second at 214.30mph. #68 Gist was 0.2secs back in third. #5 McDonald in the middle at 212.01mph. Rookie #49 Gist was fifth at 204.43mph. This was just under 10mph slower than his brother and the only time they raced against each other was in 1982. In sixth was #72 Fox at 203.64mph and the only one under 200mph was #6 Brennan in seventh at 199.04mph.

From release to the end of the five-lap Silver Race, it was #75 Goss with #8 Jones and #77 Wright tied to his tail. It was not until the start of the last lap that Goss was able to pull away finishing as they had started. First was #75 Goss with 6:57.5mins at 215.57mph. He was followed by second place #8 Jones in 7:07.9mins at 210.35mph, third place was #77 Wright at 209.50mph, #11 Schutte, #49 Gist, #72 Fox, and last was #6 Brennan in 7:30.2mins and 199.91mph in seventh.

---

17 Mosby would sell #44 (Harvard II s/n. 2914) and it would continue to race for several more years with several different pilots until it was W/O fatally in 1990 while performing aerobatics. It had raced in 24 events since 1969.

#8 Bob Jones and #39 Ed Colbert battling for position at Reno 1983, showing the closeness of Texan racing. (Bill LeSanche)

Championship (Gold) excitement started while the pilots were forming up for the race when #3 Sykes took a large bird strike in his engine forcing him out. #75 Goss was called up to race as he was the first alternate. The two Ralphs did not disappoint as from the start it was one of those races where everyone was rooting for both pilots. They flew almost as if they were in formation with Goss, hanging tight right behind both. By lap 3, Twombly was inching ahead and as lap 4 started he had the lead. The Ralphs crossed the finish line with #44 Twombly first in 6:58.8mins and at 214.90mph. #73 Rina was second in 7:00.9mins and at 213.85mph. This was the last time the two would race head-to-head, the end of nine match-ups that started in 1973. Twombly had won four and Rina three.[18] Goss was third at 13.55mph, fourth was #2 Beck, #39 Buehn was fifth, #68 Gist was sixth, and #5 McDonald came in seventh at 7:19.1mins.

Ralph Twombly's last Championship win was in 1982. Twombly would step back from T-6 racing for a few years.

1983
Reno 1983 was a slightly windy affair, but the winds didn't dampen the racing as 19 entered and 17 Texans qualified. The field was held to the 14 fastest qualifiers. The three rookies who flew under 200mph and were eliminated were #98 James Cuseo at 199.98mph, #71 Jack Todoverto at 197.76mph, and #23 Richard Yersak at 189.0mph. The year 1983 would be their only attempt at T-6 racing. By comparison, #81 Marge Hurlburt had won the 1946 75-mile race at 200.6mph while Hank Otzen won the 1968 24-mile race with a speed of 181.32mph. Those that entered but did not qualify were #44 Ralph Twombly, the 1982 winner, and #72 James Fox.

Start of the 1983 Reno Silver Race down the side to the first turn to the home pylon. (Bill LeSanche)

---
18 Ralph Rina would win a 1982 Bronze Unlimited Heat Race in Mustang #102 in his first Unlimited attempt.

#73 Ralph Rina leading the pack after turning from the home pylon at Reno 1984. (Bob Kennedy)

Top qualifier #73 Ralph Rina set a new Reno course record for the five miles at 225.56mph. He was followed by #14 Richard Sykes at 221.40mph flying a new Texan. Behind Sykes was #3 Dennis Buehn at 219.38mph, flying Sykes' old Texan. Fourth was #42 Jim Mott at 219.22mph, followed by #2 Charles Beck at 216.87mph. The remainder of the qualifiers were: rookie #94 George Catalano at 216.84mph, #11 Ray Schutte at 216.04mph, #5 Jerry McDonald at 213.78mph, #68 Jimmy Gist at 212.14mph, #8 Robert Jones at 211.91mph, #75 Al Goss at 211.64mph, rookie #9 Robert Heale at 209.96mph flying Pat Palmer's old aircraft, rookie #39 Ed Colbert at 207.71mph, and #77 Mike Wright at 205.01mph. Lap times were 1:19.8mins for first to 1:27.8mins for 14th. There was a glitch in timing, forcing some pilots to qualify twice. But when finished, it was another all-over 200mph field.

Heat-1 was a four-lap walk-way from the scatter pylon to the finish with everyone in line and #14 Sykes taking first at 224.41mph. Almost 11 seconds back in second place was #42 Mott at 217.17mph. Third was rookie #94 Catalano at 215.79mph, then #5 McDonald at 213.25mph, rookie #9 Heale at 205.22mph, #77 Wright at 205.04mph and seventh #8 Jones 31 seconds behind first place at 204.56mph.

Heat-2 was a repeat of Heat-1 from the start, with #73 Rina taking the lead and staying there to take first place at 221.74mph. Seven seconds back was #3 Buehn at 217.45mph, #68 Gist was four seconds behind Buehn at 214.80mph, #2 Beck was fourth with 213.14mph, #75 Goss followed at 211.82mph, and #11 Schutte finished at 209.41mph. Rookie Colbert was tail end at 207.07mph, which was 23 seconds back from first place.

With the disparities in speeds between the qualifiers, once they were out front, no one could catch or pass after the race started. This led to the Consolation (Silver) Race being just another train. The five-lap race would see some sparring in those behind the front two, but by mid race, finishing placements were set. Rookie #9 Heale took 7:02.4mins to win first place, #75 Goss was five seconds back, followed by #11 Schutte, #8 Jones, #77 Wright, #39 Colbert, and #2 Beck, 26 seconds back from first. Speeds ranged from 213.07mph for Heale to 200.68mph for Beck.

Sunday's five-lap Championship (Gold) Race[19] was anticipated to be hot and fast as the three fastest qualifiers were going head-to-head. Anything that happened behind them would be just an average race. However, from the start, it became obvious that this race would also be a follow-me race, as the jockeying for race position occurred on the backside of the racecourse during the pace lap. At the finish, it was #14 Sykes taking 6:38.3mins to finish first giving him an overall speed of 225.94mph. This was Sykes' first Championship win. He had raced in the first T-6 race in 1968. Second place went to another race veteran #73 Rina, who was five seconds behind at 223.16mph. In third place was #3 Buehn at 222.87mph. These three each set new Reno race speed records. Fourth was #42 Mott at 220.38mph. #68 Gist was next at 217.24mph, rookie #94 Catalano at 216.23mph, and in seventh #5 McDonald at 212.90mph. He took 7:02.7mins to finish.

When asked to explain why the racers had been so fast, Sykes said, "this airplane likes the cool temps, the high altitude and the longer racecourse. She's got speed when she can run long."

1984

Reno 1984's entrants and qualifiers were confusing, along with a change in number of laps per race and the addition of a special race. Twenty-eight pilots were entered with 20 aircraft, 18 qualified, 14 made the regular field and four raced in a special Bronze Race. Heat races were five laps over the five-mile course and the main races were six laps except the special Bronze Race, which was five laps.

Texans that were entered but not raced were #3 Richard Sykes, #6 Dennis Buehn, and rookie #66 Leonard Stonich. Pilots who entered but did not race were rookie #1 Michael Burke, #18 Randy Difani, #44 Ralph Twombly, #68 Phil Gist, #77 Richard Wright, rookie #79 Del Williams, and rookie #94 Joe McGuire.

The qualifiers in order of qualifying speeds were: #73 Ralph Rina taking 1:19.94mins at 225.169mph, #18 Dennis Buehn at 221.839mph (former #39), #2 Charlie Beck at 221.185mph, #75 Al Goss at 218.978mph, #42 Jim Mott at 218.712mph, and rookie #44 Alan Preston at 216.684mph. Texan #44 is the former Bob Mitchem 1971 winner, John Mosby's 1981 winner, and Ralph Twombly's 1982 winner. Also qualifying were: #94 George Catalano at 214.184mph, #5 Jerry McDonald at 213.270mph, #77 Mike Wright at 213.144mph, #68 Jimmy Gist at 212.766mph, #9 Robert Heale at 210.723mph, #8 Robert Jones at 209.351mph, #72 James Fox at 209.059mph, and rookie #27 Eddie Van Fossen at 207.732mph. Those relegated to the special Bronze Race were #11 Ray Schutte at 204.545mph, rookie #1 Charles Hutchins at 203.528, #6 Cliff Branch at 197.260mph, and rookie #79 John Martin with a lap time of 1:31.90mins and 195.865mph. This special race would be run after the two heat races.

Heat-1 was a start-to-finish race for six of the seven racers as #44 Preston was a DNS with mechanical problems. First through sixth places went to #18 Buehn at 219.914mph, #75 Goss at 215.347mph, #68 Gist at 214.997mph, #5 McDonald at 212.761mph, #8 Jones at 209.756mph, and rookie #27 Van Fossen at 204.969.

The timing issues that had plagued the qualifying races were back for Heat-2, which was another start-to-finish race. No times or speeds were recorded, but the finishing order was #73 Rina first, #42 Mott second, #2 Beck, #94 Catalano, #9 Heale, #77 Wright, and #72 Fox.

As a four plane, five lap fill-in race, the Bronze proved to be more exciting than either of the two heat races. The two rookies and two veterans came around for their first lap bunched up and it was a sight to see. By lap 3, #11 Schutte had pulled ahead and stayed there to finish first taking 7:10.8mins at an average of 208.923mph and $775. Rookie #1 Hutchins was second at 206.110mph, then rookie #79 Martin at 200.347mph, and fourth was #6 Branch at 199.698mph. This would be his last attempt at Texan racing.

It was flag-to-flag for the Silver Race winner #5 McDonald, who only took 8:15.9mins to cover the 30 miles at a speed of 217.777mph and collected $1,800. Second was rookie #44 Preston, who had fixed his mechanical problems, at 215.088mph. The rest of the finishers in order were #9 Heale at 215.002mph, #77 Wright at 211.350mph, #8 Jones at 209.627mph, and #72 Fox at 207.620mph. In seventh was rookie #27 Van Fossen with 8:48.9mins at 204.205mph and $1,000.

The Gold Race started with #18 Buehn and #73 Rina as if they were tied together and only yards apart. Lap by lap, #73 Rina inched forward until he finally went low and passed #18 Buehn to take first. The other five racers followed a plane's length

---

19 From here forward, the main NCAR races will be called Bronze, Silver and Gold.

Start of the 1985 Gold Race at Reno with #18 DiFani, #75 Goss, #42 Mott, #73 Rina, #27 Van Fossen, and #68 Gist. DiFani went on to take his first Reno Gold Race. (Bill LeSanche)

apart. The winning speeds for first and second were amazing with #73 Rina finishing in 8:17.1mins at 217.256mph and #18 Buehn close behind with 8:17.4mins at 217.116mph. Rina received $6,000 for first and Buehn earned $4,000 for second. The rest of the field finished in the following order: #42 Mott at 216.942mph, #94 Catalano at 214.171mph, #75 Goss at 213.215mph, and #68 Gist at 209.469mph. #2 Beck came in seventh at 8:39.4mins and 207.952mph, which paid $1,500.

1985

On August 10–11, 1985, a Demo T-6 Race was held as part of the Northwest Air Classic event at the Richland, WA, airport. The three participants raced over a 2.76-mile course. No records are available for speeds, times or placements. Those who raced were #9 Robert Heale, #75 Al Goss and #8 Robert Jones. While there was not much real racing, just the usual passing and place swapping, it did generate enough interest for planning a full race for 1986.

The 1985 Reno races saw minor changes to the racing format. There were now three heat races, a Bronze, Silver, and Gold. The number of laps remained the same, but each race would have only six contestants. The biggest change was the increase in prize money, which was the best change according to those who would be racing. The winner of the Gold Race would receive $7,000.

The weather was windy for qualifying and a few races. Qualifiers included rookie #18 Randy DiFani, who was the fastest at 224.688mph. He was followed by #73 Ralph Rina, about 4mph slower at 220.584mph. These two Texans had been the top qualifiers in 1984 with Rina first and Buehn in #18 second. Buehn sat 1985 out. Third place went to #75 Al Goss at 219.011mph. Goss was followed by #42 Jim Mott at 218.536mph, #5 Jerry McDonald at 216.189mph, #1 Charles Hutchins at 214.627mph, #44 Alan Preston at 214.424mph, #9 Robert Heale at 213.037mph, #27 Eddie Van Fossen at 212.962mph, #79 John Martin at 212.363mph, #72 Jim Fox at 211.101mph, #2 Charles Beck at 211.026mph, #77 Mike Wright at 210.049mph, #68 Jimmy Gist at 209.903mph, #8 Robert Jones at 207.380mph, #11 Ray Schutte at 205.708mph, and rookie #48 Bruce Redding at 203.057mph. Rookie #85 John Roark was the only one below 200mph at 191.938mph in his only attempt at T-6 racing.

Heat-1C was a #75 Goss race, taking only 6:59.32mins to win at 216.050mph. Six seconds back in second was #27 Van Fossen at 213.123mph, then #8 Jones at 211.323mph, #1 Hutchins at 210.136mph with rookie #85 Roark still under 200mph at 192.622mph and almost a minute slower. #2 Beck was a DNF with a sick engine.

#27 Eddie Van Fossen in the 1985 Reno Gold Race where the future eight-time Gold Race winner would finish fifth. (Bill LeSanche)

At the pylons in 1986 as #27 Van Fossen comes around to win his first Reno Gold Race at 223.450mph. Notice the pylon judges under the pylon and the photographers scattered about. The author is in this group. (Jim Daley)

Heat-1B saw #73 Rina in first at 215.142mph, followed by #68 Gist, #9 Heale, #5 McDonald, and #72 Fox, who cut pylon 5 on lap 3, was given a time penalty, and rookie #48 Reading in sixth, who was one-half minute behind first place at 198.050mph.

Heat-1A was a great race with #18 DiFani and #42 Mott battling it out throughout the entire race while the rest of the field remained about 30 seconds behind them. At the finish was #18 DiFani in first with #42 Mott in second just 0.6 of a second behind. Their speeds were 219.531mph and 218.916mph, respectively. It was a great race between the rookie DiFani and the veteran Mott. The rest of the field was #44 Preston third, followed by #11 Schutte, #77 Wright, and #79 Martin, who took 7:22.29mins at speed of 204.829mph.

The six slowest Texans competed in the six-lap Bronze Race, guaranteeing a close-run race. The three veterans entered were #77 Wright, #2 Beck, and #72 Fox. It was Wright and Beck out front from the start until Beck pulled out of the race at the end of lap 1 with a sour engine. Then it was between #77 Wright and #79 Martin, with Wright gaining the advantage on lap 5. Wright finished first at 202.528mph, followed by Martin at 200.725mph. Third was rookie #48 Redding, who had been closing on the front two Texans but ran out of laps, at 200.570mph. Fourth was #72 Fox at 200.141mph and fifth was rookie #85 Roark with 187.786mph putting him more than one-half minute behind the leader. #2 Beck received a DNF.

The Silver Race was another close-run affair, being a three-way race between #5 McDonald, #44 Preston and #9 Heale with the three seemingly tied together. The other three racers #8 Jones, #11 Schutte and #1 Hutchins following along about one half lap back. The leaders crossed the finish line in step with speeds between 216.236mph and 210.851mph with #5 McDonald first, #44 Preston second, and #9 Heale third. The judges ruled that Heale had cut pylon 2 on lap 1 and with his time penalty, Heale was moved to fourth. This placed #9 Jones third, #11 Schutte fifth and #1 Hutchins sixth.

A race to remember for a rookie would best describe the Gold Race from the scatter pylon to the end. It was an exciting race with plenty of speed and jockeying between rookie #18 DiFani, #75 Goss and #42 Mott, while #73 Rina kept pressure on all three. #27 Van Fossen and #68 Gist had their own separate race behind the others. By lap 2, DiFani had acquired the lead and held it to the end taking first in 8:28.26mins. DiFani was followed by Goss in 8:28.76mins. Their speeds were only 0.2secs difference. #42 Mott held on to third but was penalized for cutting pylon 3 on four laps and pylon 5 on lap 6. This bumped him to sixth moving #73 Rina to third, #68 Gist to fourth, and #27 Van Fossen to fifth. The payout was $7,000 for first, $5,000 for second, $4,500 for third, $4,200 for fourth, $4,000 for fifth, and $3,800 for sixth. Randy DiFani had come to make his mark at Reno.

1986

Ten Texans were entered in the Northwest Air Classic Races held August 15–17, 1986, at the Richland airport over a 4.8-mile course and only nine qualified. #41 Ralph Twombly blew a tire on landing and bent a landing gear, scraped a wingtip, and did not qualify or race.

The top qualifier was #9 Robert Heale at 229.2mph. Second was #44 Alan Preston at 222.48mph in the old John Mosby racer. These two were followed by #8 Robert Jones at 219.6mph, #97 Bruce Redding at 216.0mph, and #7 Robert Heale at 206.78mph. Heale entered and raced both his #9 and #7. Sixth place went to rookie #66 Bruce Lockwood at 205.8mph, followed by #4 David Bruce at 202.3mph, #48 Shane Theis at 200.18mph, and rookie #69 Joe Taylor in ninth at 191.2mph.

Heat-1A was a five-lap tail chase as #9 Heale led from the start with just a few passes. The Texans finished almost in the order they started. First was #9 Heale at 227.5mph, then #8 Jones, #66 Lockwood, and tenths of a second behind him in fourth was #4 Bruce, and then #69 Taylor fifth.

Heat-1B was more interesting, beginning with take-off. #44 Preston had prop problems, so he landed to fix the problem. Meanwhile, the other three racers, #97 Redding, #48 Theis and #7 Heale, flew around waiting for him to rejoin. Believing the prop problem solved, #44 took off again to join the others only to drop out with a DNS. Now with the race in full action, it was determined that #97 had false started when he jumped ahead. After a restart, it was #97 Redding start to finish at 216.6mph, with second to #48 Theis and #7 Heale third.

The six-lap Silver featured four racers and was a fast race, although they again finished in the order they raced. #44 Preston was first at 202.75mph, #4 Bruce second at 215.39mph, #7 Heale third at 204.21mph, and #69 Taylor fourth at 203.4mph.

Five pilots raced in the six-lap Gold Race. This proved to be a battle between #9 Heale, the fastest qualifier, and #8 Jones, third fastest. Both pilots really pushed each other, while the rookies fell to the back leaving #97 Redding in the middle flying alone. Heale held his lead and finished first at 230.67mph and #8 Jones was second at 222.32mph. These two were followed by #97 Redding at 218.21mph, #66 Lockwood at 208.36mph, and #48 Theis at 206.87mph.

The racing was good, despite the small number of aircraft, the crowd was happy, and plans were made for the next year. However, 1986 would be the last year of racing in Richland.

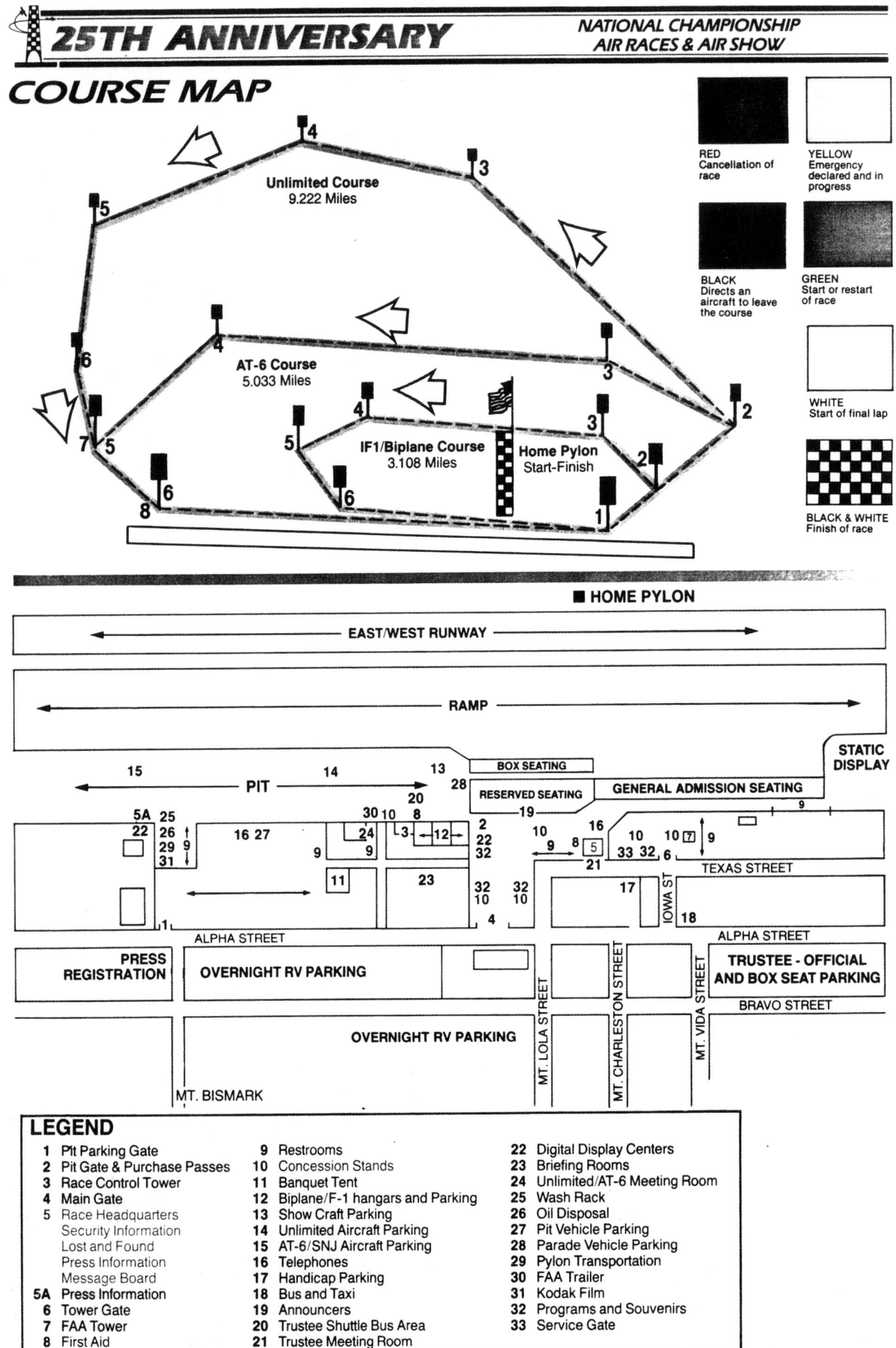

The 1988 Reno racecourse map showing the meaning of each colored flag. (Collection of Aviation Photo Services)

A chance at more prize money saw 28 entrants for Reno 1986 with 25 qualifying and 19 racing after the cut. Those entered but not qualified were #7 Bill Ellis in his only attempt at T-6 racing, #17 Gene McNeely, and #66 Lee Donham in his only attempt at Reno. Cut from the field were #72 Jim Fox, #7 Jamie MacKay, #79 John Martin, #48 Shane Theis, #6 Nick Macy, and #70 Joe Chiodo in his only Reno appearance. Macy and Chiodo were both under 200mph.

Qualifying was a hot affair with the first 15 over 210mph. The top qualifier was #9 Robert Heale at 221.474mph, with #27 Eddie Van Fossen next at 221.177mph. They were followed by #42 Jim Mott, #18 Randy DiFani at 219.276mph, and #73 Ralph Rina at 218.167mph. #88 Bruce Redding, in the first of two Texans he would qualify, came in at 218.062mph. Rookie #4 David Bruce reached 217.460mph, #44 Alan Preston[20] at 217.330mph, and #75 Al Goss at 215.983mph. #97 Bruce Redding qualified in the second Texan at 215.906mph. This aircraft would be raced by Dennis Buehn. #5 Jerry McDonald qualified at 214.907mph, followed by #68 Jimmy Gist at 214.578mph, #14 Dick Sykes at 214.018mph, #2 Charles Beck at 211.249mph, #11 Ray Schutte at 210.219mph, #8 Robert Jones at 209.951mph, and #77 Dick Wright at 208.310mph. Rookie #41 Joe Taylor reached 207.167mph in his only Reno T-6 race. In 19th place was #1 Charles Hutchins.

Cool temperatures would help everyone as Heat-1C got under way with #75 Goss and #88 Redding taking the lead. #68 Gist was in the middle and #11 Schutte was ahead of #41 Taylor. Veteran #42 Mott seemed to falter and pulled out for a DNF. #88 Redding won at 222.109mph, surpassing Goss at 220.458mph. Four seconds back was #68 Gist followed by #11 Schutte 7mph slower. #41 Taylor came in at 213.092mph and 18 seconds behind first.

The flying in Heat-1B left everyone amazed from start to finish as #27 Van Fossen flew a perfect flag-to-flag win, taking only 6:33.52mins at a speed of 230.214mph for a Heat Race. Those who followed in order were #73 Rina at 225.594mph, #2 Beck at 220.552mph, #44 Preston at 220.370mph, #5 McDonald at 219.760mph, and Wright at 211.827mph and 7:07.68mins. After the race there was talk of having #27 Van Fossen undergo another tech inspection to make sure his equipment was stock.

Heat-1A was a bit slower, but just as exciting from the scatter pylon to the finish. When the Texans came around to the home pylon, they were all in a mass gaggle. By lap 2, they had sorted themselves and raced to the finish after #9 Heale pulled out to the lead, followed by #18 DiFani. As they crossed the finish line, it was #9 Heale in first at 222.519mph, and 12 seconds behind was #18 DiFani at 220.519mph. Rookie #4 Bruce took third with 215.602mph, then #97 Buehn at 212.109mph, #14 Sykes at 211.198mph was fifth. #8 Jones was disqualified for low flying.

Results for the six-lap Bronze Race were interesting as only 27 seconds separated first and sixth and everyone flew over 200mph. Veteran #42 Mott took first and flew a prefect race reaching 212.670mph. Second was #5 McDonald, then #8 Jones, #41 Taylor, #1 Hutchins, and #77 Wright at 202.031mph.

#97 Buehn took a quick lead at the start of the Silver Race. Buehn was soon passed on lap 2 by #44 Preston and #4 Bruce, who fought closely for the next four laps. #2 Beck then fought with #97 Buehn and #68 Gist for third. #11 Schutte flew his own race at the back. When the checkered flag fell, it was #4 Bruce in first at 212.845mph. He had slipped past #44 Preston as they rounded the final pylon for home. Preston was second with 212.679mph, #97 Buehn was third at 209.781mph, followed by #2 Beck at 209.434mph, #68 Gist at 209.139mph, and, finally, #11 Schutte 205.856mph.

As the two fastest qualifiers came off the scatter pylon to start the Gold Race, they were barely a yard apart and almost wingtip to wingtip. #9 Heale and #27 Van Fossen also had #18 DiFani half a plane length behind. #73 Rina seemed to have a small technical problem as he would have normally been in the mix. Rina was further behind with #88 Reading and #75 Goss. By lap 4, Heale was in front by a prop spinner and DiFani was chewing on Van Fossen's tail feathers. At the start of lap 6, DiFani slipped back inches. As the trio rounded pylon 5, Van Fossen saw his chance, dropped low, and passed Heale for the win. Van Fossen took first at 223.450mph, second was #9 Heale at 221.393mph, #18 DiFani at 220.245mph, #88 Redding at 216.272mph, #73 Rina at 215.691mph, and #75 Goss 213.497mph. It was a really great race.

1987

Twenty-three pilots entered the 1987 Reno races, 21 qualified and 18 raced. Those not qualifying were #33 Vern Raburn and #64 James Dye. Those who qualified but did not race were #26 Linda Finch (the second women to enter since 1974) at 197.394mph, #048 Dorel Graves at 188.836mph, and #79 C. J. Stephens at 198.584mph. All three were under 200mph. Only a few years ago these would have been winning speeds. Two additional heat races were added to "allow more competition and excitement."

---

20   In 1986, Alan Preston would become the only race pilot to race in all four classes of racers during a single event: Unlimited, T-6, F-1, and Biplane.

#27 Eddie Van Fossen at 230.372mph set a new Reno qualifying record. Others qualifying at more than 200mph were: #4 David Bruce at 228.513mph, #2 Charles Beck at 226.655mph, #1 Charles Hutchins at 226.259mph, #75 Al Goss at 225.526mph, and #42 Jim Mott at 222.099mph. #44 Ralph Twombly qualified at 221.501mph. He returned to Reno after a few years away and flew the old John Mosby Texan. Also over 200mph were rookie #6 Nick Macy at 218.509mph, #18 Randy DiFani at 216.914mph, rookie #97 Tom Dwelle at 216.292mph, #8 Robert Jones at 215.597mph, #5 Jimmy Gist at 215.367mph, #88 Bruce Redding at 215.034mph, and #11 Phil "Pete" Gist at 213.615mph. Gist was filling in for Ray Schutte and this would be the second time the Gist brothers would race each other. Rookie #77 Jim Good reached 212.937mph flying Mike Wright's former T-6. #9 Robert Heale flew 212.812mph in the same T-6 Pat Palmer flew to win the 1974 Championship Race. Rookie #17 Fred Johnson at 208.142mph competed in his only T-6 race. In 18th place was #72 James Fox at 205.545mph. The difference between lap time from first to 18th was almost ten seconds, 1:18.65mins to 1:28.15mins and 30mph.

Heat-1C started under windy conditions. but the weather had little effect on the five-lap race with veteran #42 Mott and 1985 Gold Race winner #18 DiFani fighting for the lead. #2 Beck chased after them for four laps. Rookie #77 Good and #72 Fox were well behind. Normally fast, #5 Gist lagged with a poor running engine. At the flag it was #18 DiFani first, having outpaced #42 Mott in second. Their times were fractions apart with DiFani finishing in 6:56.33mins and Mott in 6:57.99mins. Beck was third, followed by #77 Good, #72 Fox and #5 Gist.

Heat-1B raced as they were to finish: #4 Bruce took first at 226.360mph, #75 Goss at 223.270mph, #6 Macy at 218.026mph and 6:55.52mins, #8 Jones at 210.806mph, #17 Johnson 210.160mph, and in sixth was #11 Gist at 207.219mph.

Heat-1C was a race from second to sixth as #27 Van Fossen took the lead from the start and stayed there to the checkered flag. The fight was between #1 Hutchins and #44 Twombly, who had not lost any flying skills during his time away from racing. In lap 4, Twombly pulled ahead into second place. #88 Redding surprised Hutchins by passing him in lap 5 to take third. #1 Hutchins took fourth, followed by #9 Heale and rookie #97 Dwelle. Times from first to sixth were 6:42.65mins to 7:09.57mins and just over 14mph difference.

Heat-2B was a five-lap fast train ride with #4 Bruce first in 6:35.32mins and 229.166mph. Second was #42 Mott in 6:38.72mins and 227.212mph. Third to sixth were: #1 Hutchins at 221.409mph, #6 Macy at 220.402mph, #77 Good at 215.870mph, and #8 Jones at 211.643mph.

Heat-2A saw #27 Van Fossen setting a pattern for start-to-finish leads and taking first at 225.616mph. While the remaining veteran pilots pushed each other for placements, they could not catch #27. Second through sixth were: #75 Goss at 221.096mph, #18 DiFani at 218.409mph, #44 Twombly at 217.863mph, #88 Redding at 215.096mph, and #2 Beck at a slow 213.096mph.

At the start of the Bronze Race, rookie #97 Dwelle was in the lead. Dwelle was followed by #5 Gist, #11 Gist, #9 Heale, rookie #17 Johnson, and #72 Fox. On lap 2, #5 Gist passed #97 Dwelle on the back side. #9 Heale easily passed #11 Gist and was headed for #97 Dwelle. Heale caught Dwelle on lap 3 with everyone else slipping further back. #72 Fox was lapped by #5 Gist as they took the final flag. #5 Gist was first at 214.259mph. Heale was not able to catch up and finished at 211.171mph in second place. This time was seven seconds behind Gist. They were followed by #97 Dwelle in third at 208.138mph, #11 Gist fourth at 207.888mph, #17 Johnson fifth at 207.705mph and one lap down was #72 Fox at 175.904mph. This was the last time the Gist brothers would race together, and both #17 Johnson and #72 Fox would not return to Reno.

Veteran winner #44 Twombly flew a winning Texan in a great Silver Race. Twombly's only challenger by mid-race was #2 Beck. #88 Redding followed close behind the two front runners. #6 Macy and #8 Jones were at the back fighting for fourth as #77 Good pulled out on lap 1 with a sour engine. Twombly retook the lead on lap 5. This startled #2 Beck, who let #88 Redding pass by. At the finish, #44 Twombly had another win at 218.032mph in 8:18.61mins. Redding was second, taking 8:22.39mins. Beck was in third place in 8:22.61mins, while rookie #6 Macy was fourth at 8:26.59mins. Finally, #8 Jones placed fifth in 8:38.99mins. This was almost 30 seconds from first place.

The two fastest qualifiers lined up for the Gold Race, but it would be #4 Bruce in the lead by the end of lap 1 with #27 Van Fossen tied to Bruce's tail. They were closely followed by #75 Goss and #42 Mott, with #18 DiFani and #1 Hutchins both a few seconds back. Van Fossen overtook #4 Bruce by the end of lap 2 and, surprisingly, so did #75 Goss, who had followed Van Fossen around Bruce. This left Mott behind Bruce, and DiFani and Hutchins behind him. Lap 4 saw Bruce move back up to second and Mott to third, then Goss, DiFani and Hutchins. As they started lap 6, Mott caught Goss. At the checkered flag it was #27 Van Fossen in 8:00.26mins and at 226.362mph. In second place was #4 Bruce in 8:01.76mins and at 225.658mph. Mott came in third at 224.780mph. In fourth place was #75 Goss at 223.496mph. At the back were fifth #18 DiFani at 219.223mph and sixth #1 Hutchins at 217.730mph. As they landed, it was determined that #4 Bruce would be placed sixth for low flying, thus bumping everyone up one place. Van Fossen had scored his first back-to-back wins.

1988

A T-6 Demonstration Race was held at the former Wendover AFB at Wendover, Utah (UT), in August 1988. "Demo races were not actual races, more of a choregraphing of passing and formation flying. Featuring between four and six Texans over a two-to-three mile temporary course, marked by identifiable landmarks," according to the T-6 Racing Association. Wendover was a typical race. The known participating racers were #6 Nick Macy, #8 Robert Jones, #27 Eddie Van Fossen and #75 Al Goss. Like most Demo Races, results are unknown.

Reno 1988 would see 21 entries, 19 qualifiers and 18 racers. Those entered but not qualified were #48 Dorel Graves and #88 Bruce Redding. #20 Linda Finch qualified but was cut to keep the field to 18. The rookies were Bud Granley flying Robert Heale's #9 (Heale would sit out 1988), #17 David Griggs, #69 Lee Oman, and #99 John Luther, which was the old #68.

For the second year in a row #27 Eddie Van Fossen was the top qualifier at 1:18.06mins for his one lap at 232.114mph. This was also a new Reno qualifying record. #7 Tom Dwelle, in his second year racing, was second at 1:19.46mins and 228.024mph in the former #97. These two were followed by the 1985 Gold winner #18 Randy DiFani at 223.744mph in third. #44 Ralph Twombly was close behind at 223.578mph. He was followed by: #6 Nick Macy at 223.193mph, #4 David Bruce at 222.508mph, #77 Jim Good at 220.236mph, #42 Jim Mott at 219.462mph, #1 Charles Hutchins at 219.382mph, #5 Jimmy Gist at 217.696mph, #75 Al Goss at 215.085mph, #2 Charlie Beck at 215.034mph, #8 Robert Jones at 214.272mph, #99 John Luther at 214.044mph, #17 David Griggs at 213.715mph, #9 Bud Granley at 211.767mph, #11 Ray Schutte at 211.241mph, and #69 Lee Oman in 18th at 209.272mph. This was almost 23mph slower than first place.

Heat-1C was delayed by the military fly-bys, but got off to a fast start with #1 Hutchins out front at the first pylon. #18 DiFani was right behind. #4 Bruce and #2 Beck flew their own race for a few laps, with Bruce steadily gaining in position. Rookies #17 Griggs and #69 Oman were at the back. Lap 4 saw DiFani slip by Hutchins as they rounded pylon 3 with Bruce following. They remained in this line up to the finish. DiFani came in first at 220.418mph, while second place went to #4 Bruce at 219.808mph. In third place was #1 Hutchins, followed by #2 Beck, #17 Griggs, and #69 Oman in sixth at 206.925mph.

Heat-1B started with #7 Dwelle in front and #6 Macy on his tail. #75 Goss was on Dwelle's wing with the other three, #11 Schutte, #42 Mott and #99 Luther bringing up the rear. Dwelle was clearly out front by lap 2, with Macy one-half plane length behind. Goss and Mott were fighting each other, leaving Luther and Schutte at the tail end. Goss overtook Mott for third and Dwelle won first, Macy was second having been only yards behind. Luther was in fifth place and Schutte in sixth. First place flew at 224.682mph in 6:43.21mins, while sixth place came in at 210.517mph in 7:10.34mins.

Heat-1A saw #27 Van Fossen pull away from the start, followed by #44 Twombly, #8 Jones, #77 Good, rookie #9 Granley, and #5 Gist. Van Fossen continued to pull away until the checkered flag. Good and Jones fought down the front straight until Gist moved up as Jones slipped back, followed by Granley. It was #27 Van Fossen who took first at 228.987mph. Following were #44 Twombly at 222.175mph, #77 Good at 219.404mph, #5 Gist at 216.375mph, #8 Jones at 216.241mph, and #9 Granley 211.946mph. The gap was 30 seconds from first to sixth.

Heat-2B started off with everyone in line. Then #7 Dwelle moved out in front. He was followed by #42 Mott, #44 Twombly, #2 Beck, #4 Bruce, and #5 Gist. By lap 4, the race had become a see-saw for third behind Dwelle and Bruce. Trailing behind were Beck, Twombly, Mott and Gist. It then appeared that Beck had soured an engine and fell back. Twombly found his second wind and moved up to second place. The race finished with #7 Dwelle first at 229.917 mph. This was

Future six-time Reno Gold Race winner #6 Nick Macy being towed back to the Texan pit area after a heat race in 1989. Macy plans to race at Reno in 2023 to attempt a seventh Gold. (Russ Hiatt)

about 1mph faster than what #27 Van Fossen had flown in Heat-1A. Second was #44 Twombly at 222.743mph, almost the same speed that he had flown in Heat-1A. Bruce came in third just 0.2secs behind Twombly. Gist finished inches ahead of #42 Mott and sixth place went to #2 Beck at 215.316mph.

Heat-2A was a runaway from the start to finish for #27 Van Fossen with everyone else bunched up behind. The first two pairs behind, and almost inseparable, were #75 Goss and #18 DiFani and #6 Macy and #1 Hutchins. #77 Good was playing catchup. Then it became Goss, Macy and Difani, while Van Fossen continued to pull away. At the flag it was #27 Van Fossen at 230.631mph and 6:32.81mins, #18 DiFani had squeezed by #75 Goss for second at 220.875mph, Goss held off #6 Macy for third at 219.144mph., Fourth place Macy came in at 218.784mph, #77 Good took fifth at 214.805mph, and #1 Hutchins came sixth at 214.693mph and 7:01.97minutes. Van Fossen set a new race record again.

With four rookies, the six-lap Bronze Race was sedate with #99 Luther taking the lead followed by veteran #11 Schutte, #17 Griggs, #9 Granley, #69 Oman, and veteran #8 Jones. Griggs and Schutte tussled a little before rookie #99 Luther took his first win at 213.850mph. Schutte followed in second place. Granley placed third and Jones fourth. Griggs was bumped to fifth for cutting pylon 3 on lap 3. This was Griggs' only Reno race. #69 Oman was sixth at 207.935mph and 8:42.82mins.

The next set of fastest pilots lined up for the Silver Race with all coming down the chute for the scatter pylon. As they rounded the pylon, it was #1 Hutchins at the front followed by #6 Macy. After Macy was the group of #5 Gist, #42 Mott, #77 Good, and #2 Beck. The race was between Hutchins and Macy, each pushing hard while Gist broke from the pack into a clear third. At the finish, only 0.48secs separated #1 Hutchins in first at 8:14.20mins and #6 Macy second at 8:14.68mins. Hutchins' speed was 219.977mph and Macy's was 219.764mph. #5 Gist took third at 216.150mph, followed by #2 Beck 214.124mph, #77 Good 214.048mph, and #42 Mott 213.590mph, placing sixth.

The fastest qualifiers were set for the Gold Race. At the scatter pylon it was #27 Van Fossen, #7 Dwelle, #18 DiFani, #44 Twombly, #75 Goss, and #4 Bruce. Bruce passed Goss on the backside of the course. Bruce caught Twombly on the next lap, where he stayed. By lap 4, it was Van Fossen one-quarter of a lap ahead of both Dwelle and DiFani. By the end of lap 5, it appeared that Dwelle might catch Van Fossen, but there were not enough laps left. Van Fossen took his third win at 229.759mph and 7:53.16mins. #7 Dwelle was second at 227.943mph and 7:56.93mins. Third was #18 DiFani 220.817mph and 8:12.32mins. #4 Bruce held on to fourth at 8:13.08mins, fifth was #44 Twombly at 8:17.55mins, and #75 Goss was sixth in 8:29.69mins at 213.711mph. The year 1988 would mark the beginning of faster speeds at Reno.

1989
A T-6 Racing Association Demonstration Race was held at Casper, Wyoming, in early June 1989 as part of the Flying Cowboy Airshow and Air Races. This was the typical Demo Race. Participants and results are not known.

Minot, North Dakota, held a T-6 Demonstration Race June 22–23, 1989. No further information is known, but it was described as the typical Demo Race.

Wendover held a second T-6 Demonstration Race on August 12–13, 1989. According to the T-6 Racing Association, this was a typical demo race. No further information is available.

The combined total purse for Reno 1989 was $500,000, with 19 Texan pilots qualifying to race for their share of the money.[21] #11 Ray Schutte qualified 19th but was cut to keep the field at 18.

The top qualifier for the third consecutive year was #27 Eddie Van Fossen at 229.701mph. He was followed again by #7 Tom Dwelle at 228.773mph. Other qualifiers were: #75 Al Goss at 224.773mph, #18 Randy DiFani at 223.056mph, #6 Nick Macy at 221.231mph, #4 David Bruce at 220.289mph, #1 Charles Hutchins at 219.276mph. He was the first under 220mph. Placing eighth through 18th were: #77 Jim Good at 218.246mph, #20 John Luther at 217.617 in a new Texan, #2 Charles Beck at 216.292mph returning after a few years away, #5 Jerry McDonald at 215.367mph, and #9 Bud Granley at 214.601mph. Rookie #44 Gifford Foley[22] was filling in for Ralph Twombly and came in at 213.715mph.

---

21 According to RARA, "In the T-6 Class prize money is paid differently than in any other Class. No money is won in any Heat Race and is only paid out in the finals. The Class choose to race in this way as it ensures that there will be no shoe-ins. Pilots have to take racing seriously each day as the results determine their positions for the one-shot money on Sunday." This meant no "sandbagging."

22 Gifford Foley would be fatally injured in this Texan in July 1990 during an airshow aerobatic routine. This Harvard had first raced at Reno in 1969 as #94 and took first place in 1971, 1981 and 1982.

#99 John Luther qualified at 212.462mph. He had already qualified #20 in 13th, and he would race both. #19 Robert Heale reached 212.089mph and was also in a new Texan. #8 Robert Jones flew 211.446mph, rookie #89 Joe Hartung finished at 204.848mph, and rookie #42 Mike Wells flew 203.194mph.

Heat-1C, -1B and -1A were predictable, with the three top qualifiers taking first place starting with #75 Goss in Heat-1C at 223.799mph. He was followed by #4 Bruce, #20 Luther, #9 Granley, #19 Heale, and #42 Wells.

Heat-1B was #7 Dwelle first at 223.034mph, #6 Macy, #5 McDonald, #77 Good, #99 Luther in his other Texan, and #89 Hartung slowest at 193.399mph.

Heat-1A was dominated by #27 Van Fossen at 224.771mph, followed by #18 DiFani, #1 Hutchins, #44 Foley, #2 Beck, and #8 Jones, who placed sixth for cutting pylon 2 on lap 1.

Gloom hung over the racecourse most of the day Friday after a Formula One pilot[23] had been fatally injured during a morning Heat Race and Heat-2B got started late.

Heat-2B was more exciting further back from the lead. #7 Dwelle and #18 DiFani at the front fought for first. The most exciting part of this race was between Jimmy Gist flying #44 (in place of Foley), #77 Good, #4 Bruce, and #5 McDonald. These four were evenly matched and it was pilot skill that made this race so interesting. The four Texans traded places through four of the five laps until #44 finally pulled ahead on the last lap. Dwelle took first place at 231.131mph, #18 DiFani was second at 221.865mph. Gist finished 1mph slower in third. #77 Good was fourth at 217.874mph, #4 Bruce fifth at 214.764mph, and #5 McDonald sixth at 213.474mph.

For a heat race, Heat-2A was a pulse pounder for all five laps. #27 Van Fossen, #75 Goss and #6 Macy came out of the chute and passed the scatter pylon as if one aircraft. Seconds back were #1 Hutchins, #20 Luther, and #9 Granley tied to each other. It was almost a fruitless chase for everyone except Van Fossen who took 6:32.87mins to fly the five laps at 230.595mph. For comparison, sixth place #9 Granley took 6:58.38mins. Second place went to #75 Goss just tenths of a mile per hour behind the lead at 230.460mph. Goss was followed by #6 Macy at 227.731mph, #1 Hutchins at 223.728mph, and #20 Luther at 220.595mph. The main six-lap final races were to prove just as exciting.

Two rookies would race in the Bronze Race, but all of the attention would be focused on veteran #2 Charles Beck. He got the jump on everyone from the start and was only challenged for the lead once by #8 Jones, and after that everyone fell into where they finished. First was #2 Beck at 215.623mph. Jones was second at 212.309mph. Jones was followed by #19 Heale at 209.015mph, rookie #89 Hartung at 208.182mph, and #99 Luther at 207.943mph. In sixth place was rookie #42 Wells at 201.882mph in his only T-6 race. This race showed that an old dog could still have a trick up his sleeve, even after being away from racing for a few years.

The first four places in the Silver Race were close and raced their own race with #1 Hutchins in the lead. Hutchins was followed by #4 Bruce, #77 Good, and #20 Luther. Behind them were #5 McDonald and #9 Granley in their own competition for fifth. At the flag it was Hutchins, Bruce, Good, Luther, McDonald, and Granley 0.6secs behind McDonald. Speeds were from 222.012mph for first place to 212.996mph for sixth.

The Gold Race was expected to be another runaway for #27 Van Fossen and from the start through the first laps it appeared that way. Then, it seemed that Van Fossen had a moment of hesitation, which #7 Dwelle took advantage of and slipped past and began to pull away. For an instant, it appeared that #75 Goss might also pass Van Fossen, but he recovered and focused his sights on Dwelle leaving Goss, #18 DiFani, and #6 Macy to themselves. #44 Foley flew by himself. Each lap saw Dwelle inching ahead until the flag fell. To everyone's surprise it was #7 Dwelle first and #27 Van Fossen second only three seconds behind. Speeds for first and second were 222.326mph and 221.118mph, respectively. Dwelle and Van Fossen were followed by #75 Goss, #18 DiFani, #6 Macy, and rookie #44 Foley in sixth at 208.939mph.

Reno 1989 was criticized as more of a formation flying event than an air-racing event, but the results from the Bronze, Silver, and Gold races proved otherwise.

1990

On June 23–24, 1990, another T-6 Demonstration Race was held at the old World War Two bomber base in Casper over a five-mile racecourse. Races were four laps each and seven mobile drilling rigs were used as pylons with the home pylon topped by an American flag. Eight Texans raced: #18 Randy DiFani, #27 Eddie Van Fossen, #7 Tom Dwelle, #77 Jim Good (who was also Air Boss and a resident of Casper), #89 Joe Hartung (flying Ed Reed's loaner SNJ that he broke on

---

23 #73 Errol Roberson was killed when his aircraft disintegrated in flight between pylon 4 and 5.

The first year #21 was entered at Reno was 1990. It was raced by Charles Hutchins and placed fourth in the Bronze Race. Hutchins would use #21 to win the 1995 Gold Race. The last Reno race for #21 was in 2008, where it finished fifth in the Silver. (Bob Kennedy)

Saturday), #22 Kenny Day, #44 Ralph Twombly (second pilot was Giff Foley), and #90 Gene McNeely. Like most of the other demo events, there was a lot of swapping places, passing, and slower race speeds. The results are unknown, and it does not seem anybody cared about them. Both spectators and pilots had a great time.

Reno 1990 would see 20 entrants, 19 qualified and 18 raced. Not qualifying was #48 Dorel Graves. #51 Ralph Rina/Gerry Miles qualified at 198.871mph but were cut to keep the field at 18.

The fastest qualifier for the fourth year in a row was #27 Eddie Van Fossen at 228.521mph. He was followed by #7 Tom Dwelle at 226.161mph, #75 Al Goss at 225.763mph, #6 Nick Macy at 224.102mph, and #5 Jerry McDonald at 222.740mph. #90 Gene McNeely at 221.668mph was fastest of the four rookies. #2 Charles Beck qualified at 221.422mph, #77 Jim Good at 218.940, #18 Randy DiFani at 216.434mph, #89 Joe Hartung at 216.382mph, #8 Robert Jones at 215.654mph, and #19 Robert Heale at 215.318mph. #59 Jimmy Gist qualified at 215.035mph in Ralph Rina's old racer #73. #21 Charles Hutchins flew at 212.265mph, also in a new Texan #99 John Luther finished at 210.623mph, followed by rookie #20 Linda Finch at 206.601mph finally making the cut to race. Bringing up the rear were rookies #22 Kenny Day at 205.514mph, and #10 Greg Morse at 203.029mph in 18th place in his only attempt at Texan racing. However, Morse did race in other classes. It was a fast field.

Heat 1C would see a 24mph gap between first place #75 Goss at 226.864mph and sixth place #10 Morse at 202.933mph. In second place was #18 DiFani at 222.112mph. Third place went to rookie #90 McNeely at 222.024mph. In fourth was #99 Luther at 215.050mph and fifth #19 Heale at 210.179mph. Goss had taken command of the race from the start with everyone else briefly battling.

Heat-1B would see rookie #22 Day out of the race early with a sour engine, leaving everyone flying behind first place #7 Dwelle. #5 McDonald was second at 221.729mph. This was 12mph slower than Dwelle. In third was #8 Jones at 217.92mph, fourth was #77 Good at 217.851mph, and #21 Hutchins took fifth at 215.287mph.

Five-lap Heat-1A belonged to #27 Van Fossen from the start with only a brief challenge from #6 Macy, who took second. #2 Beck and #59 Gist traded places several times with Beck finishing third and Gist fourth. #89 Hartung and rookie #20 Finch were fifth and sixth with 209.924mph and 209.708mph, respectively.

Heat-2B again saw #7 Dwelle take the lead to finish first at 226.566mph. He was followed by #6 Macy, #90 McNeely, #8 Jones, #77 Good, and sixth #99 Luther at 210.568mph.

Heat-2A would see #75 Goss and #27 Van Fossen briefly tussle before #27 got the upper hand around pylon 4 on lap 3 to pass and remain ahead to the finish. Van Fossen won first in 6:36.02mins for the five laps. Goss took 6:38.32mins for second place. Behind the two leaders were #18 DiFani, #2 Beck, #5 McDonald, and #59 Gist with 6:55.38mins.

From the scatter pylon through lap 4, #19 Heale and #89 Hartung pushed at each other for the lead of the Bronze Race with Heale taking first at 217.798mph and Hartung second at 215.387mph. Rookie #20 Finch was third and #21 Hutchins was fourth. Rookie #22 Day, with a fixed engine, was fifth and rookie #10 Morse was sixth at 203.308mph.

Drama was the word for the Silver Race, which started with #2 Beck and #5 McDonald out front having a great race. Further back were #59 Gist and #77 Good having their own race with #99 Luther and #8 Jones doing the same. Good slipped past Gist as did Jones by Luther; both passes were on the back side of the course on lap 5. At the checkered flag

Handout for the first Phoenix 500 Air Races in March 1994 held at the former Williams AFB with a five-mile course. There were 19 Texan qualifiers who posted good speeds. The 1995 races did not offer Texan racing. (Collection of Aviation Photo Services)

it was #5 McDonald first at 216.913mph, #2 Beck second at 216.595mph, #77 Good third, #55 Gist fourth, #8 Jones fifth, and #99 Luther sixth at 209.098mph. The judges determined that #5 had broken formation at the start and was placed last, thus moving everyone up one place giving the win to Beck.

For the second year in a row, the Gold Race provided a surprise ending. From the start, it looked like #27 Van Fossen was headed for another win, but by lap 3 he seemed to falter. This enabled #7 Dwelle to get past. On the next lap, #75 Goss flew by. Both Dwelle and Goss poured on the gas and pulled ahead, and, for a moment, it appeared that #6 Macy might also pass Van Fossen. These two would fight for the remaining laps. Meanwhile, #7 Dwelle kept his lead to take his second Gold Race win in a row, with 229.264mph. Second place went to #75 Goss at 226.775mph. Van Fossen held on for third at 223.354mph. #6 Macy earned fourth at 222.263mph. He was followed by rookie #90 McNeely at 220.751mph and #18 DiFani in sixth at 217.491mph. After the race #27 Van Fossen was asked what happened and he shrugged his shoulders and said, "Shit happens!"

1991
The toughness of the Texan was vividly demonstrated at the 1991 Reno races during qualifying, 22 entered, 21 qualified and 20 raced. After making his first practice run, but before qualifying began, #51 Jim Mott started another turn when his left wing hit the ground taking off about three feet of his aileron and jamming the controls. Considering that from wingtip to the cockpit is about 16ft, he was flying low. Able to right the Texan, and using rudder and power, he lined up on the emergency runway only to have his left wing dig in as he reduced power causing him to cartwheel and turn upside down. Mott came away with minor cuts and bruises. The Texan was heavily damaged (see Chapter 5 for details). This was a hard way to cut the field to 20 racers.

The top qualifier was #75 Al Goss with a 1:18.10mins lap at 230.013mph. #27 Eddie Van Fossen was next with 1:18.22mins and 229.660mph. They were followed by #21 Charles Hutchins at 228.928mph, #18 Randy DiFani at 226.190mph, and #6 Nick Macy at 223.600mph. Sixth place qualifier was #90 Gene McNeely at 222.823mph. McNeely had also qualified in sixth in 1990 at 221.668mph. Following McNeely were: #5 Jerry McDonald at 220.525mph, #22 Kenny Day at 220.228mph, #7 Tom Dwelle in ninth at 219.663mph in a new Texan, #2 Charlie Beck at 218.700mph, #9 Bud Granley at 218.354mph, #59 Jimmy Gist at 216.695mph, #55 David Bruce at 216.225mph, and #8 Robert Jones at 215.394mph. In 15th place was rookie #86 Sherman Smoot[24] at 214.470mph in the Texan that had been raced by Colene Giglio. #99 John Luther was at 212.315mph, #11 Ray Schutte was back in 17th at 210.130mph, #20 Linda Finch at 207.772mph, #48 Dorel Graves at 195.176mph and in 20th was rookie #73 Frank Elliott[25] with 1:33.35mins and 192.437mph. Texan #73 was Don DeWalt's first racer #74 from the 1970s. The racing field was full.

Heat-1C was a two-Texan race between #21 Hutchins and #90 McNeely until Hutchins pulled ahead and took first place at 220.667mph, with #90 McNeely at 219.915mph in second. #7 Dwelle in his new mount was third at 212.738mph, followed closely by rookie #86 Smoot at 211.790mph. Three seconds back in fifth was #20 Finch and sixth was #59 Gist.

Heat-1B was another #27 Van Fossen walk away as he took first place at 229.966mph, followed by #22 Day at 223.544mph, #6 Macy at 218.599mph, #8 Jones at 214.583mph, #9 Granley at 211.595mph, and in sixth place was #11 Schutte at 209.620mph. Thirty-eight seconds separated first to sixth.

Of the three heat races, Heat-1A was the most exhilarating, pitting four top competitors against each other to the end. From the start it was #2 Beck, #75 Goss and #18 DiFani in lock-step at the front being pushed by #5 McDonald, who was a few seconds back. All traded places throughout the race with each slipping and sliding back and forth until, finally, #75 Goss got the advantage and took first at 224.399mph. He was followed by #18 DiFani at 220.900 in second, #2 Beck at 220.715mph, #5 McDonald also at 220.715mph, #55 Bruce at 216.522mph was fifth, and #99 Luther was sixth at 202.420mph. After the race, it was judged that third place #2 Beck had been "low flying" and he was bumped to sixth. This moved McDonald, Bruce and Luther up one place. It was still a great race.

Heat-2C was a little off pace as it was an all under 200mph race. Only veteran #11 Schutte really kicked up some dust by challenging the rookies for the front before falling back. Rookie #73 Elliott would take first at 195.291mph in his only attempt at Texan racing. In second place was #48 Graves at 188.741mph, #11 Schutte with 188.598mph, #55 Bruce at 188.444mph, #99 Luther at 187.547mph, and sixth #20 Finch at 187.191mph. The next Heat Race would be back up to speed.

---

24 Sherman Smoot would go on to race Unlimiteds and was killed in a crash while testing an aircraft just two weeks before the 2022 NCAR.

25 Frank Elliott would be killed in this Texan in October 1993.

Heat-2B saw #27 Van Fossen take off like a rocket at the scatter pylon. He did not look back all the way to the checkered flag with a time of only 6:26.51mins for the five laps. The race became a contest between #22 Day, #18 DiFani and #90 McNeely for second place. #55 Bruce and #86 Smoot fought for fifth. #22 Day took second place, only 14 seconds behind Van Fossen at 224.516mph. DiFani took third at 221.718mph, #90 McNeely was fourth with 221.368mph, #86 Smoot was fifth 25 seconds back from first, with #55 Bruce sixth at 6:54.19mins.

Heat-2A was a tough race from the start for the 1990 Gold winner #7 Dwelle in his new racer as he fell back with every lap until he was tail-end-Charlie. At the front was #21 Hutchins and #75 Goss both flying a race that would see Goss take the win at 221.915mph and Hutchins second at 219.679mph. They were followed by #6 Macy, #5 McDonald, #8 Jones fifth, and #7 Dwelle in sixth at 209.171mph.

#2 Beck more than made up for his sixth-place penalty in Heat-1A. He jumped to the lead of the Bronze Race ahead of #99 Luther and #59 Gist on lap 1 and remained five seconds ahead of both from then on. Luther and Gist swapped places on lap 4 with Gist pulling a lead over Luther. This Bronze Race win was #2 Beck's fourth at Reno since his first race in 1973. #59 Gist was second at 213.445mph, almost 5mph behind Beck. In third place was #99 Luther, who was followed by #9 Granley, #11 Schutte, and in sixth #20 Finch at 204.476mph.

Another disappointment faced #7 Dwelle in the six-lap Silver Race as his new racer seemed not to have "umph" to get the job done. However, #90 McNeely, in his second year of racing, was able to put things together from the start along with #5 McDonald to take the lead. Both pilots raced in the 220mph range from lap 2 onward. In the middle were #8 Jones, rookie #86 Smoot, and #55 Bruce flying their own race before Smoot fell back just ahead of Dwelle. At the end it was #90 McNeely in first at 223.165mph, #5 McDonald second at 222.382mph, then #55 Bruce third after passing #8 Jones on lap 5, rookie #86 Smoot was fifth with 211.341mph, and sixth #7 Dwelle at 211.250mph. He was charged a $200 penalty for low flying.

Looking at the line-up for the Gold Race, it was everyone's bet that it would be another fight between #27 Van Fossen and #75 Goss. The advantage was to Goss as being the fastest qualifier. In the last six Gold Races where they had competed, Goss had only finished ahead of Van Fossen twice. From the start no one was disappointed. At the scatter pylon Goss and Van Fossen were side-by-side and remained so through the first lap and a half. Slowly, Van Fossen crept ahead until lap 4 when he was a plane length in front and stayed there to the end for another win at 227.028mph. After #27 established his lead, #75 Goss and #22 Day fought for second with Goss at 221.687mph finally edging Day at 220.702mph out for second place. It was later learned that Goss had two dead cylinders in his engine. #6 Macy was fourth at 217.508mph, #21 Hutchins fifth at 215.710mph, and #18 DiFani sixth at 209.480mph. It had taken 7:54.76mins for Van Fossen to win his fourth Gold Race.

1992

The Redmond, Oregon, Air Races were held July 3–5, 1992, at the Redmond Municipal Airport, site of the former Redmond Army Airfield. The total prize money was $25,000. Supported by and co-sponsored by the T-6 Association, 12 T-6s qualified to race the 3.478-mile course at the old bomber base. There were two heat races and a Silver and Gold Race. All the races had nine laps, 31.3 miles total, with six aircraft in each race.

The fastest qualifier was #4 Dave Bruce at 218.07mph taking only :57.43secs for his lap. #75 Al Goss was second at 216.34mph. Goss was followed by #89 Joe Hartung (one of the race organizers) at 216.30mph, #21 Kenny Day at 215.45mph, in fifth place was #5 Jerry McDonald at 215.00mph, and 77 Jim Good at 207.42mph. #9 Bud Granley at 207.35mph flew a Texan raced by Pat Palmer and Marshall Wells in the 1970s. In eighth place was #8 Robert Jones at 208.83mph. #27 Eddie Van Fossen finished ninth at 206.80mph followed by #7 Tom Dwelle at 205.14mph, and #18 Randy DiFani at 202.42mph. The only under 200mph qualifier was #90 Gene McNeely at 197.73mph and taking 1:03.66mins for his lap.

Clouds, rain and drizzle plagued both heat races, but each was fast paced. Heat-1A consisting of the odd numbered qualifiers (1, 3, 5, 7, 9, 11) saw #4 Bruce pull ahead from the start and stay there to the finish. The only real fight was between #5 and #27 for third. Bruce was first at 217.3mph and in second place was #89 Hartung at 215.38mph. Taking third was #5 McDonald at 211.16mph after passing #27 Van Fossen on lap 7. Van Fossen finished fourth at 210.80mph. In fifth was #9 Granley at 206.60mph and 0:15secs back in sixth was #18 DiFani at 201.19mph.

Heat-1B (even number qualifiers) was not as fast but still a good race for the five racers. #21 Day had engine problems and DNS. #77 Good and #75 Goss fought for the front through all nine laps, with Goss finally moving past Good on the last lap to take first at 209.96mph. Good placed second at 209.05mph. #8 Jones was third and #90 McNeely placed fourth. #7 Dwelle finished fourth but was disqualified for low flying and moved to fifth.

Rain hampered the final day of racing but did not keep the racers on the ground. After a short delay, the Silver Race began with all six racers (#21 Day had repaired his racer) off to a good start after the pace plane released them. For several laps, it was a three-way race between #27, #9 and #18 at the front and #7, #90 and #21 at the back, before #18 slipped back. This was how it remained until lap 7 when #21 dropped out with engine trouble. First went to #27 Van Fossen at 213.04mph, second was #9 Granley at 210.48mph, #18 DiFani was third at 202.11mph, fourth #7 Dwelle at 201.88mph, and fifth #90 McNeely at 201.56mph.

After another rain delay, the Gold Race got off and quickly settled into a battle between the three fastest qualifiers #4, #89 and #75. By mid-race, #89 and #75 were in the lead, opening a gap over the other four with #75 gaining the advantage over #89 at the finish. It was #75 Goss first at 219.16mph, second #89 Hartung at 216.91mph, third #4 Bruce at 214.45mph, fourth #5 McDonald at 213.57mph, and fifth #77 Good at 209.59mph. #8 Jones was sixth at 197.42mph after receiving an 18 second time penalty for a pylon cut. In spite of the weather, Redmond 1992 had provided some good racing, but it was not enough to continue.

Twenty-six Texans were entered at Reno in 1992 while only 23 qualified. The non-qualifiers were #39 Ray Dieckman, #51 Gerry Miles and F1 pilot Ray Cote. Rookies for this year were #12 Stu Eberhardt and #88 Carter Clark. Qualifying was a fantastic affair with 21 competitors over 200mph.

#27 Eddie Van Fossen was on top as the fastest qualifier at 235.223mph. He was followed by: #75 Al Goss at 232.544mph, #89 Joe Hartung at 229.484mph, #6 Nick Macy at 228.143mph, #21 Charles Hutchins at 227.277mph, #6 David Bruce at 226.561mph, #90 Gene McNeely at 225.197mph, #22 Ken Day at 224.634mph, #18 Randy DiFani at 222.878mph, and #2 Charlie Beck at 220.607mph who rounded out the top ten. They were followed by: #77 Jim Good at 219.555mph, #86 Sherman Smoot at 218.460mph, #7 Tom Dwelle at 217.561mph, #5 Jerry McDonald at 216.930mph, #20 Linda Finch at 216.303mph in her last Texan race, #9 Bud Granley at 214.240mph, #59 Jimmy Gist at 211.815mph, #9 Robert Jones at 211.217mph, #99 John Luther at 210.672mph, #11 Ray Schutte at 201.277mph, and rookie #88 Carter Clark at 200.805mph. The below-200mph qualifiers were #48 Dorel Graves at 192.892mph and rookie #12 Stu Eberhardt at 191.780mph. The gap from first to 23rd was 44mph.

Heat-1C started with #89 Hartung and #4 Bruce the only ones that had any real fight. They were first and second at the checkered flag with Hartung at 226.635mph and Bruce at 222.107mph. The rest in order were #18 DiFani third at 217.540mph, #86 Smoot at 216.345mph, #20 Finch at 211.600mph, and sixth #8 Jones with 206.431mph.

Heat-1B was almost a repeat of the previous race except there were three front runners. #75 Goss took first at 222.635mph, then #21 Hutchins at 221.674mph in second. #22 Day took third at 221.221mph. Fourth through sixth were #77 Good at 217.040mph, #5 McDonald at 216.899mph, and #59 Gist at 209.068mph.

Things stepped up a notch for Heat-1A with #27 Van Fossen out-distancing the pack by almost 7mph to take first at 230.249mph. Thirteen seconds back was #6 Macy, followed by #2 Beck at 217.952mph, #90 McNeely 217.214mph, #9 Granley 209.126mph, and #7 Dwelle at 208.998mph who appeared to be nursing a sick engine.

In Heat-2B, #75 Goss bested #27 Van Fossen's Heat-1A first place finish by three seconds at 231.578mph. #6 Macy was second at 228.852mph, followed by #4 Bruce at 226.956mph, #22 Day at 225.991mph, #2 Beck at 221.291mph, and #86 Smoot sixth at 218.684mph.

Heat-2A proved there can always be improvement when #27 Van Fossen took only 6:22.06mins to do the five-lap race at 235.094mph. #89 Hartung took 6:33.07mins. This was 11 seconds back at 228.509mph for second place. Third place went to #21 Hutchins at 222.068mph. #18 DiFani took fourth at 220.688mph., #90 McNeely took fifth at 219.910mph. Sixth place went to #77 Good who took 6:53.33mins.

There was little excitement for the Bronze and Silver races as everyone was buzzing about the Gold Race. The Bronze Race was won by #5 McDonald, who jumped ahead and stayed there at 221.641mph. McDonald was followed by #7 Dwelle at 216.517mph and #59 Gist at 215.530mph in a distant second and third. Fourth place went to #20 Finch, fifth to #8 Jones, and #9 Granley took sixth at 210.746mph.

#22 Day flew away at the start of the Silver Race and finished at 224.775mph. Second through sixth were #18 DiFani at 218.744mph, #77 Good at 217.913mph, #86 Smoot at 216.117mph, and #90 McNeely at 213.159mph. #2 Beck was given a 12-second penalty for cutting middle pylon 3 on lap 1. This placed Beck sixth with a time of 8:28.03mins for the six laps. Even with his win, this would be #22 Kenny Day's last Reno T-6 race.

The Texan fans eagerly anticipated Sunday's Gold Race. It started with pole sitter #27 Van Fossen and #75 Goss diving for the first pylon while everyone else bunched up behind. Goss and Van Fossen were wingtip to wingtip as they finished the first lap with neither able to move as they were hemmed in by #89 Hartung for several more laps. #6 Macy and

#4 Bruce fought their own battle with #21 Hutchins flying alone. By lap four, Goss had lost steam and fell back. Van Fossen appeared to have lit the fuse on *Miss TNT* and finished the six laps in 7:39.07mins at a new race record of 234.766mph. #75 Goss was second at 7:52.01mins and 228.351mph. #89 Hartung was third followed by #6 Macy, #4 Bruce, and in sixth was #21 Hutchins with 8:20.68mins and 215.275mph. A brief protest was filed after the race, which delayed the results but was disallowed.

For winning the 1992 Gold Race #27 Van Fossen took home $9,025. This is compared to the $850 #7 Ben Hall won in 1969 for the same race.

1993

Racing at Reno for 1993 began under a somber tone brought on by the fatal crash of Unlimited pilot Rick Brickert in the experimental Pond Racer during a qualifying attempt on Tuesday. Additionally, controversy plagued T-6 qualifying. Twenty-four aircraft entered with 20 qualifying. Those who did not qualify were #20 Linda Finch, #46 Richard Fields, #030 David Peeler and #51 Jerry Miles. After taking a few years away from Texan racing to compete in the Unlimited category, veteran #41 Ralph Twombly was the surprise top qualifier in a new Texan at 230.249mph. This Texan was raced as #55 in 1991. #89 Joe Hartung was next at 227.162mph and surprisingly in third was #27 Eddie Van Fossen at a slow 226.904mph. The top three were followed by: #90 Gene McNeely at 225.085mph, #75 Al Goss at 224.186mph, #21 Charles Hutchins at 223.711mph, #86 Sherman Smoot at 223.044mph, #18 Randy DiFani at 222.354mph, #77 Jim Good at 221.095mph, and in tenth was #6 Nick Macy at 220.796mph. In 11th through 20th places were #5 Jerry McDonald at 219.207mph, #2 Charles Beck at 216.878mph, #99 John Luther at 214.624mph, #55 Fred Johnson, Jr. (using Jimmy Gist's T-6) at 213.046mph, and #8 Robert Jones at 209.468mph. Rookie #7 Tom Dwelle Jr. flew his father's Texan at 207.869mph. Rookie #71 John Krawczyk at 207.604mph flew the former #11 that was first raced in 1969 by Howie Keefe, Dick Sykes and Jim Modes. Rookie #39 Ray Dieckman, who had failed to qualify in 1992, finished at 198.147mph. Rookie Canadian #64 Keith McMann flew his Harvard IV at 197.667mph. In 20th place was #48 Dorel Graves at 197.212 flying his Texan named *Slo Yeller*. After the qualifying runs, a protest was filed against Ralph Twombly for "diving to the start pylon to gain additional speed." The Race Committee reviewed the complaint and disallowed the protest, permitting racing to begin.

Heat-1C was a mellow affair between #27 Van Fossen and #21 Hutchins for the five laps with everyone else following in train. Hutchins could not catch Van Fossen who took first at 227.019mph. #77 Good was third at 217.748mph and #8 Jones was fourth at 207.480mph. #2 Beck was fifth only tenths of a second behind at 207.384mph. Rookie #39 Dieckman was sixth at 190.131mph in his first race.

Heat-1B was a similar race with #75 Goss and #89 Hartung being the only real fight, although #18 DiFani did challenge both mid-race. At the finish, it was Goss first at 228.742mph, Hartung at 226.149mph, #18 DiFani in third at 222.437mph, #5 McDonald at 220.509mph, #55 Johnson at 212.728mph, and rookie #71 Krawczyk in sixth at 203.305mph.

Heat-1C provided excitement with #6 Macy, #86 Smoot and #90 McNeely doing some wingtip-to-wingtip fighting for most of the race with everyone else further back. McNeely pulled ahead to finish first at 221.734mph, Smoot was second at 218.551mph, Macy third with 218.444mph. These speeds show the closeness of their race. Fourth was #41 Twombly at 207.087mph, then #99 Luther at 205.783mph with rookie #7 Dwelle at 204.215mph in his first race.

Heat-2C was one of the slowest races flown in a long time with only one contestant averaging over 200mph. Rookie #64 McMann took first at 201.377mph. He was followed by #48 Graves with 198.060mph. After Graves was the mid group of rookies: #71 Krawczyk third at 197.937mph, #7 Dwelle at 197.841mph, #77 Good at 197.719mph fifth, and #39 Dieckman in sixth at 192.718mph.

#21 Hutchins took the lead from the start of Heat-2B and stayed for the finish at 226.680mph. The real fighters all finished within seconds of each other. They were #18 DeFani second at 220.715mph, #89 Hartung at 220.530mph, #6 Macy at 219.743mph, #90 McNeely at 218.802mph, and behind the group in sixth was #8 Jones at 207.836mph. This race illustrates how closely matched the Texan can race with the winning factor being pilot skills.

With Heat-2A, #75 Goss and #27 Van Fossen were back in form from the start both going wingtip-to-wingtip or nose-to-tail with no visible gap. By lap 4, Van Fossen gained the advantage to take the checkered flag first at 228.852mph to Goss' second place at 226.270mph. They were followed by #41 Twombly third at 221.543mph, #77 Good at 220.525mph, #86 Smoot at 216.925mph, and sixth #5 McDonald at 216.616mph.

The five-lap Bronze Race contestants were two veterans and four rookies with #2 Beck out front from the start. Close behind Beck was #99 Luther and #55 Johnson paired together. They were followed by #7 Dwelle in the middle then #71 Krawczyk and #39 Dieckman in his aptly named *Rainbow Slug*. They finished in this order with #2 Beck being the fastest at 215.231mph and Dieckman the slowest at 194.428mph. This was Beck's second Bronze Race win.

As the six-lap Silver Race started, #90 McNeely was out front where he stayed to the finish taking his second Silver Race at 224.139mph. #77 Good tried to stay with him and was just tenths of a second behind at 223.925mph. All others finished in about the same order they started: third was #6 Macy at 221.432mph, #5 McDonald at 218.460mph, #86 Smoot at 217.526mph, and 37 seconds back from first place was #8 Jones in sixth.

The much anticipated dual between #27 Van Fossen and #75 Goss in the Gold Race did not last long. From the start it was Goss ahead of Van Fossen. By lap 3, Van Fossen had jumped into the lead with a great passing move around Goss, who suddenly found himself under attack by #89 Hartung for second place. By lap 4, Hartung had passed Goss for second and dragged #21 Hutchins with him into third. On the last lap, Van Fossen was out front and took his fourth consecutive Gold finish and sixth overall at a slow 226.885mph. #89 Hartung was second at 223.012mph, third was #21 Hutchins at 222.593mph, #75 Goss finished fourth at 221.810mph, #41 Twombly was fifth at 218.957mph, and #18 DiFani was sixth at 212.186mph.

1994

Billed as the First Annual Phoenix 500 Air Races, the 1994 races were held at the former Williams AFB,[26] now called the Mesa Gateway Airport, in Mesa, AZ, on March 18–20. The Phoenix 500 was an all-class racing event with 19 T-6s qualifying over the five-mile T-6 course. There would be five heats each with five laps and one each of the six-lap Bronze, Silver, and Gold races.

Qualifying speeds were over 200mph for 17 of the qualifiers, with #21 Charles Hutchins top qualifier at 230.21mph and #27 Eddie Van Fossen second at 228.23mph. The next three were within tenths of a second of each other with #18 Randy DiFani at 221.96mph, #6 Nick Macy at 221.52mph, and #41 Ralph Twombly at 221.126mph. Others qualifying in the 220mph range were #86 Sherman Smoot at 220.61mph and #75 Al Goss at 220.12mph. They were followed by #90 Gene McNeely at 219.93mph, #77 Jim Good at 217.16mph, #5 Jerry McDonald at 214.47mph, #4 Bud Granley at 214.23mph, #55 Fred Johnson at 213.11mph, #8 Robert Jones at 211.96mph, #99 John Luther at 210.88mph, #7 Tom Dwelle at 210.36mph, #71 John Krawczyk at 206.69mph, and #39 Ray Dieckman at 201.61mph. Rookies #42 Gregory Shelton at 199.03mph placed 18th and #302 Bill Eberhardt in 19th. The cold desert air agreed with the Texans.

Yankee Aia Pirate #7 Tom Dwelle and *Tinker Toy* #37 James Bennett arriving at Reno in 1997. *Tinker Toy* won three consecutive Silver races in 1997–99 with Bennett and then, as #7, won the 2008 Gold Race flown by Ken Dwelle. (Jim Dunn)

---

26 Williams AFB had been a T-6 training field during World War Two and Korea.

Three heat races were held on Friday, March 18, with light rain and mist. Only one contestant flew below 200mph. Heat-1C saw a 12mph difference between first place #86 Smoot at 214.69mph in 6:54.17mins and sixth placed #42 Shelton at 202.10mph in 7:19.96mins. Second through fifth places went to #18 DiFani, #77 Good, #55 Johnson, and #7 Dwelle.

Heat-1B saw an even greater speed and time gap between first and fifth with #27 Van Fossen at 222.79mph in 6:39.11mins to #39 Dieckman at 193.89mph in 7:38.60mins. Second through fourth were #41 Twombly, who had given a good chase to #27, #90 McNeely, and #99 Luther. #4 Granley exited the race on lap 1 with mechanical issues.

The last heat of the day, Heat-1A, was a rocket race from start to finish with great chases and flat-out speeds right to the end. #21 Hutchins at 227.144mph in 6:31.47mins was pushed across the line to first by second place finisher #6 Macy at 226.958mph in 6:31.79mins. They were followed by #75 Goss, #5 McDonald, #8 Jones, and taking sixth was #71 Krawczyk at 209.55mph. It was an exciting race to the end.

Rain and mist did not dampen the enthusiasm of Saturday's two heat races. Heat-2B was a contest between #6 Macy and #27 Van Fossen in a race that almost looked staged with both moving from the lead to second several times during the five laps. Van Fossen took first at 225.58mph and Macy second at 223.13mph. Third through fifth were #86 Smoot, #5 McDonald, and #90 McNeely fifth as #99 Luther dropped out on lap 1.

The afternoon Heat-2A was run in slightly better weather, a slight drizzle, and just as fast as the morning heat. It too was almost a two-horse race between #21 Hutchins and #75 Goss until #21 pulled away on lap 3 and remained there to the end. Hutchins took first at 227.32mph, #75 Goss was second at 221.10mph, followed by #41 Twombly, #18 DiFani, #77 Good, and #55 Johnson was sixth at 211.43mph.

#4 Granley, having fixed the mechanical problem, took first in Sunday's six-lap Bronze Race ahead of #8 Jones, 215.74mph to 213.62mph. The gap from first to sixth at the finish was 19mph over 30 seconds. In order of finish from third to sixth was #7 Dwelle, #71 Krawczyk, #42 Shelton, and #39 Dieckman who was the only one below 200mph at 196.29mph.

The rain increased and caused the cancellation of an Unlimited Heat Race and delayed other race starts the rest of the weekend.

The Silver produced another 200mph plus race and the time between first and second place was 0.10secs. After a delayed start, still under overcast skies, it was #18 DiFani and #90 McNeely chased by #77 Good and #5 McDonald. #55 Johnson flew alone behind the others. #99 Luther dropped out on lap 1 with a sour engine. Good and McDonald had fallen back by lap 4 and it became a DiFani and McNeely fight to the finish. DiFani came in first at 220.11mph, #90 McNeely in second at 219.66mph, #77 Good was third, and #5 McDonald fourth. In fifth place was #55 Johnson, who was penalized 12 seconds for cutting a pylon on the last lap. Even without the time penalty, he would have finished fifth at 205.23mph.

Sunday's six-lap Gold Race was the contest everyone had waited for as it pitted the two fastest qualifiers against each other. They did not disappoint. From the start under overcast skies, it was #27 Van Fossen taking an early lead with #21 Hutchins tied to his rudder. They were followed by #75 Goss, #6 Macy, #86 Smoot and #41 Twombly. With each lap, Van Fossen edged further ahead of Hutchins while all the others mixed it up swapping places. By lap 5, it was clear Van Fossen had the win. At the checkered flag it was #27 Van Fossen first at 228.469mph followed some 0:07secs back by #21 Hutchins at 224.517mph in second. In third was #6 Macy at 223.881mph. Macy would have caught Hutchins had there been one more lap. In fourth place was #75 Goss at 220.938mph, fifth was #41 Twombly at 220.631mph, and sixth #86 Smoot at 219.380mph. Time between first and sixth was 0:19 seconds.

While Phoenix is known as the Valley of the Sun, it had not lived up to its name. Regardless, the air races had been fantastic and plans were made for 1995.

In 1994, a Demo T-6 Race was held at the Paso Robles, CA, municipal airport on June 4–5. The T-6s raced over the 2.96-mile F-1 course (the real main event). #27 Eddie Van Fossen took first place. No other details are known.

July 23–24, 1994, were the dates of a T-6 Demo Race held during the Big Sky International Airshow at Billings, Montana. Known participants were #7 Tom Dwelle, Jr., #18 Randy DiFani and #77 Jim Good. Other racers and results are unknown, and it is described as the typical Demo Race.

1994 Reno started off just like 1993. At the beginning of the week, Unlimited pilot #56 Bill Speer was killed in the crash of his P-51 Mustang during a practice flight. The Texan class saw 29 entrants with 22 qualifying. Pilots who entered but did not race were #39 Ray Dieckman, #45 Gary Eller, #46 Richard Fields, #49 John Meyer, #92 Eliot Cross, and #030 David Peeler.

The qualifying speeds produced some surprises, with #21 Charles Hutchins as top qualifier at 232.996mph. He was followed by #86 Sherman Smoot at 232.905mph. The 1993 Gold winner, #27 Eddie Van Fossen, was a surprising third at 231.286mph. The next six were #6 Nick Macy at 230.900mph, #89 Joe Hartung at 229.866mph, #75 Al Goss at 228.375mph, and #37 Tom Dwelle, Jr. at 227.335mph in a Texan that had been entered with James Bennett as pilot. #90 Gene McNeely reached 225.849mph, #18 Randy DiFani at 225.310mph, and #5 Jerry McDonald at 223.906mph. The final dozen included #4 Bud Granley in a new T-6G at 222.823mph, #41 Ralph Twombly at 222.079mph, #55 Fred Johnson, Jr. at 221.177mph, and #99 John Luther at 220.039mph. #77 Jim Good tied with #99 at 220.039mph. Luther qualified on Tuesday and Good did so on Wednesday. Rookie #24 Mark Moodie was 16th at 217.324mph in his only appearance in Texan racing. #25 Jimmy Gist at 215.396mph was in a new T-6G, followed by #8 Robert Jones at 209.835mph. Rookie #7 Ken Dwelle was at 209.835mph in a Texan entered by his brother Tom Jr. The last group included #64 Keith McMann at 202.457mph, rookie #30 Bill Eberhardt was 21st at 199.445mph, 22nd was #3 Dorel Graves at 197.537mph. Graves changed his race number from #48.

The Heat-1C Race picked up the 1993 fight between #27 Van Fossen and #75 Goss. As before, they were side-by-side at the start with #41 Twombly close behind. #77 Good, #18 DiFani and #8 Jones raced each other a little further back. By lap 5, Van Fossen took first at 227.185mph. Next was Goss seven seconds back and Twombly third at 219.872mph. They were followed by #18 DiFani at 215.659mph and #77 Good at 214.332mph. Sixth went to #8 Jones who was almost 17mph slower than first place at 210.984mph.

Heat-1B was a fast five-lap race that finished bizarrely. From the start #89 Hartung and #86 Smoot flew neck-and-neck at the first pylon. They were followed by #90 McNeely and #99 Luther with #4 Granley only a prop spinner length behind. #25 Jimmy Gist was flying his own race. At the checkered flag, they finished in this order: #89 Hartung in 6:27.31mins at first, second #86 Smoot in 6:31.73mins, third #90 McNeely in 6:43.61mins, fourth #99 Luther in 6:53.18mins, fifth #4 Granley in 6:53.90mins, and in sixth was #25 Gist, whose time was 8:50.19mins with two minutes added for 11 pylon cuts. It seemed he needed to get used to his new Texan.

Midfield was where the action was for Heat-1A with #55 Johnson, #5 McDonald and #37 Tom Dwelle, Jr. putting on a great race, while #21 Hutchins and #6 Macy chased each other for first and second. Rookie #24 Moodie flew a textbook race alone in sixth at 212.909mph. When the flag fell it was #21 Hutchins first at 227.733mph, #6 Macy second at 223.817mph, #37 Dwelle Jr. third at 219.180mph, fourth #5 McDonald at 218.503mph, and #55 Johnson fifth at 215.613mph.

Heat-2C would be only the second time that two brothers would race each other as both #7 Ken Dwelle and #37 Tom Dwelle, Jr. started the race. The Gist brothers raced together in 1982. It was a two-competitor race at the front between #7 Ken Dwelle and #64 McMann while the other competitors were bunched further back. Crossing the line first was #7 Ken Dwelle at 210.076mph and second #64 McMann at 205.896mph. Third through fifth were #3 Graves at 196.268mph, #30 Eberhardt at 196.156mph, #24 Moodie at 196.028mph, and in sixth place was #37 Tom Dwelle, Jr. at 195.904mph.

#86 Smoot and #75 Goss upped the ante for Heat-2B as they charged for the start pylon in lock-step looking like one aircraft. They were closely followed by #6 Macy. As these three fought for the lead, #90 McNeely, #5 McDonald and #99 Luther battled for third one-half lap back. On lap 4, Smoot had a solid lead by almost a plane length. At this point, Goss seemed to let up to save his engine for the challenge against Van Fossen in the Gold Race. This left #86 Smoot to collect his first win at 232.003mph, #75 Goss second at 230.402mph, #6 Macy was third at 228.654mph. #5 McDonald passed #90 McNeely for fourth, and #99 Luther was sixth at 218.169mph.

Heat-2A saw #89 Hartung and #21 Hutchins trying to catch *Miss TNT* #27 Van Fossen, but to no avail. They were left to scrap for second. #41 Twombly and #37 Dwelle, Jr. flew their own race and #18 DiFani was at the tail end. Van Fossen was eight seconds ahead of second place #89 Hartung, 12 seconds ahead of third #21 Hutchins, 19 seconds ahead of fourth #41 Twombly, 23 seconds ahead of #37 Dwelle Jr. fifth, and 35 seconds ahead of #18 DiFani in sixth.

Results of the Bronze Race illustrate that pilot skills are the main ingredient in Texan racing. All six competitors, including a rookie, provided a close race. From the start the six were in a single bunch for most of the first lap. As the laps progressed, everyone found their spot and the pilot they were racing against, which provided a great race. At the flag it was veteran #77 Jim Good taking his first win at 219.679mph, second was #55 Johnson, Jr. with 217.735mph, third was rookie #24 Moodie at 216.387mph, fourth #4 Granley at 213.517mph, #8 Jones at 208.728mph, and #25 Gist at 208.728mph. It appeared that everyone had a good time.

As the pace plane led #41 Twombly, #5 McDonald, #37 Dwelle, Jr., #90 McNeely, #18 DiFani and #7 Dwelle down the chute on the way for the green flag start of the Silver Race, tragedy struck. Twombly moved out of line and slid under #5 McDonald, who did not see Twombly. Both Texans collided, taking the empennage and left wing off Twombly's aircraft. Twombly rolled inverted and crashed fatally into an unoccupied home; there was no fire. McDonald lost portions of his right wing, which jammed his controls. He was able to make a straight-in approach to land safely. The race was black flagged, and everyone was able to land safely (see Chapter 5 for details).

After meeting with the Race Committee, the Texan pilots decided to proceed with the Gold Race.

The Gold Race started a bit slower with everyone maintaining their positions until the scatter pylon, at which time #27 Van Fossen took off like a rocket. #86 Smoot and #21 Hutchins were in hot pursuit with #75 Goss falling back into the clutches of #89 Hartung and #6 Macy. The latter three swapped places until the end, while Hutchins and Smoot appeared to let Van Fossen go and raced for second place. At the end, it was #27 Van Fossen first at 224.704mph, 2mph slower than in 1993, and his fourth consecutive win and seventh overall Gold win at Reno. The battle for second was won by #21 Hutchins at 221.636mph. In third was #89 Hartung at 220.462mph. Hartung had flown around #86 Smoot who then placed fourth at 220.354mph. Fifth was #6 Macy with 219.412mph, and the bridesmaid #75 was Goss sixth at 216.495mph.

Eddie Van Fossen's last Reno Race was in 1994. He was the Texan pilot with the most wins, not bad for someone who could not qualify to race in 1984. Still the loss of veteran #41 Ralph Twombly overshadowed any celebration in the entire Texan racing community. Twombly will be missed.

1995

A January 30, 1995, news release from Superstition Racing Corp. (SRC), organizers of the Phoenix 500 Air Races, stated that a "three-day family entertainment event is scheduled for March 24–26, 1995, and features air racing in three classes: Unlimited, T-6 and Formula One." Attached to the same news release was an announcement that SRC expected to become the "new leader in air racing" and had plans to grow air racing and signed a three-year agreement with a major sponsor. Along with a new marketing division, SRC would start a new "governing body business" as a sanctioning body called Superstition Air Racing Association (SARA). "SARA is an NFL-type organization that will serve as a governing, licensing and administrative body for all race class organizations. SARA will assist in the distribution of event prize monies for all racing class organizations." There were six additional pages of SRC plans. As it came to be a short time later, SRC announced that NAA T-28s would replace the T-6 class at the 1995 races. The announcement said this change was necessary as the T-6 racing pilots could not come to an agreement on prize money and were concerned about past and future prize payouts. T-6s would not race at Phoenix again.

Shafter, CA, held a T-6 Demo Race during its annual airshow on April 20–21, 1995. Known racers were #7 Tom Dwelle, Jr., #12 Stu Eberhardt, #24 Mark Moodie, #30 Bill Eberhardt, and #75 Al Goss. It was a typical Demo Race.

Without reigning champ #27 Eddie Van Fossen in the competition, Reno 1995 was open to anybody. There were favorites such as #75 Al Goss, #89 Joe Hartung, #89 Charles Hutchins, and #86 Sherman Smoot. Old champion #51 Ralph Rina returned to make things interesting. Nineteen entered and 16 qualified to race for their share of the $65,000 prize money. Those who entered but did not qualify were #6 Nick Macy, #66 Dennis Dill and #92 Steve Clegg.

The top qualifier at 230.160mph was #21 Charles Hutchins, followed by #89 Joe Hartung at 227.738mph, #86 Sherman Smoot at 227.392mph, #90 Gene McNeely at 221.915mph, #99 John Luther at 221.286mph, and #4 Bud Granley at 220.824mph. The seventh qualifier was #75 Al Goss at 219.180mph. This was Goss' second try as a master rod broke in his first attempt and he had to change engines overnight using one from an Ag-Cat. Additional qualifiers were: #77 Jim Good at 218.780mph, #55 Fred Johnson at 218.142mph, and #8 Robert Jones tenth at 215.499mph. In 11th place was Jerry McDonald in his repaired #5 at 210.327mph, followed by #7 Tom Dwelle, Jr. at 204.067mph, and #30 entered by Bill Eberhardt, but raced by Tom Dwelle, Sr., at 203.213mph. This was the first time a father and son raced together. #51 Ralph Rina qualified at 196.392mph in 14th place. This Texan was entered several times without qualifying by Jerry Miles. In the rear were #3 Dorel Graves at 194.732mph and rookie #37 Jim Bennett in 16th at 185.196mph.

Everyone wanted to be the new king and Heat-1A was a three way towards the kingship. #75 Al Goss, #90 Gene McNeely and #21 Charles Hutchins were almost inseparable at the start and stayed that way for three laps. They were followed by #37 Bennett and #8 Jones, with #30 Dwelle, Sr. back by himself. Hutchins got past Goss and McNeely on the back side of the course and, when they came around for lap 4, Hutchins was one plane length ahead of both and stayed to the end. The finish was #21 Hutchins in 6:33.20mins and 228.433mph for the five laps. #90 McNeely had gotten around #75 Goss. Their speeds were 225.356mph and 221.783mph, respectively. #37 Bennett was fourth at 218.285mph, #8 Jones fifth at 218.158mph and #30 Dwelle, Sr. was 7:14.63mins and 206.659mph for sixth.

Heat-1B went soft by lap 3 as the second fastest qualifier #89 Hartung declared a mayday and pulled up and out with a broken pushrod. The race still provided great racing, although a little slower with #99 Luther first at 217.598mph in

6:52.78mins, #77 Jim Good at 216.967mph in 6:53.98mins, #5 Jerry McDonald at 216.841mph in 6:54.22mins. This was some very close racing. #51 Ralph Rina was fifth at 191.728mph and 7:48.48mins and seemed to be sorting things out after his time away.

The front runners at the start of Heat-1C were #86 Smoot, #4 Granley and #7 Dwelle, Jr. In lap 2, Dwelle, Jr. seemed to back off and fell back leaving #4 Granley to take first at 221.319mph. #55 Johnson was second at 216.786mph. #86 Smoot coasted to third at 204.183mph having flown with one of his landing gears hanging for the entire race. #3 Graves was fourth at 192.268mph and #7 Dwelle, Jr. fifth at 192.161mph.

Smoot seemed to have recaptured his wind for Heat-2B, as did #75 Goss with his used replacement engine. They went after each other at the start, but by lap 3, it was Smoot clearly ahead to the finish. #86 Smoot placed first at 225.832mph and second place went to #75 Goss at 214.506mph putting them both into the Gold Race. Fourth through sixth in order were #99 Luther at 213.435mph, rookie #37 Bennett 213.207mph, #55 Johnson at 210.317mph, and #51 Rina at 188.373mph.

Heat-2A was a midfield race between #5 McDonald, #4 Granley and #77 Good. Their race for third made one forget there were two other aircraft ahead battling for first place. There was some fine racing, with each defending and challenging their position at the same time. At the finish it was #77 Good in third in 6:56.54mins, #4 Granley fourth in 6:57.13mins, fifth #5 McDonald in 6:57.39mins, and #3 Graves sixth at 7:45.59mins. #21 Hutchins was first in 6:35.26mins, while second went to #90 McNeely in 6:46.70mins.

 Four aircraft were slated to start the five-lap Bronze Race, however only three raced as #89 Hartung was unable to start as his repairs were not completed in time. This race was also unique because it was the first time a father and son were racing in a finals race against each other. From the start, it was #8 Jones in the lead. #7 Dwelle, Jr. and #30 Dwelle, Sr. traded places a few times until the final flag. #8 Jones took first at 217.540mph in his first Reno win. Dwelle, Jr. was second at 203.697mph and Dwelle, Sr. placed third at 203.600mph.

Seven aircraft were scheduled for the six-lap Silver Race but only six started as #51 Rina was a non-starter. This was a race between #5 McDonald and #4 Granley from lap 1 until Granley pulled up and out on lap 2 with a hydraulic pump failure. This left McDonald to be chased by #37 Bennett and #55 Johnson. Bennett was able to close within half a plane length by lap 6 but could not catch up as he also had to keep Johnson at bay. Crossing the finish line was #5 McDonald in first place at 8:05.40mins in his first Reno win. Following were #37 Bennett in 8:05.61mins, #55 Johnson third in 8:11.04mins, #8 Jones in 8:16.32mins, and fifth #3 Graves in 9:06.90mins.

Six experienced pilots took off for the Gold Race, all determined to be crowned the new Reno Texan King. Down the chute to the first pylon, it was #21 Hutchins with #86 Smoot tied to his tail and #90 McNeely chomping at Smoot and #75 Goss eating away at McNeely. They fought this way for almost four laps until Hutchins and Smoot finally got loose from the pack. They continued their battle to the checkered flag where #21 Hutchins took first 0.21secs ahead of #86 Smoot. Their speeds were 231.430mph to 231.326mph, respectively. In third was #90 McNeely with 221.441mph, #75 Goss was fourth at 221.046mph, fifth was #77 Good at 218.593mph, and in sixth place was #99 Luther at 216.991mph.

Reno had a new Texan King, and he was from Texas.

1996
Shafter held a third T-6 Demo Race on April 10–20, 1996. Racers #44 Tom Nightingale, #51 Jerry Miles, and #86 Sherman Smoot, among others, flew during the event. Further details are unknown.

Reno 1996 would be a new contest for the king of Texans, as Charles Hutchins was killed in the crash of a friend's Harvard in May 1996 during an aerobatic routine. Hutchins was a true competitor, racing for 11 years. Twenty-two entered, 17 qualified and 18 raced. Those entered but not qualified were #5 Jerry McDonald, #6 Nick Macy, #27 Eddie Van Fossen, #33 Jerry Borchin, #B-66 Thomas Martin, and #90 Gene McNeely. The top qualifier was #86 Sherman Smoot at 229.895mph. He was followed by #21 John Krawczyk at 228.114mph flying Charles Hutchins' Texan, #75 Al Goss at 222.327mph, #4 Gene McNeely in a new T-6 at 222.052mph, and #77 Jim Good at 219.127mph fifth. #5 Jimmy Gist flew Jerry McDonald's aircraft at 218.780mph. McDonald stepped away from racing Texans for a few years. Also qualifying were #55 Fred Johnson at 217.614mph, #37 Jim Bennett at 217.114mph, #8 Robert Jones at 216.773mph, and #9 Bud Granley tenth at 216.225mph in a new aircraft. Only the third women to race at Reno, rookie #22 Mary Dilda finished at 211.665mph in Ralph Rina's old #73. #44 Lee Oman qualified at 209.346mph, #7 Tom Dwelle, Jr. at 207.365mph, #30 Bill Eberhardt at 202.206mph, rookie #92 Steve Clegg was in 15th place at 200.469mph in his only Texan race, rookie #50 Carl Penner was the first to fly below 200mph at 198.629mph, and #3 Dorel Graves was 17th at 189.854mph. After the qualifying runs were finished, the Race Committee decided to let #B-66 rookie Thomas Martin race even though he did not qualify, as this would round out the field to 18.

Rain and high winds delayed some races throughout the week; however, the Texan heat races began on schedule with Heat-1C. Three veterans against three rookies. The leaders were #75 Goss and #5 Gist from get-go, using the new start method put into practice after the 1994 accident, which brought them down the chute from the north and released them into a formation turn around the west pylon. #8 Jones was able to hold off the rookies for the entire race leaving Gist and Goss to their own race. Goss crossed first at 216.241mph, #5 Gist second at 214.829mph, #8 Jones was third at 212.577mph, #44 Oman was fourth at 205.036mph, #92 Clegg fifth at 194.656mph, and #66 Martin sixth at 184.841mph.

Heat-1B would see #21 Krawczyk in a fast aircraft, which won the Gold Race the year before. Krawczyk moved off and left everyone else to fly their own races. Rookie #22 Dilda, #77 Good and #37 Bennett flew a close race right to the end when Good and Bennett moved around and sprinted to the finish line. It was #21 Krawczyk first in 6:46.09mins for the five laps, #77 Good second in 6:58.17mins, #37 Bennett in 7:02.77mins, #22 Dilda was fourth in 7:02.98mins, #30 Eberhardt fifth in 7:36.94mins, and sixth was #3 Graves in 8:08.07mins.

Almost a full minute separated first and sixth place in the five-lap Heat-1A race with #86 Smoot in first at 6:37.07min and rookie #50 Penner sixth with 7:30.46mins. There was almost a 27mph speed difference. In between were #4 McNeely second, #55 Johnson third, #9 Granley fourth, and Dwelle, Jr. fifth.

Rookie #22 Dilda won her first heat race in Heat-2C at 208.389mph. It seems old #73 still had the "umph" to get things done. Dilda was followed by #50 Penner eight seconds back at 199.383mph, #7 Dwelle, Jr. third at 199.272mph, rookie #92 Clegg fourth at 191.722mph, #3 Graves took fifth at 181.293mph, just ahead of sixth place rookie #66 Martin at 181.209mph.

Despite the rain and wind, Heat-2B got off to a great start. As the contestants came around for lap 2, it was clear that #21 Krawczyk had a plane-and-a-half length lead over everyone. #4 McNeely and #37 Bennett were racing for second place with #44 Oman and #9 Granley dueling for fourth before Granley passed him on lap 4. At the finish it was #21 Krawczyk first at 221.942mph, #4 McNeely second at 218.524mph, #37 Bennett third at 218.222mph, #9 Granley fourth at 209.865mph, #44 Oman fifth at 206.692mph, and #5 Gist sixth at 194.466mph.

The weather was calmer for the next day's Heat-2A race and as they came around to the front straight on lap 1, it was #75 Goss in the lead with #86 Smoot one plane length back, followed by #77 Good, #8 Jones, #55 Johnson and #22 Dilda. By lap 3, they had sorted themselves out with Smoot passing Goss, Johnson passing Jones and Dilda pushing hard to catch up. They finished with #86 Smoot first 222.735mph, #75 Goss 220.910mph second, #77 Good third 214.460mph, #55 Johnson fourth 212.506mph, #8 Jones fifth 212.315mph and #22 Dilda sixth 209.821mph.

The Bronze Race was reminiscent of a lower speed 1970s race, with three professionals and three rookies. Action at the front was provided by #7 Dwelle, Jr. and rookie #50 Penner who were the only ones racing over 200mph. Dwelle, Jr. took first at 207.883mph, #50 Penner second 202.956mph, third #30 Eberhardt 197.181mph, fourth perpetual *Slo-Yeller* #3 Graves 194.042mph, #92 Clegg fifth 193.724mph and sixth #66 Martin 188.207mph.

Flying #5 *Big Red* seemed to suit Gist as he joined #8 Jones, #55 Johnson and #9 Granley in putting on a great race for the Silver. They flew a solid race with a lot of challenging and close flying. #22 Dilda and #44 Oman flew a different race for themselves. They finished with #5 Gist in first 8:10.99mins for the six laps, #8 Jones second 8:13.08mins, #55 Johnson third 8:17.57mins, #9 Granley fourth 8:20.77mins, #22 Dilda fifth 8:21.46mins, and in sixth #44 Oman 8:30.23mins.

Throughout race week there seemed to be just three pilots who had the ability to become the next Texan king and they were all in the Gold Race. By the end of the first lap, it was #86 Smoot followed by #75 Goss and #21 Krawczyk. When lap 2 was finished, it was clearly Smoot in the lead with Goss and Krawczyk contesting strongly for second place. At lap 5, after some wingtip-to-wingtip racing, Goss squeezed ahead by a fraction and stayed there to the end. At the finish, it was #86 Smoot 221.677mph and 8:06.22mins, #75 Goss second 217.232mph and 8:16.17mins, #21 Krawczyk third 216.878mph and 8:16.98mins, #4 McNeely fourth 215.344mph, #77 Good fifth 208.997mph, and sixth #37 Bennett 207.572mph and 8:59.26mins.

Smoot's reign as Texan king was brief as this was his last Texan race and he moved into the Unlimited Class. What would 1997 bring?

1997

Reno 1997 would produce some new firsts for Texan racing with 23 entered and 19 qualifying. For the first time, a wife and husband would race against each other, two women were entered with one racing, and there was another contest between two brothers. Those who entered but did not qualify were #57 Cheryl Bloom, #86 Sherman Smoot, #90 Gene McNeely (however, he would qualify and race #4), and #92 Steve Clegg. Vincent Nastro was entered with no race number listed.

Qualifying was an interesting affair. Second-time Texan racer #21 Mary Dilda was fastest in a borrowed proven winner at 229.572mph. Charles Hutchins had used #21 to win the Gold in 1995. #75 Al Goss was second fastest with 226.875mph. #6 Nick Macy returned to Reno and was third with 225.622mph. Rookie #22 Steve Dilda was fourth in his wife's Texan at 225.424mph in his only Reno racing appearance. Rookie #47 Jack Frost was fifth at 223.516mph flying the Giglio/Smoot aircraft. #4 Gene McNeely was next at 221.504mph. #14 John Krawczyk, flying a Texan that was entered by Richard Sykes, was seventh 219.100mph. #37 Jim Bennett eighth at 218.407mph, #77 Jim Good ninth at 218.195mph, and #9 Bud Granley in tenth at 217.061mph. Eleventh through 19th were: #8 Robert Jones 216.826mph, #5 Jimmy Gist again in Jerry McDonald's Texan (entered by McDonald) at 216.721mph, #44 Lee Oman at 207.608mph, #7 Tom Dwelle, Jr. at 205.868mph, #50 Carl Penner at 205.209mph, #30 Bill Eberhardt at 201.956mph, #3 Dorel Graves at 195.473mph, #66 Thomas Martin at 194.943mph, and last was #512 Ken Dwelle at 191.739mph.

#6 Nick Macy seemed to have put his time away from racing to good use as he moved into the lead from the start of Heat-1C and was able to keep #4 McNeely just behind him at every pylon turn. McNeely caught up on the straights but fell back at the turns. While further back, #77 Good and #5 Gist flew a close third and fourth race. Macy kept his lead and took first at 227.704mph, #4 McNeely in second at 222.668mph, and old hands #77 Good and #5 Gist were third and fourth at 215.773mph to 214.598mph, respectively. In fifth was #50 Penner almost 10mph slower at 204.276mph, and sixth was #66 Martin at 192.132mph.

Heat-1B proved to be a startler as rookie #47 Frost got the jump on #75 Goss after the first pylon and pulled ahead as both flew away from the rest of the field. #8 Jones flew his race midfield alone with #37 Bennett and #7 Dwelle, Jr. behind and #3 Graves at tail end. By lap 3, Goss had caught and passed Frost to take and keep the lead. Goss was first at 225.006mph, #47 Frost second at 224.904mph with an impressive time just 0.18secs back, #8 Jones 210.341mph third, #37 Bennett fourth 198.739mph, fifth place #7 Dwelle, Jr. at 198.524mph, and #3 Graves sixth at 189.458mph.

Heat-1A was one for the history books as it was the first air race featuring husband and wife competitors. #21 Mary Dilda was the fastest qualifier, and her husband rookie #22 Steve Dilda was fourth fastest. From the start, Steve hung on to Mary's tail while being lightly challenged by #14 Krawczyk, who had qualified seventh, until he fell back. By lap 3, the front pair were clearly ahead with no challengers. Mary took first at 230.935mph and it was clear she had made the right choice in flying #21, #22 Steve was second at 222.591mph, third was #14 Krawczyk at 215.753mph, #9 Granley fourth 213.197mph, #44 Oman fifth 209.229mph, and sixth #30 Eberhardt at 200.487mph.

Heat-2C was a one-sided race with #37 Bennett in charge from start to finish, taking first place at 214.424mph. Almost a full minute back in second was #30 Eberhardt at 190.353mph, third was #3 Graves at 189.730mph, #512 Ken Dwelle was fourth at 177.244mph, and #5 Gist DNF after pulling up and out on lap five with a sour engine.

Heat-2B was more to everyone's liking with #4 McNeely, #22 Steve Dilda and #75 Goss racing from the start, with #37 Bennett trying to catch the front pack. It was a truly exciting race for all five laps with Goss getting ahead by lap 3 and staying there for first at 226.538mph. Second was #22 Steve Dilda at 224.932mph and 6:39.32mins, third #4 McNeely at 224.809mph and 6:39.54mins, #37 Bennett fourth at 222.553mph, #5 Gist fifth at 216.815mph, and #9 Granley finished sixth at 214.122mph.

Again, it was a front-runners race for Heat-2A. It turned into a two-part race – part one was #47 Frost, #21 Dilda and #6 Macy all out front with each, jockeying for first. Part two was #77 Good, #14 Krawczyk, and #8 Jones. By the end of lap 2, Dilda and Macy were able to separate themselves from Frost, who settled into third in no danger from the part-two racers. #21 Dilda was able to continue to pull ahead of #6 Macy to take the checkered flag for first at 231.007mph. Macy was second at 225.407mph. He was followed by #47 Frost third at 220.477mph, #14 Krawczyk fourth at 215.919mph, #77 Good fifth at 215.396mph, and #8 Jones sixth at 213.273mph. After the race, the judges declared that #47 Frost had cut the middle two pylons on lap 2 and gave him a ten-second penalty. It had no effect on the race outcome as he had been so far ahead of the other racers.

For the Bronze Race, the Dwelle brothers swapped Texans with Ken now in #7 and Dwelle, Jr. in #512. At the first pylon it became a three-way race between #7 Ken, #44 Oman and #50 Penner, all charging ahead. This left #3 Graves, #30 Eberhardt and #512 Dwelle, Jr. behind in their own race. Eventually things settled down with #44 Oman taking first with 7:09.40mins (his first win), #7 Ken Dwelle second 7:09.99mins, #50 Penner third 7:19.99mins, #30 Eberhardt fourth 7:30.46mins, #3 Graves fifth 7:49.80mins, and #512 Dwelle, Jr. sixth over one minute back from first with 8:13.57mins.

A change of Texan was also made in the Silver Race with Lee Oman flying Bud Granley's #9. As they came around to the front straight on lap 1, it was #14 Krawczyk, #77 Good, #9 Oman and #37 Bennett in a gaggle, with #8 Jones and #5 Gist one plane length back. By lap 2, Oman and Bennett passed Good and were on the tail of Krawczyk and gaining. At lap

The 1998 Reno program cover is one of few that featured Texans. (Courtesy of the National Championship Air Races)

3, Bennett caught and passed Krawczyk. They stayed in place to the finish with #37 Bennett first at 219.846mph (his first win), #9 Oman second at 217.844mph, #14 Krawczyk third at 215.805mph, #77 Good fourth at 213.294mph, #5 Gist fifth at 212.583mph, #8 Jones sixth at 210.442mph. It was later ruled that #9 Oman had cut middle pylon 5 on lap 4 and was given a ten-second penalty, dropping him to sixth and moving everyone up one place.

Gold races are always exciting no matter what class is racing and this one was no exception. Not only were all of the top qualifiers racing, but Steve and Mary Dilda were again racing each other. From the start, it was a runaway for #21 Mary Dilda as her only close challenger at the start was #6 Macy, and he fell back and raced #75 Goss and #47 Frost for second while #22 Steve and #4 McNeely raced for fifth. As #21 Mary Dilda crossed the finish line, she became the first woman to win a Reno Gold Race. Although her time of 7:52.73mins and speed of 228.003mph for the six laps were not records, her win was a great victory. Second through sixth were: #6 Macy at 222.998mph, #75 Goss at 221.141mph, #47 Frost at 220.476mph, #22 Steve Dilda at 219.604mph, who was assessed a penalty for low flying, and #4 McNeely at 218.669mph. This would be the last race for a few years for members of the Dwelle family.

Reno got a new queen of Texan racing.

1998
Tragedy and controversy were to be had for the 1998 Reno races. An F-1 pilot died during a Heat Race and controversy swirled through Texan country. Twenty-one were entered and 16 qualified. Those entered but not qualified were: #3 Dorel Graves, #21 Tom Campau, #55 Fred Johnson, #57 Rick Drake, and #92 Steve Clegg. The fastest qualifier was #21 Lee Oman (it had been entered by owner Tom Campau) with 233.723mph. He was followed by: #47 Jack Frost also at 233.723mph, #6 Nick Macy third with 232.363mph, #75 Al Goss at 228.433mph, #22 Mary Dilda (back in her regular Texan) at 225.565mph, #8 Robert Jones at 225.395mph, #90 Gene McNeely at 224.493mph, #37 Jim Bennett at 222.161mph, #5 Jerry McDonald, back after a few years away, at 217.113mph, #9 Bud Granley at 215.111mph, #50 Carl Penner at 207.820mph, #77 Jim Good at 207.436mph, rookie #30 Jim Eberhardt (brother of Bill Eberhardt) at 197.515mph, #66 Thomas Martin at 194.436mph, rookie #44 Jim Booth at 194.079mph, and, in 16th place, rookie #57 Gary Hubler (this Texan had been entered by Rick Drake) at 192.437mph. This would be his only Reno appearance.

Now to the controversy, since Texan racing is limited to "stock engines and airframes," the Texans have been traditionally submitted to a tech inspection to ensure the planes meet the rules. When #21 so easily won the 1997 Gold Race, rumors

#75 Al Goss winning the 2000 Heat-2B Race. Goss raced at Reno from 1981 to 2009 and always flew a spectacular race. (Jerry Liang)

began to circulate (there were no tech inspections in 1997, reason unknown) that #21 may have had an advantage. So, when Lee Oman posted a 233.723mph qualifying speed in 1998, a protest was lodged to have #21 tech inspected; for this inspectors would pull out a few cylinders to look at piston dimensions for rule conformity. Lee Oman and the Texan's owner Thomas Campau refused to allow one. The Rules Committee automatically disqualified #21, which resulted in #47 Frost becoming the top qualifier as he had passed his tech inspection.

With fewer contestants, the first three five-lap heat races would have only five racers in each and all others would have six racers.

Results for Heat-1C was a race between #75 Goss and #90 McNeely, with a second race for #9 Granley and rookie #30 Eberhardt, followed by rookie #57 Hubler. At the flag, it was #75 Goss in 6:38.02mins first, #90 McNeely second in 6:44.05mins, third was #9 Granley in 7:04.52mins, fourth #30 Eberhardt in 7:36.07mins, and #57 Hubler in 8:08.77mins, almost two minutes behind first place.

#6 Macy ran away from the start of Heat-1B and stayed there to the finish. The real racing was again midfield between #8 Jones, #5 McDonald and #77 Good, with rookie #44 Booth tail-end, getting the feel of the course. They finished in racing order: first Macy at 231.244mph, second Jones at 219.099mph, third McDonald at 216.277mph, fourth Good at 216.090mph, and fifth Booth at 195.490mph, over 35mph slower than Macy.

As Heat-1A began, it was clear there would be a fight between #47 Frost and #22 Dilda, with both jockeying for the lead from the first pylon into lap 2. Frost pulled away from Dilda by the start of lap 3 and kept going to take first place. Frost set a new Reno five-lap race record with 6:21.59mins at 235.383mph. Dilda was second at 229.056mph. In third was #50 Penner at 206.444mph. In fourth was #37 Bennett at 201.747mph and in fifth was #66 Martin at 195.660mph.

Heat-2C was what Texan racing was about, with evenly matched aircraft racing relying on pilot skills for the outcome. While not the fastest race, it provided some great racing. #5 McDonald was first at 200.254mph, with #50 Penner second at 200.048mph. #90 McNeely was third at 198.536mph with #30 Eberhardt fourth at 192.144mph. Rookie #44 Booth was fifth at 186.205mph and #66 Martin placed sixth at 183.455mph.

Heat-2B was almost a repeat of -2C with the addition of fast qualifiers. #6 Macy easily won the heat at 230.042mph. #90 McNeely was second at 222.183mph, which was an almost 24mph improvement over his -2C finish. #22 Dilda took third at 213.913mph after she held off #5 McDonald at 213.740mph. Placing fifth was #50 Penner at 204.988mph and in sixth was #30 Eberhardt at 198.475mph.

Heat-2A began with #47 Frost and #75 Goss wingtip-to-wingtip until they got to the back side of the course, where Frost began to pull ahead. He continued gaining distance until the checkered flag, finishing at 230.083mph. Goss finished second at 219.882mph. A race was taking place for third between #8 Jones and #37 Bennett with some fine pilot against pilot racing. At the end, it appeared that Jones and Bennett were tied for third. However, the Race Committee determined that both had flown too low while racing and were placed back to fifth (#8 Jones at 214.710mph) and sixth (#37 Bennett at 214.813mph) and fined $200 each. This gave #77 Good third place at 213.171mph and #9 Granley fourth at 210.380mph.

Speeds for Saturday's Bronze Race were all under 200mph, with the racers evenly matched in little more than a parade. #44 Booth was a challenge to #66 Martin, with #57 Hubler right behind and #30 Eberhardt close behind Hubler. #22 Dilda and #90 McNeely kept pace with the front pack but lagged to save their engines for the Gold Race. The order of the finish was #66 Martin in first at 196.449mph, #44 Booth second at 195.832mph, #57 Hubler third at 194.795mph, #30 Eberhardt fourth at 194.485mph, and #22 Dilda fifth at 194.415mph. #90 McNeely DNF the race as he pulled out before completing lap 5.

#37 Bennett took charge of the Silver Race and flew unchallenged all the way to the checkered flag. Bennett took his second Silver Race in a row at 221.586mph. #8 Jones, #5 McDonald and #9 Granley put up a great fight for second through fourth and finished in this order. Their finishing speeds were Jones at 212.286mph, McDonald at 212.056mph and Granley at 211.254mph. #50 Penner was fifth at 203.477mph and #30 Eberhardt sixth at 193.431mph.

After finishing fourth the year before, #47 Frost was determined to win the Gold. At the start, #6 Macy was on Frost's wingtip for almost four laps. Frost had the edge by the end of lap 4 and was half a plane length ahead. This was all he needed to take his first Gold in only his second year of racing Texans. Frost's speed was 229.254mph to second place #6 Macy's 227.171mph. #22 Dilda and #75 Goss flew a wing-to-wing race for third until Goss got the better of Dilda coming out of pylon 5 on lap 6. Goss' slightly faster time was 8:05.27mins to fourth place Dilda's 8:05.78mins. #90 McNeely was fifth in 8:14.52mins and #77 Good sixth in 8:26.04mins.

In the four years since #27 Eddie Van Fossen's last win, there were now four different Gold winners. Texan racing is anything but boring with more excitement to come.

1999

Reno 1999 was another year of tragedy and controversy, with the fatal crash of Unlimited racer #38 Gary Levitz and the continuing problems of the Texan performance. Nineteen entered for a share of the $65,000 prize money, with only 17 qualifying. Those entered but not qualified were #2 Mark Henley and #92 Steve Clegg. Gene McNeely also entered #42 but did not qualify. However, McNeely did qualify and raced his regular #90. There is little or no information given about an entry by Ray Difani in a Texan named *Felix*.

#47 Jack Frost was top qualifier and set a new course qualifying record with :74.84secs and 240.032mph. This was a remarkable time. #6 Nick Macy took second with :77.03secs and 233.208mph. After being disqualified in 1998, #21 was back with its owner rookie Thomas Campau as pilot and qualifying third at 227.163mph. Campau was followed by #22 Mary Dilda at 226.647mph. During a practice run Dilda had a mayday after a bird strike in her engine broke several engine lead wires. Next was #5 Jerry McDonald fifth at 225.707mph. Sixth through tenth were: #75 Al Goss at 225.000mph, #37 Jim Bennett at 224.972mph, #90 Gene McNeely at 224.522mph, #77 Jim Good at 218.940mph, and #8 Robert Jones at 214.701mph. Eleventh through 17th: were #9 Bud Granley at 214.291mph, #30 Jim Eberhardt at 210.475mph (the brothers would alternate racing this year), #50 Carl Penner at 209.958mph, #1 Carter Clark at 201.752mph (this aircraft was previously entered as #88 but had not qualified), #44 James Booth at 201.007mph, #66 Thomas Martin at 199.978mph, and #3 Dorel Graves was 17th at 197.212mph in his return to racing.

Grumbling about engine performance and specification had begun during qualifying by several of the top contenders and started to amplify during the next three heat races.

Heat-1C was a runaway by rookie #21 Campau. His finishing time for the five laps was 6:37:38mins and 226.031mph, while second place veteran #75 Goss was 7:00:79mins and 213.456mph. Good was third at 213.339mph, fourth was #30 Eberhardt at 200.371mph, and fifth was #44 Booth at 193.645mph. #3 Graves was in his familiar sixth place at 191.233mph.

Heat-1B was a standard Texan Heat Race with one frontrunner and a midfield race for third through fifth. #6 Macy took the lead and stayed there to take first at 221.663mph. Following Macy to the finish line were the midfielders #5 McDonald at 212.804mph, #90 McNeely at 212.668mph, #9 Granley at 204.961mph, with #1 Clark in fifth at 193.992mph and fill-in #3 Graves sixth at 188.837mph.

Results of Heat-1A would see the simmering 1998 problems come to a full boil. From the first pylon, #47 Frost was off like a rocket leaving everyone behind. With Frost in the lead, it was #22 Dilda, #37 Bennett and #8 Jones racing each other for second. #66 Martin and #50 Penner raced for fifth. At the finish it was #47 Frost first at 231.668mph followed by #22 Dilda second with 219.572mph about 12mph slower. Behind Dilda was #37 Bennett at 217.099mph, #8 Jones at 212.471mph, in fifth was #50 Penner at 190.863mph, and sixth was #66 Martin at 190.733mph.

Shortly after this race, the #47 Frost and #21 Oman/Campau riff became heated with Frost asking to have several pilots (including Campau) disqualified for alleged engine out-of-spec violations. It is also reported that Campau asked first to have Frost disqualified for the same reasons. This resulted in some very "heated words" on the Texan ramp and even more once the complainants moved to race headquarters. It should be remembered that it was Frost's complaint that had gotten #21 Oman disqualified the year before. After more "heated discussions," the T-6 Race Committee disqualified #47 Frost for "unsportsmanlike conduct" and asked him to leave the race site. Frost soon left but had to return due to unspecific mechanical issues. His Texan sat at the far end of the ramp the rest of the week. #47 Jack Frost would not return to Reno.

Four similarly matched Texans raced in Heat-2B and created a very entertaining competition at the front. #90 McNeely, #22 Dilda, #6 Macy, and #75 Goss came off the scatter pylon in tight order, with no one having an advantage until lap 2 when Macy and Goss pulled ahead of McNeely and Dilda. At the back, #8 Jones and #30 Bill Eberhardt raced each other. As lap four started, it was Macy a plane length ahead of Goss. Dilda had passed McNeely, while everyone behind maintained their positions to the finish. Macy placed first at 234.787mph, #75 Goss was second at 230.391mph. They were followed by #22 Dilda at 228.999mph, #90 McNeely at 226.487mph, #8 Jones fifth at 218.817mph as he had pulled away from #30 Eberhardt at 204.299mph.

With the departure of #47 Frost, the Heat-2A race was flown with only five racers. From the start, it seemed as if #21 Campau was holding back as the rest of the field was able to stay with him throughout the race. After a short burst of speed to stay in the lead, Campau settled in for the first-place finish at 218.897mph. In second place was #5 McDonald at 217.451mph. #77 Good was third at 215.644mph, #9 Granley was fourth at 210.362mph, and fifth #37 Bennett at 195.126mph.

After a year away from Reno, #3 Graves flew a great Bronze Race along with the other five racers. All seemed to enjoy their race as there was plenty of swapping and challenging of positions. At the finish line, it was #50 Penner in

7:09.66mins for the five laps, #1 Clark took 7:23.98mins for second, #44 Booth was third in 7:32.84mins, #3 Graves was fourth in 7:50.40mins, #66 Martin was fifth in 7:50.60mins, and #30 Bill Eberhardt sixth in 7:51.44mins.

#90 McNeely and #37 Bennett flew a tight race for the Silver with Bennett looking for his third Silver win in a row. The crowd received their money's worth with this race as both frontrunners would not give even a prop's width. #8 Jones and #9 Granley put on a fine race for third while #50 Penner easily kept ahead of #30 Jim Eberhardt. Bennett and McNeely were still wing-to-wing as they started lap 4 where they remained until the flag, with #37 Bennett one-half second ahead to take his third consecutive Silver at 222.304mph. McNeely was second at 222.016mph, third went to #9 Granley at 214.210mph, fourth place #8 Jones at 213.938mph, #50 Penner cruised to fifth at 206.995mph, while #30 Eberhardt was sixth 196.909mph.

Six hungry Gold racers came down the chute in mass for the first pylon and turn. Both top qualifiers, veteran #6 Macy and rookie #21 Campau, could not be separated by a sheet of paper. As they left the rest of the field behind, #22 Dilda and #75 Goss had a hard fight with each other, leaving old friends #77 Good and #5 McDonald to fly their own race. Several times between pylons 3 and 4, Campau would nose ahead, but Macy would take it back in the turns. Macy is a crop duster by profession and knows how to make tight turns. Seven-time winner Eddie Van Fossen was also a crop-duster. Macy kept his edge and finished first at 229.396mph to rookie Campau's 228.376 second. Dilda in third at 224.560mph held off Goss, who finished fourth at 223.230mph. #77 Good placed fifth with 217.922mph and #5 McDonald sixth at 216.695mph.

Reno had another new Texan king.

2000

There were 27 entries with 23 qualifiers at Reno 2000. Those entered but not qualifying or racing were #42 Gene McNeely (he raced his #90), #47 Jack Frost, #92 Steve Clegg, and Alan Preston (no race number given.) The top qualifier was the 1999 Gold winner #6 Nick Macy at 230.891mph. Second through tenth were: #21 Tom Campau at 229.586mph, #90 Gene McNeely at 225.869mph, #75 Al Goss at 224.676mph, #37 Jim Bennett at 221.665mph, #22 Mary Dilda at 221.500mph, #77 Jim Good at 221.198mph, #4 Lee Oman at 220.652mph, #8 Robert Jones at 220.434mph in his last Texan race, #5 Jerry McDonald at 216.822mph, #9 Bud Granley at 213.300mph. Eleventh through 23rd were: #50 Carl Penner at 211.432mph, rookie #12 John Zayac at 210.559mph, #44 Lee Oman at 208.058mph flying a second Texan owned by Wayne Cartwright, #30 Jim Eberhardt at 207.309mph, Canadian #64 Keith McMann returning after a few years at 205.615mph, #444 James Booth at 204.696mph in a Texan previously raced by Booth as #44, #1 Carter Clark at 204.438mph, #3 Dorel Graves at 199.417mph in his last Texan race, #66 Tomas Martin at 198.641mph, rookie #87 Richard Siegfried at 198.552mph (this Texan last raced at Mojave in 1974 and had been heavily damaged in a take-off accident), rookie #49 John Johnson at 195.403mph, and 23rd was rookie #69 Michael Gillian. With such a full field, it was decided to add a Medallion Race between the heats.

Results of Heat-1C were #21 Campau first at 217.752mph, second #4 Lee Oman at 216.764mph, #37 Bennett at 214.000mph, #9 Bud Granley at 208.014mph, #44 McNeely at 200.698mph (the official results note "One of Lee Oman's aircraft was obviously flown by an alternate pilot, but those records are not available."), and in sixth #444 Booth at 197.002mph.

Results of Heat-1B were #6 Macy first at 226.442mph, followed by #75 Goss at 220.358mph, #77 Good at 215.456mph, #5 McDonald at 215.031mph, #64 McMann at 201.677mph. Rookie #12 Zayac was listed as DNS. He had engine trouble on the way to Reno and landed on a highway to make repairs and was plagued by continuing problems the rest of the week.

Heat-1A results were #90 McNeely at 221.687mph, #22 Dilda at 221.527mph, #8 Jones at 215.826mph, #1 Clark at 200.753mph, #30 Eberhardt at 196.266mph, and #50 Penner at 196.132mph.

The five-lap Medallion Race involved everyone that had qualified under 200mph. Veteran #3 Graves won his first race after ten years of racing at Reno at 191.786mph, proving perseverance pays off. Second place went to rookie #87 Siegfried at 191.502mph, third #66 Martin at 191.289mph, #49 Johnson at 190.643mph, and fifth #69 Gillian at 185.635mph.

Friday's last race was Heat-2B with a very close finish. #75 Goss was first in 6:39.09mins and #21 Campau second in 6:39.72mins. In third place was #22 Dilda in 6:45.63mins, followed by #4 Oman fourth with 6:48.67mins, #5 McDonald fifth in 6:57.82mins, and #1 Clark sixth in 7:27.01mins.

Results for the five-lap Heat-2A Race were #6 Macy first at 220.456mph, #90 McNeely at 220.309mph, #77 Good at 215.920mph, #8 Jones at 214.303mph, #37 Bennett at 212.620mph, and #9 Granley at 212.306mph.

Bronze Race results were #50 Penner first at 209.512mph, second was Oman now in #44 at 207.160mph, #64 McMann third at 197.485mph, fourth was #444 Booth at 196.257mph, #30 Eberhardt was fifth with a ten second penalty for cutting middle pylon 5 on lap 1 with 193.113mph, and #12 Zayac was again a DNS.

Rookie #54 Michael Pfleger qualified 17th at Reno 2011 before the races were stopped following a terrible Unlimited Race accident. (Jim Dunn)

The Silver Race featured three-time Silver winner #37 Bennett trying for a fourth consecutive win. However, #4 Oman was almost 2mph faster at the finish and took first place at 220.579mph. #37 Bennett took second at 218.484mph in his last Texan race. Placing third was #8 Jones at 217.610mph. In fourth was #5 McDonald at 217.155mph. #9 Granley was fifth at 214.715mph and sixth was #1 Clark at 200.255mph.

For the six-lap Gold, #6 Macy took only 7:49.43mins to finish first at 228.299mph. This was his second consecutive Gold. Second place went to #21 Campau at 227.717mph. In third place was #75 Goss at 226.447mph. In fourth was #90 McNeely at 222.276mph. He was followed by #22 Dilda in fifth at 218.711mph and #77 Good was sixth at 217.548mph.

With a new two-time champ, 2001 looked promising.

2001

Twenty-two Texans were entered for the 2001 Reno races. Those entered but not qualified were rookie #00 Jack Cronin, #1 Carter Clark, #42 Gene McNeely flying Mark Henley's Texan, and #444 Jim Booth. Seventeen qualified with #6 Nick Macy first at 230.891mph. Following Macy in order were: #21 Tom Campau at 229.586mph, #90 Gene McNeely at 225.869mph, #75 Al Goss at 224.676mph, #22 Mary Dilda at 221.500mph, #77 Jim Good at 221.198mph, #4 Lee Oman at 220.652mph, #5 Jerry McDonald at 216.822mph, #12 John Zayac at 210.559mph, #44 Wayne Cartwright, #30 Jim Eberhardt at 207.309mph, rookie #89 Fred Telling at 207.719mph in the former Joe Hartung Texan, #64 Keith McMann at 205.615mph, #87 Richard Siegfried at 198.552mph, #66 Thomas Martin at 198.641mph, and 17th was #68 Michael Gillian at 189.133mph. However, the horrific tragedy of September 11, 2001, had a direct effect on the Reno Air Races. All civilian flying was prohibited, and everything was grounded, including air racing, which was scheduled to start on Thursday, September 13. After events became clearer, it was hoped that qualifying would restart on September 12. The Race Committee put a plan in place to "seed" the heat races by putting together pairings for the races based on qualifying times. To fill out the field, #70 Jim Thomas was added even though he had not qualified. The Race Committee asked the FAA to grant a waiver for the race, but to no avail. The Race Committee canceled the races on September 15.

2002

Springing back from the national calamity of the previous year, Reno 2002 had 19 entrants and all qualified. The top ten were #21 Tom Campau, who was fastest at 231.071mph, #75 Al Goss at 229.026mph, #6 Nick Macy at 228.938mph, #22 Mary Dilda at 225.158mph, #90 Gene McNeely at 224.535mph, #4 Lee Oman at 220.870mph, #77 Jim Good at 219.972mph, #5 Jerry McDonald at 216.611mph, #89 Fred Telling at 214.273mph, and #9 Bud Granley at 212.995mph. Eleventh through 19th were: #444 Jim Booth at 212.059mph, #12 John Zayac at 211.934mph, #30 Jim Eberhardt at 209.941mph, #44 Wayne Cartwright at 207.165mph, #64 Keith McMann at 205.473mph, #87 Richard Siegfried at 204.485mph, #70 Jim Thomas at 199.083mph, #68 Michael Gillian at 197.346mph, and #66 Thomas Martin at 196.845mph. There was an almost 35mph gap from first to 19th. Total Texan Prize money was $77,000.

Nick Macy's black #6 *Six Cat* took the early lead in Heat-1C. Macy was able to keep half an aircraft length ahead of #4 Oman to take first place at 224.366mph. Oman placed second at 218.969mph. #89 Telling was third at 209.488, proving old #89 could still race. #12 Zayac was fourth at 204.022, having had time to fix his 2000 engine problems. In fifth was #64 McMann at 201.132mph and #68 Gillian was sixth at 189.202mph.

#90 McNeely and #75 Goss were the first pair to fight during Heat-1B. Both were trying to overtake or keep the other behind for the entire five laps until it appeared that McNeely went wide, and Goss slid by to take first. Their speeds and times were Goss 223.893mph in 6:38.89mins and second place McNeely at 223.239mph in 6:40.06mins. #5 McDonald was third at 213.755mph having flown mid-pack by himself. #444 Booth and #44 Cartwright had a fine race for fourth with Booth taking it. Their speeds and times were Booth 204.148mph in 7:17.47mins and Cartwright at 204.008mph in 7:17.77mins. #70 Thomas was sixth at 190.843mph.

As the gaggle came around to start Heat-1A, #22 Dilda was caught by surprise as #21 Campau was half a plane length ahead near pylon 3 and stayed there to finish first in 6:47.33mins with second place Dilda in 6:48.87mins. In the train behind them were #77 Good third in 6:55.05mins, #9 Granley fourth in 7:08.58mins, #30 Eberhardt fifth in 7:24.50mins, and #87 Siegfried sixth in 7:28.57mins.

Both Heat-2B and Heat-2A were raced on Friday with #75 Goss and #22 Dilda tenths of a mile per hour apart. In race -2B, #75 Goss placed first at 219.459mph and #22 Dilda placed second at 219.249mph. #4 Oman placed third at 218.311mph. Oman was followed by #5 McDonald at 210.535mph, #9 Granley at 206.533mph and close behind in sixth was #12 Zayac at 206.113mph.

Heat-2A was held a few hours later. This was the time for #6 Macy and #21 Campau to have a go at each other, with a slight challenge by #90 McNeely until lap 2, when it was just the front two. At the start of lap 2, #89 Telling pulled up and out with instrument problems and DNF. At the end it was #21 Campau first at 230.023mph, #6 Macy second at 229.138mph, #90 McNeely third at 223.121mph, #77 Good fourth at 219.551mph, and in fifth, with no hope of catching Good, was #444 Booth at 199.917mph.

After this race, Sports Class racer Tommy Rose was killed during a Heat Race.

Moved to Saturday morning, the five-lap Medallion Race started as a mass noisy gaggle with all six contestants bunched up. At pylon 4, they started to settle into their race with only #87 Siegfried and #66 Martin doing any close racing. #44 Cartwright pulled a good lead where he stayed to the end. #68 Gillian and #12 Zayac traded places until the finish. At the checkered flag #44 Cartwright was first in 7:24.69mins, #87 Siegfried second in 7:29.72mins, #66 Martin third in 7:30.84mins, #68 Gillian fourth in 7:34.86mins, #12 Zayac fifth in 7:37.15mins, and #70 Thomas sixth in 7:41.61mins. All in all, it was not a bad race.

The Bronze Race later that afternoon had the feeling of the earlier Medallion Race with four of the six Bronze racers having competed in that race. From the start, it would be a race between #30 Eberhardt and #44 Cartwright, both getting off pylon 1 together. They stayed tight to each other for the entire race, while #87 Siegfried flew alone with #64 McMann, #68 Gillian and #70 Thomas trailing behind. At the end, first was #30 Eberhardt at 204.200mph, #44 Cartwright second at 204.088mph, third #87 Siegfried at 199.573mph, #64 McMann fourth at 187.695mph, #70 Thomas fifth at 186.355mph, and #68 Gillian sixth at 184.641mph. After the race, the pylon judges gave #70 Thomas a ten-second penalty and moved him to sixth for cutting middle pylon 2 on lap 5, giving #68 Gillian fifth place.

The Silver Race was best described as a super race, featuring two veteran pilots, #5 Jerry McDonald and #77 Jim Good. Both started racing in 1978. From the start it was McDonald in the lead for the first three laps, with Good inching forward each lap. Both displayed great piloting skills from years of competition, never flying too high or wide. Overall speed would determine the winner. At the halfway mark on lap 4, Good caught and overtook McDonald, and went on to win his first Silver Race. At the finish line it was #77 Good in first at 222.106mph, #5 McDonald second at 217.230mph, #89 Telling third at 215.804mph, #9 Granley fourth at 211.862mph, fifth was #444 Booth at 207.438mph, and sixth, after a 12-second penalty for cutting pylon middle 5 on lap 2, was #12 Zayac at 206.542mph.

Wind and dust greeted the six Gold racers for the afternoon race, but it did not keep them from turning in some fast times and good racing. At the scatter pylon, it was #75 Goss, #21 Campau and #6 Macy, with #90 McNeely and #22 Dilda seconds behind and then #4 Oman. At the front, Macy and Campau moved past Goss by lap 2, having a go for each other. Further back, McNeely and Dilda were having a great fight for fourth. As the laps ticked off, Campau continued to gain on Macy until he passed him at the middle of lap 6 and took the checkered flag for his first Gold win at 231.614mph. Second was #6 Macy at 229.645mph, which was just over a minute faster than his winning 2000 time. Third was #75 Goss at 225.361mph, fourth was #22 Dilda at 221.299mph, fifth #90 McNeely at 221.189mph, and #4 Oman was sixth at 220.135mph.

Another new Texan king and a third Gold win for Race #21 with its third pilot.

2003

For Reno 2003, RARA made a change on how all classes of racing would be timed and racecourse distance measured. According to RARA (summarized):

In the past, race distance has been measured in a straight line from pylon to pylon. However, the aircraft do not race in a straight line between pylons, they race in an arc around the pylons. That's why RARA established a percent of arc that translated into distance around the pylons. Effectively, this increased the size of the race courses. Timing remains the same, so the same time over a larger course reflects an increase in speed. This new system means that all of the race speeds, including qualifying speeds, in all of the racing classes for this year's race will be faster than they would have been in previous years. In fact, most of the racers believe that it probably represents a truer air speed. Resulting in increases from 2.18 percent for F-1 and 2.56 percent for the Unlimiteds.

On the Sunday before the races started, there was a drama as Steve Dilda in the pace plane clipped a pylon with his wingtip while demonstrating to the pylon judges what a cut to a pylon looks like. He landed safely.

The fastest qualifier was #22 Mary Dilda at 239.398mph, which was a new T-6 Class qualifying record. The next nine in order were: #21 Tom Campau at 234.502mph, #6 Nick Macy at 233.123mph, #75 Al Goss at 226.427mph, #77 Jim Good at 225.427mph, #90 Gene McNeely at 222.213mph in a new G model Texan, #5 Jerry McDonald at 220.280mph, #7 Ken Dwelle at 220.120mph flying a new Texan in his first race since 1997, #89 Fred Telling at 216.359mph, #9 Bud Granley at 214.804mph. Eleventh through 17th were: #44 Wayne Cartwright at 213.771mph, #64 Keith McMann at 212.501mph, #30 Jim Eberhardt at 212.229mph, #12 John Zayac at 211.613mph, #70 Jim Thomas at 208.873mph, #444 Jim Booth at 208.206mph, and #66 Thomas Martin was 17th at just over 200mph at 200.777mph.

#44 Cartwright was added to fill out the field for Heat-1C, which started with #444 Booth, #30 Eberhardt, and #12 Zayac bunched at the front, trailed by #70 Thomas. Further back were #44 Cartwright and #66 Martin. As the front group passed pylon 5 on lap 2, the pilots were settling into their own grooves. Eberhardt passed Zayac. Booth slipped back, but not enough to be challenged by Thomas. Martin and Cartwright sailed along at the back. At the flag it was #30 Eberhardt first at 208.706mph followed by #12 Zayac second at 208.591mph, #444 Booth third at 206.723mph, #70 Thomas fourth at 203.921mph, #66 Martin fifth at 190.236mph, and sixth #44 Cartwright at 189.749mph.

It was a two against two against two race for Heat-1B. At the front was #5 McDonald and #7 Dwelle. They were followed by #9 Granley and #89 Telling. Trailing behind was #44 Cartwright and a bit further back #64 McMann. McDonald took first at 220.876mph to Dwelle's 220.456mph. Granley was in third at 214.203mph to Telling's 214.086mph. Cartwright was fifth at 211.99mph and McMann sixth at 206.274mph.

Before the start of Heat-1C, #90 McNeely declared a mayday with carburetor problems and was declared a DNS. It was obvious the race was between #22 Dilda, #6 Macy, #21 Campau and #75 Goss, leaving #77 Good to himself. This race does not usually see the pilots making an all-out effort. The way everyone pushed hard and with speeds increasing, one would have thought this was the Gold Race. Macy finally got an edge on lap 5 over Dilda and Campau and on lap 4 Goss had eased off. What a finish for a Heat Race with #6 Macy first at 236.351mph, #22 Dilda second at 235.971mph, third #21 Campau at 233.787mph, fourth #75 Goss at 227.964mph, and #77 Good fifth, 13mph behind first.

Again #44 Cartwright was added to fill in for Heat-2C. This made for an evenly matched race as all had qualified at or above 200mph. It quickly fell into pairs racing from first to sixth. At the finish was #12 Zayac taking first at 210.212mph. He was followed by #64 McMann in second place at 210.111mph, #444 Booth third at 207.320mph, #70 Thomas at 202.909mph in fourth, #66 Martin fifth at 196.455mph, and #44 Cartwright was sixth again at 196.383mph. Martin and Cartwright in the back two places had a great race between themselves.

#90 McNeely was able to compete in Heat-2B after the loan of a carburetor by Jerry McDonald. The pack was led by #89 Telling, #90 McNeely and #7 Dwelle who passed pylon 3 in a group being trailed by #30 Eberhardt, #44 Cartwright and #9 Granley. However, by lap 3, everyone except Telling and Dwelle were falling into line. At the end was #7 Dwelle in first at 218.574mph and 6:57.08mins, #89 Telling second at 218.370mph and 6:57.47mins, a close race. #90 McNeely was third with 7:04.59mins, #9 Granley fourth in 7:11.93mins, #44 Cartwright had passed #30 Eberhardt to take fifth in 7:17.25mins to sixth with Eberhardt in 7:35.89mins.

#22 Dilda would not finish the first lap of Heat-2A, pulling out with a sour engine. This left #6 Macy and #21 Campau to challenge each other with #77 Good close behind and ahead of #75 Goss. #5 McDonald hung back, perhaps to save his engine for the next race. By the start of lap 5, #6 Macy had out-distanced #21 Campau by two plane lengths and took first at 237.187mph to second place Campau at 230.465mph. Good was third at 215.760mph even after being penalised by a ten-second penalty for cutting middle pylon 1 on lap 2. Goss was fourth at 215.632mph and #5 McDonald fifth at 192.554mph. McDonald may have needed his carburetor back from McNeely.

#12 Zayac maintained a decent speed advantage throughout the entire Bronze Race and took his first win at 214.395mph. Second went to #64 McMann at 210.285mph. In third place was #444 Booth at 204.167mph. Fourth place was #70 Thomas at 202.094mph. At the back, putting on a splendid race, were #66 Martin taking fifth at 199.346mph and #44 Cartwright in sixth at 199.067mph.

His time away from Texan racing did not dampen #7 Dwelle's skills as shown in the Silver Race. An awesome battle for first place was between Dwelle, #89 Telling and #90 McNeely from the start. All three were evenly matched, and at one point on lap 3, they all passed or pulled alongside one another. #9 Granley and #44 Cartwright tangled for fourth while #30 Eberhardt settled into sixth. At the flag, it was a little more speed and a tighter turn that bought #7 Dwelle his first win at 223.015mph. He was followed by #89 Telling second at 222.765mph. In third place was #90 McNeely 221.108mph, #44 Cartwright had passed #9 Granley for fourth at 213.434mph to Granley's 212.587mph for fifth, and #30 Eberhardt sixth at 208.233mph.

The big guns were off like a shot for the start of the Gold Race. By middle pylon 5 on lap 1, it was hard to tell who had the advantage as the fastest four, #22 Dilda, #6 Macy, #21 Campau and #75 Goss, made their turn leaving #77 Good and #5 McDonald further back, but still charging. Lap after lap, each of the frontrunners seemed to gain only inches against each other until Macy finally had a 0.40secs lead over the pack and was able to stay there to take his third Gold win at 235.264mph. In second place was #22 Dilda at 233.507mph. Third was #21 Campau 0.10secs back, with #75 Goss fourth, #77 Good fifth, and #5 McDonald sixth. This was Jerry McDonald's last Reno race. It was determined that #21 had cut middle pylon 5 on lap 1 and was given a 12-second penalty, moving him to fourth place and #75 to third.

A previous Texan king was back.

2004
Unsettled weather greeted the 21 entrants for Reno 2004 with a forecast of rain and snow. The cold weather would aid in racing as the Texan flies faster when the temperature is cold. Those entered yet not qualified or racing were #21 Tom Campau, #16 Bruce Mayes in his only attempt at racing, and #736 Richard Siegfried in a Texan previously raced as #87. The top qualifier was #75 Al Goss at 238.281mph and coming in second was #22 Mary Dilda at 235.259mph. Third through tenth places went to #6 Nick Macy at 231.819mph, #77 Jim Good at 230.355mph, #90 Gene McNeely, #7 Tom Dwelle, Jr. at 224.816mph after sitting out for a few years, #89 Fred Telling at 223.485mph, rookie #20 Paul Redlich at 219.273mph, rookie #5 Joey Sanders, the new owner of Jerry McDonald's Texan, at 219.099mph, and in tenth was #9 Bud Granley at 216.969mph. Eleventh through 18th qualifiers were #44 Wayne Cartwright at 215.260mph, #70 Jim Thomas at 214.080mph, #444 Jim Booth at 212.419mph, #12 John Zayac at 211.108mph, #64 Keith McMann at 210.334mph, #30 Jim Eberhardt at 209.932mph, #68 Michael Gillian at 199.045mph, and 18th was #B66 Thomas Martin at 198.865mph.

Heat-1A was a contest between #12 Zayac and #444 Booth. #64 McMann and #30 Eberhardt followed the leaders but were not a challenge to the front two. #68 Gillian and #B66 Martin remained at the back. Booth got around Zayac to take the win. The placement was as follows: #444 Booth first at 209.662mph, #12 Zayac second at 208.798mph, #64 McMann at 205.210mph, #30 Eberhardt at 204.630mph, #68 Gillian at 198.198mph, and sixth #B66 Martin at 196.995mph.

Up next was Heat-1B with both rookies, #5 Sanders and #20 Redlich, up against four more experienced pilots – #9 Granley (racing T-6s since 1988), #89 Telling, #44 Cartwright, and #70 Thomas. By lap 3, they proved they could race by charging ahead of everyone, except Telling, and staying there. There was a brief challenge by Sanders to Redlich, but Redlich held him off. At the finish it was #89 Telling first at 219.629mph, second #20 Redlich at 217.244mph, third #5 Sanders at 216.346mph, #9 Granley was fourth at 214.492mph, #44 Cartwright was fifth at 205.859mph, and sixth was #70 Thomas at 205.684mph.

Heat-1A would be repeated twice more over the next few days as it featured the same six top qualifiers. Putting his crop-duster skills to work, #75 Goss fell into a low tight race and went full speed ahead. Goss was followed by #22 Dilda, #6 Macy and #90 McNeely. #77 Good and #7 Dwelle were well behind. At lap 3, McNeely fell back to join Good and Dwelle in the race for fourth. At the front, Goss continued to hold Dilda and Macy at bay by flying low and tight. In the end it was #75 Goss first in 6:25.075mins to second place #22 Dilda in 6:26.250mins. Third place went to #6 Macy in 6:27.467mins. #90 McNeely kept ahead of #77 Good and took fourth with 6:49.258mins. Fifth place Good finished in 6:49.309mins, leaving #7 Dwelle sixth in 6:52.067mins. The gap from first to sixth was a little over 26 seconds.

Round two of Heat-1C was a repeat of Heat-2C, only a little faster. At the finish was: #444 Booth first at 214.027mph, #12 Zayac second at 213.880mph, #64 McMann third at 210.053mph, #30 Eberhardt fourth at 209.815mph, #68 Gillian fifth at 201.688mph, and #B66 Martin sixth at 199.234mph. Martin was almost 3mph faster than his time in Heat-1C.

Heat-2B was best described as a slight change of plan from Heat-1B. It was #89 Telling in first at 212.881mph, about 7mph slower than his Heat-1B speed. #20 Redlich again second with 211.781mph, #9 Granley came in third with 211:695mph, #5 Sanders was fourth at 210.546mph, #44 Cartwright fifth at 210.501mph, #70 Thomas sixth at 205.847mph. The cold weather had an effect on equalizing everyone's performance.

Round two of Heat-1A featured the same players and same finishers as Heat-2A. Only this time #75 Goss was 3mph faster than before and took first place at 239.372mph. #22 Dilda was second at 238.833mph, then #6 Macy at 238.272mph, #90 McNeely fourth at 228.851mph, #77 Good fifth at 223.087mph and #7 Dwelle sixth at 222.185mph. The time gap from first to sixth was almost 30 seconds. Perhaps Goss had picked up a few tips from his good friend Eddie Van Fossen.

The afternoon Bronze Race was again a repeat of Heat-1C and -2C, only slightly slower than -2C. The results were the same. First was #444 Booth at 209.690mph. He was followed by #12 Zayac second at 209.129mph, third #64 McMann at 201.368mph, #30 Eberhardt fourth at 201.098mph, #68 Gillian fourth at 194.501mph, and #B66 Martin 193.846mph in sixth. This would be his last Reno race.

All six laps of the Silver Race were exciting. #89 Telling took the lead and behind him was some great racing by the other five competitors. #9 Granley, #5 Sanders, #20 Redlich, #44 Cartwright, and #70 Thomas were all fighting for second place. Between laps 4 and 5 Cartwright had caught and passed Redlich and Sanders. Then Redlich caught and passed Sanders with Thomas making continued attempts to overcome Sanders. At the flag it was #89 Telling first at 217.320mph, #9 Granley was 10 seconds back in second at 212.925mph, and third was #20 Redlich at 211.644mph who had caught and passed #44 Cartwright at the start of lap 6. Cartwright was fourth at 210.869mph, #5 Sanders held off Thomas and took fifth at 208.664mph, and #70 Thomas was in sixth at 203.988mph. After the race, #70 Thomas was fined $300 by the Contest Committee for low flying while trying to pass Sanders. Speeds in this race were fast enough to have won a Gold Race a few years back.

A great Gold Race is one that has everyone standing and cheering the racers on and that is what happened at Reno 2004. From the start, it was #75 Goss tight and low as he had been in the two previous races with #22 Dilda, #6 Macy and #90 McNeely close behind. #77 Good and #7 Dwelle were further back and running their own racing while trying to catch McNeely. At the front, Goss remained tight and low with Dilda high and wide as was #6 Macy, with #90 McNeely falling back by lap 2. Goss was flying the same race he had flown before in the heats. It appeared that Dilda had not noticed when Goss left an opening each time he rounded pylon 2. It was not until lap 4 that Dilda started to work lower while Macy continued to run high. By the time Dilda was within striking distance, the race was over. Goss had his first Gold win, at 238.079mph, after racing for 24 years. Dilda was only 1.1mph back and took second at 237.047mph. Macy placed third at 233.269mph. Back in fourth place was #90 McNeely at 223.408mph, fifth was #77 Good at 218.789mph, and #7 Dwelle was sixth at 217.789mph.

After years of racing, the new Texan king had finally won his Gold crown.

While many would say the races were lackluster with each race almost a duplicate of a previous one, it is this kind of racing that shows the following: (1) pilot skills, (2) team strategy in knowing what to do every race, and (3) preparation, the hard work put into the aircraft by pit crews and pilots to get every ounce of speed from their aircraft.

What would the next year bring?

2005

Billed as "Air Racing on the East Coast," Tunica featured T-6 races as one of three classes that raced. Held at Tunica airport on June 2–5, 2005, the races were run by the Tunica Air Racing Association (TARA) with a tight schedule. Wednesday was dedicated to course familiarization and practice. Thursday was for practice and qualifying. Friday, Saturday and Sunday were race days. Like all new events there were some problems with pylon locations, as they were in the rice paddies around the airport, and accessibility. Nine Texans showed up to race, qualifying times are not recorded. Those entered were #22 Mary Dilda, #5 Joey Sanders, #90 Gene McNeely, #68 Michael Gillian, #87 Richard Siegfried, rookie #8 Robin Crandall, #12 John Zayac, and #21 Tom Campau. Due to bad weather around the country, there were several racers who entered but did not make it to the races, including #30 Jim Eberhardt, #77 Jim Good, #20 Paul Redlich, and #89 Fred Telling. The racecourse was five miles with six laps per race.

Heat-1A results were #22 Mary Dilda first in 8:33.20mins at 188.698mph, second #5 Joey Sanders at 188.368mph, third #90 Gen McNeely at 186.791mph, fourth #68 Michael Gillian at 175.089mph, fifth #87 Richard Siegfried at 175.0892mph, and sixth rookie #8 Robin Crandall in 9:44.34mins at 171.599mph.

The Silver Heat results were #5 Sanders first at 184.774mph, second #90 McNeely at 184.753mph, third #12 Zayac at 181.124mph, fourth #87 Siegfried at 179.563mph, fifth #68 Gillian at 178.744mph, and #8 Crandall sixth at 165.186mph.

The Gold Heat results show #22 Dilda first, second was #21 Campau (who had engine problems that were fixed by Mary Dilda loaning him parts), third #90 McNeely, fourth #5 Sanders, fifth #68 Gillian, and #12 Zayac was a DNS.

Sunday's Silver Race pitted three faster against two slower racers so it was a little lop-sided. Placing first was #5 Sanders at 191.614mph, second #90 McNeely at 191.592mph, third #12 Zayac at 181.130 (including a 12-second penalty for cutting pylon 5 on lap 6), fourth #68 Gillian at 179.491mph, and fifth #8 Robin Crandall at 172.681mph in his only Texan race. His #8 Texan had been assigned #62 in 1969 but does not appear to have been raced.

The Gold Race had Sanders, McNeely and Gillian bumped up to have five racers in the race. From the start it was only #21 Campau and #22 Dilda hard charging with everyone else racing behind. At the finish it was #21 Campau first at 216.794mph, second Dilda at 215.811mph, third #5 Sanders at 191.614mph, fourth #90 McNeely at 191.592mph, and fifth was #68 Gillian at 180.202mph and 36mph slower than first place. Tom Campau had won using the parts that had been loaned to him by Mary Dilda.

TARA announced the races a success and had "high hopes" for further racing at Tunica in 2006. Unfortunately, 2005 would be the only year races were held there.

2005 Reno would see the return of a racing legend and the anticipation of a hot fight between four Gold Race winners. Twenty-one were entered and 19 would race. Those not racing were #1 Jason Somers (an F-1 and Biplane racer) who qualified at 197.038mph and #11 Carter Clark with a qualifying time of 206.328mph. The first ten qualifiers were: first #75 Al Goss at 237.403mph, #22 Mary Dilda at 236.940mph, #6 Nick Macy at 233.901mph, #21 Tom Campau at 233.451mph after a year away, #77 Jim Good at 224.172mph, #9 Bud Granley at 219.360mph, #5 Joey Sanders at 219.141mph, #44 Wayne Cartwright at 218.747mph, #90 Gene McNeely at 218.660mph, and tenth was #89 Fred Telling at 218.354mph. Qualifying 11th was racing legend #4 Dennis Buehn, who last raced at Reno in 1986, at 217.443mph, then came #12 John Zayac at 216.755mph, #444 Jim Booth at 216.067mph, rookie #55 Gary Miller at 214.375mph, #64 Keith McMann at 213.914mph, rookie #42 Chris Rushing at 210.781mph in Charles Beck's 'old' #2, which last raced in 1993, #70 Jim Thomas at 208.849mph, #30 Jim Eberhardt at 208.570mph, and 19th was #69 Lee Oman at 208.413mph, returning after a few years away.

After the first lap of Heat-1C and everyone spread out, it was rookie #42 Rushing who took control and pushed out to lead. #64 McMann and #30 Eberhardt had a fine race going by lap 2 with #70 Thomas and rookie #55 Miller trailing. #444 Booth was trying to catch up. At the end, it was #42 Rushing in first at 209.169mph followed by second and third #30 Eberhardt and #64 McMann with almost identical speeds of 205.596mph to 205.561mph. In fourth place was #70 Thomas at 202.153mph. Rookie #55 was fifth at 197.625mph with a ten second penalty for cutting pylon middle 3 on the pace lap. Booth was disqualified by the T-6 Safety Committee and Board of Directors for unsafe flying and would not race the rest of the week.

A great two-part race was Heat-1B, which featured #44 Cartwright and #5 Sanders wing-to-wing in part one for first place. Part two of the race was between #90 McNeely and #12 Zayac wing-to-wing for fourth. #4 Buehn was sandwiched between McNeely and Zayac in third position. #89 Telling was flying alone in sixth. At the finish it was Cartwright first in 6:59.008mins, Sanders second in 6:59.050mins, Buehn stayed in third in 7:05.617mins, Zayac got around McNeely for fourth with 7:06.242mins to 7:06.884 and Telling in sixth was not far behind with 7:08.650mins.

Record setting in a Heat Race is unusual, but when the Heat Race contains four Gold winners it can happen. Heat-1A was blisteringly fast from the first lap. It was formation flying for #75 Goss and #22 Dilda and #6 Macy only a yard or two back. #21 Campau had no trouble staying ahead of #77 Good. #9 Granley was unable to catch those in front of him. Still seemingly glued together Goss took first at 239.865mph setting a new Texan class record. In second place was Dilda at 239.424mph. Macy was third at 235.026mph and in fourth was Campau at 229.832mph with a sour engine. Fifth place went to Good at 218.555mph and in sixth was #9 Granley at 214.909mph.

Heat-2C was a race for the front by the two rookies #55 Miller and #42 Rushing. Behind them were #64 McMann, #70 Thomas and #30 Eberhardt enjoying their own race. #69 Oman tried several charges at those ahead of him but could not close the gap. They finished Miller first, Rushing second, McMann third, Thomas fourth, Eberhardt fifth, and Oman sixth. The time for first was 7:10.650mins and sixth was 7:33.967mins.

From the start of Heat-2B, it was #5 Sanders challenging #44 Cartwright for the lead. #89 Telling briefly held onto Sanders before falling back to defend against a closing #4 Buehn. A strong fight was going on for fifth at the back between #12 Zayac and #90 McNeely. Throughout the five laps, Cartwright countered every move Sanders made and hung on to take first 0.20secs ahead of Sanders in second place, their times being 6:57.476mins and 6:57.859mins, respectively. Third was Telling in 7:05.784mins, fourth Buehn in 7:08.934mins, fifth Zayac in 7:10.192mins, and back in sixth was McNeely in 7:10.517mins.

Heat-2A was a repeat of 2004, only with the addition of two new players. It was again #75 Goss and #22 Dilda tied to each other's wing. #6 Macy was right behind, followed by #21 Campau, #77 Good and #9 Granley. No one was giving an inch to the others. Goss hugged the inside and Dilda flew a little high looking for her chance to find a gap between Goss and any pylon. Macy had no trouble staying ahead of Campau, who was having engine problems. Old friends Good and Granley put on a good race at the back. On the last lap, Dilda made her move, but it was too late, and Goss took the checkered flag 0.20secs ahead. Speeds were again close, Goss first at 237.424mph, Dilda second at 237.388mph, Macy third at 233.442mph, Campau fourth at 229.900mph, Good fifth at 219.405mph, and sixth Granley at 214.606mph.

The Bronze Race featured the same players as Heat-2C but was faster with more overtaking and passing. Both rookies #42 Rushing and #55 Miller took the lead at the start and pushed each other until the final flag. #64 McMann and #30 Eberhardt fought for third and #70 Thomas stayed away from #69 Oman. Winning speeds were: #42 Rushing with his first Bronze in his rookie year at 216.675mph, second #55 Miller at 215.511mph, #64 McMann kept #30 Eberhardt back and took third at 206.652mph to fourth place Eberhardt's 206.002mph. Theirs was a very close race. Fifth went to #70 Thomas at 205.345mph and sixth Oman at 204.795mph.

Sometimes a race can be won in just the length of an aircraft and the Silver Race was like that for all six contestants. It was again a front race between #44 Cartwright and #5 Sanders with a little push to both by #89 Telling. #4 Buehn, #90 McNeely and #12 Zayac raced as a pack for fourth. Sanders gained 0.30secs lead by lap 5 and held off a last lap charge by Cartwright. At the flag it was #5 Sanders in 6:52.250mins and at 221.135mph in his first win in only his second year of racing. Cartwright took second in 6:52.467mins and at 221.018mph. In third place was #89 Telling in 6:53.933mins and at 220.235mph. Those at the back finished within tenths of a mph of each other. #12 Zayac took fourth at 212.596mph, #90 McNeely fifth at 212.509mph, and #4 Buehn sixth at 212.459mph. A note at the bottom of the RARA race result sheet states, "#42 Rushing removed from race results by T-6 Class Safety Committee." The only explanation would be that with his Bronze win, he was bumped into the Silver, then taken out to keep the field at six racers.

#75 Goss had the lead at the start of the six-lap Gold. #22 Dilda and #6 Macy had other ideas as both pushed Goss hard and hoped for an opening to get under or around him. By end of lap 1, Macy fell back a little and Goss seemed to slow out of his turn at pylon 7, giving Dilda the opening she needed. She swung wide around Goss at the end of lap 1 and never looked back. Meanwhile, #21 Campau[27] was nursing a sour engine while keeping #77 Good off his tail. #9 Granley didn't put up a strong challenge to Good and would finish sixth. Dilda crossed the line about seven seconds ahead of #75 Goss to take her second Gold win at 237.180mph. Goss was second at 233.659mph. Macy was third at 231.040mph, #21 Campau kept fourth place at 227.221mph, and #77 Good was fifth at 216.728mph.

Mary Dilda had paid attention and won her crown back.

2006

Twenty-two pilots entered and 22 qualified, however #1 Jason Somes did not race after qualifying 22nd at 195.977mph, the only one under 200mph. With the large number of racers each race would have seven contestants, except the Silver and Gold with eight each. #22 Mary Dilda sat out the races.

Top ten qualifiers were: #75 Al Goss at 237.558mph, #6 Nick Macy at 235.816mph, #43 Dennis Buehn at 228.095mph in a Texan he raced in 2005 as #4, #37 Zayac at 226.303mph in a Texan last raced at Reno in 1975 as #72, #90 Gene

---

27 On the way home from Reno, #21 Tom Campau had a complete engine failure when two cylinders let go and the engine seized. He had to belly land in a cornfield causing significant damage. Texan #21 made it home on the back of a truck.

McNeely at 225.698mph, #21 Rick Siegfried at 222.892mph in a Texan rebuilt from the 2005 accident and with a new owner, #77 Jim Good at 220.022mph, #9 Bud Granley at 219.757mph, #444 Jim Booth at 219.141mph, and rookie #8 Ken Gottschall at 218.485mph in a plane last raced by Robert Jones in 2000. Eleventh through 21st qualifiers were: #5 Joey Sanders at 217.313mph, #44 Wayne Cartwright at 215.558mph, #55 Gary Miller at 215.177mph, #64 Keith McMann at 215.093mph, #70 Jim Thomas at 214.710mph, #20 Paul Redlich at 214.667mph, #42 Chris Rushing at 214.501mph, #30 Jim Eberhardt at 210.577mph, #12 Tom Martin at 209.970mph in John Zayac's Texan, #69 Lee Oman at 207.580mph, and #68 Michael Gillian at 205.477mph was last.

Heat-1C 5 was won by #70 Thomas at 218.874mph, second #20 Redlich at 218.638mph, third #42 Rushing at 216.145mph, fourth #30 Eberhardt at 210.895mph, fifth #69 Oman at 210.379mph, sixth #12 Martin at 207.845mph, and seventh #68 Gillian at 201.699mph.

Heat-1B had #9 Granley first at 218.541mph, second #5 Sanders at 212.931mph, third #444 Booth at 212.761mph, fourth rookie #8 Gottschall at 212.369mph, fifth #44 Cartwright at 210.915mph, sixth #55 Miller at 210.878mph, and seventh #64 McMann at 208.126mph.

Heat-1A results were #75 Goss first at 232.623mph, second #6 Macy at 231.814mph, third #90 McNeely at 219.058mph, fourth #21 Siegfried at 216.060mph, and fifth #77 Jim Good at 213.554mph. #37 Zayac was unable to start and #43 Buehn was disqualified by the Contest Committee for low flying.

The Heat-2C winners were #20 Redlich first in 7:03.683mins, #70 Thomas was second in 7:05.059mins, #42 Rushing third in 7:08.667mins, #30 Eberhardt fourth in 7:17.317mins, #69 Oman fifth in 7:19.900mins, #68 Gillian sixth in 7:38.666mins, and #12 Martin seventh in 8:18.400mins.

Heat-2B places stood as #5 Sanders first at 215.007mph, #9 Granley second at 214.253mph, #444 Booth third at 211.021mph, #44 Cartwright fourth at 210.291mph, #8 Gottschall fifth at 210.289mph, #55 Miller sixth at 208.102mph, and #64 McMann seventh at 204.960mph.

Heat-2A would have only six racers, as #75 Goss had engine problems after taking off and was forced to return before the race started and was a DNS. His crew found metal in the oil putting him out of the races. This left #6 Macy to take the win at 234.347mph. In second place was #43 Buehn at 228.135mph, #90 McNeely third at 220.889mph, #77 Good fourth at 216.638mph, #21 Siegfried fifth at 216.162mph, and #37 Zayac was sixth at 194.917mph.

The Bronze Race went to #20 Redlich in his second year at Reno with a winning speed of 219.665mph. In second place was #42 Rushing at 217.123mph. He was followed by third #70 Thomas at 212.183mph, fourth #30 Eberhardt at 205.936mph, fifth #12 Martin at 203.360mph, sixth #69 Oman at 202.971mph, and seventh #68 Gillian at 197.223mph.

The Silver Race with eight contestants had third-year racer #5 Sanders take his second Silver Race in a row at 221.717mph. #9 Granley placed second at 218.966mph and this would be Granley's last race for a few years. Third place went to #444 Booth at 215.296mph. Booth was followed by rookie #8 Gottschallin fourth at 215.190mph, fifth was the Bronze Race winner #20 Redlich at 213.739mph, sixth #55 Miller at 213.621mph, #64 McMann seventh at 212.876mph, and eighth #44 Cartwright at 211.709mph.

Sunday's Gold Race had eight contestants; however, #75 Goss was a DNS. First place went to #6 Macy at 235.609mph making this his fourth Gold win. In second was #43 Buehn at 229.100mph. #90 McNeely was third at 222.926mph, #37 Zayac was fourth at 221.060mph, #5 Sanders was fifth at 218.674mph, #77 Good sixth at 218.587mph, and #21 Siegfried seventh at 215.848mph.

Macy proved he still had king-making powers.

2007

This would be another tragic year for Reno, with three fatal injury crashes in race week. The accidents took place on three separate days and the pilots were #3 Steve Dari in the Biplane Class, #4 Brad Morehouse in the Jet Class, and #95 Gary Hubler in the F-1 Class. Hubler had raced Texan #57 at Reno in 1998. For the Texan races, there were 23 entrants, 19 qualifiers and 21 racers. Those entered but not qualifying or racing were #21 Richard Siegfried, #33 Dennis Buehn who qualified in another Texan, and #55 Gary Miller.

Second place 2006 Gold winner #43 Dennis Buehn was the top qualifier at 237.939mph for his one lap of the 5.0646-mile course. A spilt second behind was #75 Al Goss at 237.011mph followed by #22 Mary Dilda in third at 234.671mph, and #6 Nick Macy in fourth at 233.718mph. Fifth through tenth were #2 Ken Dwelle back after a few years off at 231.049mph, #37 John Zayac at 230.125mph, #90 Gene McNeely at 226.734mph, #5 Joey Sanders at 226.123mph, #9 veteran Tom Dwelle, Sr. at 224.916 (he lasted raced Texans at Reno in 1997), #8 Ken Gottschall at 221.856mph in tenth. Eleventh through 20 were #89 Fred Telling at 218.004mph, #44 Wayne Cartwright at 215.681mph, #64 Keith McMann at 214.665mph, rookie #88 Doug Dotter at 213.324mph (this Texan had been raced as #2 Charles Beck and #42 Chris Rushing), rookie #28 John Lohmar at 213.032mph (this Texan had raced as #20 John Luther and #26 by Linda Finch), #70 Jim Thomas at 210.732mph, #30 Jim Eberhardt at 210.448mph, #50 John Krawczyk at 210.409mph (returning after last racing in 1997; his Texan had raced Mojave 1975 as #2 Dennis Buehn), #69 Lee Oman at 201.969mph, and 20th was #11 Carter Clark at 201.634mph. Veteran #77 Jim Good did not qualify, but raced.

The first race was Heat-1C and it had two DNSs, #11 Clark and #77 Good. It was a smart race from start to finish with the competition being for second place. Rookie #28 Lohmar shot out front leaving #50 Krawczyk, #70 Thomas and #30 Jim Eberhardt to fight for second, while #69 Oman remained in fifth. At the flag it was #28 Lohmar first with 6:57.367mins, second was #30 Eberhardt in 7:06.577mins, #70 Thomas in 7:06.643mins third, #50 Krawczyk fourth in 7:08.846mins, and #69 Oman fifth in 7:17.788mins. #11 Clark would not race due to an accident when another aircraft taxied into his tail, shredding his rudder and left horizontal stabilizer.

Proving he had not lost any skills during his time away from Texan racing, #7 Dwelle, Sr., who had been racing in the Unlimited Class, cruised to an easy win in Heat-1B at 225.267mph. Dwelle, Sr. was followed by #5 Sanders at 219.331mph, #8 Gottschall was third at 218.201mph, rookie #89 Jerry Borchin was fourth at 216.117mph (in his only race, flying Fred Telling's Texan), fifth was #44 Cartwright at 212.515mph, sixth #64 McMann at 207.788mph, and seventh rookie #88 Dotter at 203.930mph.

First race for the top qualifiers was Heat-1A. It was a great show by four-time Gold winner #6 Macy, racing legend #43 Buehn, Gold winner #75 Goss, two-time Gold winner #22 Dilda, #90 McNeely, #37 Zayac, and #2 Ken Dwelle. From the start it was Macy, Buehn and Goss, with Dilda about one-quarter of a lap back. Zayac, Dwelle and McNeely were having a go at each other by lap 2. At the front, Macy still had the lead with Buehn closing every one-half lap while Goss and Dilda raced for third. Lap 4.5 saw Buehn pass Macy for the lead, and he stayed there to the finish. Buehn was first at 236.039mph, #6 Macy second at 235.774mph, third went to #75 Goss at 233.623mph, Dilda took fourth at 230.075mph, #2 Dwelle passed #37 Zayac on lap 4 to place fifth at 225.541mph, with Zayac sixth at 223.736, and #90 McNeely seventh at 222.483mph. The gap from first to seventh was just over 13.5mph.

Rookie #28 Lohmar took his second heat win in Heat-2C at about 2mph slower than his first win. Second place was #30 Eberhardt 7.5mph behind at 209.100mph, #70 Thomas third at 207.287mph, #50 Krawczyk was fourth at 206.997mph, fifth was #69 Oman at 203.032mph, #77 Good was sixth at 202.889mph, while #11 Clark was a DNS.

Heat-2B was canceled due to the crash of Gary Hubler. Those scheduled to race were rookie #88 Dotter, #64 McMann, #44 Cartwright, #89 Telling, #8 Gottschall, #5 Sanders, and #7 Dwelle, Sr.

Only a few miles per hour slower, Heat-2A featured the same pilots finishing in the same order as Heat-1A. First was #43 Buehn at 234.348mph, #6 Macy second at 234.258mph with a closer margin, #75 Goss third at 230.951mph, #22 Dilda at 229.020mph fourth, #2 Ken Dwelle fifth at 225.271mph, #37 Zayac sixth at 222.311mph, and #90 McNeely seventh at 220.771mph.

Taking his first Bronze Race was rookie #28 Lohmar at 217.027mph without a real challenge. Lohmar was followed by #30 Eberhardt second at 209.601mph and about 14 seconds back, third was #70 Thomas at 207.942mph, #50 Krawczyk fourth at 207.630mph, fifth #69 Oman at 205.051mph, #77 Good sixth at 204.989mph, and #11 Clark was again a DNS.

The competitors in the Silver Race made up for their missed Heat Race and went full bore. It was a fine race with #5 Sanders going for his third consecutive Silver win. He was challenged from the start by 1990 Gold winner #7 Dwelle, Sr. #89 Telling chased both for half the race and #8 Gottschall hung on briefly to Telling. #44 Cartwright, #88 Dotter and #64 McMann had a good tussle for fifth. Sanders tried hard but could not catch Dwelle, Sr., who took first by just over 10 seconds ahead of Sanders. This would be #7 Dwelle, Sr.'s first Silver win and his last Texan race at Reno. #5 Sanders stayed ahead of Telling for a full second at 221.145mph. Telling who placed third at 220.290mph never let up and had there been one more lap might have caught Sanders. Fourth was #8 Gottschall at 217.182mph, #44 Cartwright fifth at 213.307mph, #64 McMann sixth at 212.556mph and, after cutting pylon 1 on lap 1, was seventh place #88 Dotter at 211.706mph.

There was no doubt that the Gold Race would be between #43 Buehn and #6 Macy, who was going for his fifth Gold. #75 Goss looked for his second Gold with #22 Dilda thrown into the middle. This left #2 Dwelle, #37 Zayac, and #90 McNeely to race among themselves and stay out of the way of the front runners. By lap 2, Buehn had half a plane length over Macy, with Goss and Dilda falling back with no hope of catching Macy or Buehn. Macy was not about to give up, but neither was Buehn as he wanted his first Reno Gold and he pulled ahead. At the flag, Buehn had almost a one-half lap over Macy. Winning times and speeds were #43 Buehn in 7:45.632mins at 234.940mph for first, and #6 Macy in 7:46.900mins at 234.301mph in second. Macy was followed by #75 Goss in 7:53.665mins at 230.955mph in third, #22 Dilda fourth in 8:02.966mins at 226.507mph, #2 Dwelle in 8:08.372mins at 224.000mph placing fifth, #37 Zayac in 8:18.624mins at 219.394mph sixth. and #90 McNeely in 8:19.950mins at 218.813mph. There was a 16mph difference from first to last.

After racing at Reno since 1973, Dennis Buehn had his first Gold win.

2008

Race week started off on a sad note as F-1 rookie Erica Simpson was killed during practice. There were 23 entered, 21 qualified and 23 pilots raced. Those entered but not qualified were #1 Carter Clark, as he would race another Texan, and #92 Larry Tueber. The top qualifier was #6 Nick Macy at 243.083mph, trying for his fifth Gold. Taking second was #7 Ken Dwelle at 239.203mph. He was followed by #37 John Zayac at 238.836mph, #75 Al Goss at 237.540mph, #43 Dennis Buehn at 236.616mph (he would qualify but not race), #90 Gene McNeely at 234.385mph, #89 Fred Telling at 227.181mph, #28 John Lohmar at 225.447mph, #42 Chris Rushing at 222.650mph, and tenth #8 Ken Gottschall at 221.611mph. Eleventh through 18th were #77 Jim Good at 220.674mph, #64 Keith McMann at 220.184mph, #5 Joey Sanders at 219.654mph, #21 Gary Miller at 219.568mph (this would be #21's last race as it was W/O in a fatal accident with another pilot in July 2009), rookie #94 Adrianus Clermont at 219.126mph (this Texan has raced since 1986 under other numbers and pilots), #70 Jim Thomas at 281.735mph, #50 John Krawczyk at 216.825mph, and rookie #66 Vic McMann at 215.626mph. Vic McMann is the younger brother of #64 Keith McMann. In 19th place was #30 Jim Eberhardt at 211.172mph, then #69 Lee Oman at 206.781mph, and twenty-first went to rookie #56 Scott Dockter at 203.133mph.

Heat-1C was won by rookie #94 Clermont at 219.319mph. In second place was #50 Krawczyk at 215.622mph, #70 Thomas was third at 212.283mph, #66 Vic McMann placed fourth at 211.864mph, #30 Eberhardt fifth at 209.466mph, #69 Oman sixth at 206.875mph, and #56 Dockter was seventh with 203.940mph.

Heat-1B was won by #28 Lohmar in first with 225.225mph. In second place was #42 Rushing at 220.126mph, third #8 Gottschall at 219.552mph, #21 Miller was fourth at 219.165mph, #77 Good was fifth at 217.799mph, sixth was #5 Sanders at 217.712mph, and #64 Keith McMann placed seventh at 211.536mph.

#6 Macy placed first in Heat-1A at 236.887mph. He was followed in second place by #7 Dwelle at 236.411mph, #75 Goss at 232.264mph in third, #43 Clark in fourth at 228.057mph flying Dennis Buehn's Texan, fifth went to #37 Zayac at 227.999mph, in sixth was #90 McNeely at 223.806mph, and rookie #89 Duane Woods placed seventh at 223.719mph in Fred Telling's Texan.

The top four finishers from Heat-1C exchanged places for Heat-2C. #50 Krawczyk was first at 217.254mph, #94 Clermont second at 216.254mph, #66 Vic McMann third at 211.442mph, #70 Thomas fourth at 209.920mph, fifth #30 Eberhardt at 207.472mph, sixth #69 Oman at 203.963mph, and seventh went to #56 Dockter at 203.111mph.

In Heat-2B, #28 Lohmar won his second Heat Race for the week at 219.332. He was followed by #8 Gottschall in second at 214.070mph, third was #77 Good at 211.724mph, fourth #5 Sanders at 209.707mph, Rick Siegfried replaced Gary Miller in #21 to take fifth at 208.476mph, #42 Rushing was sixth at 205.179mph, and #64 Keith McMann was seventh at 204.577mph.

Heat-2A was won by #6 Macy at 239.654mph, #75 Goss second at 236.044mph, #37 Zayac third at 230.814mph, fourth was #7 Dwelle at 227.608mph plus a 20-second penalty for cutting middle pylon 2 on lap 2 and middle pylon 3 on lap 3. #90 McNeely was fifth at 223.879mph, #89 Telling was sixth at 223.659mph, and in seventh was #43 Clark at 191.132mph. Clark received a 90-second penalty for cutting middle pylon 2 on laps 4 and 5, middle pylon 3 on laps 4 and 5, middle pylon 3 on laps 4 and 5, and middle pylon 1 on laps 3, 4 and 5. This may be a record for pylon cuts.

Saturday's six-lap Bronze Race was a close race between #50 Krawczyk in first at 214.984mph and rookie #94 Clermont in second place at 214.942mph. They were followed by #66 Vic McMann in third at 211.840mph, in fourth #70 Thomas at 210.212mph, #30 Eberhardt at 209.154mph in fifth, #69 Oman at 204.609mph, and #56 Dockter in seventh at 203.474mph.

With #28 Lohmar winning both his Heat races, his win of the Silver Race at 224.101mph capped off a great week for him. Second place was #8 Gottschall at 221.567mph, #77 Good was third at 219.294mph, fourth #5 Sanders at 219.177mph, fifth was #21 Siegfried at 218.873mph, sixth #42 Rushing at 215.040mph, and seventh was #64 McMann at 211.560mph.

#7 Ken Dwelle set a new speed record with his Gold Race win at 244.523mph. This was his first Gold and his last Texan race. In second place was #75 Goss further back at 237.855mph. In third was #37 Zayac at 234.142mph. Fourth place went to #90 McNeely at 230.556mph. #89 Telling was fifth with 227.515mph in his last Texan race. #43 Clark was sixth at 227.295mph and four-time Gold winner #6 Macy was a DNF, having pulled out of the race with a broken prop shaft.

This year would mark the end of the Dwelle family's Texan racing career. It was nice to end it with a Gold crown.

2009

Nineteen Texans were entered and qualified, with 17 pilots qualifying and 18 racing. Once again #6 Nick Macy was top qualifier at 239.350mph. Macy was followed by: #43 Dennis Buehn at 238.968mph, #75 Al Goss at 234.814mph, #37 John Zayac at 230.106mph, fifth was #90 Gene McNeely at 228.218mph, #28 John Lohmar at 227.006mph, #5 Joey Sanders at 226.780mph, #56 Scott Dockter at 222.408mph in Ralph Rina's #73, #8 Ken Gottschall at 222.286mph and in tenth place #77 Jim Good at 220.138mph. Eleventh through 19 qualifiers were #42 Chris Rushing at 219.339mph, #50 John Krawczyk at 281.447mph, #64 Keith McMann at 215.483mph, #94 Nick Macy at 214.291mph in a Texan raced by Ott Clermont in 2008, #66 Bud Granley at 213.522mph (he qualified this Texan for Vic McMann who would do the racing), #30 Jim Eberhardt at 209.875mph, #69 Lee Oman at 204.017mph, #26 Jim Thomas at 202.840mph in a new unraced Texan, and in 19th place was #57 Scott Dockter in his regular Texan at 193.374mph. This Texan raced as #56 in 2008.

Heat-1C had #94 Macy first in his new Texan at 219.888mph, almost 20mph slower than he usually raced. In second was #66 Vic McMann at 208.524mph, in the first race in which the McMann brothers would race against each other. #30 Eberhardt placed third at 207.730mph, #69 Oman fourth at 198.630mph, #26 Thomas fifth in his new Texan at 198.550mph, sixth #57 Dockter at 196.151mph, and #64 Keith McMann was a DNF with sour engine.

Moving up a notch in speed saw #8 Gottschall win Heat-1B at 226.103mph, with second place #5 Sanders at 224.309mph with a ten-second penalty for cutting pylon 3 on lap 2. In third place was #77 Good with 224.196mph, #56 Dockter was fourth at 219.576mph, fifth was #42 Rushing at 219.549mph, and sixth #50 Krawczyk at 218.102mph.

Heat-1A had five contestants for the five-lap race as #37 Zayac was a DNS. The heat was won by #6 Macy at 241.094mph with second going to #43 Buehn at 235.442mph. #75 Goss third at 235.367mph. #28 Lohmar placed fourth at 223.972mph. #90 McNeely was given a ten-second penalty for cutting pylon 4 on lap 1 followed by a disqualifying penalty by the Race Safety Committee for unsafe flying.

The five-lap Heat-2C Race was back to seven contestants with #94 Macy again taking first at 219.787mph. Following Macy were: #66 Vic McMann second at 212.065mph, #30 Eberhardt at 209.391mph, after repairs #64 Keith McMann fourth at 209.336mph, #69 Oman fifth at 199.653mph, #26 Thomas sixth at 199.573mph, and seventh #57 Dockter at 198.907mph. This was some close racing.

From the times and speeds posted for Heat-2B, there had been a smart race between first-place finisher #8 Gottschall in 6:49.348mins and at 222.909mph and second place #5 Sanders with 6:49.725mins and at 222.704mph, #77 Good was third at 218.593mph, and #56 Dockter fourth at 218.185mph. These two Texans raced against each other a number of times during the days of the battles of the two Ralphs. In fifth place was #42 Rushing at 215.303mph, and #50 Krawczyk sixth at 214.770mph. Texan #5 (former #25), #56 (former #73), and #77 (former #41) had all raced against each other for the first time at Reno in 1973.

For the fastest qualifiers, Heat-2A was a good work-up for the Gold on Sunday as #6 Macy took first at 236.749mph, #43 Buehn second at 231.636mph, #75 Goss third at 231.636mph, fourth #28 Lohmar at 224.093mph, #37 Zayac fifth at 224.012mph, and #90 McNeely at 219.677mph.

There was a sizable spread between first and seventh for the Bronze Race with #94 Macy first at 215.512mph and seventh #57 Dockter at 197.136mph. This was like racing in the 1970s. Second through sixth winners were #66 Vic McMann at 207.376mph, #64 Keith McMann third at 207.369mph, #30 Eberhardt fourth at 206.169mph, #69 Oman fifth at 200.437mph, #26 Thomas was sixth at 197.267mph, this would be his last Texan race. After the race, #94 Macy forfeited the win so as to move up to the Silver Race. This moved everyone up a spot, giving #66 Vic McMann the Bronze win and his brother second place.

Macy's move up from the Bronze was for naught in the Silver, as it was a race between #8 Gottschall and #5 Sanders. Posting 8:01.344mins and 227.482mph for the six-lap race for first was #8 Gottschall, with #5 Sanders second place 8:01.514mins and 227.401mph. #42 Rushing was third at 220.132mph, #77 Good fourth at 219.358mph in his last Reno race, fifth went to #50 Krawczyk at 217.732mph, sixth went to #56 Dockter at 217.056mph, and former Bronze winner #94 Macy was seventh at 216.625mph.

#6 Macy made up for the Silver by taking first in the Gold in 7:40.928mins and 237.557mph. Second place was #75 Goss in 7:45.678mins at 235.134mph. In third was #43 Buehn in 7:53.614mins at 231.194mph, fourth #28 Lohmar in 8:02.910mins at 226.744mph, fifth #37 Zayac in 8:03.116mins at 226.647mph, and #90 McNeely sixth in 8:04.107mins at 226.183mph.

This was #6 Nick Macy's fifth Gold win.

2010

Reno started off with a gloom as veteran racer #75 Al Goss had been killed in a non-racing accident in March, a real hard charger who is missed. Seventeen Texans entered, and 18 pilots raced, with #6 Nick Macy being the top qualifier and setting a new qualifying speed record of 1:14.628mins and 244.539mph for his one lap of the 5.0693-mile course. #43 Dennis Buehn was second with 1:17.291mins and 236.114mph, #37 John Zayac third at 233.444mph, followed in order by #66 Vic McMann 227.806mph, #88 John Lohmar 227.029mph in a Texan renumbered from #28 to #88, #5 Sanders at 225.670mph, #50 John Krawczyk at 224.961mph, #42 Chris Rushing at 224.775mph, #64 Keith McMann at 224.620mph, #56 Duane Woods was tenth at 224.385mph. Eleventh through 18th were #8 Ken Gottschall at 223.604mph, #90 Lee Oman at 222.021mph flying Gene McNeely's Texan as Gene would sit this year out, #94 Rick Siegfried at 216.224mph, #33 Carter Clark at 213.156mph, #57 Scott Dockter at 210.204mph, #30 Jim Eberhardt at 208.396mph, #1 Carter Clark at 205.242mph in his original Texan, and #69 Wayne Cartwright at 203.115mph. This Texan was entered by Lee Oman with Cartwright qualifying and Oman racing. This would be Cartwright's last Reno race.

The first race was a little lop-sided Heat-1C with #94 Siegfried and #33 Clark greatly outdistancing the rest of the field from the start with both staying close to the end. #57 Dockter and #30 Eberhardt challenged each other for third while #69 Oman flew back in fifth. At the flag, it was #94 Siegfried in first at 223.515mph, #33 Clark second at 220.425mph, #57 Dockter stayed ahead of #30 Eberhardt for third with 214.559mph to Eberhardt's 213.916mph, fifth was #69 Oman at 208.309mph, while Krawczyk in Clark's #1 was a DNS.

Krawczyk made up for his previous DNS by winning Heat-1B at 224.648mph with #42 Rushing just under 2mph slower in second at 222.951mph. They were followed closely by #56 Woods at 222.571mph in third, #90 Oman fourth at 222.254mph, fifth was #64 McMann 216.572mph, and sixth #8 Gottschall at 216.409mph. This was a good race.

Heat-1A saw Gold winner #6 Macy pull out at the end of lap 1 with a burned piston, leaving the fight between #37 Zayac and #43 Buehn, with #88 Lohmar chasing both. #5 Sanders and #66 McMann were further back about 8mph slower. #43 Buehn had the edge and passed Zayac, taking first with 237.904mph to Zayac's 231.128mph. #88 Lohmar held off #5 Sanders for third at 226.478mph to fourth place Sanders' 218.858mph, and #66 McMann coasted to fifth with 216.203mph, perhaps saving his engine for the next heat and a chance in the Gold.

Heat-2C was a repeat of Heat-1A, only slightly slower, with all six contestants finishing in the same order. In first was #94 Siegfried at 221.410mph, #33 Clark second at 217.919mph, third #57 Dockter at 213.629mph, #30 Eberhardt fourth at 212.198mph, fifth #69 Oman 206.792mph, and sixth #1 Krawczyk at 206.671mph. Even though it seemed to be the same race as before, Texan racing is never boring as this kind of challenge highlights how much skill is required to race equal configured aircraft against each other.

#90 Oman seemed to like his new mount better than his regular #69 as he kept #90's nose right on #50 Krawczyk's wingtip for the entire Heat-2B Race. By the end of lap 4, they were only tenths of a mile per hour apart with #42 Rushing pushing both, but unable to catch them. The finishing times tell it all. First was #50 Krawczyk in 6:48.215mins, second #90 Oman in 6:48.710mins, third #42 Rushing in 6:50.905mins, then came #8 Gottschall fourth in 6:55.192mins, fifth #64 McMann in 7:07.015mins, and sixth was #56 Woods in 7:07.842mins.

No one could guess how the outcome of Heat-2A would affect the Championship Race. Macy had repaired the engine in #6 but was unable to keep up with the rest at the start. It was #43 Buehn at the start down the chute for the first pylon turn with #37 Zayac, #88 Lohmar and Macy behind. #5 Sanders was just behind the front group, with #66 McMann half a plane length back. Buehn continued to pull ahead and at the finish he was first, flying over 6mph faster than second place #37 Zayac at 234.927mph. In third was #88 Lohmar at 234.237mph. #6 Macy was next but was disqualified for crossing the deadline at the start and had his time wiped. This gave #5 Sanders fourth place at 223.894mph and #66 McMann fifth at 222.565mph.

#94 Siegfried took the win in the Bronze Race as he had in his two heat races at a speed of 224.475mph. He was again followed by #33 Clark second at 219.475mph, #57 Dockter third at 216.817mph, #30 Eberhardt fourth at 214.411mph, fifth #69 Oman at 210.640mph, and #1 Krawczyk sixth at 210.551mph.

The six-lap Silver Race started at 10:22am on Sunday, with the winds picking up after a beautiful week. Siegfried was bumped up to the Silver Race with his winning of the Bronze Race, so there were seven starters. From the pylon 1 turn, it was a race between #42 Rushing, #90 Oman and #50 Krawczyk. Rushing fell back on lap 3 to race against #8 Gottschall and #56 Woods, leaving Oman and Krawczyk to themselves. By lap 5, Oman was a plane length ahead and by the end of the lap had added another one-half length. The fight was in the middle for third with Rushing just able to stay ahead until the flag. At the finish it was #90 Oman first at 228.139mph, #50 Krawczyk second at 226.514mph, and third #42 Rushing at 222.881mph. Close behind at 222.372 was #8 Gottschall and in fifth was #56 Woods at 222.300mph. Placing sixth was #64 McMann with 216.973mph and seventh place was #94 Siegfried at 216.614mph. Oman forfeited his win to move into the Gold giving the Silver win to #50 Krawczyk.

By the time the Texan Gold Race was to start, the winds were 35mph, well over the safety limit. With both the Texan and Unlimited pilots in agreement, the final Gold races for both classes were canceled. Under the rules, the winners and placements of Heat-2A for both classes would be declared the final results for the Gold races. This gave #43 Buehn the Gold title win with #37 Zayac second, #88 Lohmar third, #5 Sanders fourth, #66 McMann fifth, #6 Macy sixth, and #90 Oman seventh.

Everyone agreed safety first.

2011

Reno 2011 would see the greatest tragedy in the history of air racing. An aircraft crashed into the stands, killing 10 and injuring 69 more. Texans were not involved, so presented are the results of racing up until the event was canceled.

There were 18 Texans entered with 17 qualifying and 17 pilots racing. Ralph Rina entered #73 but did not qualify or race. His original #73 was raced as #22 by Duane Woods. Top qualifier was #37 John Zayac at 240.248mph, followed by #43 Dennis Buehn at 239.989mph. #6 Nick Macy at 238.786mph was third. Fourth was #88 John Lohmar at 238.182mph. Fred Telling entered #89, but it would be qualified in fifth at 234.289mph and raced by Lee Oman. #90 Gene McNeely was back after a year away and qualified at 227.791mph placing sixth. Taking seventh was #22 Duane Woods with 225.083mph in a Texan raced the year before as #56. Eighth through 17th were #50 John Krawczyk at 224.684mph, #8 Ken Gottschall at 223.672mph, #66 Vic McMann at 222.650mph (his brother Keith would sit out this year), #5 Joey Sanders at 222.332mph, #33 had Rick Siegfried at the stick at 221.970mph, #42 Chris Rushing at 220.796mph, #94 had Michael Gillian returning with 215.817mph, #30 Jim Eberhardt at 207.202mph, #69 Lee Oman in his regular Texan at 205.635mph, and 17th was rookie #54 Michael Pfleger at 201.314mph.

Some fine racing took place in Heat-C with everyone giving a good show. #42 Rushing took first at 218.001mph. Second went to #94 Gillian at 214.454mph, having not lost his racing skills while away. In third was rookie #54 Pfleger at

In his first Reno Texan race in 2013, #78 Tom Baber taxies in, followed by #22 Chip Wood. While it was Baber's first race, #22 is the former #73 Texan that Ralph Rina first raced at Mojave and Reno in 1973. (Mike Henniger)

198.365mph. Fourth was taken by Oman in #69 at 198.037mph, while #5 Sanders was fifth at 197.037mph, and sixth went to #50 Krawczyk with 196.981mph.

Ralph Rina had to be proud of his old #73 as it took first place in Heat-1B flown by Woods as #22 and at 231.587mph. Woods was followed by #50 Krawczyk in second at 228.770mph. In third was #66 McMann at 227.891mph. #5 Sanders was fourth 227.106mph, followed by #33 Siegfried in fifth at 221.013, and #8 Gottschall, who finished sixth with a 30-second penalty for cutting pylon 5 three times.

Last race for the 15th was Heat-1A with the top qualifiers competing. The trio of #6 Macy, #43 Buehn and #37 Zayac grouped together until lap 2. By then, it was Buehn pulling away leaving Macy and Zayac battling for second, while Lohmar and Oman fought for fourth. At the flag it was #43 Buehn first, seven seconds ahead of #6 Macy, who was only 11/10ths of minute ahead of #37 Zayac in third. #88 Lohmar kept fourth at 226.682mph. Fifth place went to #89 Oman at 223.852mph. #90 McNeely was sixth at 217.452mph.

On Friday the 16th, the first Texan race was Heat-2C at 11:27am. It was #42 Rushing from start to finish as he had only a brief challenge from #94 Gillian. The final placement was: #42 Rushing at first 217.130mph, second #94 Gillian at 210.749mph, third #30 Eberhardt at 201.519mph, #54 Pfleger fourth at 198.506mph, #69 Clermont (for Oman) fifth at 198.216mph, and #50 Krawczyk sixth at 197.947mph.

Heat-2B set off at 1:10pm and was a smooth race easily won by #22 Duane Woods at 227.754mph. In second was #50 Krawczyk at 224.668mph. Third went to #66 McMann at 224.126mph, who had ridden Krawczyk the entire race but just could not gain the prop spinner length that separated them. In fourth was #5 Sanders at 220.428mph. Fifth went to #33 Siegfried at 219.928mph with #8 Gottschall sixth at 219.675mph.

Catastrophe struck at 4:26pm shortly after RARA made the right decision to cancel the remaining races. Would the races return?

2012

After much sorrow, hard work and, safety improvements, Reno 2012 happened. Changes made to the T-6 racecourse included fewer sharp turns and a slightly shorter course of 4.9657miles. This meant that during a five-lap race, contestants would fly a total of 24.8285 miles, and six-lap races would total 29.7942 miles. All classes made safety and briefing improvements.

Seventeen pilots were entered, 17 qualified and 18 raced. At 241.089mph, #6 Nick Macy was the top qualifier taking 1:14.149mins for his lap, while second-place qualifier #43 Dennis Buehn was 240.279mph and 1:14.399mins. Third through fifth were #37 John Zayac at 236.967mph, #88 John Lohmar at 234.397mph, #89 Lee Oman at 232.746mph, again qualifying Fred Telling's Texan. In sixth place, flying in a new Texan, was #14 Chris Rushing at 231.825. Rushing flew Richard Sykes' old #14. #90 Gene McNeely finished at 227.402mph as he shared racing duties with his rookie son Greg. Following McNeely were #50 John Krawczyk at 225.120mph, #9 Joey Sanders at 224.777mph, and #64 Keith McMann who was back at 220.458mph in tenth. Eleventh through 14th were #66 Vic McMann at 218.068mph and 1:20:997mins, rookie #33 Terry Adams at 217.009mph (he was third pilot to race #33 in three years), rookie #42 Rob Sandberg at 213.701mph competing in Charles Beck's old #2, and #73 legendary racer Ralph Rina at 212.426mph. Rina won his last Reno Gold Race in 1984 at 217.256mph. #54 Michael Pfleger finished 15th at 211.875mph, then #69 Lee Oman at 204.872mph, and 17th was rookie #59 Nathan Harnagel at 194.257mph and 1:32.025mins. This was Harnagel's only Texan event as he would move over to the Jet Class.

There might have been déjà vu during Heat-1C after rookie #42 Sandberg jumped into the lead ahead of Rina in #73. Rina had chased this Texan many times when Charles Beck raced it at Mojave and Reno in the 1970s. Sandberg and Rina had the race to themselves for four of the five laps. At the flag it was #42 Sandberg winning his first Heat Race at 208.553mph and #73 Rina second at 207.954mph. #54 Pfleger was third at 198.316mph, after a 10-second penalty for a pylon cut. Thirty seconds behind was #69 Oman in fourth at 185.969mph. Then came the other two rookies, #59 Harnagel fifth at 185.281mph and #90 Greg McNeely sixth at 185.141mph, almost one minute behind first place.

After a few years seemingly under the weather, #5 Sanders dominated Heat-1B with the win at 226.201mph. Second place finisher #90 Greg McNeely had a 10-second penalty for a pylon cut and came in at 221.008mph. #66 Vic McMann was third at 219.511mph to his fourth-place brother #64 Keith at 216.954mph, fifth was rookie #33 Adams at 215.181mph, and #50 Krawczyk was a DNS.

The weather was hot all week but #6 Macy's win in Heat-1A was blistering at 246.047mph. #43 Buehn was second at 243.866mph. They had walked away from everyone by lap 2. Their closest challenger was #88 Lohmar who tried to keep up, but fell back, and took third with 239.697mph. Fourth went to #89 Oman at 234.556mph, who had fought to keep #37 Zayac behind him for the entire five laps. Zayac finished fifth at 234.270mph and #14 Rushing was sixth at 229.572mph.

#90 Greg McNeely was a DNS for Heat-2C. #73 Rina again chased #42 Sandberg for four of the five laps before Sandberg crossed the line first for his second heat win at 221.657mph to Rina in second at 216.470mph. #54 Pfleger was third at 212.600mph. In fourth place was #69 Oman at 205.371mph and finishing fifth was #59 Harnagel at 195.251mph.

Heat-2B would see rookie #33 Adams as a DNS and #5 Sanders the winner at 232.219mph. Sanders was followed by second place #90 Gene McNeely six seconds back at 227.539mph. One second back, McNeely in third place was #66 Vic McMann at 227.411mph. Vic McMann was again ahead of his brother Keith in #64, who placed fourth at 220.801mph. #50 Krawczyk had solved his Heat-1B problems and finished fifth right behind #64 at 220.739mph.

#37 Zayac was a DNS for Heat-2A. This did not matter to #6 Macy or #43 Buehn who were locked in a fast fight for first. #14 Rushing, #88 Lohmar and #89 Oman fought their own race for third. Again, it was Macy first in 6:07.394mins to Buehn's 6:08.382mins in second place. #88 Lohmar took a charge at the front two but came up short and took third in 6:13.856mins. In fourth place was #89 Oman in 6:24.741mins and #14 Rushing in 6:30.480mins placed fifth.

The year 2012 would be a good one for rookie #42 Sandberg, as he swept both of his heat races and the Bronze Race (211.893mph), staying ahead of #73 Rina (208.095mph) for all three races. This was not a bad display from Rina either, since he had not raced since 1995. #90 Gene McNeely was a DNS and #54 Pfleger was third at 189.983mph. In fourth place was #69 Oman at 189.685mph and rookie #59 Harnagel was fifth at 187.953mph.

A rejuvenated #5 Sanders ran away from the pack to take his third Silver Race win at 228.151mph ahead of rookie #90 Greg McNeely in second at 223.360mph. This was a good showing in his rookie year. Third went to #66 Vic McMann at 220.013mph. In fourth place was #50 Krawczyk at 220.013mph. Following in fifth was #64 Keith McMann at 213.392mph and finally in sixth was rookie #33 Adams at 213.102mph. Sanders bumped up to the Gold Race with this win.

All things being equal in a Texan race, it comes down to position and skills to win. For winning the Gold, #43 Buehn had longevity skills and #6 Macy had position and winning skills. From the start, it was obvious that Macy and Buehn meant business, as they were tied together through lap 3 when Macy started inching ahead and Buehn fell back to hold off #88 Lohmar. Lap 4 saw #89 Oman overtake #14 Rushing while #5 Sanders flew at the back. #6 Macy blitzed across the finish to take his sixth Gold Race and set a new speed record at 247.317mph. Buehn held off Lohmar for second at 244.948mph. Lohmar was third at 243.887mph. #89 Oman took fourth at 235.156mph, #14 Rushing fifth at 234.475mph, and #5 Sanders sixth at 223.614mph.

Macy was now one Gold win away from tying with all-time champion #27 Eddie Van Fossen who earned seven Reno wins. Macy held hopes for a win in 2013.

2013

This was the 50th anniversary of air racing at Reno, but only the 43rd for Texans. There were no Texan races in 1964–67 or in 1979–80. Nineteen entered, 17 qualified and 18 raced. Those entered, but not qualified or racing, were #59 Nathan Harnagel and #64 Keith McMann. Keith McMann's final race had been in 2012, as was Harnagel's.

Gold winner #6 Nick Macy was again the top qualifier at 243.722mph, with #43 Dennis Buehn second at 242.756mph. #88 John Lohmar was next with 234.896mph. #14 Chris Rushing was fourth fastest at 232.634mph and in fifth was #37 Zayac at 230.237mph. Also qualifying were: #89 Gene McNeely at 230.193mph, in seventh #5 Joey Sanders at 229.007mph, eighth was #90 Gene McNeely at 228.492mph (his son would race), #50 John Krawczyk at 224.726mph, and tenth #66 Vic McMann at 219.416mph. This group was followed by #42 Rob Sandberg at 215.963mph, #54 Michael Pfleger at 210.171mph, #12 Terry Adams at 209.858mph, #69 Lee Oman at 203.967mph, 15th was rookie #78 Thomas Baber at 202.063mph, next was #49 John Johnson at 199.575mph. Johnson last raced in 2000 in another Texan carrying #49. The other under 200mph racer was #22 Duane Woods in 17th at 197.782mph.

For most of the 24.8285 miles, total distance of the five-lap Heat-1C, #54 Pfleger and #12 Adams flew a good race staying in contact with each other. These two were well ahead of #69 Oman, #22 Woods and #78 Baber, all bunched up for third. #49 Johnson was almost alone by lap 4. By the end of lap 4, Pfleger had a one-half plane length lead over Adams, where he stayed to take the Heat win at 216.462mph, with Adams second place at 213.549mph. In the middle were #69 Oman placing third at 206.463mph, #22 Woods was fourth at 206.234mph, #78 Baber was fifth at 206.203mph (a close set of racing), and #49 Johnson came in sixth at 202.993mph.

#5 Sanders and #90 Greg McNeely fought each other hard and managed to keep #50 Krawczyk behind them during Heat-1B. #66 McMann and #42 Sandberg trailed the others about 10mph slower. Sanders caught a break coming out of pylon 5 on lap 5 as #90 McNeely faltered coming out of the turn. Sanders was able to take the win at 227.999mph, leaving

Veteran #5 turning the pylons during the 2018 Reno races, flown by William Walker. #5 has been racing since 1970 and has raced under #25, #5, and #51 throughout the years. (Mike Henniger)

McNeely second at 226.827mph, then followed about six seconds back by #50 Krawczyk at 223.111mph, #66 McMann in fourth at 215.565mph, and #42 Sandberg brought up the rear in fifth at 213.223mph.

It was full throttle from the start of Heat-1A for both #6 Macy and #43 Buehn for three laps, but then Macy's engine let go, forcing him out. He landed safely. This allowed Buehn to back off and save his engine. #43 Buehn took first at 237.813mph to #88 Lohmar's second at 234.043mph. #14 Rushing finished third at 228.328mph just over one second ahead of fourth place #37 Zayac at 227.674mph. In fifth place was #89 Gene McNeely. With no new engine Nick Macy's racing was over for 2013. This gave everyone else hope of moving up.

Heat-2C was another contest between #12 Adams and #54 Pfleger at the front and everyone else racing for third. Pfleger caught Adams on the backside on lap 4 where he stayed to take the flag in first at 209.629mph. Seconds behind was #12 Adams at 209.236mph, then #22 Woods third at 204.553mph, and #69 Oman fourth at 203.026mph. Oman was followed by fifth place #78 Baber at 201.944mph and sixth #49 Johnson at 198.456mph.

Heat-2B belonged to #5 Sanders from lap 2, as he pulled away from the pack and stayed. The old Joey was back and earned first place at 240.323mph to second place #90 Greg McNeely at 237.502mph. #50 Krawczyk placed third at 234.081mph. In fourth was #66 McMann at 228.214mph. Thirty seconds and about 18mph slower in fifth was #42 Sandberg.

#88 Lomar tried for five laps to catch #43 Buehn in Heat-2A, but Buehn kept the fuse lit and finished first at 242.334mph, followed by #88 Lohmar at 235.440mph. In third was #14 Rushing at 233.049mph. Rushing flew a good race against Lohmar. #37 Zayac was fourth at 230.040mph and fifth place #89 Gene McNeely finished at 228.243mph.

#54 Pfleger grabbed the Bronze in 8:22.110mins for the six laps by a narrow edge to second place #12 Adams' 8:25.408mins. Third place went to #22 Woods who was halfway to Adams' prop at 8:25.673mins. In fourth was #69 Oman in 8:41.507mins. #49 Johnson was fifth at 8:41.602mins. Five seconds back in sixth was #78 Baber with 8:46.018mins. This would be #49 Johnson's last Texan race.

#5 Sanders took the Silver for his fourth Silver Race at 229.134mph. The first race win of #5 was the Gold at Mojave in 1974. #90 Greg McNeely was second at 226.883mph. Third went to #50 Krawczyk at 222.036mph. Krawczyk would step away from Texan racing for a few years after this race. In fourth was #66 McMann at 215.304mph and fifth was #42 Sandberg at 214.225mph.

Sunday's Gold Race was a great race even without Nick Macy racing. #88 Lohmar really gave #43 Buehn a race for the money. Without Macy in between, Lohmar caught Buehn by lap 2, but could not inch forward. For the next three laps, they were almost wingtip to wingtip. Buehn added his last burst of speed and crossed the finish line for his fourth Gold just 0.9 mile per hour over #88 Lohmar with 245.559mph to 244.638mph. Those in third through fifth also had a close race with #14 Rushing finishing third at 239.082mph. In fourth place was #37 Zayac at 237.293mph and #89 Gene McNeely finished fifth at 235.186mph.

With Texan racing, you can never be sure of the outcome.

2014

Several events put a damper on the 2014 Reno races. The first was the death of Sports Class racer Lee Behel on the opening day of qualifying, Monday, September 14. Second were the forest fires around the area causing some visibility issues due to smoke. Fifteen pilots qualified in 16 Texans. Fastest qualifier was the 2013 Gold winner #43 Dennis Buehn at 243.177mph. He was followed by #88 John Lohmar at 242.004mph, #14 Chris Rushing at 235.877mph, #6 Nick Macy at 234.584mph, and #89 Gene McNeely at 230.695mph. Four-time Silver winner #5 Joey Sanders was sixth at 225.681mph and #90 Greg McNeely placed seventh at 224.486mph. #2 Thomas Baber was eighth at 220.343mph in a Harvard that had been raced by Terry Adams in 2013 as #12. Nineth place went to rookie #42 Kevin Sutterfield at 217.091mph. In tenth place was rookie #94 Chris LeFave at 214.566mph. Texan #94 had been raced by four other pilots and with three other race numbers since 2008. #25 Terry Adams placed 11th at 213.915mph in a Texan that had been raced in 1994 by Jimmy Gist. #73 Ralph Rina was 12th at 209.358mph, having sat out in 2013. #54 Michael Pfleger placed 13th at 208.966mph. #87 Rick Siegfried was 14th at 205.733mph. #69 Lee Oman was 15th at 202.371mph and in 16th place was #19 Dennis Buehn at 201.476mph. This Texan would be raced by Thomas Baber. #66 Vic McMann sat out this year.

Veteran #73 Rina and #54 Pfleger had a fine Heat-1C race. They stayed well ahead of #19 Baber who had his hands full keeping #87 Siegfried and #69 Oman behind him. Rookie LeFave was a filler and flew at the back and was not classified as being a faster qualifier. In the end it was Rina in first at 212.332mph. Pfleger placed second at 212.130mph with Baber in third at 201.675mph. Oman came in fourth at 200.858mph and Siegfried behind at 200.823mph. Again, this race featured some good racing.

Heat-1B would see both rookies, #94 LeFave and #42 Sutterfield, have a good contest for fourth, with #5 Sanders and #90 Greg McNeely having a fight for the lead. In the end it was Sanders first at 228.842mph and #90 McNeely second at 226.790mph. Third went to #2 Baber at 220.461mph. #42 Sutterfield was fourth at 215.356mph. #94 LeFave came in fifth at 213.083mph and #25 Adams was sixth at 212.280mph.

The five contestants for Heat-1A finished in the same order they qualified in: #43 Buehn first at 239.770mph, #88 Lohmar at 235.906mph, #14 Rushing at 234.855mph, #6 Macy at 229.715mph, and #89 Gene McNeely fifth at 229.299mph. Macy's time was 6:26.712mins compared to McNeely's 6:27.413mins, while first place Buehn had 6:10.495mins.

Heat-2C would see #73 Rina and #54 Pfleger again dueling for first. Rina pushed past to the win at 208.699mph to Pfleger's 208.646mph. There was a swapping of positions from third through fifth. This time it was #87 Siegfried third at 191.489mph, #19 Baber fourth at 191.005mph, #69 Oman fifth at 190.882mph with #94 LeFave as a DQ filler.

It looked like another winning year for #5 Sanders when he took first in Heat-2B at 229.794mph in 6:26.580min. However, #90 Greg McNeely was not about to let Sanders go unchallenged, staying close and finishing second at 229.550mph and 6:26.991mins. Third was rookie #42 Sutterfield at 219.016mph. In fourth was #2 Baber at 217.863mph in his second race of the day. Fifth place went to #94 LeFave at 215.960mph and in sixth was #25 Adams at 214.366mph.

#6 Macy's engine gremlins resurfaced during Heat-2A as he was forced to fall back after a decent start keeping up with frontrunners #43 Buehn and #88 Lohmar. By lap 3, Macy was passed by #14 Rushing, who then set off to catch Lohmar, even though there were not enough laps left to truly have a chance. Buehn crossed the finish line with a time of 6:11.735mins to second place #88 Lohmar's 6:13.922mins. In third place was #14 Rushing in 6:14.799mins, followed by #6 Macy fourth in 6:25.602mins, and #89 Gene McNeely fifth with 6:25.755mins.

It seemed that everybody passed everybody during the six laps of the Bronze Race, except filler #94 LeFave. At the front it was again #73 Rina and #54 Pfleger at each other the entire race, only milliseconds apart. Two-time Reno Gold winner Rina gave it his all and took first, and his fourth overall Reno win, at 204.166mph and 8:42.125mins to second place #54 Pfleger's 204.157mph and 8:42.149mins. It was quite a race. #87 Siegfried was third at 190.294mph followed by #69 Oman fourth at 197.137mph, #19 Baber fifth with 186.874mph and 9:30.439mins. #94 LeFave was last unclassified.

Although #5 Joey Sanders' Texan is painted red, he loves silver. It was #5 from the start of the Silver, keeping a few steps ahead of #90 Greg McNeely all the way to the finish. The real fight was for third to sixth places, with these four having a really good race to the end. At the flag it was #5 Sanders at 229.367mph for his third consecutive and fifth overall Silver win. Greg McNeely was second at 227.889mph. In third place was #2 Baber at 217.457mph in his last Texan race. Fourth went to #94 LeFave at 215.371mph. LeFave flew in a total of six races during the week. Adams placed fifth at 213.720mph in his last Texan race. Rookie #42 Sutterfield took sixth at 212.289mph with a 12-second penalty for cutting pylon 2 on lap 2.

From the release of the Gold racers down the front straight, #43 Buehn had a slight lead over #88 Lohmar until pylon 1 then pulled away and did not look back. As hard as Lohmar tried, he could not keep up or even pass and had to hold off #14 Rushing who kept challenging. In the end, it was #43 Buehn first at 239.163mph for his third Gold win and second in a row. Lohmar held off #14 Rushing for second at 237.853mph. If Lohmar had not had to fight against Rushing, he might have taken the Gold. #14 Rushing was third with 237.293mph. It is possible he might have taken second place, if there had been one more lap. In fourth was #6 Macy at 231.702mph and #89 Gene McNeely was fifth at 227.975mph.

Reno 2014 was another great year of racing.

2015

Reno 2015 had 17 entered, 16 qualified and 17 raced. #6 Nick Macy was back as the fastest qualifier at 238.524mph. Macy was followed by #88 John Lohmar second at 234.749mph, #43 Dennis Buehn third with 232.296mph, #89 Gene McNeely was the last of the 230mph qualifiers at 231.037mph, and Silver winner #5 Joey Sanders was fifth at 229.761mph. Returning after a year away was #37 John Zayac in sixth with 227.895mph. #14 Chris Rushing was seventh at 225.546mph and #90 Greg McNeely at 223.858mph was eighth. #25 Duane Woods was back placing ninth at 221.627mph. In tenth place was #50 Rob Sandberg returning at 219.361mph and racing John Krawczyk. In 11th was #66 Vic McMann with a speed of 213.076mph after sitting out two years. Next was #94 Chris LeFave at 208.397mph, then #42 Kevin Sutterfield at 208.036mph, 14th was #54 Michael Pfleger at 203.621mph, rookie #2 Eric Woelbing was 15th at 201.620mph, and 16th was #69 Lee Oman at 188.973mph. Rookie #22 Chad Morgan did not qualify, but he would race.

Rookie #22 Morgan was a DNS for Heat-1C, leaving the other five to put on a good race from the start, almost in formation, until pylon 3 where #94 LeFave and #42 Sutterfield began to stretch the field out. #2 Woelbing gave chase for a few laps but could not catch up and did not have to work hard to stay in third. #69 Oman was never a challenge to #54 Pfleger in fourth. Finishing order was #94 LeFave first at 216.670mph, second #42 Sutterfield at 213.763mph, and third #2 Woelbing at 211.391mph. Pfleger placed fourth at 206.670mph after a 10-second penalty for cutting pylon 5 on lap 2, and fifth was #69 Oman at 194.204mph.

Heat-1B began as five laps with five racers coming out of the chute for the start. Before the scatter pylon, #50 Sandberg pulled up and out for a DNF (sour engine). By end of lap 1, #14 Rushing had a commanding lead, where he stayed to the checkered flag taking first at 241.432mph, surprising for a B Heat Race. Second was #90 Greg McNeely at 229.973mph, third #25 Woods at 217.071mph, and fourth #66 McMann at 214.058mph, a little over 27mph slower than first place.

Speeds in Heat-1A races were usually around 240mph, but speeds this time were only in the mid-230s. #6 Macy was first at 234.149mph. #43 Buehn was second at 234.012mph. In third was #88 Lohmar at 231.269mph. Taking fourth was #5 Sanders at 225.308mph. #37 Zayac took fifth at 225.043mph, while #89 Gene McNeely was a DNS.

In Friday's Heat-2C, both rookies showed they had what it takes to race Texans with good performances. From the start, it was #94 LeFave out front, where he stayed to win at 218.845mph. Then came rookie #2 Woelbing in second at 215.777mph. #54 Pfleger placed third with 213.690mph, but had #22 Morgan right behind in fourth at 213.629mph. #69 Oman was fifth at 196.051mph and #42 Sutterfield was a DNS.

Rushing throttled back #14 a bit, possibly to save his engine, in Heat-2B, but kept it up enough to beat #90 Greg McNeely to the finish line with a 230.589mph to 229.252mph victory. Third was #66 McMann at 219.980mph and fourth went to #25 Woods at 216.738mph. #50 Sandberg had solved his problem from Thursday and finished fifth at 197.760mph.

Heat-2A was #43 Buehn's turn to take first by only a fraction of a mile per hour over second place #6 Macy with 235.314mph to 235.174mph. Their times were 6:17.511mins to 6:17.736mins, respectively. Ten seconds back in third was #88 Lohmar in 6:27.737mins. He was followed by #37 Zayac in 6:28.492mins in fourth. In fifth was #89 Gene McNeely in 6:33.307mins and #5 Sanders in sixth with 6:38.095mins.

The second race of the day on Saturday was the six-lap Bronze. This race was another DNS for #42 Sutterfield as he was unable to fix his engine, and this was his last attempt at Texan racing. Rookie #22 Morgan and #94 LeFave both had good starts and hung on to each other for a few laps, staying tight. Woelbing again made a brief chase until he had to give up to defend against #54 Pfleger, who was moving up, leaving #69 Oman back in fifth. The finish was close with #94 LeFave keeping #22 Morgan behind to take first at 220.828mph to Morgan's 220.377mph. Despite some fine racing on his part, this was Chad Morgan's only Texan adventure. Third place went to rookie #2 Woelbing at 216.521mph. Fourth went to #54 Pfleger at 214.433mph and #69 Oman was fifth at 198.660mph.

The Silver Race may have seemed strange as #5 Sanders was not in it. Only five pilots would race the six laps. The front two were #14 Rushing and #90 Greg McNeely and they finished in under eight minutes. They took first and second at 233.372mph and 225.921mph, respectively. At 8:05.385mins and 219.620mph, #66 McMann was third, followed by #25 Woods fourth at 216.087mph in his last Texan race. #50 Sandberg was fifth at 206.515mph. #14 Rushing bumped up to the Gold, which enabled everyone else to move up a place in the Silver and made #90 McNeely the winner.

In any racing class, it is said one has to be bold to race in the Gold. This was proven with this race and, while slower than more recent gold races it was exciting. As the competitors came down the front for the start, it was seven Texans tied together as if one aircraft. They only separated to make the first pylon turn, which saw #43 Buehn in the lead with #6 Macy, #14 Rushing, #88 Lohmar, #90 Gene McNeely, #37 Zayac and #5 Sanders strung out behind almost parade style. The line up remained this way for four laps until Rushing closed on Macy and passed. In back, Zayac got around McNeely, and it stayed this way to the finish. Buehn took his fourth Gold at 238.073, with Silver-race winner and bump-up #14 Rushing finishing second at 231.808mph. #6 Macy took third with a close 231.730mph. In fourth was #88 Lohmar at 227.726mph. Taking fifth was #37 Zayac at 227.348mph in his last Texan race. Sixth place went to #89 Gene McNeely at 226.428mph and #5 Sanders was seventh at 221.276mph. Reno 2015 was a safe year with great racing.

2016
Reno 2016 had 15 qualifiers and 15 pilots race. #6 Nick Macy was fastest at 251.792mph setting a new qualifying record. #43 Dennis Buehn was second at 249.277mph. Buehn was followed in order by #90 Greg McNeely at 241.560mph, #88 John Lohmar at 240.023mph, #5 Joey Sanders at 235.038mph, #14 Chris Rushing at 233.187mph, #50 John Krawczyk returned after a few years and posted 231.564mph in seventh, #89 Gene McNeely at 229.556mph, and in ninth was rookie #9 Pete Stavrides at 227.440mph. This Texan has been racing since 1968 and was last raced by Bud Granley in 2006. In tenth place was #2 Ralph Rina at 225.626mph in a Texan raced by Eric Woelbing in 2015. In 11th place was #27 Eric Woelbing at 225.126mph flying Eddie Van Fossen's eight-time Gold winner. Was there any magic speed left in it? Next was #94 Chris LeFave at 220.002mph, followed by #54 Michael Pfleger at 208.557mph, #69 Lee Oman at 200.123mph, and 15th was #58 rookie Thom Vaughn at 194.708mph.

Heat-1C had six Texans circulating, but only three were racing. The other three were not competing as field fillers. After five laps, it was #54 Pfleger first at 209.716mph, second #69 Lee Oman at 196.043mph, and third rookie #58 Vaughn at 193.911mph. The three faster fillers were #88 Lohmar at 209.896mph, #2 Rina at 209.438mph, and #94 LeFave at 209.126mph.

Heat-1B was a competitive race with six contestants. #89 Gene McNeely was first at 226.352mph, followed by rookie #27 Woelbing in second at 219.715mph. Taking third was #50 Krawczyk at 219.678mph. In fourth was rookie #9 Stavrides at 217.455mph. Fifth place went to #94 LeFave at 212.532mph, and #2 Rina placed sixth at 212.524mph.

All six of the top qualifiers raced in Heat-1A, with both six-time Gold winners #6 Macy and #43 Buehn up against four that wanted their first. The Heat was won by #6 Macy at 238.561mph. In second place was #43 Buehn at 236.131mph, followed by #14 Rushing in third at 234.777mph. #90 Greg McNeely finished fourth at 223.235mph. #88 Lohmar was fifth at 222.465mph and #5 Sanders was sixth at 221.931mph.

Two non-competing Texans were in Heat-2C, which had only three actual racers. #54 Pfleger finished first at 210.661mph. #69 Oman was second at 195.494mph, while #58 Vaughn was disqualified as he had cut a pylon and had gone too low. The non-competing Texans were #2 Rina at 210.378mph and #94 LeFave at 210.213mph.

Heat-2B had #89 Gene McNeely winning at 233.212mph. He was followed by #27 Woelbing second at 230.618mph, third was #50 Krawczyk at 224.240mph, and #9 Stavrides fourth at 221.278mph. Both the Heat-2C fillers were at the back with #2 Rina fifth at 218.732mph and #94 LeFave sixth at 216.156mph.

Heat-2A saw #6 Macy take first at 236.717, and it appeared Macy was back to winning after a few years in the doldrums. #14 Rushing was second at 236.654mph. #43 Buehn was third at 230.277mph. Buehn was followed by fourth #90 Greg McNeely at 224.122mph, fifth #88 Lohmar at 224.058mph, and #5 Sanders was again sixth at 223.256mph.

The Bronze Race was unique in the history of Reno racing. There were again five Texans with the same group as Heat-2C for the six laps. #2 Rina and #94 LaFave were non-competing, leaving #54 Pfleger, #69 Oman and #9 Stavrides racing. At the finish it was #54 Pfleger first at 210.602mph. In second was #69 Oman at 192.701mph and #9 Stavrides as a DNF. Pfleger bumped up to the Silver giving first place to #69 Oman.

The Silver Race also became strange as rookie #9 Stavrides, who had only finished two races, was in the Silver Race, now with seven contestants. At the finish, it was #89 Gene McNeely in first at 228.838mph, earning his third Silver win. Second place went to #27 Woelbing at 227.093mph. #50 Krawczyk was third at 221.823mph in his last Texan race. Fourth was #2 Rina at 215.793mph, followed by fifth place #94 LeFave at 213.601mph. Bump-up #54 Pfleger was sixth at 207.112mph. Rookie #9 Stavrides was disqualified with a 36-second penalty for three pylon cuts.

A slower-than-usual Gold Race saw some great competition at the front, as shown by the winning speeds and times. #14 Rushing won his first Gold Race in 7:41.088mins and 231.193mph. In second was #6 Macy in 7:41.266mins and 231.104mph in what was almost a wingtip-to-wingtip finish. Buehn earned third with 7:41.650mins and 230.912mph. Neither he nor Macy would receive their seventh win this year. In fourth was #90 Greg McNeely at 222.856mph. Fifth place went to #88 Lohmar at 221.835mph and a 12-second penalty for a pylon cut. #5 Sanders placed sixth with 218.384mph. Joey would step away after this race for a few years and return in 2021.

Two classic race planes came out of retirement in 2016 and a new Texan king was crowned.

2017

Reno 2017 had 16 pilots and aircraft qualify, with six-time Gold champion #6 Nick Macy again the top qualifier at 232.623mph. Macy was followed by the other six-time Gold winner, #43 Dennis Buehn, at 230.222mph. #88 John Lohmar was third at 229.131mph, followed by #90 Greg McNeely fourth at 223.409mph. Greg's father, #89 Gene McNeely, earned fifth place at 222.169mph. This was a new father-son record. Returning after sitting out a year was #66 Vic McMann in sixth at 219.928mph, followed by #27 Eric Woelbing in seventh at 218.809mph. The first rookie to qualify was #50 Vitaly Pecherskyy at 216.934mph in John Krawczyk's T-6. #2 Chris LeFave was ninth at 216.658mph. He was the fourth pilot to race #2 since 2014. In tenth was #9 Pete Stavrides at 212.685mph, then #54 Michael Pfleger at 192.771mph, rookie #7 Mike Scott 190.890mph, #73 Ralph Rina at 189.878mph flying a new #73, #58 Thom Vaughn at 188.471mph, rookie #49 Bill Muszala at 187.287mph, and 16th was #69 Lee Oman at 186.021mph.

Heat-1C was taken by #54 Pfleger at 199.360mph, followed in second by #73 Rina at 195.895mph. Rookie #7 Scott placed third at 190.599mph and 7:35.736mins. Fourth went to #58 Vaughn at 190.516mph and 7:35.934mins. These two had a close race, as did #49 Muszala in fifth at 184.206mph and 7:51.552mins and sixth place #69 Oman at 184.188mph and 7:51.598mins.

Heat-1B had an even spread from first to fifth. #66 McMann was first at 219.630mph. #27 Woelbing placed second at 217.315mph. In 1983, #27 *Miss TNT* qualified for the first time at 207.732mph. Rookie #50 Pecherskyy was third at 216.341mph. Fourth went to #2 LeFave at 212.413mph and #9 Stavrides was a DNF after only one lap. He was unable to fix his problem and would not race any more in 2017.

Although Heat-1A was won by #6 Macy at 227.601mph, it was the race between #90 Greg and #89 Gene McNeely that drew all the attention. It was son over father with #90 Greg fourth at 213.779 in 6:46.319mins to #89 Gene's fifth at 213.770mph and 6:46.336mins. Gene had taught Greg well. Second place was #88 Lohmar at 225.211mph and #43 Buehn at 222.209mph placed third.

Heat-2C was a repeat of -1C, only slower, with everyone finishing in the same order. First place went to #54 Pfleger at 197.687mph, followed by second #73 Rina at 197.509 only 0.40secs behind. Third was #7 Scott at 190.523mph, followed by fourth place #58 Vaughn at 190.348mph. In fifth was #49 Muszala at 181.189mph and finally #69 Oman at 181.108mph.

It appears that #66 McMann had a handy lead from the start of Heat-2B and was able to stay there to the end, taking first place at 224.646mph. McMann was followed by #27 Woelbing in second at 222.247mph. The gap from first to second was a little over four seconds. In third place was #2 LeFave at 218.118mph. Fourth went to #89 Gene McNeely at 218.075mph, as a replacement for #9, with #50 Pecherskyy a DNF after two laps.

Saturday's Heat-2A was also a repeat, only stepped up a notch in speed and perhaps a sign of what was to come in the Gold Race. #6 Macy was again first at 232.424mph, and in second was #88 Lohmar at 230.830mph. Third went to #43 Buehn at 228.506mph. In fourth was #90 Greg McNeely at 216.423mph and fifth was #89 Gene McNeely at 216.350mph.

Veteran racer #73 Ralph Rina would win his third Reno Bronze Race, taking 8:56.045mins for the six laps, with #54 Pfleger second with 8:59.279mins. #69 Oman was third in 9:02.918mins, followed by #7 Scott fourth in 9:15.719mins in his only T-6 attempt. Fifth place went to #58 Vaughn in 9:15.789mins in his last T-6 race. Vaughn and Scott flew a close race. Back in sixth place was #49 Muszala in 9:23.735mins.

#66 McMann took his first win at Reno in the Silver Race at 221.387mph, with #27 Woelbing at 219.756mph. They were followed by third-place finisher #2 LeFave at 217.355mph with rookie #50 Pecherskyy in fourth at 217.265mph. #89 Gene McNeely was tail end as a non-competing (N/C) entrant at 216.969mph.

The surprise winner of the Gold Race was #88 Lohmar at 225.470mph and 7:42.301mins, just milliseconds over #6 Macy at 225.434mph and 7:42.375mins. Third went to #43 Buehn at 222.717mph and 7:48.017mins. Fourth was #89 Gene McNeely at 213.974mph with 8:07.139mins and his son #90 Greg McNeely placed fifth at 213.499mph and 8:08.222mins.

Nick Macy and Dennis Buehn would have to wait another year for a seventh win.

2018

Reno 2018 had 16 pilots entered, 15 qualified and 15 raced. #66 Vic McMann was entered but DNQ and DNR. Top qualifier was 2017 Gold winner #88 John Lohmar at 243.030mph in a T-6 that had been first qualified by Linda Finch in 1988 at 205.802mph. Second fastest was #14 Chris Rushing returning after being away with a speed of 238.061mph. Third was six-time Gold winner #43 Dennis Buehn at 236.030mph. Fourth was six-time Gold winner #6 Nick Macy at 232.408mph. In fifth place was #2 Chris LeFave at 225.617mph and sixth was #27 Eric Woelbing at 222.132mph. Seventh was #89 Gene McNeely at 222.070mph. Rookie #5 William Walker III took eighth at 221.738mph, flying Joey Sanders' T-6. Ninth was #9 Pete Stavrides at 220.822mph, with #90 Greg McNeely next at 218.982mph. #50 Vitaly Pecherskyy was 11th at 217.673mph. In 12th place was #73 Ralph Rina flying just below 200mph at 197.714mph. #69 Lee Oman was 195.828mph, then #49 Bill Muszala at 194.004mph, and in 15th place was #54 Michael Pfleger at 189.010mph in a new Harvard.

Heat-C had four racers and one N/C and was won by #73 Rina at 191.714mph. He was followed by #2 LeFave at 191.025mph but he was the N/C, so second place went to #69 Oman at 186.373mph. In third was #49 Muszala at 185.841mph and fourth was #54 Pfleger at 182.143mph.

#27 Woelbing would put *Miss TNT* back where it belonged in first place in Heat-1B at 222.052mph. Following in second place was #89 Gene McNeely at 221.373mph. Rookie #5 Walker was third at 217.454mph. Fourth was #90 Greg McNeely at 217.445mph. In fifth was #9 Stavrides again racing against its old adversary #5 at 214.262mph and sixth was #50 Pecherskyy at 210.379mph.

The 2017 Gold champion #88 Lohmar took Heat-1A at 237.303mph. Second went to #14 Rushing at 236.358mph. Seven seconds back in third was #6 Macy at 231.898mph. He was followed seven seconds back in fourth by #43 Buehn at 227.960mph and fifth #2 LeFave at 223.008mph.

#66 Vic McMann hugging the pylon while being chased by #88 John Lohmar during Heat-1A at the 2019 Reno races. (Mike Henniger)

With #54 Pfleger a DNS for Heat-2C there were two N/C racers as fill-in and only #73 Rina who took first at 192.222mph. Second was #69 Oman at 191.861mph and in third was #49 Muszala at 191.423mph. The N/C racers were #2 LeFave at 194.089mph and #50 Pecherskyy at 191.509mph.

None of the Texans racing in Heat-2B had ever beaten #27 in a race, so it was no surprise that #27 Woelbing took first at 225.872mph. He was followed by #89 Gene McNeely second at 225.208mph. Third #90 Greg McNeely at 221.786mph and 6:31.651mins placed just ahead of fourth place #5 Walker's 221.785mph and 6:31.653mins. This was a close race. In fifth was Stavrides at 213.709mph and 6:46.453mins to sixth #50 Pecherskyy at 213.629mph and 6:46.604mins proving not all close racing is at the front.

Lined up for Heat-2A were #88 Lohmar, #14 Rushing, #6 Macy, #43 Buehn, and #2 LeFave, however this race was canceled due to high winds.

The Bronze was the fourth victory for #73 Rina at 193.968mph. In second place was #69 Oman at 193.738mph followed by third #49 Muszala at 193.320mph. At 193.243mph was #2 LeFave, but he was an N/C. Fourth went to #54 Pfleger at 188.865mph.

Old #27 racked up another win with first place in the Silver Race. Eric Woelbing finished at 227.590mph. In spite of winning this race, this would be his last T-6 event. Second went to #89 Gene McNeely at 226.171mph, followed by #90 Greg McNeely in third at 224.512mph. In fourth was #5 Walker at 219.647mph, #9 Stavrides was fifth at 217.311mph, and sixth #50 Pecherskyy at 217.178mph.

#88 John Lohmar won the Gold Race for the second year in a row. Lohmar was challenged by #14 Rushing right behind and within striking distance. Lohmar finished in 7:35.947mins and 228.612mph to Rushing's 7:36.149mins and 228.511mph. Third was #6 Macy at 225.676mph, followed by #43 Buehn at 223.145mph fourth and fifth #2 LeFave at 218.087mph.

Could two-time Gold-winner #88 John Lohmar make it three in a row?

2019

While 15 Texans entered, only 14 qualified for Reno 2019. However, 15 raced. At the top was #14 Chris Rushing, second in the 2018 Gold Race, at 233.706mph. Second fastest was #43 Chris LeFave at 232.773mph in Dennis Buehn's #43. Third was #6 Nick Macy at 231.439mph. Fourth was #66 Vic McMann at 229.422mph, returning after not qualifying in 2018. Fifth was two-time Gold winner #88 John Lohmar at 229.189mph. In sixth was #5 Rick Siegfried at 221.258mph, replacing William Walker III. Seventh was #90 Greg McNeely at 220.688mph. McNeely was followed by #50 Vitaly Pecherskyy eighth at 219.358mph, and ninth #89 Gene McNeely at 218.042mph. Tenth was #2 Michael Pfleger in Chris LeFave's T-6 at 217.605mph. The under 200mph group began with 11th place #49 Bill Muszala at 195.190mph, #69 Lee Oman at 195.043mph, and #73 Ralph Rina at 192.743mph. In 14th was #33 Dennis Buehn at 192.636mph in a new Texan. Greg McNeely entered #98 but it DNQ, though it then did race. There were no rookie pilots this year.

Wednesday, September 11, saw racing under way with Heat-1C won by #49 Muszala at 200.921mph. He was followed by second #69 Oman at 198.277mph, third #33 Buehn at 195.837mph, fourth LeFave in Rina's #73 at 195.748mph, and fifth was #98 Greg McNeely at 195.739mph.

The next day had Greg McNeely back in #90, winning Heat-1B at 220.238mph. Second was #5 Siegfried at 220.228mph. Their times were very close, with McNeely finishing in 6:34.404mins and Siegfried in 6:34.421mins. Third went to #50 Pecherskyy at 219.478mph. In fourth was #89 Gene McNeely at 218.116mph, while #2 Pfleger was fifth at 214.990mph.

Six-time Gold winner #6 Macy was a DNS for Heat-1A, leaving #14 Rushing to a flag-to-flag win at 236.311mph. Back in second was #43 LeFave at 230.195mph. In third was #66 McMann at 225.465mph and two-time Gold winner #88 Lohmar placed fourth at 225.343mph.

Heat-2C had Rina back in #73 where he finished second to #49 Muszala's first. About a tenth of a second back in third was #98 Greg McNeely at 194.130mph. In fourth was #69 Oman at 191.529mph and close behind him was #33 Buehn at 191.164mph.

Hard close racing took place during Heat-2B as the separation between all flyers was mere tenths of a second apart. First place was #90 Greg McNeely in 6:40.246mins followed by second #5 Siegfried in 6:40:894mins. Third went to #50 Pecherskyy in 6:40.896mins. In fourth was #2 Pfleger in 6:41.059mins and fifth was #89 Gene McNeely in 6:41.531mins.

The Heat-2A racing really took place in third and fourth places. At the front was #14 Rushing first at 235.390mph. Second was #43 LeFave at 229.543mph. In third was #66 McMann at 228.251mph. In fourth place was #88 Lohmar at 228.128mph. In fifth and flying a careful race was #6 Macy coming in at 220.751mph.

#88 John Lohmar and #14 Chris Rushing, both Gold Race winners, flashing passed a pylon for the 2019 Gold Race. It was won by #14 Rushing at 238.051mph. (Mike Henniger)

Taking his fifth Bronze Race and third in a row was #73 Ralph Rina at 194.115mph, followed by #98 Greg McNeely at 193.846mph. In third was #49 Muszala at 193.156mph. Fourth place went to #69 Oman at 185.438mph and fifth to #33 Buehn at 185.322mph. It is fitting that #73 Ralph Rina would win as this would be his last Reno race. It is always nice to go out with a win. This would also be #33 Dennis Buehn's last Reno race. Both Rina and Buehn had started racing in 1973 at Reno.

Another last race for a veteran racer was the Silver Race, featuring father and son Gene and Greg McNeely. This would be Gene's last race. His son, #90 Greg, would take first place at 223.468mph. In second was #50 Pecherskyy at 222.978mph. #2 Pfleger was third at 221.523mph, also in his last race. Fourth place went to #89 Gene McNeely at 221.310mph. #5 Siegfried was fifth at 212.082mph with a 24-second penalty for two pylon cuts.

A new champion was crowned after the Gold Race. It was #14 Chris Rushing, who was a rookie in 2005, at 235.081mph. In second place was #43 LeFave at 233.067mph. Placing third was #88 Lohmar at 229.715mph. Fourth was #66 McMann at 229.714mph and #6 Macy was a DNF after two laps.

With the retirements of Dennis Buhen and Ralph Rina, the only veteran aircraft racing is #5. This Texan first raced in April 1970 at Ft. Lauderdale, FL, as #25. The aircraft's longevity is a testament to the strength of the North American Texan.

2020

There were no races held at Reno in September 2020 due to the COVID-19 pandemic.

2021

Reno 2021 returned without #6 Nick Macy. Twelve T-6s were entered. All qualified and 13 raced. Top qualifier was the 2019 Gold Race winner #14 Chris Rushing at 236.67mph, followed in second by #88 John Lohmar at 228.142mph. Third place went to rookie #43 Joel Stinnett at 226.573mph, in Dennis Buehn's Gold-winning T-6. In fourth was #66 Vic McMann at 224.156mph, fifth was #50 Vitaly Pecherskyy at 223.498mph, sixth was #90 Greg McNeely at 223.254mph, seventh was #5 Joey Sanders at 218.522mph (returning after some time away), eighth was #49 Bill Muszala at 200.885mph. Ninth through 12th were all under 200mph, starting with #4 Chris LeFave at 198.208mph in a T-6 that had raced as #44 in 2007. Tenth place went to rookie #25 Jason Karlin at 194.748mph. In 11th was another rookie, #73 Loren Marburg, at

190.823mph in a Texan Ralph Rina flew to win his last race in 2019. In 12th was #69 Lee Oman at 187.886mph. This small field meant everyone raced.

Heat-1C started at 2:05pm and was finished 15 minutes later, having been won by #49 Muszala at 201.803mph. In second place was #4 LeFave at 200.088mph, third was rookie #25 Karlin at 194.257mph, fourth was rookie #73 Marburg at 191.926mph. Fifth place #69 Oman at 190.890mph was almost 11mph slower than Muszala in first.

Heat-1B was canceled as there were not enough pilots to race.

Thursday's Heat-1A entrants were all the fastest qualifiers with defending Gold champ #14 Rushing taking first at 237.963mph. Rushing was followed by two-time Gold winner #88 Lohmar at 230.989mph, then rookie #43 Stinnett in third 228.285mph, fourth was #66 McMann at 220.221mph, fifth #90 McNeely at 219.676mph, sixth #50 Pecherskyy at 217.368mph, and seventh #5 Sanders at 217.323mph.

The only race on Friday was Heat-2C with five racers. #49 Muszala took first again at 202.627mph, then #4 LeFave second at 199.879mph. In third, was #25 Karlin at 194.171mph. Fourth place went to #69 Oman at 192.978mph. This time Oman was ahead of #73 Marburg, who placed fifth at 191.259mph.

In Heat-2A, everyone found some extra speed, as it was a faster race than Heat-1A with the winner finishing three seconds faster for the five laps. First was #14 Rushing at 239.201mph, second was #88 Lohmar at 232.190mph, third was #43 Stinnett at 230.414mph, and fourth was #66 McMann at 224.339mph. In fifth place was #50 Pecherskyy at 222.237mph. #5 Sanders came in sixth after flying around #90 McNeely at 222.148mph. McNeely placed seventh at 218.246mph.

Due to the lack of contestants, the standard Bronze and Silver races were replaced with a six-lap race named the Classic. The finish was the same as in Heat-2C, with #49 Muszala taking first at 202.496mph, then #4 LeFave at 197.597mph, #25 Karlin at 194.198mph, #69 Oman at 193.660mph, and #73 Marburg at 193.253mph.

#14 Rushing found the groove for the Gold Race and put some distance between himself and the rest of the field. At the finish he was first in 7:23.814mins and 234.862mph. Behind Rushing and placing second was #88 Lohmar in 7:36.760mins and at 228.862mph. Close behind was rookie #43 Stinnett who took third in 7:38:151mins at 227.513mph. #66 McMann placed fourth in 7:49.771mins at 221.885mph, and fifth #50 Pecherskyy in 7:52.137mph at 220.773mph. In sixth was #90 McNeely in 7:52:165mins at 220.760mph. Pecherskyy and McNeely flew a very close race. In seventh was #5 William Walker III in 7:58.667mins at 217.761mph. He took over for Joey Sanders.

This was #14 Chris Rushing's second Gold in a row.

2022

The 2022 Reno race week was plagued by wildfire smoke, which saw some heat races canceled because of near zero visibility. There were 16 Texans entered, 16 qualified and all raced. Six-time Gold winner #6 Nick Macy returned in 2022, looking for the elusive number seven win. The top three qualifiers were all Gold winners with #14 Chris Rushing in first at 236.590mph, #6 Nick Macy second at 232.838mph, and #88 John Lohmar third at 232.242mph. In fourth place was #43 Stinnett at 226.804mph, fifth #66 Vic McMann at 223.968mph, sixth #50 Vitaly Pecherskyy at 223.661mph, and seventh #5 Joey Sanders at 221.019mph. Taking eighth place and back in his regular #2 was Chris LeFave at 220.739mph. Placing ninth was #90 Greg McNeely at 210.419mph and in tenth was #49 Bill Muszala at 200.253mph. Those contestants under 200mph were 11th #73 Loren Marburg at 198.824mph and 12th rookie #4 Craig Meyer at 194.615mph, in an AT-6A with no racing history. #69 Lee Oman at 193.635mph was 13th. In 14th was #25 Jason Karlin at 193.509mph. Fifteenth place went to rookie #13 Brian Reberry at 190.490mph. This Texan had been raced by LeFave as #4 in 2021. In 16th and final place was rookie #21 Ben York III at 190.229mph. This aircraft had raced before as #54 by Michael Pfleger.

There were seven racers in Wednesday's Heat-1C starting at 3:26pm. This was the only heat race until Saturday. The results show a three-part race from the start. #49 Muszala was at the front to the finish, taking first place at 199.167mph. Part two was the race between second-place finisher #73 Marburg at 196.358mph and rookie #4 Meyer in third at 191.760mph. Racers in fourth through seventh place were practically tied to each other. In fourth place was #69 Oman in 7:47.828mins and 185.684mph, fifth #25 Karlin in 7:47.900mins at 185.655mph, sixth rookie #13 Reberry in 7:48.451mins at 185.437mph and seventh was rookie #21 York in 7:48.602mins and at 185.377mph. This race showed that not all hard racing goes on at the front.

With the smoke causing cancellation of some full races, the one v one T-6 Drag Races were held. These are a one-lap race over a 3½-mile course between two racers. They are flagged off from a standing start and the first one around the course to the finish pylon is declared the winner. Drag races were first held at Mojave in 1976 and have been run at Reno on a few occasions, however, the most recent results have not been recorded. The 2022 pairings and results were #1 Race,

#69 Oman (w) vs #73 Marburg; #2 Race, #25 Karlin vs #90 McNeely (w); #3 Race, #2 LaFave (w) vs #43 Stinnett; and #4 Race, #25 Karlin (w) vs #73 Lohmar (in Marburg's T-6).

Full course racing resumed on Saturday with Heat-1B at 9:53am and there was less smoke. It was a close race for the four that were racing as #69 Oman was a N/C. First was #50 Pecherskyy at 222.996mph, second was five-time Silver winner #5 Sanders at 222.170mph. In third was #2 LaFave at 221.330mph and fourth was #90 McNeely at 221.144mph. Oman's speed was listed as 191.775mph.

The second Saturday race, Heat-1A, was off at 12:35pm. It was won by two-time Gold winner #14 Rushing at 229.616mph. He was followed in second place by six-time Gold winner #6 Macy at 221.825mph. In third was two-time Gold winner #88 Lohmar at 220.240mph, fourth was #43 Stinnett at 216.860mph, fifth was #66 McMann at 213.102mph. #50 Pecherskyy was a DNS.

Sunday's five-lap Classic Race began at 10:51am with seven contestants racing. It was a repeat of Heat-1C with fourth through seventh places again putting on a great race. All were in the 7:40mins and 187mph range. Fourth place went to #60 Oman, fifth to #25 Karlin, sixth to #13 Reberry and #21 York was in seventh. Those at the front were all a little closer than before with #49 Muszala taking first at 199.967mph, second was #73 Marburg at 195.692mph, and in third place was #4 Meyer at 195.963mph.

#50 Pecherskyy led from the start of the six-lap Silver Race and flew a high-and-wide race to stay ahead of #90 McNeely, who had no problem with #2 LeFave behind him as he was keeping five-time Silver winner #5 Sanders at bay. #25 Karlin and #69 Oman were N/C and cruising around at the back in the 180mph hour range. At the finish it was #50 Pecherskyy, followed by #90 McNeely second at 222.305mph, then third #2 LeFave 220.268mph and fourth #5 Sanders 220.111mph. After the finish #50 Pecherskyy decided to bump up to the Gold and forfeited the win to #90 McNeely for his third win and second in a row and bumping everyone up a place.

They say the noise of a T-6's prop tips going supersonic at high speed is loud enough to set off car alarms in the parking lot and the noise is one reason why people enjoy the Texan races so much, along with the close flying. The 2022 Gold Race did not disappoint. With three multiple Gold Race winners out front intent on increasing their totals, the outcome was unknown for almost three laps. #14 Rushing began pulling away and stayed in front to finish first in 7:13.955mins and 240.213mph. In second was #6 Macy in 7:28.831mins at 232.251mph. Macy would have to wait another year for a try at winning number seven. Third went to #88 Lohmar in 7:31.036mins at 231.116mph, fourth #43 Stinnett in 7:40.122mins at 226.552mph. #66 McMann was fifth and #50 Pecherskyy was sixth at 223.8mph and 223.2mph, respectively. This was Rushing's fourth Gold and third in a row.

A gaggle of Texans as they race toward home pylon during the 2022 Gold Race at Reno. They are #14 Chris Rushing, #88 John Lohmar, #66 Vic McMann, #43 Joel Stinnett #50 Vitaly Pecherskyy, and just out of the photo is #6 Nick Macy. Chris Rushing would take first place. (Mike Henniger)

While there was celebration in the T-6 Class pits, the 2022 races ended on a somber note after the fatal crash of Aaron Hogue's L-29. The Jet and Unlimited Gold races were canceled.

The grand adventure that started at Cleveland in 1946 may come to an end as RARA announced that 2023 will be the last air races to be held at Reno/Stead. RARA is hopeful of finding another venue to hold the "World's Fastest Motorsport."

2023

Reno 2023 was graced with beautiful weather and warm and clear skies. However, there was a gray mood across the ramp at the realization that 2023 would be the final races held in the "Valley of Speed." There were 19 Texans entered, 16 qualified, and 17 raced. Of the 19, #27 Eric Woelbing was a no-show, which was a shame as it would have been great to have *Miss TNT/Pole Dancer*, the champion Texan (eight Gold wins), participate in the last races. The 16 qualifiers included three rookies. Top qualifier was four-time Gold winner (going for his fifth win and fourth in a row) #14 Chris Rushing at 236.504mph taking 1:13.460mins. Next was #66 Vic McMann at 229.228mph, third was six-time Gold winner (going for his seventh win) #6 Nick Macy at 227.150mph, fourth two-time Gold winner #88 John Lohmar at 226.622mph, followed by #50 Vitaly Pecherskyy at 225.003mph, #43 Joel Stinnett sixth at 224.036mph, three-time Silver winner #90 Greg McNeely seventh at 216.818mph, eighth at 212.573mph was #2 Chris LeFave, followed by #25 Jason Karlin in ninth at 199.590mph, tenth was #49 Bill Muszala at 197.937mph, 11th was rookie #388 Aaron Singer at 197.554mph, next was #69 Lee Oman at 195.158mph, #48 Brian Reberry in a new Texan was 13th at 188.840mph, #73 Loren Marburg was 14th at 187.897mph, 15th was rookie #19 Michael Sisk at 185.744mph and 16th was rookie #999 Job Savage at 179.239mph, taking 1:36.930mins for his lap. Both #21 Ben York III and #5 Gordo Sanders blew engines during qualifying. #5 Sanders had a spare engine and was able to race without qualifying while #21 York had to sit out the last Reno races. #5 has never failed to race in an event it has been entered in since it started racing in 1970. It first raced at Reno in 1972 and it is fitting that it should race at the final National Championship Races.

Besides the regular Heat and Medal races, one-lap Drags were held, providing great entertainment for all. Results were: #43 Stinnett (w) vs #48 Reberry; #73 Marburg vs #69 Oman (w); #25 Karlin vs #90 McNeely (w); #69 Oman vs #2 LeFave (w); #43 Stinnett (w) vs #69 Oman; #90 McNeely vs LeFave (w); and #43 Stinnett vs #2 LeFave (w).

Heat-1C was five laps for a total of 24.123miles, with #25 Karlin taking first at 197.863mph and #49 Muszala at a close second with 197.663mph. #48 Reberry at 189.119mph came third, then came rookie #19 Sisk at 188.917mph in fourth, while #73 Marburg was a DNS with engine issues.

Heat-1B featured the middle qualifiers, which had #90 McNeely taking first at 216.611mph, second was #2 LeFave at 208.927mph even after a 10-second penalty for a pylon cut, rookie #388 Singer was third at 197.451mph. He was followed in fourth by #69 Oman at 191.526mph with rookie #999 Savage fifth at 179.198mph almost 20mph slower. #5 Sanders was a DNS as he was changing engines. After his first test flight after changing engines, he was met by the fire trucks on landing, necessitating more work.

Heat-1A for the fast runners was an all-over 215mph affair, with first place finisher #14 Rushing posting 234.345mph, having taken the lead at the start. He was followed in second by #66 McMann at 222.892mph half a lap behind, #88 Lohmar was third at 222.847mph and #6 Macy at 222.284mph in fourth. These two had some close racing between them for a Heat race. #50 Pecherskyy was fifth at 219.619mph and #43 Stinnett sixth at 217.126mph.

The Texan ramp at the last Reno National Championship Air Races in September 2023 at Stead, where Texan racing had begun in September 1967. (Jim Dunn)

Heat-2C saw two separate races, with #25 Karlin and #49 Muszala out in front. Karlin was first to pylon 1 low and tight and Muszala was half a plane back. The front two were followed by #73 Marburg and #19 Sisk with #48 Reberry charging by lap 3. Lap 4 saw Karlin and Muszala wingtip to wingtip, and Reberry passing Marburg and Sisk. As they all started lap 5, it was Karlin still low and tight with Muszala a prop spinner back. As they crossed the line for the flag, it was #25 Karlin first at 197.544mph and 7:19.740mins, second was Muszala at 197.541mph and 7:19.541mins. Third went to #48 Reberry at 190.630mph, fourth to #19 Sisk at 190.367mph, while #73 Marburg was fifth at 189.986mph. A really great race.

Heat-2B had fast close racing from the start, with #90 McNeely and #2 LeFave at the first pylon side by side, then came #388 Singer, #69 Oman, and #999 Savage. #5 Sanders had started in sixth, but by lap 2, he had moved to third and started moving up against LeFave. Singer, Oman, and Savage were well behind the leaders for the rest of the race. At the flag, it was #90 McNeely at 218.913mph first and 6:36.816mins, then #2 LeFave second at 218.778mph. Third was #5 Sanders at 216.035mph (if there had been one more lap he may have caught LeFave). Fourth was #388 Singer at 202.411mph, while in fifth was #69 Oman at 180.749mph, and close behind him in sixth was #999 Savage at 180.538mph and 8:01.161mins.

Heat-2A was a showdown of the three fastest qualifiers. From lap 1, it was #14 Rushing, #66 McMann and #88 Lohmar, then #6 Macy, #50 Pecherskyy, and #43 Stinnett. By lap 4, Lohmar had caught McMann but lost ground by pylon 5. Macy was able to get around Lohmar and hold on, but he could not catch McMann. At the flag, it was #14 Rushing first at 234.422mph, #66 McMann second at 224.424mph, then #6 Macy third at 223.582mph, fourth was #88 Lohmar, then fifth Percherskyy, then #43 Stinnett at 219.068mph. After things settled, it was announced that #88 Lohmar had been DQ for unsafe flying, which moved everyone up. A fine race overall.

The last ever Bronze Race at Reno was not a disappointment, with #25 Karlin out in front from the start, followed closely by #49 Muszala around pylon 1. They were trailed by #48 Reberry, #19 Sisk and #73 Marburg. By lap 2, Karlin and Muszala were even but with Karlin still on the inside, Sisk and Marburg were almost tied together, while Reberry was alone at the back. Lap 4 had Karlin and Muszala less than a half a plane separating them. At the backside of the course, Muszala pulled a slight lead but could not hold it. Meanwhile, Marburg passed Sisk. As they came around for the final lap, Muszala passed Karlin and took first. Winning times and speeds were #49 Muszala first at 196.297mph and 7:22.534mins, second #25 Karlin at 196.268mph and 7:22.598mins, third was #73 Marburg at 191.364mph, fourth rookie #19 Sisk at 191.292mph, and fifth #48 Reberry at 187.980mph and 7:42.112mins.

The last Silver Race was a #90 McNeely race from start to finish. The main race was between #2 LeFave and #5 Sanders, while #388 Singer, #69 Oman and #999 Savage held a good race for themselves at the back. Lap 3 was where the action took place, with LeFave and Sanders wing to wing at pylon 5 and Sanders staying there. Lap 5 saw McNeely lapping Savage, and then Sanders gaining on McNeely with everyone hoping he would catch him, but McNeely held on to even pass Oman. At the flag it was #90 McNeely first at 219.280mph, #5 Sanders second at 217.568mph, #2 LeFave third at 215.046mph, fourth was #388 Singer at 202.245mph, fifth went to #69 Oman at 186.944mph and sixth to Savage at 181.633mph. It was later announced that #90 McNeely had cut a pylon and was given a 12-second penalty but, because of his lead, he kept first place.

The final Reno Gold Race started on time and had #14 Rushing in front by pylon 1, followed by #66 McMann and #6 Macy hugging the pylon, with #88 Lohmar following and then #50 Pecherskyy and #43 Stinnett. Lap 3 is where Macy made his move on McMann and got his nose out front, while #88 also tried to move around both but could not hold on out of the turn. Lap 5 had Macy slightly ahead and McMann and Lohmar neck and neck in third. As lap 6 started, it was clear that Rushing would take his fifth Gold Race, as he was almost half the course ahead of Macy. Macy would be second, as McMann and Lohmar were not close. At the flag it was #14 Chris Rushing first at 234.063mph with #6 Nick Macy second at 226.126mph, third went to #66 Vic McMann at 223.670mph, fourth #88 John Lohmar 223.608mph, while #50 Vitaly Pecherskyy was fifth at 220.486mph and #43 Joel Stinnett was sixth at 220.395mph. These two had flown a tight race but unfortunately were overlooked by the front action.

Cheers went up as #14 Rushing crossed the line taking his fifth Gold and fourth in a row. However, within minutes of the cheering, there was a loud gasp from the crowd as they witnessed two Texans come together on approach to runway 8 and then fall to earth in clouds of dust. It took several minutes to determine who had crashed and then the realization set in that it had been #14 Chris Rushing and #6 Nick Macy. Fire rescue crews rushed to the site of the crashes, and it was determined that both pilots had perished. The RARA canceled the remaining races. It was truly a terrible way for the Reno races to finish.

After all the long years of following air racing, this is truly a very sad ending to the longest running air races in history and I feel a great loss for all the pilots that gave their lives for the "World's Fastest Motorsport." The roar of Texans in the Valley of Speed has been silenced forever.

Chapter 4
Photo Gallery

Part 1 – Postwar Photo Gallery

#23 NX57805, AT-6A aac s/n. 41-15872, on arrival at the 1947 NAR Cleveland with new three-bladed prop. Dot Lemon did not qualify and sat out the races for 1947, hence no race number applied. The aircraft raced in 1946 as #72. (B. J. Matthews via Nicholas A. Veronico)

#23 NX57805 at the 1948 Nationals, also raced by Dot Lemon, and sporting a Kendall Oil logo, the sponsor for the 1948 races. (via Nicholas A. Veronico Collection)

At the 1948 Nationals, #23 NX57805 placed third in the finals and Dot Lemon won US$750. The last year #23 raced was 1948 and its fate post-racing is unknown. (via Dan Hagedorn Collection)

#31 N66134, SNJ-3 BuNo. 6927, at the 1948 Nationals raced by Kaddy Landry. The plane is shown in a dark paint scheme sponsored by the Jess Bristow Air Shows of Miami. Landry would place second in the finals and take home $1,250. Note: this photo was taken in 1948, but the film was developed in 1998. (Emil Strasser)

#31 from the opposite side. Landry had flown to first place at the Miami races earlier in the year. (via Dan Hagedorn Collection)

#31 in a light color scheme at the 1949 Nationals, again raced by Kaddy Landry and now sponsored by NUTA's, a flying service based in Miami. While the requirement for all racers was to be stock, those with only slightly modified canopies could race. (Leo J. Kohn via Dan Hagedorn)

#31 from the opposite side. Landry would place second again in the finals behind Grace Harris. The post-racing life of #31 would see it remanufactured and sold to the South African Air Force (SAAF). It is reported to be back in the US under rebuild. (via Nicholas A. Veronico Collection)

#35 NC57584, SNJ-3 BuNo.5575, at the 1946 Cleveland Nationals, raced stock by aerobatic pilot Arlene Davis. *Miss Mulligan II* placed fourth in the finals and Davis collected $500. Davis was listed as an alternate pilot to race in place of Jane Page in 1947 but did not race. The fate of #35 post-racing is unknown. (Emil Strasser, exposed 1946 and developed 1998)

#36 NX63760, SNJ-2 BuNo. 2019, at New York City, New York (NY), post-race in 1947. Entered by Bella Heineman in the 1947 Halle Trophy Race at Cleveland, the stock SNJ failed to qualify. The aircraft would later go to the Peruvian Air Force and its fate is unknown. (Leo J. Kohn via Dan Hagedorn)

#42 N62382, SNJ-2 BuNo. 2039, at the 1946 Nationals in Cleveland as a semi-stock aircraft. Note the extended exhaust pipe used for skywriting. It may have been used by Edna Whyte for an airshow routine before being modified for racing. (Leo J. Kohn via Dan Hagedorn)

#42 NX62382 at the Nationals in 1947. After heavy modification work, the plane was ready for the Halle Trophy Race with Edna Whyte as pilot. It is unknown if these modifications were strictly for air racing or some other purpose. Whyte would place third in the finals and take home $750. (via Tim Weinschenker Collection)

#42 NX62382 seen from the opposite side for a better view of modifications. The only year it raced was 1947. (via Tim Weinschenker Collection)

#42 N62382 in its post-race career as a skywriter and demonstration aircraft for the Skytypers Inc. at Long Beach, CA, 1995. It would be written-off (W/O) in a fatal accident at Melville, NY, in May 2018. (Roger Cain)

#44 N90641, AT-6A aac s/n. 41-461, raced from 1947 to 1949 at the Cleveland Nationals by Grace Harris. For the 1947 races, the Texan had an overall natural metal finish with red trim. Shown here is the 1948 paint scheme of overall gold and bronze. In the 1947 races, Harris placed second in the Halle Race and took home $1,000. (Emil Strasser)

#44 again at the 1948 Nationals. Grace Harris flew almost a walk-away race after a shaky start to take first place and the $2,250 prize money. (Emil Strasser)

#44 at the 1949 Nationals wore an overall gold scheme with red trim. Like the other 1949 contestants, Harris flew as a stock Texan except for the canopy as called for in the 1949 rules. She finished first in the finals and received $2,500. Post-racing career, #44 went to the Royal Iraqi Air Force and its fate in unknown. (Leo J. Kohn via Dan Hagedorn)

#45 N65560, SNJ-3 BuNo. 5519, raced by Betty Skelton at the 1949 Nationals, where she placed fourth in the finals with a sick engine. The paint scheme of #45 was an overall crimson red with gold trim. In between the races, Skelton and Kaddy Landry flew aerobatic/comedy routines. (Leo J. Kohn via Dan Hagedorn)

#45, as required, was stock except for the canopy. Texan N65560 would vanish into the great Texan buy-back of the 1950s and its fate is unknown. (via Tim Weinschenker Collection)

#49 NX61269, AT-6A aac s/n. 41-234, at the 1947 Cleveland Nationals. This A model had been re-engined with a Ranger V-770-9 engine rated at 575hp. It was raced by Dori Marland in 1947 but was forced out of the final race with fuel problems. It was not badly damaged when it bellied in. (via Nicholas A. Veronico Collection)

#49 was towed back to the Cleveland airport after its belly landing and repaired. In 1948, it was raced by Betty Clark, who had better results with it, placing fourth in the finals and collecting $500. (via Dan Hagedorn Collection)

#49 did not qualify to race in 1949 as it was not stock. It appears to still be in flyable shape when photographed here in the early to mid-1950s. (via Tim Weinschenker Collection)

#49 in the California Bay area in 1959. Note the chain locking on the aft canopy. Its fate after this photo is unknown. (William T. Larkins)

#54 at the 1947 Cleveland Nationals raced by Betty Clark. *Chum Seat Special* was one of only two Texans modified with a turbocharger and the only one to race. Clark would drop out of the finals with a sick engine on lap 2. The aircraft got its name by having a second seat behind the pilot. Note the small square window. (Emil Strasser)

#54 at Cleveland in 1947. It was the only Texan to race with an open canopy, and with the turbocharger engine, it would have been very noisy for Betty Clark. This Texan would be remanufactured to stock and sold to Mexico. Its fate is unknown. (Harold G. Martin via Dan Hagedorn)

#61 NX74108, XAT-6E, aac s/n. 42-84241, was the only Texan with a Ranger engine built by North American. Its Ranger V-770-9 engine produced 575hp. It qualified first at 223.3mph for the 1947 Nationals. It was raced only once at Cleveland by Marge McGrath, who was forced to drop out of the finals with a sour engine. (via Tim Weinschenker Collection)

#61 qualified first at 223.3mph in 1947 but did not finish in the finals. Built for test comparisons against the standard P&W-powered Texans, there were not enough improvements to warrant production. It was later sold to the Colombian Air Force and its fate is unknown. (via Dan Hagedorn Collection)

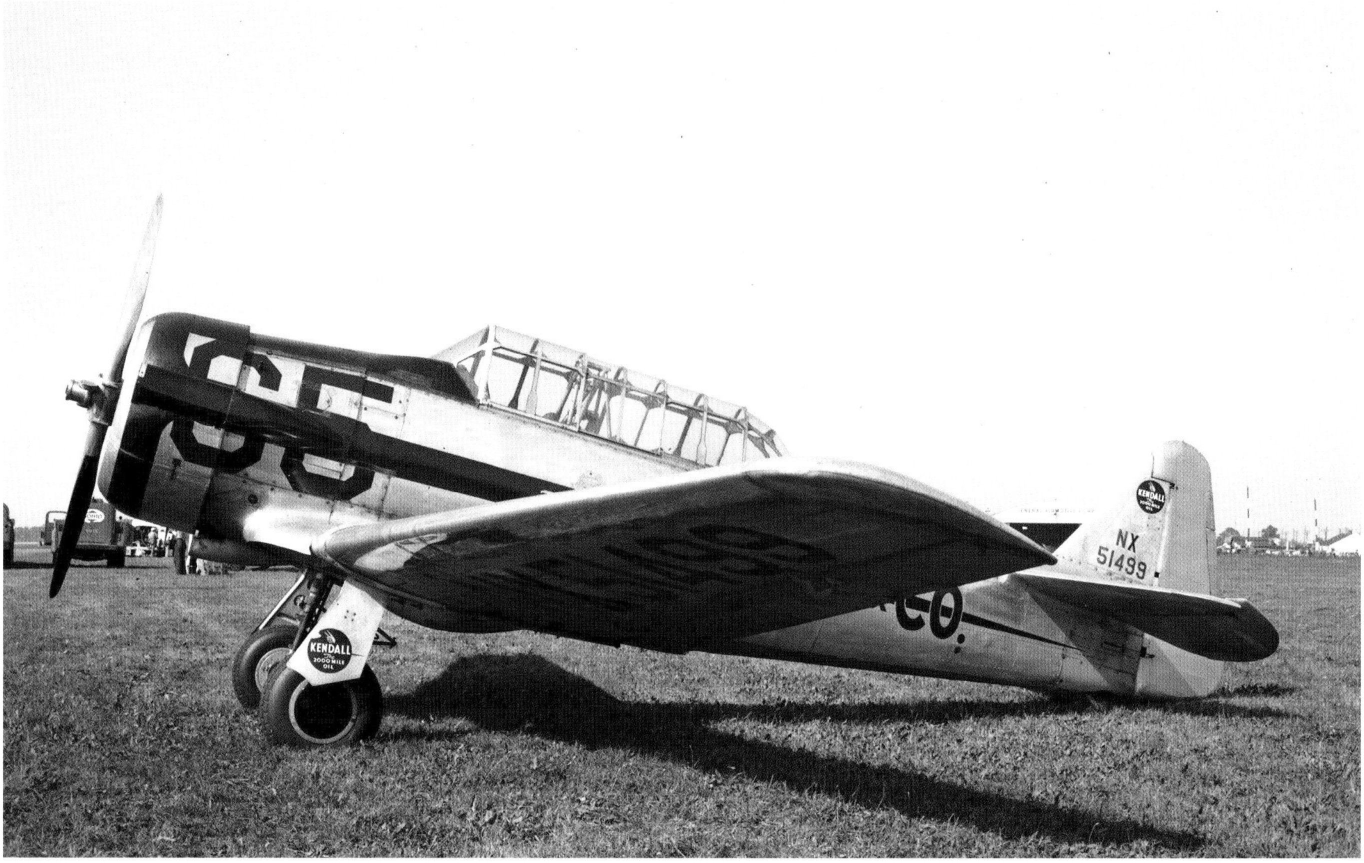

#65 NX51499, AT-6 acc s/n. 40-2113, raced by Anna Logan at Cleveland Nationals in 1947 and 1948. Logan qualified seventh and finished fifth in 1947, winning $250. She was less fortunate in 1948 being listed as a DNS for the finals. The fate of the aircraft after the races is unknown. (Harold G. Martin via Dan Hagedorn)

#72 NC57805, AT-6A aac s/n. 41-15872, raced in the 1946 Halle Trophy Race by Dot Lemon was straight stock and would place fifth in the finals, collecting $250. Texan #72 would race in the 1947 and 1948 races as Race #23. (Emil Strasser).

#75 NX63770, AT-6A aac s/n. 41-16743, was raced by Ruth Johnson in all four of the Cleveland National Air Races 1946–49. In 1946, Johnson raced it in a stock configuration with a three-bladed prop. She finished third and collected $750. (Tim Weinschenker Collection)

By 1947, #75 had been highly modified and would take Johnson to first in the finals after she took the lead on lap 2 for the final Halle Trophy Race. She collected $2,500. WIKK was a radio station in Erie, Pennsylvania (PA). (via Dan Hagedorn Collection)

#75 flown by Ruth Johnson at the 1948 Kendall Trophy Races would have engine problems and drop out of the finals on lap 3. Johnson's luck was no better in 1949, as she again dropped out of the finals with a sick engine. Johnson and #75 were the only racers to race in all four of the postwar Cleveland Air Races. The fate of #75 post-racing is unknown. (Tim Weinschenker Collection)

Above: #79 NX65619, SNJ-3 BuNo. 6827, was entered by Betty Skelton in the 1947 Cleveland Halle Trophy Races but did not qualify or race. Owned by the National Air Shows company, Skelton would put on an aerobatic display between races. She won several national aerobatic titles. The name under the canopy is Clem Honkamp. The aircraft would later be sold to the Swedish Air Force and its fate is unknown. (Harold G. Martin via Dan Hagedorn)

Left: #81 NC51497, AT-6A aac s/n. 41-16280, was raced by Marge Hurlburt to first place in the inaugural Halle Trophy Race at Cleveland in 1946. Hurlburt is standing in front of #81 after finishing the final race wearing a grey dress with red trim. The aircraft was owned by Tanner Flying Service of Ohio and loaned to Hurlburt. She was fatally injured flying another Texan in July 1947 and the fate of #81 is unknown. (Emil Strasser Collection)

#83 NX57799 *The Weaker Six*, AT-6A aac s/n. 41-15915, raced by Jane Page at Cleveland in 1947. Page raced in the Bendix Race finishing ninth and still qualified and raced in the Halle Trophy Race. She placed fourth and took home $500. This photo taken post-race has the #83 race number still just visible after being washed. (Tim Weinschenker Collection)

#83 was raced by Nancy Corrigan for the 1948 Kendall Trophy Race, her only race, where she placed fifth in the finals and won $250. Corrigan's sponsor was The Corrigans of Cleveland, O, who were not related to her. The fate of #83 is unknown. (Harold G. Martin via Dan Hagedorn)

#91 NX55941, SNJ-4 BuNo. 9985, was raced at Cleveland in both the Kendall 1948 and the Women's Trophy Race 1949 by Helen McBride. For the 1948 race, McBride finished sixth, which placed her out of the money, as that was only paid out up to fifth place. (via Nicholas A. Veronico Collection)

In 1949, #91 was considered stock even with the modified canopy, enabling McBride to race in the Women's Trophy Race, where she placed third. (Leo J. Kohn via Dan Hagedorn)

#91 as it appears today, fully restored as a stock SNJ-4. This photo was taken in January 2023. Texan #91 is the only flying survivor of the postwar Cleveland NAR. (Roger Cain)

This photo shows an aircraft similar to #96 NX63829, AT-6A aac s/n. 41-784. #96 was entered by Dora Jean Dougherty in the 1947 Nationals but did not race. The AT-6A was later sold to the Chilean Air Force but is believed to have crashed before delivery. (Emil Strasser)

#28 NX19446, SNC-1 BuNo. 6290, was entered in the 1949 Nationals by Jane Page. Under the rules for the Women's Trophy Race, all participants had to be stock, but cut-down canopies were allowed. Powered by a 420hp Wright R-975, it is hard to say how it would have fared against the Texan as protests by the other pilots kept it from racing. It was the first production aircraft of the series, and its fate is unknown. (via Nicholas A. Veronico Collection)

Part 2 – A New Era Photo Gallery

#0 N3254G at Reno 1969, raced by Hugh Glassburn. *Miss Janet Sue* had its best finish at Ft. Lauderdale in 1970 where it placed second in the Consolation Race. (Emil Strasser)

#1 N9525C post race at Bakersfield in 1968. It was raced in the 1967 Reno Demo Race by Walter Morrison and placed third. It later raced as #3. (Russ Hiatt)

#1 N7295C at Reno 1968, raced by Hank Otzen. He took first place in the first fully sanctioned Texan race. (H. C. Lineberger via Doug Slowiak)

#1 N7061C at Mojave in 1978, raced by Jim Furlong. *Head Hunter* earned its best finish, a fourth in the Silver Race, at Mojave 1978. (Bob Kennedy)

#1 NX42BA at Reno 1984, raced by Charles Hutchins. He took second in the Bronze Race and went on to take first in the 1988 and 1989 Silver races – the aircraft's best results. NX42BA was W/O in July 2002. (Bob Kennedy)

#1 N3169G was raced by John Krawczyk at Reno in 2010. Its best finish was second in the 1999 Bronze Race flown by Carter Clark. It has also raced as #11 and #88. (Bob Kennedy)

#1 N8540P at Reno in 2005, where it was entered by Jason Somes. He would qualify but did not race and did the same in 2006. It also raced as #51. (Jerry Liang)

#2 N2861G was raced by W. S. Halfhill at Reno in 1968, where it finished sixth in the Consolation Race. It has also raced as #5. (Ron Olsen)

#2 N447CL raced at Reno in 1969 by Walter Morrison and placed fifth in Heat-2. Morrison made a live radio broadcast during the races for KGIL radio. Later, it was registered as N164CL. (Jerry Liang)

#2 N2821G was flown by Bruce Payne at Reno 1972 and placed fourth in the Medallion Race. It also raced as #2 and #2A. (Emil Strasser)

#2A N711AP, at Mojave 1973, was raced by Bruce Payne, where it finished third in Bronze, its best finish. The aircraft is N2821G with a new registration number. (Russ Hiatt)

#2 N777AP, also at Mojave in 1973, was entered by Calvin Conroy. The aircraft did not qualify or race and is often confused as being N711AP. (Ron Olsen)

#2 N9789Z raced at Mojave by Dennis Buehn in 1975 and finished sixth in the Gold Race. The aircraft also raced as #50 and is now racing with a new registration number. (Jerry Liang)

#2 N86WW at Reno in 1981. *California Medfly* was raced by Charles Beck and took third in the Gold Race. (Emil Strasser)

#2 N86WW at Reno in 1984, now called *Honest Entry*, was raced by Charles Beck. It would take first in the 1990 Silver Race, which was its best finish. It also raced as #42 and #88. (Bob Kennedy)

#2 N2863G at Reno in 1994, as *Honest Entry II*, was flown by Charles Beck. It was entered but did not qualify or race. It also raced as #7. (Bob Kennedy)

#2 N8044H was entered by Mark Henley at Reno in 1999 but did not qualify. It also raced as #42. This photo is from Oshkosh, Wisconsin (WI), in 1999. (John Kerr)

#2 N4485 was raced at Reno in 2007 by Ken Dwelle. Its best place was fifth in the 2007 Gold Race. Also, it has raced as #7. (Roger Cain)

#2 N1465 at Reno 2016 raced by Ralph Rina. Its best finish was fifth in the 2018 Gold Race flown by Chris LeFave. It is still racing and has also raced as #12. (Kenneth Smith)

#2 N1465 at Reno in 2022 was raced by Chris LeFave and took second in the Silver Race. It was also raced as #12. (Jim Dunn)

#3 N2860G won the 1967 Demo Race at Reno flown by Hank Otzen. There were two races and Otzen won both. It also raced as #46. (Emil Strasser)

#3 N9525C raced for 13 years, beginning at Reno 1968, flown by Richard Sykes. Its best Reno finish was third in the Gold Race for 1968 and 1978. (Robert J. Pauley via Nicholas A. Veronico Collection)

#3 N9525C at Mojave in 1976, the year after Richard Sykes won the Silver Race. This would be its best finish. (Russ Hiatt)

#3 N9525C at Reno in 1983 in its last race, flown by Dennis Buehn. It finished third in the Gold Race. It also raced as #1. (Bob Kennedy)

#3 N42JM at Reno in 1996. It was raced by Dorel Graves as #3 from 1994–2000. In 1996, he qualified 17th and finished fourth in the Bronze Race. His best finish was first in the Bronze Race in 2000. It has also raced as #048 and #48. (Mike Henniger Collection)

#4 N6975C raced in the 1967 Reno Demo Race, where it took fifth in the final race flown by Dick Gregory. Also, the aircraft raced as #37. (Emil Strasser)

#4 N8158H was raced by Don Phillippi at Reno in 1968 and finished third in the Championship Race. (Ron Olsen)

#4 N8158H also raced in St. Louis in 1969, placing fourth in the Gold. It was a DNS in the Gold at Reno in 1971. The aircraft also raced as #43. (Emil Strasser)

#4 N6979C was entered by Kirk McKee at Reno 1976. It did not qualify or race, so McKee raced another aircraft, #76. (William T. Larkins)

#4 N144KM was entered at Reno in 1977 by Kirk McKee and again it did not qualify or race. This photo was taken at Watsonville, CA, in May 1980. It was W/O in a fatal accident in May 1985. (Bob Kennedy)

#4 N17498 qualified in 13th at Reno 1981 by Charles Neeley but did not race. It also raced as #47. (Emil Strasser)

#4 N8540Z took first in the Silver Race at Reno in 1986 flown by David Bruce. It also took third in the Gold Race at Redmond, Oregon (OR), in 1992. Also, the aircraft raced as #41 and #55. (Bob Kennedy)

#4 N4269E at Reno in 1994, raced by Bud Granley. He took fourth in the Bronze at Reno and also first in the Bronze at Phoenix. Chris LeFave flew #4 at Reno in 2021 where he took second in the Classic Race. The Texan also raced as #13 and #44. (Jim Dunn)

#4 N3171P at Reno 2000, raced by Lee Oman, who took first in the Silver Race. Note that both N4269E and N3171P are painted similarly and the two are often confused with each other. This one also raced as #43. (Bob Kennedy).

#4 N57493 *Emily* at Reno 2022, raced by rookie Craig Meyer, who placed third in the Classic Race. (Jim Dunn)

#5 N2861G was raced by Don Gulotta during the 1967 Reno Demo Race. Gulotta would take second in the final race. It was also raced as #2. (Emil Strasser)

#5 N5208V at Reno 1968, where James Williams raced it to fifth place in the Championship Race for its best finish. (Ron Olsen)

At Reno 1969, #5 N5208V qualified 21st, so James Williams was cut and did not race. It would be his last attempt at Texan racing. Note the registration number color has changed from the image above. (Emil Strasser)

#5 N7404C at its first appearance with the Red Baron Racing Team at Mojave 1974. It was raced by Roy McClain to sixth in the Gold Race. (Russ Hiatt).

#5 N7404C at Mojave 1976 after placing third in the Gold by McClain. This was its best Mojave finish. (Russ Hiatt)

#5 N7404C at Reno in 1983, now as *Big Red*, was raced by Jerry McDonald. By this time, #5 had two fifth places in the Reno Gold races. (Bob Kennedy)

#5 N7404C at Reno in 1990. Jerry McDonald had won his first Silver Race in the 1984 Reno Races and had a second first in the 1985 Silver Race at Reno. (Russ Hiatt)

#5 N7404C at Reno in 2000 with Jerry McDonald. McDonald would race *Big Red* until Reno 2003, where he placed sixth in the Gold Race. (Bob Kennedy).

#5 N7404C at Reno in 2016. Joey Sanders took over racing *Big Red* in 2004. He has won five Reno Silver races so far, and continues to race. In 2023, Sanders finished second in the Silver Race. *Big Red* has also raced as #25 and #51. (Kenneth Smith)

#5 N3653G took over the #5 race number in 1978. At the 1979 races, where this photo was taken (note the C-133 behind), Cliff Branch would place third in the Silver Race. Its best finish was a fourth in the Gold Race at Mojave in 1978. It also raced as #14. (Bob Kennedy)

#6 N5489V raced in the 1967 Reno Demo Race flown by Victor Baker and placed sixth. By the 1968 Reno Races, when this photo was taken, Baker was the fastest qualifier, but only finished fifth in the Championship Air Race. (H. C. Lineberger via Doug Slowiak)

#6 N5489V at Ft. Lauderdale in 1970, where Baker would take fourth in the Consolation Race. Its best finish was second in the 1970 St. Louis Consolation Race. (Robert F. Pauley via Nicholas A. Veronico)

#6 N5489V at Cape May in 1971 before the start of the fatal Heat-2B Race. Baker had qualified eighth and would crash on lap 3. (Kenneth Smith Collection)

#6 N2885G at its second Reno Race in 1973, flown by Art Bowles. Its best finish was first in the 1972 Wilson, North Carolina, Consolation Race. It would be W/O on its way home after the 1973 Graham races. (Ron Olsen)

#6 N7446C raced at Reno in 1978 with Charles Gilbert, placing fourth in the Medallion Race. It also raced as #43. (Dennis Buehn Collection)

#6 N98474 was raced at Reno in 1982 by James Brennan and in 1984 by Cliff Branch, who placed fourth in the Bronze Race. It is shown here at Reno in 1982 as *Italian Stallion*. It is not the same *Italian Stallion* that raced at Reno in 1985. (Bob Kennedy)

#6 N1363R was entered by Dennis Buehn at Reno in 1985, but he did not qualify or race *Italian Stallion*. Note the markings similar to N98474. (Bob Kennedy)

#6 N2897G qualified 24th by Nick Macy at Reno in 1986, but did not make the cut and did not race. (Bob Kennedy)

#6 N2897G at the 1998 Reno races, where it took second in the Gold Race. Nick Macy was one year away from his first Gold win in 1999. (Bob Kennedy)

#6 N2897G was raced by Nick Macy at Reno in 2014. By this time, Macy had six Gold Race wins. Note the long scoreboard on the side of *Six-Cat*. (Jerry Liang)

#6 N2897G is still racing, shown here at Reno in 2022. Nick Macy won second in the Gold Race. In 2023, Macy finished second in the Gold Race moments before he was killed in an mid-air collision when landing. (Jim Dunn)

#7 N2863G at the 1967 Reno Demo Race, where it was flown by Darryl Greenamyer to fourth in the final race. It also raced as #2. (Emil Strasser)

#7 N203V at Reno in 1969, raced by Ben Hall. Hall had qualified 13th but did not race in 1968. In 1969, he would take first in the Gold Race. He would also take first in the Gold Race at the 1970 Ft. Lauderdale Races. #7 was the first Harvard II to race in Closed Course Pylon Racing. (Emil Strasser)

#7 N203V in Seattle, Washington (WA), between races in 1971. It would later race at Miami and Graham in 1973. (Dan Hagedorn Collection)

#7 N611F at Reno in 1974, flown by Colene Giglio. She was the first woman since 1949 to race in Texan Closed Course Pylon Racing. Giglio would qualify 17th and finish fifth in the Medallion Race. (Emil Strasser)

#7 N611F at the 1979 Mojave races, where Giglio would take her second win in a Silver Race. She took her first Silver at Mojave in 1976. (Bob Kennedy)

#7 N611F *"Humm-Baby"* was entered by Jamie MacKay at Reno in 1986 where it qualified 21st, but it did not race. It also raced as #47 and #86. (Bob Kennedy)

#7 N5632V qualified in 15th at Reno in 1982 by William Meier, but was cut and did not race. (Bob Kennedy)

#7 N29939 was entered at Reno in 1986 by Bill Ellis, but did not qualify or race. It carried a Sanders decal. Its former Spanish Air Force markings were similar to those shown on N3931Z and it was coded 744-187. (Emil Strasser)

#7 **N7979C** raced at Richland, WA, in 1986, flown by Robert Heale. It finished third in the Silver Race. It is shown on the ramp at Reno in 1987, but it was not entered or raced. (Emil Strasse).

#7 **N97AW** *Tinker-Toy* was raced by members of the Dwelle family from 1987 to 2008. Tom Dwelle, Sr. used it to take first in the 1989 and 1990 Reno Gold Races. Ken Dwelle flew it to win the 2008 Reno Gold Race. The aircraft is shown here at Reno in 1989. It also raced as #37, #97, and #97. (Russ Hiatt)

#7 N8204H *Yankee Air Pirate* was another Dwelle family racer. This photo is from Reno 1993 where Tom Dwelle, Sr. took fourth in the Bronze Race. (Bob Kennedy)

#7 N8204H at Reno 1993. #7 had finished fourth in the Silver Race at Redmond in 1992 flown by Tom Dwelle, Sr. (Jim Dunn)

#7 N4485 taxies out at Reno in 2003 with Ken Dwelle at the controls. *Kitchen Pass* would take first in the Silver and Tom Dwelle, Sr. would be sixth in the 2004 Gold Race. It also raced as #2. (Jim Dunn)

#7 N2996Q was raced by Mike Scott at the 2017 Reno races where he finished fourth in the Bronze Race. (Jim Dunn)

#8 N7078C was entered in the 1968 Reno races by Robert Drews but did not qualify or race. Shown is a similar SNJ, BuNo. 6924. (American Aviation Historical Society [AAHS] Collection via Jerry Liang)

#8 N7804B was raced at Ft. Lauderdale in 1969 by Bill Lumley. It was his only Texan race and he qualified seventh. Shown is #8 in its post-race paint scheme. It also raced as #81. (via Dan Hagedorn)

#8 N4983N raced at the 1970 Ft. Lauderdale event a year after this photo was taken. Fred Edison qualified 17th and finished third in the Special Trophy Race. It also raced as #68, #69, and #74 (shown). (Robert F. Pauley via Nicholas A. Veronico Collection)

#8 N6601C at Mojave 1975, where Chan Stokes took second in the Medallion Race and later first in the 1975 Reno Consolation Race. At Lincoln, CA, in 1976, he placed first in the Championship Race, but was bumped to fifth for five pylon cuts. Also, it raced as #33. (Russ Hiatt)

#8 N7412C was raced at Reno in 1977 by Ron Helve, where he finished third in the Medallion Race. Helve would later win the 1982 Unlimited Gold Race at Reno in #4 *Dago Red*. It also raced as #13. (Bob Kennedy)

#8 N7038C *Fertile Turtle* at Reno in 1978. It was raced by Dimitry Prian in his first race, where he qualified 11th. During the first lap of the Consolation Race, he collided with #74 and both aircraft crashed fatally. The aircraft also raced as #38 and #43. (Jerry Liang)

#8 N4RC at Reno in 1982, the year after Robert "Bob" Jones first raced it as a rookie in 1981. *Rent-A-Dent* was second in the 1982 Silver Race. Jones raced for 20 years and was a consistent Silver Race contestant. He raced to second in the Richland Gold Races in 1986. Also, it was raced as #80. (Bob Kennedy)

#8 N4RC had a new sponsor by Reno 1990, also a car rental agency. Jones would take a fourth in the Silver Race. (Russ Hiatt)

#8 N4RC taxies in at Reno 1997 with a totally new paint scheme. Jones would race until 2000, placing third in the Silver Race. (Jerry Liang)

#8 N4RC was under new management at Reno 2010 and raced by Ken Gottschall, who took over in 2006. Ken would give #8 its only win in the 2009 Reno Silver Race. The aircraft was retired after the 2011 Reno event, having raced for 29 years. (Bob Kennedy)

#8 N6427D was raced at Tunica, Mississippi (MS), in 2005 by aerobatic pilot Robin Crandall. There he placed sixth in the Silver Race, aiming to take part of the $50,000 total Texan prize money. It was also raced as #62. (Robin Crandall)

#9 N5199V at its first race at Reno 1968, raced by Phil Livingston, who would finish third in the Championship Race. The aircraft raced for 32 years with eight different pilots under five different names and at five different events. (Ron Olsen)

#9 N5199V was raced by Pat Palmer at Reno 1973 as *Gotcha!* and would finish third in the Gold Race and first in the Gold at Mojave the same year. Palmer would win the 1974 Reno Gold Race in his last year racing #9. (Jerry Liang)

#9 N5199V at Reno 1976 but now raced by Marshall Wells and named *Cum'n Thru*. Wells and Palmer were friends and when Palmer bought his new Texan, N999LP, he sold *Gotcha!* to Wells. (Emil Strasser)

#9 N5199V, raced by Marshall Wells and named *Cum'n Thru!*, is in a gold/bronze paint scheme at Reno 1977. Wells would place third in the Consolation Race. Wells' best finishes in #9 were first in the 1976 Reno Consolation Race and first in the 1976 Lincoln Championship Race after the initial first place winner was bumped back for pylon cuts. (Charlene Aro)

#9 N5199V as *Lickety Split* at Reno 1983, raced by Robert Heale to first place in the Consolation Race during his rookie year. His only other win was first place in the Gold at Richland in 1986. #9 was raced at Reno in 1998 by Bud Granley to fourth in the Silver Race. Granley took over #9 in 1989, with Lee Oman racing it once in 1997. Oman's best finish was sixth in the Gold Race in 2005. (Bob Kennedy)

#9 N5199V returned to Reno in 2016, raced by Pete Stavrides, and was a DNF in the Bronze Race. (Kenneth Smith)

#9 N5199V at Reno 2018, its last year raced. Stavrides finished fifth in the Silver Race. (Mike Henniger)

#10 N1046C, in its second race in August 1969 at Cleveland, was raced by Don Barrett. It raced earlier in the month at St. Louis. It placed fifth in the Consolation at St. Louis and second in the Consolation at Cleveland and was entered, but did not qualify, at Reno in September 1969. (Robert F. Pauly via Nicholas A. Veronico Collection)

#10 N1046C is shown at Ft. Lauderdale in 1970 where it finished fifth. Note the addition of the checkerboard tail, which was painted red and white. (Robert F. Pauly via Nicholas A. Veronico Collection)

#10 N1046C was raced by Jim Wilson at Reno in 1974. Wilson placed fifth in the Championship Race, and this would be #10's last race. Note the rag stuck into the air intake. Texan N1046C would be W/O ten years after the Cape May accident, July 1981, at an airshow. (Emil Strasser)

#10 N39403 at its only appearance in Texan racing in 1990 at Reno. *Bad Juju* was raced by Greg Morse and finished sixth in the Bronze Race. (Russ Hiatt)

#11 N9060Z is at Reno in 1968 for the first full-scale Texan races and was flown by Howie Keefe to sixth place in the Championship Race. (Ron Olsen)

#11 N9060Z would be raced again by Howie Keefe at the 1970 Ft. Lauderdale races. *"Miss Sky Prints"* had new nose art and would take first place in the Special Trophy Race. (Robert F. Pauley via Nicholas A. Veronico Collection)

#11 N16730 at Cleveland in 1969. *Miss Sky Prints II* would qualify fifth and finish fifth in the Championship Race. Keefe would also qualify for the 1969 Reno races but was cut after qualifying 23rd. It also raced as #71. (Robert F. Pauley via Nicholas A. Veronico Collection)

#11 N16730 at Mojave 1979, where Calvin Conroy did not qualify, but #11 was raced by Dick Sykes to fifth in the Silver. Conroy and Jim Modes co-raced #11 throughout the 1970s and the best finish was by Modes, a sixth in the 1973 Mojave Gold. (Russ Hiatt)

#11 N16730, at Reno 1986, was now raced by Ray Schutte. He took first in the 1984 Reno Bronze Race and finished sixth in the Silver. Ray qualified 20th in 1992 at Reno but was cut and it would be the last time he would race. (Bob Kennedy)

#11 N9785Z, at Cape May June 6, 1971, was raced by Ernest Opp, who had qualified 13th. The Texan was also used as a pace-plane. This was Opp's second race; he had raced at Wilson in May and qualified eighth. The plane also raced as #88 under a different registration number. (Kenneth Smith Collection)

#11 N3169G seen after a ground collision at Reno in 2007, raced by Carter Clark. Clark qualified 20th but was unable to make repairs in time to race. (Roger Cain)

#11 N3169G *Daring Diane* shown from the opposite side at Reno 2007. Temporary repairs were made, and Clark flew it home. It raced as #1 and #88 as well. (Roger Cain)

#12 CF-RZO was the first Harvard IV to race in Closed Course Pylon Racing. Jim Strang raced in five events from 1970 to 1971. This photo is at the 1971 Cape May races where he scored his best finish with a third in the Championship Race. (Kenneth Smith Collection)

#12 CF-RZO was the first Canadian-registered Texan to race in Closed Course Pylon Racing and is shown after retiring from racing at Dayton, OH, in 1972. Jim Strang flew in the 1971 Jacksonville Demo Race and placed third. (R. A. Burgess via Doug Slowiak)

#12 N612MD turning the pylons at Mojave in 1975. M. D. Washburn raced for only two years, 1974–75, at two events in Mojave and Reno. For 1974, he finished fifth in the Gold at Mojave and third in the Reno Consolation Race. In the Mojave 1975 race, he was third in the Gold. It was during the 1975 Reno Heat-2 that he clipped a pylon and fatally crashed. (Jerry Liang)

#12 N91AM qualified 23rd by Stu Eberhardt at Reno in 1992, but was cut to keep the field to 20. (Bob Kennedy)

#12 N12KY was raced by John Zayac at Reno 2002, where he would finish sixth in the Silver Race. Zayac's best finish in #12 was first in the Reno Bronze Race in 2003. The aircraft was also raced by Tom Martin in 2006 to a fifth in the Bronze Race. (Bob Kennedy)

#12 N1465 was raced by Terry Adams at Reno in 2013 and took second in the Bronze Race. It also raced as #2. (Jerry Liang)

#13 N7412C was entered at Reno twice, once in 1968, when it qualified 16th, and in 1969, when it qualified 23rd by Joseph Andrade, and both times it was cut. This photo is from 1968. Also, it was raced as #8. (Ron Olsen)

#13 N4269E has raced under other race numbers, such as #4 and #44, but it is shown here at Reno 2022. It was raced by Brian Reberry, who finished sixth in the Classic Race. (Jim Dunn)

#14 N2886G was raced once at Reno in 1969 by Rudy Malaspina. He qualified fourth and took sixth in the Championship Race. This Texan was W/O in September 1976 after making a low pass at an airshow. (Emil Strasser)

#14 N3653G wore a US Navy three-tone blue paint scheme at Reno in 1973 when raced by Fred Sebby. He finished sixth in the Bronze after cutting three pylons. Entered in the 1973 Reno races, it qualified 20th and was cut. It also raced as #5. (Ron Olsen)

#14 N57418 *Mystery Ship* at Reno in 1983, raced by Richard Sykes. He took first in the Gold Race and set a new five-mile course record at 225.94mph. John Krawczyk raced #14 in 1997 and took second in the Silver. (Bob Kennedy)

#14 N57418 *Baron's Revenge* was raced by Chris Rushing at Reno 2015. Chris had four Gold Race wins in 2016, 2019, 2021, and 2022. It is a fitting tribute to Chris Rushing's late father-in-law Richard Sykes. Chris won his fifth Gold Race in Reno 2023, but he was tragically killed moments after winning the race when his aircraft collided with another. (Jerry Liang)

#15 N9801C was raced by Fred Sebby at Mojave in 1975 and called *Blue Canoe II*. Sebby would take fifth in the Silver and also second in the 1975 Reno Medallion. He did not qualify for 1976 Mojave. If a comparison is made between Sebby's #14 N3653G and this aircraft, one understands why they are often confused as the same Texan. (Bob Kennedy)

#16 N7471C in a post-race photo at Oshkosh, WI, in the 1970s. This Texan appeared at the 1969 Reno races with #16 painted on its side and a dark paint scheme with the name *Crazy Ed's*. After a thorough search, no records can be found that it raced at any event. (via Nicholas A. Veronico Collection)

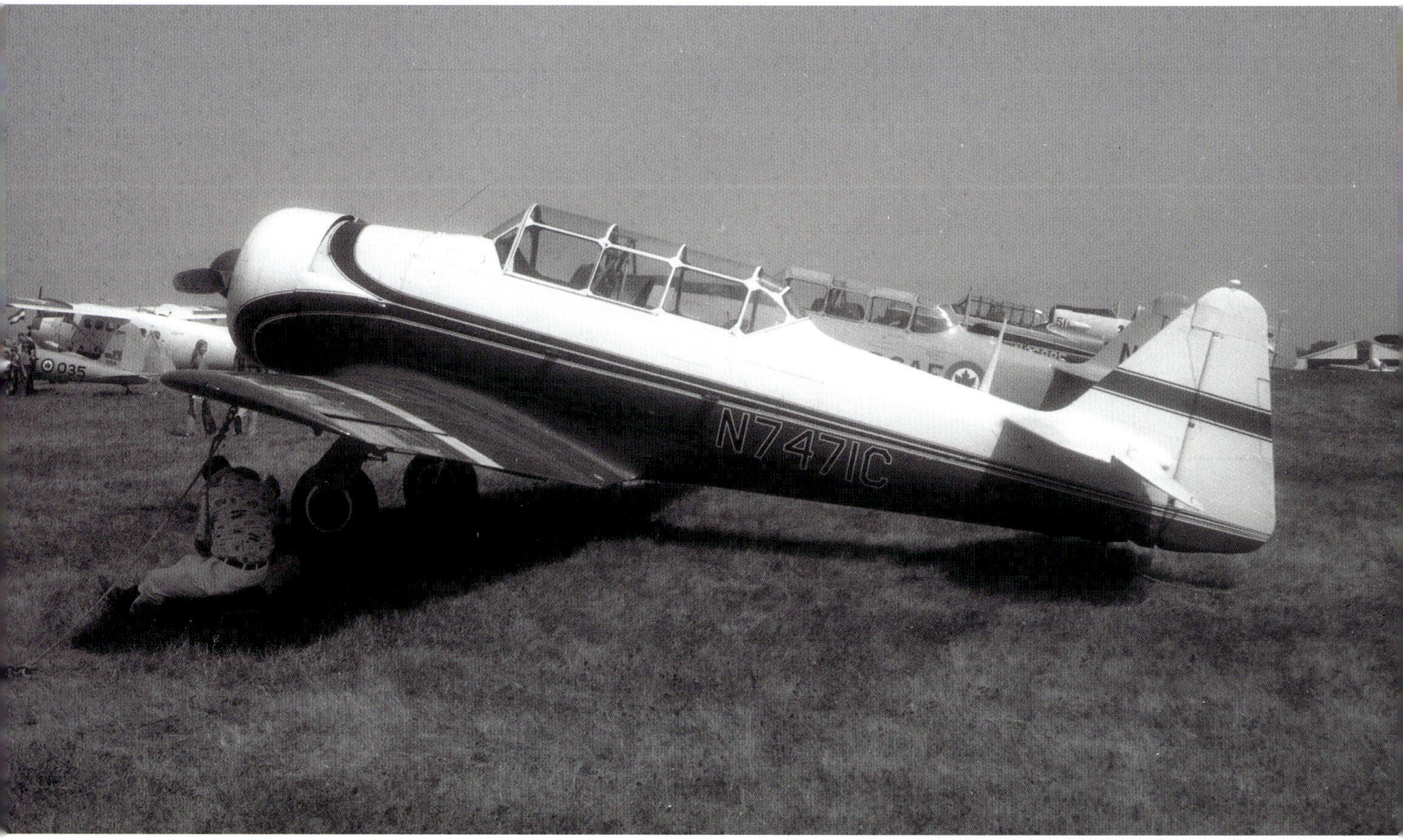

#16 N86116 was entered by Bruce Mayes at Reno in 2004, but did not qualify. (Jim Dunn)

#17 N5198V was raced only once and that was by rookie John Moriarty at Ft. Lauderdale in 1969. He qualified fifth. It is seen two months later at Morristown, NJ, still wearing its race number. (Bob O'Dell via Dan Hagedorn)

#17 N8212E is seen at Oshkosh in 1990 after its racing career. It raced twice and both times at Wilson. In 1971, Jozef Huysman qualified 10th and, in 1972, he qualified fifth. He finished second in the Consolation Race. (William "Bill" Jesse)

#17 N711AP *"Speedy Gonzales"* was entered in the 1975 Reno races with a #17 taped over its #2, similar to how the "A" had been added to its number at Mojave in 1973. It was entered by James Raymond but did not qualify or race. (Russ Hiatt)

#17 N3931S was entered by Gene McNeely at Reno in 1986, but it did not qualify. (Bob Kennedy)

#17 N3931S was at Reno again in 1987 raced by Fred Johnson, who finished fifth in the Bronze Race. It would be raced in 1988 by David Griggs, who placed fifth in the Bronze. It also raced as #55. (Russ Hiatt)

#18 N30JF was first raced at Cape May in 1971, where Jim Flanagan qualified 14th. Later that year, he raced at Reno, as shown here. Jim's best finish was Reno 1972 with second in the Medallion Race. He was also a DNF at Miami in 1973 and qualified 12th at Graham in 1973. The aircraft also raced as #76. (Emil Strasser)

#18 N57318 was entered by Dennis Buehn at Reno in 1984 but did not qualify. However, in 1985, when raced by Randy DiFani, it finished first in the Gold and would race in another seven Gold Races from 1985 to 1994, with only two third places. DiFani took first in the Silver at the 1994 Phoenix race. Also, the Texan raced as #39 and #45. (Bob Kennedy)

#19 was registered as N6424D in 1989 and N694US in 1990. It was raced both years at Reno by Robert Heale. It finished third in the 1989 Bronze Race and first in the 1990 Bronze Race, shown here. The aircraft was raced as #41, #69, and #94 as well. (Russ Hiatt)

#19 N2269U was qualified for the 2014 Reno races by Dennis Buehn but was raced by Thomas Baber to fifth in the Bronze Race. (Roger Cain)

#19 N260CF was flown by rookie Michael Sisk at Reno 2023, where he qualified 15th at 185.744mph and finished fourth in the Bronze. (Jim Dunn)

#20 N3272G at Reno in 1990, raced by Linda Finch. She was the second women to race in the new era of Texan pylon racing. She entered #20 at Reno in 1988, qualifying 19th but was cut. In 1990, she finished third in the Bronze Race. It also raced as #26, #28, and #88. (Russ Hiatt)

#20 N7471S and Paul Redlich would race at Reno in 2004 and again in 2006. Redlich finished third in the 2004 Silver Race (when this photo was taken). A fifth in the Silver Race in 2006 would be his last Texan race. (Jerry Liang)

#21 N3261G was raced by John Trainor at Cape May in 1971, where he finished sixth in the Championship Race. His best finish was at the 1969 Ft. Lauderdale races when he took first in the Championship Race. (Dick Phillips via Dan Hagedorn)

#21 N125JD, on the ramp at Reno 1993, was raced by Charles Hutchins to third in the Gold Race. Hutchins would take first in the 1995 Gold and Mary Dilda would take first in the 1997 Gold. (Bob Kennedy)

#21 N212TC qualified first at Reno 1998 flown by Lee Oman. A major controversy led to the aircraft being disqualified from racing that year. The new owner of #21, Tom Campau (note new registration number), would race it at Tunica in 2005 and take first in the Gold Race. (Russ Hiatt)

#21 N212TC at Reno in 2006 with another new owner. It was raced by Rick Siegfried and finished seventh in the Gold Race. (Jerry Liang)

#21 N620AJ was raced by rookie Ben York III at Reno in 2022. York qualified seventh and finished seventh in the Classic Race. It also raced as #54. (Jim Dunn)

#22 N3518G is on its belly after having landing gear trouble at the February 1969 Ft. Lauderdale races. B. F. McKinney had taken fourth in the Championship Race. The aircraft was repaired and raced the remainder of 1969. (Robert F. Pauley via Nicholas A. Veronico Collection)

#22 N3518G is repaired and racing at the August 1969 St. Louis races, where it finished second in the Consolation Race. Its best finish would be fifth in the 1969 Reno Race. McKinney would race a new Texan in 1970. (Robert F. Pauley via Nicholas A. Veronico Collection)

#22 N555Q, seen here post-racing, had been raced by B.F. McKinney in the 1970 Ft. Lauderdale races. It qualified 15th and took second in the Special Trophy Race. (AAHS via Jerry Liang)

#22 N7065C/N22KD changed registration numbers between its first two years and was raced by Kenny Day. It is shown at Reno in 1990 as N7065C where it placed fifth in the Bronze. Day's best finish was first in the 1992 Reno Silver Race, and the aircraft flew as N22KD. (Russ Hiatt)

#22 N73RR was raced by Mary Dilda, the third women to race Texan in the new era, at Reno in 1998. She would place fourth in the Gold Race. First raced at Reno in 1996 by Dilda, it would race off and on until 2015. It also raced as #56, #59 and #73. (Bob Kennedy)

#22 N73RR at Reno in 2000, where Mary Dilda would finish fifth in the Gold Race. Mary would use #22 to win the 2005 Reno Gold Race and take second at the 2005 Tunica Race. It last raced in 2015 by Chad Morgan. (Jerry Liang)

#23 N89013 may have raced in the 1979 Mojave drag races by Dennis Buehn, seen here on the ramp. It was entered in the 1983 Reno races by Richard Yersak, where it qualified 17th but was cut. (Bob Kennedy)

#24 N7976C *Mustang*, on the ramp at Reno 1969, was raced by Gerald Swayze, who finished sixth in the Medallion Race. His best finish was at St. Louis in 1969 with a fourth in the Consolation Race. The paint scheme is the early Confederate Air Force (CAF) colors as this Texan was associated with that organization, which has since been renamed the Commemorative Air Force. (Jerry Liang)

#24 N3682F was raced by Gerald Swayze at Reno, shown here in 1973. It would place fourth in the 1973 Consolation Race and sixth in the 1974 Consolation Race. (Ron Olsen)

#24 N7613C would only be raced once by Mark Moodie at Reno in 1994. It finished third in the Bronze Race. It is seen here on the ramp during the Demo Races held at Shafter, CA, in 1995. (Bob Kennedy)

#25 N7404C at Reno in 1972. The photograph appears to show that there were plans to change #25's registration number to N25RM before Roy McClain obtained the Texan. McClain would take first place in the Gold Race. While owned by Tony Murgia, its best finish was third in the 1970 St. Louis Championship Race. (Emil Strasser)

#25 N7404C at the 1973 Reno races, where Roy McClain would finish first in the Medallion Race. The aircraft would change race numbers in 1974 to #5 and continues to race under this number. It has also raced as #51. (Ron Olsen)

#25 N8048E in its first race at Reno in 1994, raced by Jimmy Gist to fifth in the Bronze Race. (Bob Kennedy)

#25 N8048E returned to Reno in 2014 after last racing in 1994. Shown in 2015, it was raced by Duane Woods to fifth place in the Classic Race. (Jerry Liang)

#25 N3680F was raced by Jason Karlin at Reno in 2021–23. Karlin finished fifth in the Classic Race in 2022, when this photo was taken. (Jim Dunn)

#26 N3272G qualified 20th in the 1987 Reno races by Linda Finch in her first attempt at Texan racing. Finch was cut and did not race. It also raced as #20, #28 and #88. (Jerry Liang)

#26 N726KM, still wearing its former SAAF markings, was raced by Jim Thomas at Reno in 2009 to sixth place in the Bronze Race. This was his only entry. (Jerry Liang)

#27 N127VF at its first Reno race in 1984 where Eddie Van Fossen would qualify 14th and place seventh in the Consolation Race. While not a first-place winner that year, by 1986 Eddie would win three consecutive Gold races at Reno. Eddie and *Miss TNT* would go on to win five more Gold races, four at Reno and one at Phoenix. (Bob Kennedy)

#27 N127VF on its way to Reno in 1987 to win the Gold Race. Eddie Van Fossen would win his last races, both Gold, at Reno and Phoenix in 1994. It was a fitting way to retire. As of 2022, Eddie and *Miss TNT* remain the all-time Texan Gold winners with eight. (Bob Kennedy)

#27 N127VF was raced as *Pole Dancer* by its new owner Eric Woelbing, who purchased the aircraft from Eddie Van Fossen. Woelbing placed second in the Silver Race at Reno in 2016. (Jim Dunn)

#27 N127VF had reverted to *Miss TNT* by Reno 2018. Eric Woelbing had better luck with that name as he took first in the Silver Race. (Jim Dunn)

#28 N3272G has had great luck at Reno beginning in 2007. John Lohmar placed first in the 2007 Bronze Race. This was followed by first in the 2008 Silver and fourth in the 2009 Gold. It also raced as #20, #26, and #88. (Jerry Liang)

#30 was first entered as N62510 "Nicayank" by Hugh Alexander at Reno in 1969. It qualified 27th and was cut. Next, it flew at Ft. Lauderdale in 1970 and took third in the Consolation Race. By the 1970 Wilson Regional Air Races, N62510 had become N30HA and it finished first in the Consolation Race. It raced at Cape May in 1971, where this photo was taken, and placed second in the Championship Race. (Kenneth Smith Collection)

#30 N30HA returned to Reno in 1971 and Hugh Alexander would finish second in the Medallion Race. Alexander's best finish would be at the 1972 Wilson races, where he would finish first in the Championship Race, which was his last race. (Emil Strasser)

#030 N7437C was entered in the 1993 Reno races by David Peeler but did not qualify or race. The aircraft did not return. This photo shows N7437C at the 2001 SUN 'n FUN Fly-In sporting the same paint scheme worn at Reno. (John Kerr)

#30 N666SS/N116SE is another Texan racer that changed its registration during its racing career. Shown here as #30 N666SS at Reno in 1994, it was raced by Bill Eberhardt and would place fourth in Heat-2. The aircraft was raced once by Tom Dwelle, Sr. in 1995. (Bob Kennedy)

#30 N116SE in its new blue paint scheme at Reno 2010. Jim Eberhardt would be the principal pilot for most of the 17 years that #30 raced. Its best finish was first in the 2002 Bronze Race with Eberhardt in command. Also, it raced as #302. (Bob Kennedy)

#31 N90629 at Madera, CA, in 1979, flown by Wes Tolle. There is no proof that it ever raced. *Lickety Split* had raced in 1978 as #90. (Bob Kennedy)

#33 N733L was raced by Leo Volkmer at the 1969 Reno Races where he placed second in the Medallion Race. John Moriarty raced it at Fort Lauderdale in 1970 and qualified tenth but was disqualified for low flying. (Emil Strasser)

#33 N1974M had been raced as #96 by Richard Minges until the start of the 1971 racing season. He raced at Wilson in May and took first in the Championship Race. The next race on the schedule was Cape May in June. Minges qualified sixth. During lap 1 of Heat-2B, he collided with Don Barrett and fatally crashed. This photo was taken at Cape May the morning of the accident. (Dennis Buehn Collection)

This is a surplus AT-6F, much like #33 N6601C, which was entered at Reno in 1974 by Marshall Wells and qualified 20th but was cut and did not race. The Texan had a race number change to #8. (William T. Larkins)

#33 N9800C was entered by Jerry Borchin at Reno in 1996 but did not qualify. This photo was taken in 1999. (Jerry Liang)

#33 N2757 is sitting back in the hangar area at Reno in 2010 after it had been raced by Carter Clark and placed second in the Bronze Race. Its best race was sixth in 2012 with Terry Adams. (Bob Kennedy)

#33 N4434N turning the pylons at Reno 2019. *Money Rat/Money Trap* was raced by six-time Reno Gold-winner Dennis Buehn to fifth in the Bronze Race. (Roger Cain)

#35 N7448C was the first Texan raced by Jay Quinn and he raced it at Reno in 1969. He qualified 16th and finished third in the Medallion Race. Shown here at the Merced, CA, airshow. (Jerry Liang)

#35 N9735Z taxiing out at Cape May in June 1971, piloted by Jay Quinn and hoping to qualify. (Dennis Buehn Collection)

#35 N9735Z at the 1971 Cape May races, where Jay Quinn qualified seventh. This photo was taken the morning of the fatal accidents. #35 *Jay Bird* was W/O on lap 3 of Heat-2B. (Kenneth Smith Collection)

#35 N3653G was entered at the 1974 Mojave races by Fred Sebby, but it was relegated to racing in the drag races only. (Emil Strasser)

#37 N6975C was raced at Reno by Dick Gregory in 1968 and qualified seventh and finished fourth in the Consolation Race. This was its best finish. Its paint scheme is described as avocado green with gold lettering. The plane is shown in 1973 when raced by Jim Metcalfe. It also raced as #4. (Ron Olson)

#37 N97AW aloft over Reno in 1997 where Jim Bennett would win the first of his three consecutive Silver Races. *Tinker Toy* also raced as #7 and #97. (Jim Dunn)

#37 N3666F wore this paint scheme at its first Reno outing in 2006, raced by John Zayac. He would take a fourth in the Gold Race. (Jerry Liang)

#37 N3666F sitting on the ramp in 2010. John Zayac would make his best finish at Reno in 2010, placing second in the Gold Race. Also, it raced as #72. (Bob Kennedy)

Above: #38 N7038C is seen in a typical paint scheme and painted canopy on the ramp at Reno 1968. It was raced by James Writz to second in the Consolation Race, its best finish. It also raced as #8 and #43. (Ron Olsen)

Left: #38 N7090C taxiing out at Reno 1972, raced by Don Gaylan. He would take fifth in the Medallion Race, its best finish. It only raced in 1971 and 1972. (Jerry Liang)

#39 N57318 racing at Reno in 1983 where it would finish sixth in the Consolation Race flown by Ed Colbert. *Ruthie's* best finish was in 1982, when Dennis Buehn raced to fifth in the Gold Race. It also raced as #18 and #45. (Bob Kennedy)

#39 N3258G getting ready for a race at Reno in 1993 flown by Ray Dieckman. He finished sixth in the Bronze Race. In 1994, Ray would finish sixth in at the Phoenix races. (Bob Kennedy)

#40 N1040C sits with its support equipment on the ramp at Reno in 1973. If a work stand was needed, any 55-gallon drum was used. Stan Gnesa qualified 19th but was cut and did not race. (Ron Olsen)

#40 N1040C *The Martin Fabric Clip Special*, raced by Stan Gnesa, is seen taxiing out at Reno in 1977. Gnesa qualified 1sixth and finished fifth in the Medallion Race. (Jerry Liang)

#41 N8206E was the first of Ralph Twombly's #41s. It is shown at the 1969 Cleveland races, which was Twombly's first race. He qualified eighth and finished third in the Consolation Race, which was its best finish with this registration. It was repainted and reregistered as N41BT at the start of 1971. (Robert F. Pauley via Nicholas A. Veronico Collection)

#41 N41BT is undergoing engine maintenance on the line at Cape May in 1971. Ralph Twombly qualified tenth, started Heat-2B, and finished fifth in the Championship Race. Ralph's best finish in this #41 was third in the 1972 Wilson Championship Race. It also raced as #77. (Kenneth Smith Collection)

#41 N9831C was Ralph Twombly's third #41, which he raced 1977–79. Shown on the ramp during the 1979 Mojave races. *Spooled Up* carries "National Champion T-6 Racing Class 1977–1978" on its side. Twombly finished first in the 1977 Reno Gold Race, second in the 1978 Reno Gold Race, first in the 1978 Mojave Gold Race, and second in the 1979 Mojave Gold Race. It was raced as #98 as well. (Bob Kennedy)

#41 N6424D at Reno 1986, raced by Joe Taylor who would finish fourth in the Bronze Race. The Texan also raced as #16, #69, and #94. (Bob Kennedy)

#41 N8540Z is seen with Ralph Twombly climbing out after arriving at Reno in 1994. Twombly attempted to race this Texan at Richland in 1986 but blew a tire on landing and bent the gear. He took fifth in the 1993 Reno Gold Race and fifth in the 1994 Phoenix Gold Race. Ralph qualified 12th at Reno in 1994, but he was fatally injured at the start of the Silver Race, colliding with #51 Jerry McDonald. (Bob Kennedy)

#42 N3274G on the ramp at Reno 1973, raced by Jim Mott to second in the Championship Race. Mott had taken first in the 1972 Reno Medallion Race. Mott would win the Gold Race at Mojave 1974, which was his best finish. (Ron Olsen)

#42 N3274G *Miss Chief* arriving at the 1976 Mojave races. Mott would qualify seventh but was unable to race after a prop strike following a drag race. (Jerry Liang)

#42 N3274G at Reno 1983, raced by Jim Mott to fourth in the Gold Race. In 1981, Jim qualified #42, but it was raced by Ralph Twombly, who won the Silver Race. This Texan now lives in Australia as VH-OVO. (Bob Kennedy)

#42 N42DQ made its only race appearance at Reno in 1989. It was raced by Mike Wells and placed sixth in the Bronze Race. It also raced with new registration number N77TX. (Jerry Liang)

#42 N77TX on the ramp at Reno in 1991. It did not race that year. Raced in 1994 by Greg Shelton, it finished fifth in the Bronze Race as *Artic Fox* at Phoenix. (Emil Strasser)

#42 N8044H was entered in both the 1999 and 2001 Reno races by Gene McNeely but did not qualify or race in either year. It is shown here at the 2001 SUN 'n FUN expo. It also raced as #2. (John Kerr)

#42 N86WW, raced by Kevin Sutterfield at Reno in 2015, was a DNS for the Silver Race. Its best finishes were first in the 2005 Bronze with Chris Rushing and first in the 2012 Bronze with Rob Sandberg. Shown is the old #42 that was first raced at Reno in 1977 by Charles Beck. Also, it was raced as #2 and #88. (Jerry Liang)

#43 N9789Z at Graham in 1972, raced by Dennis Buehn. This was his first in #43. Buehn placed fifth in this set of Demo races. (Dennis Buehn Collection)

#43 N7038C qualified 21st for Reno 1972 by Dennis Buehn but was cut and did not race. (Jerry Liang)

A repainted #43 N7038C is on the ramp at the 1974 Mojave races. Dennis Buehn would place sixth in the Consolation Race but was bumped back to seventh with a pylon cut. It also raced as #8 and #38. (Russ Hiatt)

#43 N7446C raced only in the 1976 Mojave Drag Races. Dennis Buehn was first in the final race against #11 Jim Modes. Also, it was raced as #6. (Bob Kennedy)

#43 N8158H was another of Dennis Buehn's #43s. He is taxiing out at Reno in 1976. *Midnight Miss II* would take first in the Medallion Race. It raced as #4 as well. (Jerry Liang)

#43 N3171P *Midnight Miss III* takes off at Reno 2006, raced by Dennis Buehn to second the Gold. Buehn raced it to win six Gold races at Reno over the next nine years, with the first win in 2007. (Mike Henniger)

#43 N3171P at Reno 2015, where Dennis Buehn would win his last Gold Race. The aircraft is still racing and placed fourth in the 2022 Gold Race with its current owner Joel Stinnett. It also raced as #4. (Alan Hess via Mike Henniger)

Art Carlson is in John Mosby's #44 N1395N at Cleveland in 1969. Carlson would qualify third and take fourth in the Championship Race. Besides Carlson, Howie Keefe would also race it. Carlson was racing it in Heat-2B at Cape May in 1971 when the race was red flagged due to the two fatal crashes. (Robert F. Pauley via Nicholas A. Veronico Collection)

#44 N1395N at Reno in 1971. It was raced by John Mosby to third in the Special Make-Up Race. Mosby was also at Reno in 1969, but qualified 26th and was cut from the race. (Jerry Liang)

#44 N194A at Reno in 1973, raced by Jack Lowers for owner Jim Mosby. Lowers finished first in the Consolation Race. John Mosby had taken over this Texan from Bob Mitchem who had raced it as #94. (Ron Olsen)

#44 N194A was raced by Ralph Twombly at Mojave in 1976 for John Mosby. Twombly qualified eighth with *"Miss Behavin"* and took first in the Gold Race. (Emil Strasser)

#44 N194A at Reno in 1978, actually being raced by John Mosby this time. He would qualify fourth and place sixth in the Championship Race. (Emil Strasse).

#44 N194A raced at the 1986 Reno races by Alan Preston, who placed second in the Silver Race. Preston placed first in the 1986 Richland Silver Race in this Texan. (Bob Kennedy)

#44 N44ZZ, formerly N194A, was raced at the 1987 Reno Races by Ralph Twombly. He took first in the Silver Race. It also raced as #94. (Bob Kennedy)

#44 N75964 was raced by Tom Nightingale at the April 1996 Shafter Demo Race held as part of the annual Warbird show. (Bob Kennedy)

#44 N4269E raced at Reno in 2005. It was flown by Wayne Cartwright to second in the Silver Race. Lee Oman had used #44 to win the 1997 Bronze Race, its only win. It also raced as #4. (Bob Kennedy)

#44 N7522U at Reno in 1998, raced by Jim Booth to second in the Bronze Race. Jim would take third in the 1999 Bronze Race. Booth would later use #44 as the Reno pace plane. It also raced as #444. (Bob Kennedy)

#45 N57318 was used by John Mosby at the 1971 Cape May races. He did not qualify but was allowed to race. N57318 is shown here at El Mirage, CA, airport in 1981. It also raced as #18 and #39. (Bob Kennedy)

#45 N7679C is here at Brown Field, CA, in May 1948, a decade before it was entered in the 1994 Reno races by Gary Eller. It did not qualify. (Bob Kennedy)

Left: #46 N2860G raced at Mojave in 1973, flown by Charles Beck to second in the Bronze Race. Beck and Jim Striwalt would alternate racing #46 from 1973 to 1976. The aircraft also raced as #3. (Russ Hiatt)

Below: Richard Fields entered #46 N7055H twice at Reno, in 1993 and 1994. Both years it did not qualify or race. The Texan is seen here at Santa Maria, CA, in August 1994. (Russ Hiatt)

Above: #47 N302V *Miss Seattle* taxiing out at Reno 1971, raced by Ron Kostelnik. Ron qualified fifth and finished fifth in the Championship Race. The aircraft would crash fatally on its way back to Seattle after the races. (Emil Strasser)

Right: #47 N611F taxiing out at Reno 1998, flown by Jack Frost. Frost would win the 1998 Gold Race and he placed fourth in the 1997 Gold. After being the fastest qualifier in the 1999 races, Frost was disqualified for "unsportsmanlike conduct" and asked to leave the races. It also raced as #7 and #86. (Bob Kennedy)

#48 N3194G was raced at Reno in 1971 by George Burdick, where he qualified 20th and placed first in the Make-Up Race. This Texan was W/O in 1972. It is shown here in 1962 before it was raced. (Russ Hiatt)

#48 N48BC raced twice at Reno and is seen here in 1986 being raced by Shane Theis. While Theis qualified 23rd, he did not race. His best finish had been the month before at the 1986 Richland races where he finished fifth in the Gold. (Emil Strasser)

#048/48 N42JM is being towed back to the Texan pits at Reno in 1991. Dorel Graves had qualified 19th and would finish second in Heat-2C. Graves had entered the Reno 1987 races as #048 and had qualified 21st but was cut. It also raced as #3. (Russ Hiatt)

#48 N2983 would be entered in the 2018 Reno races by John Johnson but would not qualify or race. *Playtime* is seen on arrival in 2018. It raced as #49 as well. (Kenneth Smith)

#48 N6625C taxiing in at Reno 2023 where it was raced by Brian Reberry, who qualified 13th at 188.840mph and finished fifth in the Bronze. (Jim Dunn)

#49 N21JD on the ramp at the 1979 Mojave races where John Kirkland qualified first and took third in the Gold Race. The Texan was first raced at Reno in 1977 by John Allcorn and finished fourth in the Consolation Race. (Bob Kennedy)

#49 N21JD at Reno 1982. It was raced by Phil Gist where it placed fifth in the Silver Race. It had been entered at Reno in 1981 by John Hunt, but it did not qualify due to damage before the start of the races. (Bob Kennedy)

#49 N2864D was entered in the 1994 Reno races by John Meyer. It would not qualify or race. Also, it was raced as #64. (Bob Kennedy)

#49 N29931 taxiing in at Reno in 2000. It was raced by John Johnson to fourth in the Medallion Race. This is the same N29931 that Jim Mott cartwheeled at Reno 1991 as #51. (Jerry Liang)

#49 N2983 showing how speed tape is put to use in racing. *Playtime* is shown at Reno 2013 being turned around the pylons by John Johnson. He took fifth in the Bronze Race. As mentioned, it also raced as #48. (Roger Cain)

#49 N7296C taxiing out to start a race at Reno in 2018, raced by Bill Muszala. He would take third in the Bronze Race and also in the 2019 races. (Mike Henniger)

#49 N7269C rounding the pylons at Reno 2022, piloted by Bill Muszala to first in the Classic Race. He also took first in the 2021 Classic Race. (Jim Dunn)

#50/502 N502 at Reno 1968. It was qualified by legendary Unlimited Race pilot Commander Walt Ohlrich, United States Navy (USN). Texan #502 had its number briefly changed to #50. It qualified 14th but did not race as Ohlrich was also racing his Grumman F8F Bearcat. (Ron Olsen)

#50 N17400 rounding a pylon at Reno 1969, raced by George Sanders. He qualified 16th and finished fifth in the Medallion Race. This was the only time the faded Canadian Harvard raced. (Emil Strasser)

#50 N8539L was raced by Carl Penner at Reno in 1998. Penner raced *Big Wind* for five years at Reno with a best finish of two Bronze Race wins in 1999 and 2000 and two fifth place Silver Races in 1998 and 1999. (Bob Kennedy)

#50 N4763 at Reno in 2009, where it finished fifth in the Silver raced by John Krawczyk. He had won the 2008 Bronze Race and would race #50 until 2013. (Mike Henniger)

#50 N4763 at Reno in 2022, after placing first in Heat-1B raced by Vitaly Pecherskyy. He would finish sixth in the Gold Race, which was #50's second Gold Race finish. It also raced as #2. (Jim Dunn)

#51 N7404C is the former #5 *Red Baron*. The remains of the name painted on the side of the Texan are still visible at Mojave in 1978. New owner Jerry McDonald qualified seventh and took first in the Silver Race. In 1978 and 1979, Cliff Branch used #5 on his Texan. N7404C would get #5 back in 1981. It also raced as #25, and #5. (Bob Kennedy)

#51 N8540P was entered at Reno in 1990 by Ralph Rina and qualified 19th but *Killer Hunt* was cut and did not race. Shown undergoing maintenance at Chino, CA, in August 1990. It was also raced as #1. (Russ Hiatt)

#51 N29931 seen after recovery to the 1991 Reno ramp area. The aircraft was cartwheeled by Jim Mott during a practice lap. Mott dragged a wingtip in *Yaba Daba Do* causing control damage and crashed on landing. Mott had qualified 21st. This also raced as #49. (Russ Hiatt)

#51 N2676P, also named *Yaba Daba Do*, was entered at Reno in 1992 by John Marlin/Jerry Miles, but did not qualify or race. Note the similar paint schemes on all three Texans. (Emil Strasser)

Reno 2017 was the last year #54 N1364J was raced by Michael Pfleger when he placed second in the Bronze Race. Pfleger's best finishes were first in the 2013 Bronze Race and sixth in 2016 Silver Race. (Jim Dunn)

#54 N620AJ was raced at Reno in 2018 by Michael Pfleger. He qualified 15th and placed fourth in the Bronze Race. It also raced as #21. (Mike Henniger)

#55 N2864G is at Cleveland in 1969 with Len Tanner, who qualified ninth and finished fifth in the Consolation Race. The plane would have its best finish at Wilson in 1970 when Jack Lowers took second in the Consolation Race. (Robert J. Pauley via Nicholas A. Veronico Collection)

#55 N3203G had been entered at Reno in 1976 as *Lil Maria*, but engine troubles kept Bob Dodson from racing. It is shown here several years later at Oshkosh, WI. (Emil Strasser)

#55 N8540Z qualified 13th at Reno in 1991 flown by David Bruce. He would place third in the Silver Race. It also raced as #4 and #41. (Bob Kennedy)

#55 N3931S/N5FJ at its first appearance at Reno 1993. It was raced by Fred Johnson to third in the Bronze Race. Its civil registration changed to N5FJ in 1995 and it placed third in the Silver Race. Also, it was raced as #17. (Bob Kennedy)

#55 N7648E *Trophy Hunter* taxiing out at Reno 2005, raced by Gary Miller to second in the Bronze Race. In 2006, it was called *Big Daddy* and took sixth in the Silver Race. (Jerry Liang)

#56 N101GB was raced by Scott Dockter at Reno 2008. *Deuce of Hearts* placed seventh in the Bronze Race. The Texan also raced as #57. (Jerry Liang)

#56 N73RR at Reno 2010, raced by Duane Woods to fifth in the Silver Race. The plane was raced by Scott Dockter in 2009. In the 1970s, Ralph Rina raced it as #73. It also raced as #22 and #59. (Bob Kennedy)

#57 N3257G on the ramp at Reno 1969, when it was raced by Cdr Ohlrich. He qualified 16th and finished fourth in the Medallion Race. (Emil Strasser)

#57 N3257G was entered at Reno in 1973 by James Wirtz and qualified 25th but was cut and did not race. (Harold Bailey via Ron Olsen)

#57 N2831D finished sixth in the 1981 Reno races flown by Ed Colbert. The aircraft carried a side number of #577, which was shortened to #57. Shown here at Compton, CA, in 1980. (Bob Kennedy)

#57 N997RD in the Texan pits during Reno 1998. Gary Hubler finished third in the Bronze Race. In 1997, Cheryl Bloom entered #57 but did not qualify. (Russ Hiatt)

#57 N101GB is being towed out for a Heat Race at Reno in 2010. It was raced by Scott Dockter to third in the Bronze Race. With the exception of race numbers, the paint scheme was the same as when it raced as #56. (Bob Kennedy)

#58 N7058C takes off for a Heat Race at Reno 2016 by Thom Vaughn. He raced in Heat-1C and also Heat-2C before being disqualified. Vaughn returned to Reno in 2017 and placed fifth in the Bronze Race. (Kenneth Smith)

#59 N73RR *Blue Bayou* on the Reno 1991 ramp being raced by Jimmy Gist. Gist finished third in the Silver Race that year, second in the 1991 Bronze Race, and third in the 1992 Bronze Race. It also raced as #22, #56 and #73. (Bob Kennedy)

#59 N651SH *Dulcinea* raced only once and that was at Reno in 2012, where it was raced by Nathan Harnagel to fifth in the Bronze Race. (Jerry Liang)

N6427D was assigned #62 for the 1969 racing season and was to be flown by Jack Wimer, however, there is no proof it ever raced under this number. It did race as #8. (Norm Taylor via Dan Hagedorn Collection)

#64 N2864D was raced at Mojave in 1976 and flown by Ben Harrison, who did not qualify or race. He raced at Reno in 1997 and placed fourth in the Medallion Race. This photo was taken at Harlingen, TX. It also raced as #49. (Jerry Liang)

#64 CF-WLO was only the second Canadian-registered Texan (Harvard) to race in closed course pylon racing. Keith McMann is being towed into the pits at Reno 1994, his second year there. He finished second in Heat-2C. (Russ Hiatt)

#64 CF-WLO taxies in after not qualifying at Reno in 2013. This was McMann's last attempt at Reno. His best finish was fifth in the 2012 Silver Race. (Jerry Liang)

#65 N7657C was named *Yuras* when entered in the 1972 Reno races by Don Weinberger. He qualified 17th but decided not to race. This was his only attempt at Texan racing. This photo shows it at an airport sometime later. (Dan Hagedorn Collection)

This photo shows a stock SNJ, similar to #66 N7078C. The aircraft was entered in the 1969 Reno races by Robert Drews but did not qualify or race. It also raced as #8. (AAHS via Jerry Liang)

#66 N66JL sat out the 1973 Reno races on the ramp, as its owner, Jack Lowers, raced John Mosby's #44. Lowers' best finish in #66 was fourth in the 1971 Cape May Championship Race. (Ron Olsen)

#66 N1666T *Lusty Lady* was entered in the 1984 Reno races by Stoney Stonich but did not qualify or race. (Bob Kennedy)

#66 N1466 at Merced, CA, in the 1970s. There is no record of it racing in the 1970s, but it has a "Quaker State" motor oil racing sticker and clipped wingtips. (Russ Hiatt)

#66 N1466 during the 1986 Reno races where it was entered but did not race. It was raced the month before at Richland by Bruce Lockwood, earning fourth place in the Gold Race. (Bob Kennedy)

#66 N7520U was entered by Dennis Dill in the 1994 Reno races and did not qualify or race. It is shown with a three-bladed prop. (Bob Kennedy)

#B66 N8993 taxiing out for a Heat Race at Reno in 1998, raced by Thomas Martin. That year the aircraft's best finish was first in the Bronze Race. Martin would race until 2004. (Bob Kennedy)

#66 N4802E readied for a Heat Race at Reno 2010, raced by Vic McMann. *Time Machine* would finish fifth in the Gold Race that year. (Bob Kennedy)

#66 N4802E, sporting its black overall scheme, takes off for a heat race at Reno in 2021. Vic McMann took fifth in the Gold Race. He earned first in the 2017 Reno Silver Race. (Mike Henniger)

#68 N8048J had its first year at Reno in 1981, raced by Jimmy Gist. *Texas Red* took third in the Silver that year. Gist would race in five Gold Races between 1982–85, with his best finish fourth in 1985. It also raced as #99. (Emil Strasser)

#68 N4983N, in the Texan pits at Reno 2002, was raced by Michael Gillian to fifth in the Bronze Race. Gillian's best finish was fifth in the Gold Race at Tunica in 2005. It had first been entered as #74 at Cleveland in 1969, and also raced as #8 and #69. (Bob Kennedy)

#69 N9649C was raced once under this race number by Richard Minges at St. Louis in 1969. He qualified first and finished first in the Championship Race. The aircraft survived its racing career and is shown at Titusville, FL, in 1987. It was also raced as #96. (Mike Jones)

#69 N3646G on the ramp at Reno in 1973, raced by Robert Suacci. He would race #69 at both Reno and Mojave in 1973. Suacci finished fourth in the Reno Championship Race and fourth in the Mojave Champ. Its best finish was first in the 1974 Mojave Silver Race. (Ron Olsen)

#69 N6424D *Taylor Maid* was raced at Reno 1988 by Lee Oman to sixth in the Bronze Race. Joe Taylor finished fourth with it in the 1986 Richland races. It also raced as #19, #41, and #94. (Russ Hiatt)

#69 N4983N taxiing out at the 2000 Reno races, flown by Michael Gillian to fifth in the Medallion Race. Also, the aircraft raced as #8, #68, and #74. (Jerry Liang)

#69 N3173L at Reno 2013 was raced by Lee Oman to fourth in the Bronze Race. Oman earned first in the Bronze for 2016 by way of others bumping up or DNFs. (Mike Henniger)

#70 N7463C rounding the pylons at Reno 1969 by William Turnbull, who had qualified 11th and took third in the Consolation Race. Also raced as #70 N706F. (Emil Strasser)

#70 N706F changed registration numbers and pilots between 1969 and 1970. *Ol' Betsy* is on the line at Reno 1971, raced by Fred Saunders to fourth in the Consolation Race. (William T. Larkins)

#70 N706F, sporting a new paint job for Reno 1973, was raced by Calvin Early, who placed sixth in the Championship Race. This was #70's best finish. (Ron Olsen)

#70 N10597 raced once and that was at Reno in 1986 by Joe Chiodo. He qualified 25th and was cut. (Bob Kennedy)

#70 N2269T taxies out to start the 2002 Reno Bronze Race flown by Jim Thomas. He would finish sixth in that race. Thomas' best finish was sixth in the 2004 Reno Silver Race. (Bob Kennedy)

#71 N6414D only raced at the 1969 Cleveland races, flown by Texan rookie Richard Foote. He qualified 11th and finished fourth in the Consolation Race. Foote was also a transcontinental Mustang racer. (Robert F. Pauley via Nicholas A. Veronico Collection)

#71 N6972C placed fifth in the 1978 Medallion Race after qualifying 17th. Jim Fox was also at Mojave 1979 but sat out the races. It also raced as #72 and #77. (Jerry Liang)

#71 N7011C's only attempt at racing was the 1983 Reno races where Jack Todoverto qualified 16th but did not race as the field was cut to 14. (Bob Kennedy)

#71 N16730 was raced with this number for both the 1993 Reno and 1994 Phoenix races by John Krawczyk rather than its original #11. Krawczyk placed fourth in the Bronze at Phoenix. It is shown on the ramp at Reno as #11. (Bob Kennedy)

#72 N3666F was raced by Bill Turnbull at Reno in 1973. *CAF Blunderbirds* would place third in the 1971 Gold Race. Turnbull won the Gold Reno Race in 1973. It also raced as #37. (Ron Olsen)

#72 N6972C at Reno in 1984, raced by Jim Fox with a new paint scheme and new race number. Fox finished sixth in the Silver Race, which was his best finish. It also raced as #71 and #77. (Bob Kennedy)

#73 N73RR at Mojave 1973, where Ralph Rina would qualify second and finish third in the Gold Race. Mojave 1973 would be the first battle of the Ralphs when both Ralph Rina and Ralph Twombly would race against each other for the Gold prize. This photo is on the Reno ramp in 1973. (Ron Olsen)

#73 N73RR on the ramp at Mojave in 1979, which was the last Mojave race. Ralph Rina would place fourth in the Gold Race. Rina raced in all six of the races held at Mojave and earned two third places in the Gold races. (Bob Kennedy)

#73 N73RR after finishing second in the 1983 Reno Gold Race where Rina also set a new class speed record. Rina won two Gold races, Reno 1978 and 1984. The aircraft also raced as #22, #56, and #59. (Bob Kennedy)

#73 N7765C qualified 20th at Reno in 1991 by Frank Elliott and raced in Heat-2C. It took first place but did not advance further. It also raced as #74. (Jim Dunn)

#73 N51KT hosting a familiar pilot and number. This #73 was raced at Reno in 2012 and 2014 by Ralph Rina. Rina took first in the 2014 Bronze Race. *Strip Teeze* is shown in 2013 at Porterville, CA. (Jerry Liang)

#73 N158JZ placed second in the 2022 Classic Race at Reno and was raced by Loren Marburg. Ralph Rina used it from 2017 to 2019 to win three Bronze races. (Jim Dunn)

#74 N6900G is wearing an overall white scheme with red trim at Reno in 1968. It was qualified by Leroy Penhall to 15th but did not race. Penhall was also a Mustang and jet race pilot. (Ron Olsen)

#74 N4983N was entered at Cleveland in 1969 by Fred Edison, but it developed an engine oil leak and did not qualify. It also raced as #8, #68, and #69. (Robert F. Pauley via Nicholas A. Veronico Collection)

#74 N7765C *Hot Knotts* raced at the 1973 Reno races by Don DeWalt. He qualified 17th and finished sixth in the Medallion Race. (Ron Olsen)

#74 N7765C *The Exorcist* at Reno 1974, again raced by Don DeWalt. He would finish fourth in the 1974 Consolation Race. It also raced as #73. (Jerry Liang)

#74 N74DW bending around the pylons at the June 1976 Mojave races flown by Don DeWalt. He would have his new #74 painted in time for the Reno races. He took third in the Mojave Silver Race. (Emil Strasser)

#74 N74DW *Exorcist*, now having been painted, on the ramp at Reno 1976, where Don DeWalt would place sixth in the Gold Race. This is the Texan DeWalt was flying when he was hit by #8 during lap 1 of the 1978 Reno Consolation Race and was fatally injured. (Emil Strasser)

#75 N832N qualified 26th but was cut. Barrie Simonson was not able to race in the 1973 Reno races. He would return in 1974 and 1975 and race in the Consolation races. (Ron Olsen)

#75 N7985C *Warlock* at the 1982 Reno races, raced by Al Goss to third in the Gold Race. It was in 1981, Al's rookie year, that he placed sixth in the Gold Race. The aircraft was reregistered N75AG in 1992. (Bob Kennedy)

#75 N75AG shows off its scoreboard in 2007. Al Goss would place third in the Reno Gold Race. (Jerry Liang)

#76 N30JF showing the bicentennial spirit at Reno in the 1975 race. It was flown by John Gerber, who qualified 17th and placed first in the Medallion Race. Kirk McKee was third in the 1976 Reno Medallion Race and John Gerber took fourth in the Silver Race at Mojave. It also raced as #18. (Emil Strasser)

#77 N6972C in 1975 at the Modesto, CA, airport long after it had been entered in the 1968 Reno races by Harold Jolliff. He qualified 17th but did not race. It was also raced as #71 and #72. (J. L. Sherlock via Doug Slowiak)

#77 N41BT was raced at Mojave in 1978 by Jack Francis. *The "Wildcatter"* was raced to third in the Silver Race, but would be relegated to only racing in the 1979 Mojave drags. (Bob Kennedy)

#77 N41BT at Reno in 1984, where Mike Wright would race it to fourth in the Consolation Race. Wright would race #77 for another two years, with a best finish of first in the 1985 Reno Bronze Race. (Bob Kennedy)

Jim Good taxies out #77 N41BT at Reno 2008. He finished third in the Silver Race. Good also raced #77 in the 1990 Casper, Wyoming (WY), 1992 Redmond, and 1994 Phoenix races, the latter of which he placed third in the Silver Race. Good's best finish in #77 was first in the 2002 Reno Silver Race. It also raced as #41. (Jerry Liang)

#78 N3579 *"Patches"* comes in for a landing after a heat race at the 2013 Reno races, the only year it raced. Thomas Baber flew it to sixth in the Bronze Race. (Mike Henniger)

#79 N51979 heads home after qualifying 19th, but getting cut and not racing at Reno in 1987. C. J. Stephens did not try to race again. (Bob Kennedy)

#80 N60380 shortly after qualifying ninth in the 1971 Reno races by Bud Collins; however, Collins chose not to race. (via Nicholas A. Veronico Collection)

#80 N4RC *Sampson* was raced by Bud Collins at Reno in 1973, where it qualified seventh and finished fourth in the Consolation Race. Collins had entered the race in 1972 and 1974 but did not qualify. It also raced as #8. (Harold Bailey via Ron Olsen)

#81 N7804B had this race number assigned in 1969, but there is no record of it racing with this number or being flown by William Lumley or Richard Jensen. It is shown at Oshkosh post-racing. It was also raced as #8. (John Kerr)

#85 N85JR *Blue Six* only raced once and that was at Reno in 1985. John Roark qualified 18th and finished fifth in the Bronze Race. (Emil Strasser)

#86 N611F raced its first year at Reno in 1991 by Sherman Smoot. He finished fifth in the Silver Race. Smoot later moved to the Unlimited Class. (Bob Kennedy)

#86 N611F *Bad Company*, now sporting an overall black paint scheme, is in the Texan pits at Reno in 1993. Sherman Smoot again earned fifth in the Silver Race. Smoot's best finish in #86 would be first in the 1996 Reno Gold Race. It also raced as #7 and #47. (Bob Kennedy)

#87 N87H at Mojave in 1974, raced by Fred Kohler. Kohler had qualified 17th, which relegated him to only racing in the drags. During the race, he applied full power but forgot to release his brakes and stood *Bandersnatch* on its nose, bending the prop and breaking the nose case. Further damage was done shortly after while trying to ferry it back home. (Bob Kennedy)

#87 N87H taxiing out for a race at Reno 2002, flown by Rick Siegfried. He would finish third in the Bronze Race. This Texan had first raced at Reno in 1971, where it had qualified 24th and placed fifth in the Make-Up Race by Fred Kohler. It was also raced as #736 and was used as a pace plane in 2023. (Jerry Liang)

#88 N13631 at the 1968 Reno races, raced by Bob Metcalfe, who qualified ninth and finished third in the Consolation Race. It was his first time racing. The aircraft carried a blue/gray camouflage scheme with its race number in red. (Ron Olsen)

#88 N13631 at Reno 1973, where Bob Metcalfe qualified 11th and finished third in the Consolation Race. Metcalf's best finish was first in the 1973 Mojave Silver Race. He also raced at Graham in 1973, but his results are unknown. (Ron Olsen)

Bruce Redding taxies in #88 N88RT at Reno 1986. He pushed hard all weekend and made it into the Gold Race, where he took fourth. (Bob Kennedy)

#88 N88RT, after receiving a great racing paint scheme, on the ramp at Reno in 1987, raced by Bruce Redding. He would qualify in the Silver Race and finish second. The plane was entered in the 1988 race but did not qualify or race. It also raced as #11. (Emil Strasser)

#88 N3169G was entered in the 1992 Reno races by Carter Clark, who qualified 21st but was cut and did not race. It also raced as #1 and #11. (Bob Kennedy)

#88 N86WW *Double Trouble* being raced by Doug Dotter at Reno in 2007. This was his only Texan race, but he placed seventh in the Silver Race. The Texan also raced as #2 and #42. (Jerry Liang)

N3272G, now #88 and raced by John Lohmar, at Reno in 2010. *Radial Velocity* took third in the Gold Race. Over the next four years the aircraft would finish fourth or better in Gold races. (Bob Kennedy)

#88 N3272G at Reno in 2021, showing its scoreboard that includes two Gold Race wins in 2017 and 2018, won by John Lohmar. In 2021, Lohmar would place second in the Gold Race. It also raced as #20, #26, and #28. (Jim Dunn)

#89 N8993 raced at the 1971 Wilson races and qualified 11th. John Silberman's results are not known, and he only raced once in Texans. This aircraft also raced as #66. (Bob Kennedy)

#89 N604R was raced by Joe Hartung at Reno 1990. Hartung placed second in the Bronze Race that year. His best finish in *"Boomer"* was second in the 1993 Reno Gold. (Bob Kennedy)

#89 N604R *Baby Boomer* taxiing at Reno 2015. It would finish sixth in the 2015 Gold Race with Gene McNeely flying. Fred Telling would take a first in the 2004 Silver Race. (Jerry Liang)

#89 (#2) N817NP was loaned to Joe Hartung by Ed Reed to race in the 1990 Casper Demo Race. Results are not known, and it might have won as #2, but because Hartung's usual number was #89, there is doubt. Shown here at Pine Bluff, Arkansas (AR), in 1987. (John Kerr)

#90 N90629 qualified sixth at Mojave by Larry Havens in 1978. He raced in the Drags but did not start the Silver Race. The previous month, Larry raced at Reno and finished second in the Medallion Race where the race number was painted red. It also carried Race #31. (Russ Hiatt)

#90 N991GM on the ramp at the 1990 Reno races where Gene McNeely would qualify sixth and finish fifth in the Gold Race. McNeely also raced at Casper that year. (Bob Kennedy)

#90 N991GM *Undecided* wearing the marking of the North American Team at Reno 1999. Gene McNeely was a member of this demonstration team. McNeeley took second in the Silver Race. (Bob Kennedy)

#90 N991GM in the markings of the AeroShell demonstration team at Reno 2002. McNeely finished fifth in the Gold Race. His best finishes in this Texan were all at Reno, including two Silver first places in 1991 and 1993, in addition to third in the 1995 Gold. (Jerry Liang)

#90 N4269Q was a new Texan that Gene McNeely first raced at Reno in 2005. It is now raced by his son, Greg McNeely, and is seen here taxiing out for the start of the 2022 Silver Race, when Greg took first place. Greg also had fourth place in the 2016 Gold Race. In 2023, Greg placed first in the Silver Race. (Jim Dunn)

This image shows a stock Texan, which is what #92 N8FU would have been. It was entered but did not qualify at the 1994 Reno Race with pilot Elliot Cross.

#92 N94SC on the Reno ramp in 1995, where Steve Clegg was entered but did not qualify. Clegg had better luck in 1996 when he qualified 15th and placed fifth in the Bronze Race. (Jim Dunn)

#94 N194A *Little Hummer* taking a turn around the 1969 Reno race pylon before it received its scarlet red paint scheme. Its race number is painted red. Pilot Bob Mitchem qualified 15th and finished first in the Consolation Race. Mitchem finished first in the Championship Race at the 1969 Cleveland races earlier in the month. (Emil Strasser)

#94 N194A at Cape May in June 1971, wearing its famous red paint. (Dennis Buehn Collection)

#94 N194A at Cape May in 1971, where Bob Mitchem would take first in the Championship Race. Later in the year, he would set a new national class qualifying speed record and a winning speed record at the 1971 Reno races. It also raced as #44. (Kenneth Smith Collection)

#94 N90650 *Nuthin' Fancy* was raced by rookie George Catalano at Reno 1983. During Catalano's first year, he qualified sixth and placed sixth in the Gold Race. His only other Texan race was Reno 1984 where he took fourth in the Gold Race. (Bob Kennedy)

#94 N694US was raced by Ott Clermont at Reno 2008. Clermont would place second in the Bronze category in his first race attempt. (Jerry Liang)

#94 N694US was raced by Chris LeFave to first place in the 2015 Bronze Race. Notice the placement of the silver speed tape. This aircraft also raced as #19, #41, and #69. (Jim Dunn)

#96 N9649C was the first Texan raced by Richard Minges. He qualified sixth for the 1969 Ft. Lauderdale races. Minges would be second in the Championship Race. He would get a new Texan by the 1969 St. Louis races. It is shown here in its post-racing career. (Mike Jones)

#96 N1974M at Santee, North Carolina (NC), in May 1969 before Richard Minges applied his race number to his new racer. (Roger Besecker via Dan Hagedorn Collection)

#96 N1974M at the 1969 St. Louis Race, where Richard Minges would take first in qualifying and first in the Championship Race. (Robert F. Pauley via Nicholas A. Veronico Collection)

#96 N1974M with Richard Minges taxiing in at Reno 1969. He would place second in the Championship Race. Minges was also an F-1 race pilot and often raced both aircraft at the same events. By 1971, Minges was racing N1974M as #33. (AAHS Collection via Jerry Liang)

#96 N3188G *1 Kielbasa* was raced at Mojave in 1976 by Mike Sukosky for the second year. Sukosky placed sixth in the Silver Race after being penalized for a pylon cut. (Emil Strasser)

#96, now named *Doozie*, at Reno 1978, where Mike Sukosky qualified 18th and took third in the Medallion Race. (Jerry Liang)

#97 N9799Z at Reno. In 1969, it was flown by Jack Briggs but did not race that year. In 1973, Gordon Richardson qualified 23rd but was cut. Richardson would place fourth in the 1973 Mojave Bronze Race after four pylon cuts. It also raced as #7 and #37. (Ron Olsen)

#97 N97GM would be entered at Mojave 1979 by Gary Meermans but did not race. It also raced as #7 and #37. (Bob Kennedy)

#97 N97AW at Reno 1986 with its third registration number. Tom Dwelle, Sr. raced it to third in the Bronze Race. It would have better luck through the years as #7 and #37. (Bob Kennedy)

#98 N9831C *Hrududu!* was raced by Jim Landry, who qualified sixth for the 1976 Reno races. Landry took fourth in the Championship Race, the aircraft's best finish. It also raced as #41. (Emil Strasser)

#98 N5500V would have been easy to follow around the racecourse in its overall yellow paint scheme. It was entered by James Cuseo at Reno in 1983, but qualified 15th and was cut as the field was held to 14. Cuseo did not attempt to race again. (Bob Kennedy)

#98 N101FT did not qualify for the 2019 Reno races but was allowed to race. *"Almost Perfect"* was raced by Greg McNeely to fill in the field of racers. McNeely took second in the Bronze Race and then first in the Silver Race in his regular #90. (Mike Henniger)

On Saturday morning at Cape May 1971, #99 N3626F was raced by Ed Snyder and would be W/O on lap 3 of Heat-2B. Snyder raced in seven events from 1969 to 1971, with most of his finishes in the championship races. (Kenneth Smith Collection)

#99 N83H was raced only once and that was at the 1973 Miami race by John Card, who qualified in last place at 183.6mph. He raced in Heat-1B, but placed last as he could not get his landing gear to retrack and was disqualified by the judges for extremely low flying. He never raced again. The aircraft is shown flying in 1984. (Bob Kennedy)

#99 N999JP at Mojave in 1977, being raced by Pat Palmer. He took second in the Championship Race. Palmer introduced his new *Gotcha!!* in Mojave in 1975 and took first in the Championship Race. He would also race it at Reno in 1975, qualifying first and taking first in the Championship Race. (Emil Strasser)

#99 N999JP tucked under the wing of the massive C-133 transport at Mojave 1979 after winning Pat Palmer's last Gold Race. His total with #99 was four. (Bob Kennedy)

#99 N8048J in its second year being raced by John Luther at Reno 1989, where he would take fifth in the Bronze Race. The Texan's best finish was its rookie year of 1988 when Luther took first in the Bronze Race. The plane's last year racing was when it competed in its only Gold Race and finished sixth. It also raced as #68. (Russ Hiatt)

#302 N666SS was entered by Bill Eberhardt for the 1994 Phoenix races and qualified 19th at 187.813mph but did not race. Shown here in 1985 at Bakersfield. It also raced as #30. (Bob Kennedy)

#388 N49388 was qualified by rookie Aaron Singer in 11th for Reno 2023 at 197.554mph. Singer finished fourth in the Silver Race. (Jim Dunn)

#444 N7522U was raced by Jim Booth at Reno 2002. Jim would place fifth in the Silver Race. His best finish in #444 was first in the 2004 Reno Bronze Race. In 2005, he was disqualified after a heat race for unsafe flying. It also raced as #44 and would become a pace plane at Reno. (Bob Kennedy)

#512 N9035Z was raced by Tom Dwelle, Jr. at Reno 1997. He would race against his brother Ken in the Bronze Race and finish sixth. Ken Dwelle finished 2nd. (Jim Dunn)

#999 N3931R qualified 16th at 179.239mph at Reno 2023, flown by rookie Job Savage. Savage finished sixth in the Silver Race. (Jim Dunn)

N3941Y, the Beck-Statler *Wildfire* racer, was to race in the Unlimited Class. It was modified from an unknown Texan airframe. It is shown taxiing at Mojave in September 1983. (Bob Kennedy)

N3941Y would have been raced by Charles Beck. It flew a few times and was an on-again, off-again project until the death of Bill Statler in 2005. It had a P&W R-2800 engine. (Bob Kennedy)

Pace plane N9785Z was flown by Ernest Opp, who used his Texan at several races, notably at Cape May and St. Louis in 1970–71. The plane is shown in its post-racing career at Shaw AFB, NC, in 1979. (Norm E. Taylor via Doug Slowiak Collection)

Pace plane NX72375 was used by several pilots including Dennis Buehn for pacing between 1983–88. It is shown here at Reno 1983. (Bob Kennedy)

Pace plane N1038A was used by Laird Doctor for pacing at Reno during the 1990s. Here, it taxies out at Reno 1997. (Bob Kennedy)

Pace plane N7520U was flown by Larry Klassen and Laird Doctor during the late 1980s and early 1990s. This is a Reno ramp shot in 1994. (Bob Kennedy)

Pace plane N39403 was another Texan used by Laird Doctor in the 1996–98 years. Seen here on the 1998 Reno ramp. (Bob Kennedy)

Pace plane N3261G was used by Steve Dilda in the 1999–2004 timeframe. Dilda may have also used it at Tunica in 2005. It is shown at Reno 2002. (Bob Kennedy)

Pace plane N7522U had been a racer (#444) before becoming a pace plane, flown by Jim Booth 2007–10 and 2013. This is Reno 1999. (Bob Kennedy)

Pace plane N717UP was flown by Rob Sandberg in 2016, 2018, 2019, and 2022. It is here on take-off at Reno 2022. (Roger Cain)

Chapter 5
Accidents, Pace Planes, Pilots and Sponsors

Accidents

Of all the classes of air racing, the Texan class has had the fewest accidents, aside from the usual minor gear-up, bent props and ground loops, involving fatalities. Presented are the factual reports from the National Transportation Safety Board (NTSB) and, where available, personal accounts of the accidents.

While numerous race pilots have been killed in Texan accidents over the years in transit to/from races or during airshows, those accidents are not included. Only accidents during an air race are listed. Accidents are listed by year.

August 31, 1947; National Air Races Cleveland; #49 AT-6A (Modified) NX61269; Non-injury; Pilot Dori Marland. During the final lap of the Halle Trophy Race, the aircraft was forced to make a gear-up belly landing off airport resulting in minor damage. Probable cause: fuel mismanagement, out of gas. (Note: it was rumored that with the re-reengining of the Texan with the Ranger engine it had never run smoothly. It was raised to its gear and towed back to the airport and later repaired and raced in the 1948 races by another pilot.)

June 5, 1971, 3:40pm; Cape May National Air Race, North Cape May; #10 SNJ-5 N1046C; Non-injury; Pilot Don Barrett. During the start of the competition, #33 collided with #10 in flight, causing damage to rudder and aft portion of canopy of #10. #10 landed safely without further damage. Probable cause: pilot of other aircraft misjudged clearance between aircraft. NTSB: NYC71AN118 (Note: N1046C was repaired and flew at Reno in September 1971. It was W/O in July 1981 with two fatalities in a non-racing accident.)

June 5, 1971, 3:40pm; Cape May National Air Races, North Cape May; #33 T-6D N1974M; Fatal; Pilot Richard Minges. During the start of the race on lap 1 at pylon 3, #33 overtook and hit the rudder and canopy of #10, causing the loss of 10ft

#49 NX61269 resting on its belly in a field at the 1947 Cleveland NAR after Dori Marland had fuel-management problems. Marland was unhurt and #49 was lifted onto its gear and towed back to the airport. It was rebuilt and raced by Betty Clark in the 1948 NAR. (via Nicholas A. Veronico Collection)

#10 N1046C after its collision with #33 during Heat-2B at the 1971 Cape May air races. Pilot Don Barrett was able to land while #33 crashed fatally. #10 was repaired and continued to race until 1974. (Kenneth Smith Collection)

of the left wing from #33. A fire ensued after the impact and the aircraft was destroyed. Probable cause: pilot in command misjudged clearance. NTSB: NYC71AN118 (Note: a Texan using this registration number is currently flying.)

June 5, 1971, 3:44pm; Cape May National Air Races, North Cape May; #6 T-6D N5489V; Fatal; Pilot Victor Baker. During the cancellation of the race on lap 3 due to a previous accident, #6 pulled up and slightly to the right straight into #99's path of flight causing a vertical collision with the propeller of #99 resulting in the separation of the tail of #6. #6 spun into the ground and the aircraft was destroyed. Probable cause: inadequate clearance of aircraft during closed course air race. NTSB: NYC71AN119 (Note: this Texan was not rebuilt, and registration was canceled.)

June 5, 1971, 3:44pm; Cape May National Air Races, North Cape May; #99 SNJ-5 N3626F; Fatal; Pilot Ed Snyder. During the cancellation of the race on lap 3 due to a previous accident, #6 pulled up into the flight path of Race #99. The Texan collided with the tail of #6 causing both aircraft to crash into the ground and the aircraft were destroyed. Probable cause: inadequate clearance of aircraft during closed course air race. NTSB: NYC71AN119 (Note: this Texan was not rebuilt, and registration was canceled.)

June 5, 1971, 3:44pm; Cape May National Air Races, North Cape May; #35 SNJ-4 N9735Z; Fatal; Pilot Joseph "Jay" Quinn. During the cancellation of the race on lap 3 due to a previous accident, #6 and #99 collided ahead of #35. #35 flew through the debris while trying to avoid a collision with the other aircraft and crashed into the ground. The aircraft was destroyed. Probable cause: evasive maneuver to avoid collision during low-level closed course air race. NTSB: NYC72AN091 (Note: this Texan was not rebuilt, and registration was canceled.)

The following is a brief summarized account by the late air-race chronicler John Tegler of the tragedy at Cape May:

As the pace plane pulled up for the start, the first four headed around the #1 pylon. They were followed by #33 Minges who had already pulled ahead of #10 Barrett in fifth place leaving #10 Barrett in sixth. As they approached the #1 pylon #33 Minges was slightly ahead and above, and to the right of #10 Barrett on the outside. It appeared that #33 Minges was not aware of the fact that #10 Barrett was just behind and below him, and in an attempt to catch the front four ahead snapped his left wing down abruptly to turn into the #1 pylon and struck the canopy of #10 Barrett. The outer partition of his left wing tore off and he rolled inverted over #10 Barrett and went straight in. #10 Barrett, his canopy a mass of twisted metal and broken glass and his rudder jammed after being hit by parts of his canopy, climbed for altitude in an attempt to bail out but found it impossible to get through the smashed canopy. With little or no rudder control #10 Barrett was able to get safely on the ground.

    Meanwhile, the other four who were ahead of the accident and had not seen [the incident] continued to race, which was the proper procedure. #44 Carlson who had been behind #33 and #10 immediately pulled up and off the course. The front four, #41 Twombly, #6 Baker, #99 Snyder and #35 Quinn, came around to complete the first lap [and] could probably see the smoke from #33's crash but continued to race. As they entered the back straight on the third lap #41 Twombly noticed two aircraft circling above the course and thought maybe the aircraft were clearing the course (these two were the pace plane #11 Opp and #44 Carlson.). Twombly pulled back on the power and slowed down, this allowed the other three to pass him. #6 Baker and #99 Snyder were above him and #35 Quinn below. As the three lead aircraft rounded #6 pylon and started down the main straight someone fired a red flare from the area of the F.A.A. trailer adjacent to the runway. At this time #6 Baker was in front with #99 Snyder in second above and behind him. #35 Quinn was third below and behind #99. Apparently #6 Baker caught sight of the flare and immediately pulled up to clear the course as required. In doing so, he pulled up into the path of #99 Snyder and they collided. #99's prop cut the entire empennage from #6 and both fell into the ground in a shower of debris. #35 Quinn apparently hit or was hit by the debris and also crashed in a gentle left-hand turn. #41 Twombly who was still behind managed to avoid the falling debris and climbed away. #11 Opp, #44 Carlson and #41 Twombly landed safely.

It is speculated that the first accident was a racing accident and if the flare had not been fired and the race was allowed to continue, the second accident could have been avoided.

October 12, 1974; California National Air Races, Mojave; #87 T-6D N87H; Minor injuries; Pilot Fred Kohler. During the start of a drag race, the pilot applied full power, but failed to release the brakes and stood the aircraft on its nose and caused minor damage to engine and prop. Sometime later it appears that a more serious accident occurred resulting in

Aftermath of the fatal collisions at Cape May in June 1971. There is perhaps some small comfort in the knowledge that the four pilots who died were doing what they loved. (via Dennis Buehn Collection)

The poor-quality photo shows the moment after M. D. Washburn in #12 N612MD collided with pylon 1 on the first lap of the 1975 Reno Heat Race, causing major damage to his wing. As he made the turn, he was too close to the pylon, and he crashed fatally. (via Emil Strasser Collection).

The remains of #12 are in the secure storage compound at Reno 1975, showing the results of the impact and fire. This SNJ was later rebuilt and is now displayed in a museum. (Jerry Liang)

#8 N7038C seconds after impact. Note fuel streaming out of right wing. Pilot Dimitry Prian was fatally injured on impact with #74 Don DeWalt. (via Emil Strasser Collection)

major damage, perhaps related to a brake issue. There is no official FAA or NTSB report on file. (Note: this Texan was repaired and raced again starting in 2000.)

September 12, 1975, 12:40pm; National Championship Air Races, Stead; #12 SNJ-5 N612MD; Fatal; Pilot Marlin D. "MD" Washburn. During the first lap for a heat race, the pilot was flying low and collided with the race pylon during the closed course race. This caused the separation of the left wing. A fire ensued on impact and the aircraft was destroyed. Probable cause: pilot in command misjudged clearance. NTSB: OAK76FXQ16. (Note: there is currently a Texan flying with this registration number.)

September 16, 1978, 2:36pm; National Championship Air Races, Stead; #8 SNJ-4 N7038C; Fatal; Pilot Dimitry Prian. During a closed course pylon race, the aircraft collided at the fifth pylon turn with #74 causing the loss of the empennage behind the cockpit and outer portion of the right wing. The aircraft was destroyed on impact with terrain. Probable cause: pilot in command misjudged clearance. NTSB: OAK78DA055. (Note: there is a Texan currently flying with this registration number.)

September 16, 1978, 2:36pm; National Championship Air Races, Stead; #74 T-6G N74DW; Fatal; Pilot Don DeWalt. During a closed course pylon race, #74 collided at the fifth pylon turn with #8, causing the loss of the entire right wing. The aircraft rolled left and impacted the terrain, and the aircraft was destroyed. Probable cause: pilot in command misjudged clearance. NTSB: OAK78DA055. (Note: Don DeWalt was pulled alive from wreckage but died later at the hospital. Aircraft not rebuilt and the registration number was canceled.)

September 11, 1991, 5:00pm; National Championship Air Races, Stead; #51 T-6G N29931; Minor injuries; Pilot Jim Mott. The aircraft was flying on the racecourse during trials and seemed to enter a turn at one of the pylons at a lower-than-normal altitude. The left wing contacted the ground. The pilot was able to recover to level flight and made a left base turn to runway 18. As the aircraft turned from base to final, it continued to bank to the left until the left wing

#74 N74DW seconds after impact, streaming fuel from its right wing. Note the impact has caused the left gear to extend. Don DeWalt survived the impact but succumbed to his injuries on the way to the hospital. (via Emil Strasser Collection)

contacted the ground and aircraft cartwheeled. About 3ft of the left aileron was found at the pylon, where the first wing contact occurred. The pilot said the aileron controls were jammed and he could only control the aircraft in roll by use of the rudder and power changes. As the aircraft turned on final for the runway, the pilot reduced power. The aircraft did not respond fast enough, and the left wingtip contacted the ground. The aircraft sustained substantial damage. Probable cause: the failure of the pilot to maintain an adequate clearance between the aircraft and the ground while maneuvering around a pylon, which resulted in a loss of control during landing. NTSB: LAX91LA392. (Note: this Texan was repaired and raced again as #49 in 2000.)

September 18, 1994, 10:10am; National Championship Air Races, Stead; #41 SNJ-4 N8540Z; Fatal; Pilot Ralph Twombly. Two airplanes, #41 and #5, collided while participating in an air race near the airport. #41's left wing and empennage separated in flight and crashed into a residence; #5 landed at the airport without further incident. The post-accident wreckage examination and video tapes of the occurrence showed that #41 overtook and struck #5's right wing from below. #41 pitched up, the empennage separated, and the left wing folded. #41 then began to cartwheel and spin until it crashed. Probable cause: the pilot of #41 misjudged the distance between his aircraft and #5. Twombly's diverted attention on the start of the air race is a factor in this accident. NTSB: LAX94LA368. (Note: a Texan is reported as flying in Denmark with this aircraft's BuNo.)

September 18, 1994, 10:10am; National Championship Air Races, Stead; #5 SNJ-4 N7404C; No injuries; Pilot Jerry McDonald. During the start of an air race, two aircraft collided about two miles west of the Reno-Stead Airport. Both aircraft were beginning a local visual flight rules air race. #41 entered an uncontrolled descent and collided with a nearby home and was destroyed. #5 sustained substantial damage, but the pilot landed at Reno-Stead Airport without further incident. The aircraft's left aileron and wingtip separated from their respective attach points. The right wing's leading edge, from the tip to 10.5ft inboard, sustained substantial damage. The pilot experienced severe vibrations. The consensus of ground witnesses was that #41 overtook #5 and struck #5 with its left wing low. A participating race pilot reported that the aircraft were to be lined up abreast of each other at the beginning of the race. He said that #41 moved out of position before the airplanes reached the visible staging area. When the airplanes reached the staging area, #41 appeared to move back into position, but the pilot overcorrected the alignment and struck #5. Probable cause: pilot of other misjudged the distance between his aircraft and #5. NTSB: LAX94LA368. (Note: this Texan was repaired and is currently racing.)

September 17, 2023, 2:15pm; National Championship Air Races, Stead; #14 T-6D N57418; Fatal; Pilot Chris Rushing. At the conclusion of the Gold Race, #14 Rushing and #6 Nick Macy collided while landing at runway 8, resulting in both Texans crashing to the ground. #14 Chris Rushing had just won the Gold Race, with #6 Macy coming in second. The collision resulted in #14 receiving left wing damage and its tail assembly being severed and nosing over. #6 flew on for a few seconds before also nosing over.

September 17, 2023; 2:15pm; National Championship Air Races, Stead; #6 T6G N2897G; Fatal; Pilot Nick Macy. After crossing the finish line, #6 Macy and #14 Rushing collided when landing and crashed to the ground. Both pilots were killed. Rushing had just won the Gold Race, with Macy in second place. #6 flew for a few seconds after impact and then nosed over.

Pace Planes

When Pylon Air Racing resumed after World War Two, the sport returned to the racehorse starting method used prewar. This involved all contestants lined up abreast across the field or on dual/parallel runways. The starter dropped the flag, and everyone charged off for the first (scatter) pylon. While fraught with danger, there were few accidents but some mild confusion. The use of air starts with a pace plane came about partly due to confusion at the St. Louis Air Races in 1969. The small size of the runway required contestants to take off in two groups in opposite directions and then form up to race. Other events like Mojave and Reno used racehorse starts at first. Mojave first used a pace plane and pace lap in 1979, while Reno began doing so in 1975. All Texan races thereafter after would use this method. Records for aircraft used as pace planes are not very good. On several occasions, Bob Hoover used his P-51D Mustang as the starter. Later, a designated pilot and aircraft were used. See Chapter 6, Table 2, for the known Texans used as pace planes. Many more Texans served as pace planes, but there are no records of them.

Ralph Rina conducts a T-6 pilot briefing on the ramp at Reno 1975. (Harold Loomis via Dennis Buehn)

Pilot Profiles

Pilots who race Texans are of diverse backgrounds from a variety of career fields. While most have aviation-related careers, they all have certain things in common: the love of flying, the love of a challenge and adventure, and, most of all, the love of North American Aviation's rugged, fun to fly, noisy, fast, and beautiful Texan. Beauty is in the eye of the beholder.

Victor Baker; #6; Attorney; Los Angeles, CA. Victor first raced in the 1967 Reno Demonstration Race and took sixth place. Baker was fifth in Reno Championship Race in 1968, first in 1969 Reno Medallion, fifth in 1969 Championship St. Louis, second in the Consolation Race in 1970 at St. Louis, and third in the 1970 Ft. Lauderdale Consolation Race. Victor Baker was killed at the 1971 Cape May race. He was 42 years old.

Charles Beck; #2 and #46; Building Contractor; Los Angeles, CA. Charles Beck was a fighter pilot in World War Two and flew Corsairs in Korea. He was a long-time member of the Air National Guard. Beck was a cofounder of the Condor Squadron at Van Nuys, CA. This is the group that put on the first Reno Texan air race in 1967. Beck first entered Reno in 1973 and qualified 24th but was cut to keep the field to 18. He placed second in the 1973 Mojave Bronze Race, fifth in the 1975 Mojave Medallion Race, second in the 1978 Mojave Gold, and sixth in the 1979 Mojave Gold. He fared better at Reno with several third and fourth places in the gold races until he won the 1991 Bronze and 1993 Bronze. He was last entered at Reno 1994 but did not qualify or race. He raced for 19 years, including several years in the Unlimited Class. He was involved in the development and building of the Beck/Statler Unlimited air racer based on a Texan airframe in the 1980s. Charles Beck passed away in March 2009.

Dennis Buehn; #43 (this was the most used race number of the 16 he either entered or raced); Aircraft Restorations; Fallon, NV. Dennis Buehn was introduced to aviation by working as a seaplane baggage boy on Catalina Island. After a career in the US Navy, he became involved with air racing by working on several Unlimited air racers. He was a crew member on #42 Jim Mott's Texan. Mott encouraged Buehn to buy a Texan of his own. Buehn owned 39 Texans and by his own account had been associated with well over 200. His restoration company specializes in Texan and HU-16 flying boats. He entered his first Texan, #43, at Graham, TX, in 1972. He went on to fly in Reno in 1972 in a different #43 and qualified 21st but was cut to keep the field at 18. He was 27 years old. He was back in 1973 and finished third in the Medallion Race. He had better luck at the 1973 Mojave races, taking second in the Gold Race. This was his best finish in the three years he raced there. His Reno record from 1973 to 2019 (he did not race there continuously) has been a first in the 1976 Medallion, his first win, and six Gold Race wins. His last race was in 2019 when he finished fifth in the Bronze.

Betty Clark; #54 and #49; Pilot; Denver, CO; 28 years old in 1947. She was nicknamed "Buzz Betty" from her days as a WASP pilot after she reportedly made two generals and three colonels hit the dirt when she misjudged her altitude during a low pass. Betty Clark began flying in 1942 while working as an X-ray technician. Her interest in aviation began with her father, who was a glider builder and pilot. Clark served in the WASP for two years, enlisting in May 1943 and ferrying B-25s, B-26s, P-63s and P-51s. Her first air race was at the NAR in Cleveland (#54) in 1947 where she qualified fourth but was forced out of the final race on lap 2 with engine trouble. Returning in 1948 and racing #49 (the Ranger-powered Texan that Dori Marland had crashed in 1947), she finished fourth in the final race. She worked in Los Angeles in the aircraft business before managing the Rifle Airport in Rifle, CO, until 1979. Betty Clark passed away in August 1999.

Nancy Corrigan; #83; Flight Instructor; Columbia, MS; 36 years old in 1948. Nancy Corrigan was born in Owenduff in Achill, Ireland, and emigrated in 1929. She started flying in 1932 while working as a nursemaid in Cleveland, OH, to pay for flying lessons. She subsidized her income by modeling with the Powers modeling agency in New York for about ten years. Corrigan earned her pilot's license after less than five hours of flying. When the US entered World War Two, she became a primary pilot trainer for the army at Spartan College and later Stephens College. After the war, she earned her commercial pilot's license. She was only the second women to do so at the time. Early on, she had vowed that one day she would compete in the Cleveland National Air Race. She got her chance in 1948 while still teaching flying at Stephens College. She raced #83, which had been raced in 1947 by Jane Page, and placed fifth in the final race. Nancy Corrigan passed away in 1983.

Don DeWalt; #74; Sales Restaurant Equipment; El Monte, CA; 41 years old in 1978. DeWalt was an all-out competitor and also raced in the F-1 Class. His first Texan race was Reno 1972 where he qualified 19th but was cut to keep the field at 18. When another racer decided not to race, DeWalt bumped up and finished sixth in the Medallion Race. At the 1973 race, DeWalt qualified 11th and finished fifth in the Silver. DeWalt was only able to place sixth in the 1973 Reno Medallion Race. His first win was at the 1973 Miami races where he took first in the Consolation Race. In 1974, he took fourth in the Silver at Mojave and fourth in the Consolation at Reno. He would sit out the races in 1975 to prepare his new #74. He qualified second in #74 at Reno and placed sixth in the 1976 Reno Championship Race and third in the Mojave Silver. His only Texan race in 1977 was at Reno in which he finished sixth in the Gold. He qualified second at Reno in 1978 and took sixth in the F-1 race just before the start of the Consolation Race. It was during this race that Don DeWalt was killed in a collision with Race #8.

Mary Dilda; #21 and #22; Commercial Pilot; Memphis, TN; 48 years old in 2007. It was only natural Mary Dilda would learn to fly as she grew up in an aviation family. She earned her private pilot's liccnse at age 18 and became a certified instructor at 20. After college, she joined the Air Force and flew medical evac and cargo type aircraft. She flew larger cargo types during the First Gulf War. After leaving the Air Force, she flew for a charter company before moving to FedEx. Dilda bought her Texan, #22 (formerly Ralph Rina's #73), in March 1996 and raced it in September, becoming only the third woman to race Texans. She placed fifth in the Reno Silver Race for 1996. This was her first race. In 1997, she was able to use #21, a proven winner, and took first in the Gold. She returned to flying #22 in 1998 and took fourth in the Gold. This win was followed by third in the 1999 Gold, fifth in Gold for 2000, and fourth in Gold 2002. She also took second in the 2002 Gold Jet Race in #22 L-39. In 2003, she placed second in the Gold and first in the Jet Gold. Dilda won second in the 2004 Gold Race. She would win her second Gold Race in 2005 and also place 2nd in the Tunica races that year. Her final Texan race was in 2007, where she placed fourth in the Gold. Mary Dilda made history by being the only wife to race against her husband (Steve in #22) in Texan racing. They raced against each other in the 1997 Gold Race in which Mary came first and Steve fifth.

Dwelle Family; # 2, #7, #7, #30, and #512; Businessmen/Professional Pilots. The Dwelle family is unique in the history of T-6 racing. It is the first to have raced father against sons and only the second set of brother-against-brother racers. Tom Sr. learned to fly in his father's BT-13 before joining the Air Force in 1960 and flying combat missions in Vietnam. His first Texan was #7, which he initially raced at Reno in 1997, finishing third in the Bronze. He returned to Reno in 1988 and took second in the Gold, followed by back-to-back first places in the 1989 and 1990 Gold Races. Tom Sr. also raced #7 *Yankee Air Pirate* to sixth in the 1991 Silver Race. He raced Unlimiteds for several years and returned to Texans to win the 2007 Silver Race in #7 *Tinker Toy*. Tom Sr. is retired from the oil industry, but still flies the family A-36 Bonanza that his father bought.

Ken Dwelle began flying in 1986 and became an Air Force fighter/instructor pilot, flying F-16s and F-117s, and later flew for an airline. His first Reno Race was in 1994 where he placed sixth in the Silver in #7 *Yankee Air Pirate*. He took first in the 2003 Silver Race in #7 *Kitchen Pass*, and in 2008 won the Gold Race in #7 *Tinker Toy*.

Tom Dwelle, Jr. received his private pilot's license in 1989 and was the family's first professional pilot. Tom flew with several airlines and his first Reno Race was in 1993, in which he finished fourth in the Bronze in #7 *Yankee Air Pirate*. Dwelle was also third in #37 *Tinker Toy* at Reno 1994, and first in the 1996 Bronze in *Yankee Air Pirate*. He raced both #7 and X-512 in separate races for 1997. Dwelle placed seventh in the 2004 Gold Race with #7 *Kitchen Pass*. Both brothers continue to fly for the family business. The Dwelles are truly lovers of the Texan and a remarkable racing family.

Linda Finch; #26 and #20; Medical Facilities Manager; Pilot; San Antonio, TX; 41 years old in 1992. Linda Finch is perhaps best known for recreating Amelia Earhart's around-the-world flight in a restored 1935 Lockheed 10E. She completed the flight in 73 days in 1997. She earned a pilot's license in 1979. In the 1980s, she purchased a Texan, which she restored and began flying at airshows. Finch also took up air racing as #26, later changing the number to #20. At the 1987 Reno Races, she qualified 20th but was cut to keep the field at 18. Flying as #26 in 1988, she qualified in 19th and was again cut. Finally making the field in 1990, she finished third in the Bronze. Finch took sixth in the 1991 Bronze Race and fourth in the 1992 Bronze. This was her second-best finish and her last Texan race. Besides Texans and Lockheed 10s, Linda Finch is qualified to fly the CAF P-47 and F4U.

Colene Giglio; #7; Flight Instructor; Long Beach, CA; 37 years old in 1974. When Colene Giglio entered the 1974 Reno Races, she became the first woman to race in the Texan Class since 1949. Racing came naturally to Giglio after years of instructing. She qualified 17th and finished fifth in the Medallion Race. She raced at Mojave the same year, qualifying 12th and finishing sixth in the Consolation Race. Giglio took fourth in the 1975 Reno Consolation Race and third in the Mojave Medallion Race. She had better luck in 1976 with a fourth in the Consolation at Reno and her first win at Mojave in the Silver. Reno was the only location for a Texan race in 1977. There she qualified 12th but was unable to race due to engine problems. This was her last Reno race. Giglio raced at Mojave in 1978 where she qualified fifth and took fifth in the Gold Race. She last raced in 1979 and took her second win at Mojave in the Silver Race. After racing, she continued to work as a flight instructor, working at Eagle Aviation in Long Beach, CA, where she would become the president of the company before retiring in the 1990s.

Jim Good; #77; Mechanic/Aircraft Restorer; Casper, WY; 54 years old in 1987. Jim Good was a true gentleman and fine pilot. His aviation career began as an airline transport pilot. He was also a skilled airframe and powerplant and inspection authorized mechanic, who built and restored airplanes including warbirds. His first job was with Christler Flying Service, a forest fire air tanker service. He used his commercial license to fly for an oil company conducting pipeline patrols, hence his ability to fly low around the pylons. Good developed a passion for air racing and raced the first time at Reno in 1987 and he qualified 15th but was a DNF in the Silver with a rough engine. In 1988–93, he raced in the Silver with two second places in 1990 and 1993. He took seventh place in the Gold at the 1992 Redmond Races and third in the Silver at Phoenix in 1994. Good help organize, run and race in the 1989–90 Casper Races. His luck changed in 1994 when he won his first race, the Bronze at Reno. He would race in the Gold from 1995–2000. His second win came in 2002 with a first in the Silver. Between 2003 and 2009, he had three fifth places in the Gold races. Good's last race was in 2009 when he took fourth in the Silver. At retirement, he had more than 40,000 hours flying time. Before passing away in 2016, Jim Good was inducted into the Wyoming Aviation Hall of Fame.

Al Goss; #75; Crop Duster; Bakersfield, CA; 39 years old in 1981. The term "always a bridesmaid, never the bride" could well have been Al Goss's endearing title. His first race was at Reno in 1981 in which he qualified tenth and finished sixth in the Gold. In 1982, he won the Consolation Race and then bumped up to the Gold where he finished third. He was second in the 1983 Consolation Race, which would be the last time he would finish in any race other than Gold races. Goss raced in 25 Gold races, finishing between sixth and second (nine times in second place). He won his first and only Reno Gold Race in 2004. Goss raced at Richland in 1985, Redmond in 1992 (qualified second and took first in the Gold), and Phoenix in 1994, taking second in the Gold. Goss was a true sportsman, as he enjoyed racing and proved that you do not have to win every race to be a great pilot. Al Goss was killed in 2010 at the age of 69 in the crash of his beloved *Warlock*.

Bud Granley; #4, #9, and #66; Airline Pilot/Airshow Performer; Bellevue, WA; 48 years old in 1985. Granley joined the RCAF in 1956 and flew Harvards, T-33s, and F-86s. Upon retirement from the airlines, he has become a renowned airshow pilot, flying Mustangs, Warhawks, Thunderbolts, and Spitfires. He began his racing career flying Unlimiteds at Reno in 1985. By 1988, he had moved to Texans, racing #9 and taking third in the Bronze Race (this Texan had been racing since 1968). Throughout his 18 years of racing Texans, Granley raced in one Gold race, ten Silver Races (with second place in 2004 and 2006), and four Bronze Races (with a first in the 1994 Phoenix races.) His last race was Reno 2009 in #66 in which he qualified 15th.

Grace Harris; #44; Corporate Executive Officer; Kansas, MO; 41 years old in 1947. Grace Harris got her love of flying after taking a ride with an itinerant barnstormer and a flight instructor during World War Two. She attended her first postwar air race in 1946 as a spectator and decided she wanted to race. Harris purchased her Texan from famed test pilot Vance Breese and modified it to race. Her first race was in 1947 at Cleveland where she qualified third and finished second in the finals. She would take first place in 1948. For the 1949 races, she had to remove the previous modifications on her aircraft, as the requirement for 1949 was that racers had to be stock. Harris won the 1949 races at a slightly slower speed. Grace Harris continued to fly and later became interested in Sports Car Racing, and is more famously known for winning a number of races during her six years in the sport. Harris set up an aviation scholarship in her name for female pilots as part of the International Society of Women Airline Pilots. Grace Harris passed away in 1994 at age 91.

Marge Hurlburt; #81; Flight Instructor; Willoughby, OH; 31 years old in 1946. In her early life Marge was a schoolteacher and took flying lessons in her spare time. Being a qualified pilot by the start of World War Two, she was recruited into the WASP as a ferry pilot and target tow pilot. Postwar, she became a flight instructor. Hurlburt entered the inaugural National Air Races at Cleveland in the 1946 Halle Trophy Race in a loaned stock Texan and took first place. She also raced in the Texan demo races during the 1946 and 1947 All Women's Airshow in Miami. In 1947, she was loaned a Goodyear FG-1D by her close friend Cook Cleland and set a new international women's speed record of 337mph. While preparing her own Texan for racing, Hurlburt took a job with an airshow company doing an aerobatic routine and was killed at an airshow on July 4, 1947.

Ruth Carter Johnson; #75; Flight Instructor; Clyde, OH; 28 years old in 1949. Johnson learned to fly while attending college and, in 1943, she enlisted in the WASP (Class 43-W-5) and ferried P-39s and P-40 fighters across the country. After discharge, she worked for a private flying school before beginning her racing career at Cleveland in 1946. Her stock Texan took third behind Hulburt and Page. For 1947, she had modified her Texan and was the second fastest qualifier and took first in the final. Johnson's luck changed for the 1948 races as she had to drop out on lap 3 with a sick engine. The same happened in 1949 when she was a DNF. Ruth Johnson and #75 are the only pilot/aircraft combination to have competed in all four of the postwar Cleveland races. She continued as an airport manager and flight instructor, at one time owning a flying service in Chino, CA, in the late 1960s and 1970s. After a life in aviation, she passed away in April 1997.

Robert "Bob" Jones; #8; Airline Pilot; Federal Way, WA; 46 years old in 1981. After serving in the US Navy as a fighter pilot, Bob Jones joined United Airlines. Jones entered and qualified eighth at Reno in 1981, finishing fifth in the Consolation Race. He raced at Reno for 19 years in six Bronze races (best finish second in 1982 and 1989) and 11 Silver races (best finish second in 1996 and 1998). Jones also raced at Richland in 1985 and 1986, where he qualified third and took second in the Gold for 1986. At the Redmond races in 1992, he qualified eighth and placed sixth in the Gold. At the 1994 Phoenix races, he qualified eighth and finished second in the Bronze. His last Reno race was in 2000 in which he finished third in the Silver. Robert Jones retired from United Airlines after 31 years of flying.

Katherine "Kaddy" Landry; #31; Airshow Performer/Mechanic; 31 years old in 1948. Landry received her pilot's license in 1940 while in college through the Civilian Pilot Training Program. She graduated with a PhD in education. Entering the WASP in 1943, she flew with target-towing squadrons. Postwar, she moved to Florida and taught flying while also performing aerobatics with Jesse Bristow Air Show Co. She took first in the 1947 aerobatic championship during the All Women's Air Show in Tampa. Landry placed ahead of Marge Hurlburt in the 1947 races at the same show. In 1948, she took first in Miami before going to Cleveland where she finished second in the Kendall. The race was held on September 5, her 31st birthday and she raced #31. She was second in the Cleveland Nationals in 1949 while still performing in stunt flying and aerobatic shows. Later, she went back into education and was an associate professor at the University of Florida, retiring in 1987. Kaddy Landry Steele passed away in June 2003.

Dorothy "Dot" Lemon; #72 and #23; Barnstormer/Flight Instructor/Businesswoman; 40 years old in 1946. Dot soloed at age 16 after being taught by a barnstormer and took up the profession for a number of years. She later became an advertising agent and a sales manager for Hayes Aviation. By the late 1930s, she was running a flight school in Florida and, by 1940, was the chairperson for the Florida chapter of the Ninety-Nines. Lemon and her husband provided flight training during World War Two. She entered her first Cleveland Air Race in 1946 and finished fifth in the finals. She was unable to qualify and sat out the races in 1947. She had better luck in 1948 when she finished third in the finals. In the 1960s, she served as the president of the Institute of Navigation. By 1964, Lemon had moved to Venezuela to run a gold mine. Dot Lemon passed away in 1986 in Caracas, Venezuela.

Nick Macy; #6 and #94; Ag Pilot; Tulelake, CA; 30 years old in 1986. Coming from an ag pilot family, Macy soloed at age 16 and earned his pilot's license at 18. While attending the University of Nevada at Reno, he would go to the races where he developed an interest in racing. He first entered the Reno races in 1986, qualifying 24th but was a DNR after being cut. He was back in 1987, qualifying eighth and finishing fourth in the Silver. He credits his racing skills to his years as an ag pilot. Macy's Reno-racing record is impressive: six Gold wins (his first was in 1999), eight second place Golds, a second in the Silver in 1988, and the record for fastest qualifying time of 251.792mph in 2016. He was the fourth fastest qualifier at Phoenix in 1994 and finished third in the Gold. Adding to his laurels is his 2009 Reno appearance at which he qualified and raced two Texans, qualifying #6 in first and then #94 in 14th. He took first place in #6 in the Gold and seventh place with #94 in the Silver. He raced at Reno in 2022 at which he finished second in the Gold. Nick returned to Reno 2023, at which he finished second in the Gold. Minutes after the race finished, he was killed in a landing accident.

Dori Marland; #49; Model/Actress; Los Angeles, CA; 26 years old in 1947. Dori Marland was born as Dori Marie Jugle but used her father's middle name Marland for her stage and professional career. After graduating from high school, she won a swimsuit contest with a prize of a trip to California. She enrolled in the Pasadena Playhouse, eventually going to Paramount Pictures. After Pearl Harbor, she wanted to do something for the war effort. She, like other actresses, did pin-up pictures. Her father told her about the flying training program for women and she went to Denver where she took lessons and built-up flying hours. After obtaining the required hours, she applied to the WASP and was accepted. Marland graduated in the 43-W-8 class and was tasked with engineering and testing in Arizona. She later went to Florida for training in the B-26 for which she flew target-towing and air gunnery flights. Marland met and married Flying Tiger ace Colonel Herbert Morgan, though they would later divorce. She returned to California and modeled. Her father encouraged Marland to continue flying and, in 1947, a friend offered her a chance to race in the Cleveland Air Races. She raced in 1947 in the Ranger engine modified #49 and was forced to drop out due to fuel management problems. It was her only air race. She would marry a Douglas Aircraft test pilot and lived in Muroc, CA, for a while. She would go on to a variety of careers including mother, real estate and mail sorter before retirement. Dori Marland passed away in April 2013, and while her racing career was short, as the National WASP World War Two Museum stated, "her life was a testament to patriotism, hard work and persistence."

Roy "Mac" McClain; #25 and #5; Flying Service/Crop Duster; Eufaula, AL; 39 years old in 1975. Mac McClain hit the racing scene in 1972 at the Wilson races, flying Tony Murgia's former #25 and proceeded to qualify fourth and finish second in the Championship Race. From there he went to the Reno races and qualified third and finished first in the Championship Race. McClain followed this up in 1973 with a second in the Championship Race at Miami, a first in the Gold at Reno, a second in the Gold at Mojave, and raced at Graham in November. This was a full year of racing for the rookie. Beginning in 1974, he split his time between racing the Red Baron RB-51 and the now renumbered #5 Texan. He was the fastest qualifier at Reno and finished second in the Gold. He was also the fastest qualifier at Mojave but would be a DNF in sixth. With his effort being put into the RB-51 in 1975, he placed fifth in the Gold at Mojave and fifth in the Gold at Reno. During his last year racing, McLain took second in the Gold at Mojave, but first in the Gold with the RB-51 at the same race. Roy McClain helped bring several major sponsorships to the sport of air racing. Health issues forced him to retire from racing and he passed away in 1982 at age 45.

John Mosby; #44, #45 and #94; Publisher; St. Louis, MO; 38 years old in 1969. Mosby's first race was at the 1969 St. Louis races, at which he qualified 11th but was eliminated after finishing fourth in a Heat Race. From there, it was Reno 1969 and he qualified 26th and was cut. Mosby did not have any better luck at the 1979 Ft. Lauderdale races, where he was the fastest qualifier but only made it to sixth in Heat-2B. He had back-to-back races at Wilson and Cape May in 1971. At Wilson, he qualified sixth and was eighth in the Championship Race as a fill-in. He went to Cape May in a new Texan, was a DNQ but was allowed to race (his results are unknown). Mosby's second attempt at Reno was in 1971 at which he qualified 21st and finished third in the Make-Up Race. In 1972, Mosby bought Bob Mitchem's #94 and renumbered it as #44. This resulted in him being the fastest qualifier and finishing second in the Championship Race. His first win was at Miami in 1973. He did not race at Reno in 1973, but another pilot raced his Texan. He next raced at Mojave in 1975, qualifying 11th and taking second in the Gold. He competed again at Reno in 1976, taking third in the Gold. In 1977, he qualified 14th but was a DNS at Reno. Mosby did take sixth in the Gold in 1978. Mosby's last Texan race was at Reno in 1981, at which he qualified first and took first in the Gold, and set a new Reno speed record at 222.78mph.

Jim Mott; #42 and #51; Electrical Contractor; Long Beach, CA; 41 years old in 1971. Jim Mott raced in both Texan and Unlimited classes. His first Texan race was at Reno in 1971, qualifying 18th and finishing third in the Medallion Race. In 1972 at Reno, he placed first in the Medallion Race after that the winner was bumped to fifth for pylon cuts. In 1973, he qualified first and took second in the Reno Gold, and later fourth in the Mojave Consolation Race. His placement at the 1973 Graham races is not recorded. After taking third in the 1974 Reno Gold, Mott took first at Mojave. This was his only Gold win. In 1976, he had engine problems and pylon cuts at Mojave. Mott only placed sixth in the Consolation Race. This was his last year racing at Mojave. He placed third in the Gold at Lincoln but was bumped to fourth with a pylon cut. His Reno results for 1976 were fifth in the Medallion Race and third in the Consolation Race after being bumped up as a fill-in. Mott would race in the Reno Gold races eight times over the years, placing between third and fourth. In the 1986 Reno races, he won the Bronze Race and took sixth in the 1988 Silver. From 1989–90, he raced his #42 *Sea Fury* in the Unlimited Class. Mott returned to Texans in 1991 in #51, but while doing a practice lap, he dug a wingtip and cartwheeled while landing. This was his last Texan race. Jim Mott passed away a few years ago and his #42 Texan is now flying in Australia.

Jane Page (Hlvacek); #54, #83 and #28; Professional Pilot/Businesswoman; Burbank, CA; 26 years old in 1948. Jane Page learned to fly while attending the University of Arizona. She was later a WASP pilot, Class 43-W-7, and flew as a staff pilot for 19 months. After discharge, she worked with her husband in a greenhouse business and engaged in flying as a hobby. Her first race was the 1946 Halle Trophy Race at Cleveland, where she finished second in #54 behind Marge Hurlburt. In 1947, Page helped organize and fly in the first All Women's Airshow in Tampa. The airshow featured a Texan Demo Race which she took fourth. For the 1947 Cleveland races, she raced #83 and took fourth in the finals. That year she had also raced a Lockheed F-5G in the Bendix race and placed ninth. Page planned to race Bill Odom's former YP-47M in the 1948 Bendix and let Nancy Corrigan race her #83. Due to mechanical issues, Page was a DNS for the Bendix, while Corrigan placed fifth. For the 1949 Women's Trophy Race at Cleveland, Page entered a modified Curtiss SNC-1 trainer (#28), but after protest from the other pilots she was not allowed to race. Her post-racing career was still in flying, as she earned her commercial airline pilot's license and flew for several airlines and charter operators. Jane Page was a life member of the Ninety-Nines and passed away in April 2006.

Pat Palmer; #9 and #99; Aero Engineer; Seattle, WA; 37 years old in 1975. When Pat Palmer raced for the first time at Reno in 1971, his #9 had previously raced at Reno in 1968–69. Palmer qualified seventh and finished third in the Consolation Race. He was then placed into the Championship Race as the first alternate after Richard Sykes stood his Texan on its nose during the racehorse start. Palmer finished second in the Championship Race. At Reno in 1972, he finished second in the Consolation Race, which would be his lowest finish. In 1973, he raced at Reno taking third in the Championship Race, while qualifying first at the inaugural Mojave races and then taking his first Gold win of five total. His 1974 record was first at Reno in the Championship Race and second in the Mojave Gold. This was the last year he raced #99. It would later be raced by Marshall Wells and last raced at Reno in 2018. With his new #99, he qualified third at Mojave in 1975 and took first in the Gold. He qualified first at Reno and first in the Gold Race. In June 1976, Palmer took second in the Gold at Mojave and first in the Reno Championship Race. Racing at Reno in 1977, he placed second in the Championship Race. At his last Reno and last Texan race in 1978, Palmer took fifth in the Gold. He was entered in the 1978 and 1979 Mojave races but was a DNQ and DNR. Palmer had a very impressive record.

Ralph Rina; #73, #51, #2, and #73; Airline Captain/Flight Standards Trainer; Hawthorne, CA; 31 years old in 1973. Ralph Rina's first race in #73 was at Reno in September 1973 in which he qualified 12th and finished sixth in the Consolation Race. He went on to Mojave in October, where he qualified third and took first in the Bronze and third in the Silver after bumping up, and raced at Graham in November. He was back at Reno in 1974 taking his second win in the Consolation Race and then fourth in the Gold at Mojave. The races at Mojave were in June 1975. There, Rina took second in the Silver but was bumped to first after the winner was charged with pylon cuts. In September 1975, Rina qualified second and finished fourth in the Gold at Reno. June 1976 brought Rina a fourth in the Gold at Mojave and later he was the fastest qualifier and earned second in the Gold at Reno. Rina would take third in the 1977 Reno Gold Race. His first Gold win was at Reno in 1978 and he placed third in the Mojave Gold. Only Mojave held Texan races in 1979, and he was fourth in the Gold. This was the last of the races held in Mojave. From 1981–83, Rina would finish second in the Gold at Reno before taking his second Gold win in 1984. In 1985 and 1986, Rina took third and fifth in the Gold, respectively. It should be noted that Rina also raced Mustang #102 in 1986. After 1986, Rina stepped away from racing until 1990, when he entered #51 and qualified 19th, but was a DNR. He stepped away again until 1995 and entered #51, qualifying 14th and racing in Heat-2B, but was a DNS for the Silver. After another pause, he entered a new #73 in 2011, but was a DNQ. He won second in the Bronze in 2012. He was a DNR in 2013 but came back in 2014 to win the Bronze. Rina was again a DNR in 2015 but took fourth in the Silver in #2 in 2016. Rina then began a streak of three consecutive Bronze wins at Reno for 2017, 2018, and 2019 flying #73 before retiring from racing. Ralph Rina passed away in April 2023

Chris Rushing; #42 and #14; Retired USAF/Avionics Business; San Clemente, CA; 47 years old in 2005. Rushing was a chief master sergeant with the 146 Airlift Squadron. This unit was co-located at the Van Nuys Airport where the Condor Squadron Headquarters is located, so it is only natural that Chris became associated with that group. He was also married to the daughter of one of the Condor Squadron cofounders, Richard Sykes. Rushing purchased Charles Beck's #2 in 2005 and renumbered it as #42 for his first race at Reno in 2005. He qualified 16th and earned his first racing prize when he finished first in the Bronze. In 2006, he was second in the Bronze Race, followed by a sixth in the 2008 Silver Race. He placed third in the Silver for 2009, third in Silver for 2010, and first in Heat-2C in the shortened 2011 races. Rushing began racing #14, which was his late father-in-law's old racer, in 2012, and took fifth in the Gold Race. In 2013 and 2014, he finished third in the Gold Races. His second win came in 2015 in the Silver Race before bumping up to the Gold event and placing second. Rushing won his first Gold Race in 2016, then finished second in the 2018 Gold. He followed this up with a first in the Gold in 2019, 2021 and 2022. For 2023, he finished first in the Gold Race for his fifth Gold win at Reno. Minutes after the conclusion of the race, Chris was killed in a landing accident. Rushing was the President of the Condor Squadron up until his death in 2023.

Joey "Gordo" Sanders; #5; Retired USAF/Flight Instructor/Flying Service Owner; Jasper, AL; 46 years old in 2004. Sanders flew RF-4s and KC-135 while in the ANG/USAF, retiring as a lieutenant colonel. He retired after 30 years of flying for FEDEX. Sanders began racing his historic #5 (formerly #25 and #51) at Reno in 2004, qualifying ninth and finishing fifth in the Silver. He took his first of six silver race wins at the 2005 Tunica races and also his first Reno Silver win. He raced in five gold races with his best finish a third at Tunica, where he bumped up after winning the Silver. Sanders took a break from racing between 2016 and 2021. He raced in 2022 and finished third in the Silver, which was his 11th Silver race. In 2023, he finished second in the Silver Race, keeping #5's record of finishing every Championship Race.

Betty Skelton; #79 and #45; Aerobatic Pilot/Racecar Driver/Businesswoman; Pensacola, FL; 21 years old in 1947. Skelton soloed at age 12 and received her private pilot's license at 16. Betty applied for the WASP, but the group was disbanded before she was old enough to join. She raced twice at Cleveland. The first time was in #79, but she did not qualify. She returned to Cleveland again in 1949 in #45 where she finished fourth in the finals. Skelton is more widely known for her success in the US Female Aerobatic Championship, which she won three times (1948, 1949, and 1950) and as a racecar driver, earning four Woman's Land Speed Records among others. Betty Skelton passed away on August 31, 2011.

Richard "Dick" Sykes; #3 and #14; Lawyer; Toluca Lake, CA; 44 years old in 1968. Growing up in Southern California, Dick, like most boys in the 1940s, wanted to fly. He enlisted in the Army Air Corps during World War Two and became a fighter pilot flying P-38s. Sykes became a cofounder of the Condor Squadron in 1965. He entered his #3 for the first time at Reno in 1968 and qualified second and took second in the Championship Race. He placed third in the 1969 Reno Consolation Race and, in 1971 (there were no 1970 Reno T-6 races), stood his Texan on its nose during the start of the Gold Race. With pylon cuts, Dick went from fourth in the Consolation Race to sixth at Reno in 1972. In 1973, Sykes and fellow race pilots organized the Mojave Air Races to be run after Reno, at which he placed second in the Consolation Race. In Mojave, Sykes qualified 16th and took fifth in the Championship Race. He did not race at Reno in 1974, but he did race at Mojave, where Charles Beck qualified Sykes' #3 and took second in the Silver. In June 1975 at Mojave, he finished first in the Silver, but was bumped back to fifth for two pylon cuts. At Reno, Sykes finished fifth in the Consolation Race. A sixth in the Gold at Mojave in 1976 was followed by a fifth in the Reno Championship Race. Sykes was second in the Consolation at Reno in 1977. In 1978, he was third in the Championship Race and a DNF at Mojave. In the last Mojave Race in 1979, Sykes would be fifth in the Gold. There were no Texan race at Reno that year. Returning to Reno in 1981, he was fourth in the Gold. He had a DNF in the 1982 Reno Championship Race after taking a large bird strike in the engine. Sykes changed Texans in 1983 for Reno (#14) at which he would take his only Gold win after qualifying second fastest. His last race was Reno 1986 at which he qualified 13th and 5th in Heat-1A in #14. Richard Sykes passed away in August 2008. His #14 was raced by his son-in-law Chris Rushing until his death at Reno 2023.

Ralph Twombly; #4, #41 (x4), #42 and #44; Professional Pilot; Wellsville, NY; 45 years old in 1969. Twombly learned to fly in World War Two with the US Army and flew charter work postwar and later was a corporate pilot. He owned his own flying service. Twombly first entered Texan racing in 1969 at the revived Cleveland races. There he qualified eighth and finished third in the Consolation Race in his first #41. Returning in 1970, he placed fourth in the Trophy Race at Ft. Lauderdale, was a DNF at Wilson in the Gold Race (prop spinner problems), and was fourth in the St. Louis Consolation Race. In 1971, Twombly raced at Jacksonville, placing fourth, then at Wilson, placing first in Consolation Race as a fill-in, but taking his first Gold win. He raced at Cape May and was in the fatal Heat-2B race but went on to take fifth in the Championship Race. Twombly also raced at Reno for the first time, qualifying 12th, but was a DNF in the Consolation Race. In 1972, he was at Wilson and placed third in the Championship Race and third in the Consolation Race at Reno. He was again busy in 1973 with third in the Consolation Race at Miami, second in the Medallion Race at Reno, second in the Silver Race at the inaugural Mojave races, and was the third fastest qualifier at Graham. In 1974–94, Twombly raced at Mojave, Reno, Richland (where he entered but was DNQ-DNR after landing gear problems), Casper, and Phoenix (fifth in Gold). He would race Unlimiteds in 1989–90, win his second Gold Race at Mojave in 1976, his third at Reno 1977, and his fourth at Mojave in 1978. Twombly raced at 13 of the 16 locations that held Texan races and raced in 33 title races (Medallion, Consolation, Silver, and Gold) using seven Texans. His last race was the Silver at Reno in 1994 when he was killed in a mid-air collision at the start. Ralph Twombly was 70 years old. He was a dedicated Texan race pilot.

Eddie Van Fossen; #27; Ag Pilot/Businessman; Bakersfield, CA; 43 years old in 1984. Van Fossen joined the US Army after graduating from high school. While in the Army, he took flying lessons and earned a private license. After leaving the Army, he took up crop dusting as a profession and would run his own dusting service by 1979. After purchasing an ex-Honduran Texan and fully restoring it, Van Fossen qualified 14th and took seventh in the 1984 Silver Race at Reno. In 1985, he qualified ninth and finished fifth in the Gold, which would be his lowest Reno Gold finish in the next nine years. Van Fossen and #27 *Miss TNT* would use the proven style of racing to win races. The motto was "Fly Low, Fly Fast, Turn Left." Van Fossen and #27 *Miss TNT* took the first of eight Gold Race wins in 1986. Their record stands today. The first place wins were in 1986–88. Van Fossen placed second in 1989 to everyone's surprise. Although they qualified first in 1990, they finished third. Races in the years 1991 and 1992 earned additional first places. There was another first in the Silver 1992 Redmond races and a first in 1993, In 1994, first was won at Phoenix and he also won first in the last Gold Race at Reno in 1994. The plane and pilot also raced at Casper in 1990. In 1993, Van Fossen and *Miss TNT* were awarded the Pulitzer Trophy by the National Aeronautic Association for their successes. While Van Fossen retired from air racing in 1994, *Miss TNT* (named *Pole Dancer*) last raced in 2018.

Edna Gardner-Whyte; #42; Professional Pilot/Instructor; Fort Worth, TX; 45 years old in 1947. Gardner-Whyte was a registered nurse who fell in love with flying and made it a career, receiving her pilot license in 1931. She had vast experience in air racing by winning numerous races before World War Two. During the war, she was an instructor at various flight schools and owned several over the years. Her only entry in Texan racing was at the 1947 Cleveland Races in which she qualified fifth and finished third in the finals. Edna would continue to fly and race after Cleveland, winning the All Women's International Air Races four times. She also raced at Cleveland in the 1968 Women's Stock Plane Race and at Reno in 1968 in the same class of racing. Edna Gardner-Whyte passed away in February 1992. Her #42 was restored back to a stock configuration and flown by the Skytypers Demo Team until being W/O in a fatal accident in May 2018.

Sponsors

Unlike the Unlimited Class, Texan racing events have had few major sponsors and most of the individual contestants have only local sponsors. Bardhal Oil Products sponsored some Mojave races, Schlitz Brewing Co. sponsored the Cape May races, the Halle Brothers Department Store sponsored the 1946–47 races, but Texan racing gets by with the smaller sponsors. Casinos and hotels, tool companies, motor oils and gasoline companies (Quaker State, Pennzoil, Getty Oil, Phillips 66), Champion Spark Plugs, waxes and finishes, aircraft repair companies, and fixed base operations (FBOs).

The following was written on the cowling of #99 at Reno in 1976, as recorded by Emil Strasser: "NOTICE: Radial aircraft engine fumes cause an unusual form of mental debilitation resulting in excess expenditure on racing airplanes, incoherence and eventual commitment to a padded hanger. E. Sorenson, Esq." When asked why they race, most Texan race pilots say they do it for the action, excitement and the fun.

Chapter 6
Tables

#44's racing scoreboard. (Emil Strasser)

Table 1: Race Events

All known events that featured Texan racing: either full races or demonstration races in chronological order. Included last are all known proposed races that would have had Texan racing.

Event Name	Location	Date(s)	Course Size	Number of Laps	Total Distance	Comments
National Air Races	Cleveland, Ohio	August 30–September 2, 1946	15 miles	5	75 miles	Postwar
National Air Races	Cleveland, Ohio	August 20–September, 1947	15 miles	5	75 miles	Postwar
National Air Races	Cleveland, Ohio	September 4–6, 1948	15 miles	5	75 miles	Postwar
National Air Races	Cleveland, Ohio	September 3–5, 1949	15 miles	5	75 miles	Postwar
National Championship Air Races	Reno/Stead, Nevada	September 23–24, 1967	2.5 miles	6	15 miles	Exhibition Race
National Championship Air Races	Reno/Stead, Nevada	September 1968–69	3 miles	6/8	18/24 miles	
Florida National Air Races	Fort Lauderdale, Florida	February 13–16, 1969	3 miles	6	18 miles	
St. Louis National Air Races	Chesterfield, Missouri	August 8–10, 1969	3 miles	6/8	18/24 miles	
National Air Races	Cleveland, Ohio	August 29–September, 1969	2.5 miles	8/10	20/25 miles	
Florida National Air Races	Fort Lauderdale, Florida	April 16–19, 1970	3.189 miles	10	31.89 miles	
Wilson Regional Air Races	Wilson, North Carolina	July 25–26, 1970	2.43 miles	10/8	24.3/19.4 miles	
St. Louis National Air Races	East Alton, Illinois	September 5–7, 1970	2.5 miles	8	20 miles	
Herlong Field Air Races	Jacksonville, Florida	April 25, 1971	UNK	UNK	UNK	Demonstration Race
Wilson Regional Air Races	Wilson, North Carolina	May 15–16, 1971	2.43 miles	12	29.1 miles	
Cape May National Air Races	Cape May, New Jersey	June 2–6, 1971	2.5 miles	8	20 miles	
Bartow Air Races	Bartow, Florida	September 1971	UNK	UNK	UNK	Demonstration Race
National Championship Air Races	Reno/Stead, Nevada	September 1971–78	3 miles	6/8	18/24 miles	
Wilson Regional Air Races	Wilson, North Carolina	May 20–21, 1972	2.43 miles	8	19.4 miles	The Richard Minges Memorial Air Races
Rosser Ranch Air Races	Graham, Texas	June 23–25, 1972	3.5 miles	6/8 laps	28 miles	PRPA race
The Great Air Races	Miami, Florida	January 16–21, 1973	3 miles	8	24 miles	Held at Tamiami Airport
California Air Classics	Mojave, California	October 18–21, 1973	3.763 miles	6/8	22.6/30 miles	
Rosser Ranch Air Races	Graham, Texas	November 2–4, 1973	3.5 miles	6/8 laps	28 miles	PRPA race
California National Air Races	Mojave, California	October 9–13, 1974	3.763 miles	6	22.6 miles	Also included 1 lap Drag Races
California Air Races	Lincoln, California	May 1975	3 miles	UNK	UNK	Demonstration Race

Event Name	Location	Date(s)	Course Size	Number of Laps	Total Distance	Comments
California National Air Races	Mojave, California	June 18–20, 1975	3.685 miles	6/8	22.1/29.4 miles	Also included 1 lap Drag Races
California Air Races	Lincoln, California	May 15–16, 1976	3 miles	6/8	18/24 miles	Also included 1 lap Drag Races
California National Air Races	Mojave, California	June 19–20, 1976	3.5 miles	6	21 miles	Also included 1 lap Drag Races
California National Air Races	Mojave, California	October 27–29, 1978	3.685 miles	5/6	18.4/22.1 miles	Also included 1 lap Drag Races
California National Air Races	Mojave, California	June 23–24, 1979	3.685 miles	5/6/8	18.4/22.1/29.4 miles	Also included 1 lap Drag Races
National Championship Air Races	Reno/Stead, Nevada	September 1981	5.207 miles	4	20.8 miles	
National Championship Air Races	Reno/Stead, Nevada	September 1982–99	5 miles	4/5	20/25 miles	
Northwest Air Classics	Richland, Washington	August 10–11, 1985	2.76 miles	UNK	UNK	Demonstration Race
Northwest Air Classics	Richland, Washington	August 15–17, 1986	4.8 miles	6	28.8 miles	
Wendover Air Races	Wendover, Utah	August 1988	UNK	UNK	UNK	Demonstration Race
Flying Cowboy Airshow and Air Races	Casper, Wyoming	June 1989	UNK	UNK	UNK	Demonstration Race
Minot Air Races	Minot, North Dakota	June 22–23, 1989	UNK	UNK	UNK	Demonstration Race
Wendover Air Races	Wendover, Utah	August 12–13, 1989	UNK	UNK	UNK	Demonstration Race
Flying Cowboy Airshow and Air Races	Casper, Wyoming	June 23–24, 1990	5 miles	4	20 miles	
Redmond Air Races	Redmond, Oregon	July 3–5, 1992	3.478 miles	6/9	20.8/31.3 miles	
Phoenix 500 Air Races	Mesa, Arizona	March 18–20, 1994	5 miles	5/6	25/30 miles	
Paso Robles F-1 Races	Paso Robles, California	June 4–5, 1994	2.96 miles	UNK	UNK	Demonstration Race on an F-1 course
Big Sky International Airshow	Billings, Montana	July 23–24, 1994	UNK	UNK	UNK	Demonstration Race
Minter Field Warbird Show	Shafter, California	April 20–21, 1995	UNK	UNK	UNK	Demonstration Race
Minter Field Warbird Show	Shafter, California	April 19–20, 1996	UNK	UNK	UNK	Demonstration Race
National Championship Air Races	Reno/Stead, Nevada	September 2000–11	5.06 miles	5/6	25.3/30.3 miles	
Tunica Air Races	Tunica, Mississippi	June 2–5, 2005	5 miles	6	30 miles	

National Championship Air Races	Reno/Stead, Nevada	September 2012–13	4.93 miles	5/6	24.6/29.5 miles	
National Championship Air Races	Reno/Stead, Nevada	September 2014–23	4.82 miles	5/6	24.1/28.92 miles	Also included 1 lap Drag Races
Proposed Air Races						
Cape May Air Races	Cape May, New Jersey	June 2–6, 1970				Canceled three weeks before they were to start
T-6 Invitational	Ontario, California	July 2–4, 1971				To be held at the Ontario Speedway, but were cancelled
T-6 Demonstration	Mosport, Ontario Canada	July 24–25, 1971				Canceled
Las Vegas Air Races	Las Vegas, Nevada	June 8–10, 1984				Canceled
Seattle Air Races	Seattle, Washington	August 3–4, 1991				Canceled
Abbotsford Air Races	Abbotsford, British Colombia, Canada	August 10–11, 1991				Canceled
New Orleans Air Races	New Orleans, Louisiana	October 26–27, 1991				Canceled
Phoenix 500 Air Races	Mesa, Arizona	March 24–26, 1995				T-6 Racing Canceled
Tunica Air Races	Tunica, Mississippi	June 1–4, 2006				Canceled
Marana Air Races	Marana, Arizona	October 20–22, 2006				Canceled

Table 2: Assigned Race Numbers

Each Texan raced was/is assigned a race number by the pilot/owner for the aircraft for a designated race or as requested by the pilot/owner for time period based on the availability of the number. Some Texans used the same race number throughout their racing career, while others used multiple numbers. No two aircraft were allowed to use the same number during a race. Not every Texan assigned a race number raced and are noted. (Example: SNJ- 5 N9824C, at one time, carried a large #88 but this was an ad for an Oldsmobile dealer.) Assigned race numbers are in numerical order.

ENT Entered, **QUL** Qualified, **DNQ** Did Not Qualify, **DNR** Did Not Race, **DMG** Damaged, **W/O** Written Off. **BL** Billings, **CLV** Cleveland, **CM** Cape May, **CY** Casper, **FL** Fort Lauderdale, **GR** Graham, **MI** Miami, **MV** Mojave, **PX** Phoenix, **RD** Redmond, **R** Reno, **RW** Richland, **StL** St. Louis, **SH** Shafter, **TU** Tunica, **WL** Wilson

Race #	Registration #	A/C Name	Model	Mil S/N.	Race	Pilot(s)	Other Race #
					Postwar Closed Course Pylon Racers National Air Races, Cleveland Ohio 1946–49		
23	NX57805		AT-6A	41-15872	NAR CLEVELAND 1947 (DNQ) STOCK, 1948 3-BLADED PROP	DOT LEMON	#72
31	NX66134	NUTA'S MIAMI, FL; JESS BRISTOW AIRSHOWS	SNJ-3	6927	NAR CLEVELAND 1948-49 CROPPED CANOPY	KADDY LANDRY	
35	N57584	MISS MULLIGAN II	SNJ-3	5575	NAR CLEVELAND 1946-47 STOCK	ARLENE DAVIS	
36	NX63760		SNJ-2	2019	NAR CLEVELAND 1947 (DNQ) STOCK	BELLA HEINEMAN	
42	NX62382		SNJ-2	2039	NAR CLEVELAND 1947	EDNA WHYTE	
44	NX90641		AT-6A	41-461	NAR CLEVELAND 1947–49 CROPPED CANOPY	GRACE HARRIS	
45	NX65560		SNJ-3	5519	NAR CLEVELAND 1949 CROPPED CANOPY	BETTY SKELTON	
49	NX61269	SPENCER CHEMICAL CO.; WAXWING	AT-6A	41-234	NAR CLEVELAND 1947, 1948 RANGER ENGINE (DMG 1947)	DORI MARLAND (1947), BETTY CLARK (1948)	
54	NX64448	CHUM SEAT SPECIAL	AT-6A	41-277	NAR CLEVELAND 1946–47 CROPPED CANOPY, TUBRO-CHARGER	JANE PAGE (1946), BETTY CLARK (1947)	
61	NX74108		XAT-6E	42-84241	NAR CLEVELAND 1947 CROPPED CANOPY RANGER ENGINE (NAA FACTORY BUILT)	MARGE McGRATH	
65	NX51499	MAVEC & Co.	AT-6	40-2113	NAR CLEVELAND 1947-48	ANNA LOGAN	

#	N-number	Name	Model	Serial	Event/Notes	Pilot	Race #
72	N57805		AT-6A	41-15872	NAR CLEVELAND 1946 STOCK	DOT LEMON	#23
75	NX63770	MISS WIKK	AT-6A	41-16743	NAR CLEVELAND 1947–49 CROPPED CANOPY, 3 BLADE PROP (1946 AS #41)	RUTH JOHNSON	
79	NX65619		SNJ-3	6827	NAR CLEVELAND 1947 (DNQ) STOCK	BETTY SKELTON	
81	NC51497		AT-6A	41-16280	NAR CLEVELAND 1946	MARGE HURLBURT	
83	NX57799	THE WEAKER SIX	AT-6A	41-15915	NAR CLEVELAND 1947–48 CROPPED CANOPY	JANE PAGE (1947), NANCY CORRIGAN (1948)	
91	NX55941	MIKE	SNJ-4	9985	NAR CLEVELAND 1948–49 CROPPED CANOPY	HELEN McBRIDE	
96	NX63829	LADY BIRD	AT-6A	41-784	NAR CLEVELAND 1947 (DNR)	DORA JEAN DOUGHERTY	
28	NX19446	LITTLE WILLI	SNC-1	6290	NAR CLEVELAND 1949 (ENT-DNQ-DNR)	JANE PAGE	
Closed Course Pylon Racers 1967–2021							
0	N3254G	MISS JANET SUE	SNJ-5	112034	RENO 1968–69, 1971; FT. LAUDERDALE 1970	HUGH GLASSBURN	
1	N9525C	CONDOR	SNJ-4	27307	RENO 1967 DEMO	WALTER MORRISON	#3
1	N7295C	HEAD HUNTER	SNJ-5	90735	RENO 1968	HENDRIK OTZEN	
1	N7061C	SILVER BABY	SNJ-4	27386	MOJAVE 1978, 1979 (DRAGS)	JIM FURLONG	
1	N42BA	MISS UNIVERSE	HRV IIa	EX287	RENO 1984–89	MICHAEL BURKE (1984–85) CHARLES HUTCHINS	
1	N8540P	DARING DIANE	T-6D	44-81646 (1)	RENO 2005 (WHITE #1, QUL-DNR), 2006 (ORANGE #1, QUL-DNR)	JASON SOMES	#51
1	N3169G	HALFHILL TEXAN	SNJ-6	111974	RENO 1999–2000, 2008, (QUL-DNR), 2010	CARTER CLARK, JOHN KRAWCZYK (2010)	#11, #88
2	N2861G	KGH RADIO SPECIAL	SNJ-6	112157	RENO 1968	W. S. HALFHILL	#5
2	N447CL	OMNI TEXAN	SNJ-5	85056	RENO 1969	WALTER MORRISON	
2	N2821G*	GREAT AMERICAN; SPEEDY GONZALES	T-6G	52-8211	RENO 1972	BRUCE PAYNE	#2A
2A*	N711AP*		T-6G	52-8211	MOJAVE 1973	BRUCE PAYNE	2
2*	N711AP	OMNI	T-6G	52-8211	MOJAVE 1973; MIAMI 1973; RENO 1973 (QUL-DNR)	CALVIN CONROY, BRUCE PAYNE	#2, #17
2	N777AP		SNJ-5	43924	MOJAVE 1973 (*Note: 1 Confusion as to which aircraft raced at MV-73.) (*Note 2 N2821G, N711AP, N777AP all carried #2)	CALVIN CONROY	

Race #	Registration #	A/C Name	Model	Mil S/N.	Race	Pilot(s)	Other Race #
2	N9789Z		HRV II	AJ731	MOJAVE 1975	DENNIS BUEHN	#43, #50
2	N86WW	CHALLENGER II; CALIFORNIA MEDFLY; TRY HARDER; HONEST ENTRY	SNJ-4	27255	MOJAVE 1978–79; RENO 1977–78, 1981–93	CHARLES BECK	#42, #88
2	N2863G	HONEST ENTRY II	SNJ-6	112168	RENO 1994 (ENT-DNQ-DNR)	CHARLES BECK	#7
2	N8044H	MISS TANNER	T-6G	51-14791	RENO 1999 (ENT-DNQ)	MARK HENLEY	#42
2	N4485	KITCHEN PASS	T-6	44-81646 (2)	RENO 2007	KEN DWELLE	
2	N1465	BARE ESSENTIALS	HRV IV	20248	RENO 2014–19, 2022–23	THOMAS BABER (2014), ERIC WOELBING (2015), RALPH RINA (2016), CHRIS LeFAVE (2017–18, 2022–23), MICHAEL PFLEGER (2019)	#12
3	N2860G		SNJ-6	112130	RENO 1967 DEMO	HANK OTZEN	#46
3	N9525C	TWO-FIVE CHARLES; ANGELS DESIRE	SNJ-4	27307	MOJAVE 1973–76, 1978–79; RENO 1968–69, 1971–73, 1975–78, 1981–83	RICHARD SYKES, DENNIS BUEHN (R-1983)	#1
3	N42JM	SLO-YELLER	T-6G	51-15048	RENO 1994–97, 1999–2000	DOREL GRAVES	#48, #048
4	N6975C		SNJ-5	51677	RENO 1967 DEMO	DICK GREGORY	#37
4	N8158H		SNJ-5	90918	RENO 1968–69, 1971–72; ST. LOUIS 1969–70	DON PHILLIPPI, DON REYNOLDS	#43
4	N6979C	ANTISAPATION	T-6D	42-85408	RENO 1976 (ENT DNQ-DNR)	KIRK McKEE	
4	N144KM		T-6A	41-16066	RENO 1977 (DNQ-DNR)	KIRK McKEE	
4	N17498 (1)	HALL RACER	T-6G	49-3221*	RENO 1981	CHARLES NEELY	#47
4	N8540Z	DASH ONE; SLO THUNDER	SNJ-4	27849	RENO 1986–89, 1992; RICHLAND 1986; REDMOND 1992	DAVID BRUCE	#41, #55
4	N4269E	FOUR PLAY	T-6G	53-4601	RENO 1994–95, 2021; PHOENIX 1994	BUD GRANLEY (PX-1994), CHRIS LeFAVE (R-2021)	#13, #44
4	N3171P	FOUR PLAY	T-6	SAAF7320 17320*	RENO 1996–97, 2000–02, 2005	GENE McNEELY (1996–97), LEE OMAN (2000–02), DENNIS BUEHN (2005)	#43
4	N57493	EMILY	T-6A	41-0242	RENO 2022	CRAIG MEYER	
5	N2861G		SNJ-6	112157	RENO 1967 DEMO	DON GULOTTA	#2
5	N5208V		SNJ-4	27768	RENO 1968–69	JAMES WILLIAMS	

5	N7404C	RED BARON; BIG RED	SNJ-4	51542	MOJAVE 1974–76; RENO 1974–75, 1981–2016, 2018–19, 2021–23; REDMOND 1992; PHOENIX 1994; TUNICA 2005 NOTE: DMG 1994 DURING RACE	ROY McCLAIN, JERRY McDONALD (R-1982; RD-1992; PX-1994), JIMMY GIST, JOEY SANDERS (R-2004–16, 2021–22; TU-2005), WILLIAM WALKER III (R-2018, DNQ 2023 RACED), RICK SIEGFRIED (R-2019)	#25, #51
5	N3653G	BABY	SNJ-4	27280	MOJAVE 1978–79; RENO 1978	CLIFF BRANCH	#14
6	N5489V	CONDOR II	SNJ-5	90646	RENO 1967–69; ST. LOUIS 1969–70; FT. LAUDERDALE 1970; CAPE MAY 1971 NOTE: W/O DURING CAPE MAY RACE	VICTOR BAKER	
6	N2885G	WHITE LIGHTNING	T-6G	49-2965	RENO 1972–73; WILSON 1972; MIAMI 1973; GRAHAM 1973	ARTHUR BOWLES	
6	N7446C	CHARLES ANGEL	T-6D	44-81819	RENO 1978	CHARLES GILBERT	#43
6	N98474	ITALIAN STALLION	HRV IV	20257*	RENO 1982, 1984	JAMES BRENNAN, CLIFF BRANCH	
6	N1363R	ITALIAN STALLION	T-6G	MM53833	RENO 1985 (DNQ-DNR)	DENNIS BUEHN	
6	N2897G	SIX CAT	T-6G	49-3492	RENO 1986 (QUL-DNR), 1987–94, 1997–2019, 2022–23; WENDOVER 1988; PHOENIX 1994 NOTE: W/O 2023 RENO	NICK MACY	
7	N2863G		SNJ-6	112168	RENO 1967 DEMO	DARRYL GREENAMYER	#2
7	N203V	MISS MERIDIAN PAVERS; 6 KILLER TOO	HRV II	2784	RENO 1968–69, 1971–72; FT. LAUDERDALE 1970; MIAMI 1973; GRAHAM 1973	BEN HALL, JACK LOWERS (MI-1973; GR-1973)	
7	N611F	EAGLE I; HUMM-BABY	SNJ-6	112323	MOJAVE 1974–76, 1978–79; RENO 1974–77, 1986 (QUL-DNR);	COLENE GIGLIO, DENNIS BUEHN (MV-1979 DRAGS), JAMIE MacKAY (R-1986)	#47, #86
7	N5632V		T-6G	52-8218	RENO 1982 (QUL-DNR)	WILLIAM MEIER	
7	N29939		T-6G	49-3034	RENO 1986 (ENT-DNQ-DNR)	BILL ELLIS	
7	N7979C	Old No.7	SNJ-5	84827	RICHLAND 1986	ROBERT HEALE	
7	N97AW	TINKER TOY	HRV II	2970	RENO 1987–90, 2007–2008; CASPER 1990	TOM DWELLE, Sr., TOM DWELLE Jr., KEN DWELLE (R-2007–08)	#37, #97, #97
7	N8204H	YANKEE AIR PIRATE	T-6G	49-3284	RENO 1991–97; REDMOND 1992; PHOENIX 1994; BILLINGS 1994	TOM DWELLE, Sr., TOM DWELLE, Jr. (R-1993, 1995)	
7	N4485	KITCHEN PASS	T-6	44-81646 (2)	RENO 2003–04	KEN DWELLE (2003), TOM DWELLE (2004)	#2

Race #	Registration #	A/C Name	Model	Mil S/N.	Race	Pilot(s)	Other Race #
7	N2996Q	MISS KATHY	T-6G	49-3071	RENO 2017	MIKE SCOTT	
8	N7078C		SNJ-4	26755	RENO 1968 (ENT-DNQ)	ROBERT DREWS	#66
8	N7804B		SNJ-5	51819	FT. LAUDERDALE 1969	WILLIAM LUMLEY	#81
8	N4983N		T-6D	44-81453	FT. LAUDERDALE 1970	FRED EDISON	#68, #69, #74
8	N6601C	DO IT	T-6F	44-81757	MOJAVE 1975–76; RENO 1975–76 (DNQ-DNR); LINCOLN 1976	CHAN STOKES	#33
8	N7412C		SNJ-4	27404	RENO 1977	RON HELVE	#13
8	N7038C	MISS FERTILE TURTLE	SNJ-4	27536	RENO 1978 NOTE: W/O DURING RACE	DIMITRY PRIAN	#38, #43
8	N4RC	THE PHOENIX; RENT-A-DENT; ALL STAR RENT A CAR; GRACE 8	SNJ-6	111957	RENO 1981–2000, 2006–2011; RICHLAND 1985–86; WENDOVER 1988; REDMOND 1992; PHOENIX 1994	ROBERT JONES, KEN GOTTSCHALL (R-2006-11)	#80
8	N6427D	ROLLING THUNDER	SNJ-4	51629	TUNICA 2005	ROBIN CRANDALL	#62
9	N5199V	SUNSET SPECIAL; MISS SEMPER FI; GOTCHA #1; CUM'N THRU; LICKETY SPLIT; GOTCHA	SNJ-5	43875	RENO 1968–69, 1971–1977, 1983–92, 1996–2000, 2002–06, 2016–18; MOJAVE 1973–76, 1978–79 (ENT-DNR); LINCOLN 1976; RICHLAND 1985–86; REDMOND 1992	PHILLIP LIVINGSTON (R-1968–69), PAT PALMER (1971–74), MARSHALL WELLS (1975–79), ROBERT HEALE (1983–87), BUD GRANLEY (1988–2006), PETE STAVRIDES (2016–18)	
10	N1046C	GO-MAN-GO	SNJ-5	85080	CLEVELAND 1969; RENO 1969 (ENT DNQ-DNR), 1971–72 (ENT-DNQ-DNR), 1973–74; FT. LAUDERDALE 1970; ST. LOUIS 1969–70; CAPE MAY 1971 (DMG); MIAMI 1973; GRAHAM 1973	DON BARRETT (1970–71), CALVIN EARLY (MI-1973)	
10	N39403	BAD JUJU	SNJ-4	43794	RENO 1990	GREG MORSE	
11	N9060Z	MISS SKY PRINTS	SNJ-5	43835	RENO 1968; FT. LAUDERDALE 1970	HOWIE KEEFE	
11	N16730	MISS SKY PRINTS II; COME ON ELEVEN; HELLO 11	HRV II	3198	CLEVELAND 1969; ST. LOUIS 1969; RENO 1969, 1971–78, 1982–89, 1991–92; MIAMI 1973; MOJAVE 1973–76, 1978–79 (ENT-DNR) NOTE: DURING MOJAVE 1975 CAL WORTHINGTON RACED AS #1 "SPOT" IN DEMO	HOWIE KEEFE (CLV-1969; StL-1969; R-1969), JIM MODES (R-1971, 1973, 1975, 1977; MV-1973–76, CAL CONROY (R-1972, 1974–76, 1978) RAY SCHUTTE (R-1982-86, 1988–92), PETE "PHIL" GIST (R-1987)	#71

#	Reg	Name	Model	Serial	History	Owner/Pilot	Race #
41	N8206E		SNJ-5	90789	CLEVELAND 1969; FT. LAUDERDALE 1970; ST. LOUIS 1970; WILSON 1970	RALPH TWOMBLY	#41, #77
41	N41BT	SHATZI; POPI'S PLANE	SNJ-5	90789	RENO 1971–76; CAPE MAY 1971; WILSON 1971–72; JACKSONVILLE 1971; MOJAVE 1973–75; MIAMI 1973; GRAHAM 1973	RALPH TWOMBLY	#41, #77
41	N9831C	SPOOLED UP	SNJ-6	112180	RENO 1977–78; MOJAVE 1978–79	RALPH TWOMBLY	#98
41	N6424D	FLY-BY-U	SNJ-4	51360	RENO 1986	JOE TAYLOR	#19,#69,#94
41	N8540Z	SLO THUNDER	SNJ-4	27849	RENO 1993–94 (W/O DURING RACE 1994); RICHLAND 1986; PHOENIX 1994	RALPH TWOMBLY	#4, #55
42	N3274G	TAR BABY; MIS-CHIEF	SNJ-5B	43647	RENO 1971–78, 1981, 1983–88; GRAHAM 1972–73; MOJAVE 1973–76, 1978; LINCOLN 1976	JIM MOTT (R-1981 QUL), RALPH TWOMBLY (R-1981 RACED)	
42	N42DQ	DQ BLIZZARD	T-6C	41-16320	RENO 1989	MIKE WELLS	
42	N77TX	ARTIC FOX	T-6C	41-16320	PHOENIX 1994	GREG SHELTON	
42	N8044H		T-6G	51-14791	RENO 1999 (ENT-DNQ), 2001 (ENT-DNQ)	GENE McNEELY	#2
42	N86WW	SUGARFOOT; HONEST ENTRY; DEFECTOR	SNJ-4	27255	RENO 2005–06, 2008–15	CHRIS RUSHING, ROB SANDBERG (2012–13), KEVIN SUTTERFIELD (2014–15)	#2, #88
43	N9789Z		HRV II	AJ731	GRAHAM 1972	DENNIS BUEHN	#2, #50
43	N7038C	MIDNIGHT MISS	SNJ-4	27536	RENO 1972 (QUL-DNR), 1973–75; MOJAVE 1973–74, 1976	DENNIS BUEHN	#8, #38
43	N7446C	WARBIRDS WEST	T-6D	44-81819	MOJAVE 1976 (QUL-DNR)	DENNIS BUEHN	#6
43	N8158H	MIDNIGHT MISS	SNJ-5	90918	RENO 1976	DENNIS BUEHN	#4
43	N3171P	MIDNIGHT MISS III	T-6	SAAF7320 17320* 133660*	RENO 2006–19, 2021–23	DENNIS BUEHN, CHRIS LeFAVE (2019), JOEL STINNETT (2021–23)	#4
44	N1395N	SKY PRINTS SPECIAL	SNJ-4	51584	RENO 1969 (QUL-DNR), 1971; ST. LOUIS 1969; CLEVELAND 1969; FT. LAUDERDALE 1969–70; CAPE MAY 1971; WILSON 1971	JOHN MOSBY, HOWIE KEEFE (FtL-1969), ART CARLSON (CLV-1969; CM-1971)	
44	N194A	SKY PRINTS SPECIAL; MISS BEHAVIN	HRV II	2914	RENO 1972–73, 1975–78, 1981–82, 1983 (ENT-DNQ-DNR), 1984–86; MIAMI 1973; MOJAVE 1975–78; RICHLAND 1986; WILSON 1971	JOHN MOSBY, RALPH TWOMBLY (MV-1976; R-1982–83), JACK LOWERS (R-1973), ALAN PRESTON (R-1984–86; RW-1986)	#44, #94

Race #	Registration #	A/C Name	Model	Mil S/N.	Race	Pilot(s)	Other Race #
44	N44ZZ	MISS BEHAVIN	HRV II	2914	RENO 1987–89; CASPER 1990	RALPH TWOMBLY, GILLFORD FOLEY (R-1989)	#44, #94
44	N75964		SNJ-4	10116	SHAFTER 1996	TOM NIGHTINGALE	
44	N4269E	SIX SHOOTER	T-6G	53-4601	RENO 1996–97, 2000 (DNQ-RACED), 2001–2007	LEE OMAN (1996–97), WAYNE CARTWRIGHT (2000–07)	#4
44	N7522U	MY T-6	HRV IV	20423	RENO 1998–99	JIM BOOTH	#444, PP
45	N57318		T-6A	41-16302	CAPE MAY 1971 (DNQ-RACED)	JOHN MOSBY	#39
45	N7679C		T-6G	49-3310	RENO 1994 (ENT-DNQ)	GARY ELLER	
46	N2860G	TURKEY 46	SNJ-6	112130	MOJAVE 1973–76; RENO 1973–76	CHARLES BECK, JIM STIRWALT (R-1975; MV-1976)	#3
46	N7055H		T-6C	42-4071	RENO 1993–94 (ENT-DNQ-DNR)	RICHARD FIELDS	
47	N302V	MISS SEATTLE	T-6G	49-3221	RENO 1971	ROD KOSTELNIK	#4
47	N611F	FROST BITE	SNJ-6	112323	RENO 1997–99	JACK FROST	#7, #86
48	N3194G		SNJ-5	91089	RENO 1971; GRAHAM 1972	GEORGE BURDICK (R-1971), CLIFF PUTMAN (GR-1972)	
48	N48BC	BUMPIN DUNKIN; MISS T	T-6A	41-558	RENO 1985–86 (QUL-DNR); RICHLAND 1986	BRUCE REDDING (R-1985), SHANE THEIS (R-1986; RW-1986)	
48	N42JM	SLO-YELLER	T-6G	51-15048	RENO 1990 (ENT-DNQ), 1991–92 (QUL-DNR), 1993	DOREL GRAVES	#3, #048
048	N42JM		T-6G	51-15048	RENO 1987 (ENT-QUL-DNR)	DOREL GRAVES	#3, #48
48	N2983	PLAY-TIME	T-6D	42-86272*	RENO 2018 (ENT-DNQ-DNR)	JOHN JOHNSON	#49
48	N6625C	THE OTHER WOMAN	T-6G	49-3100	RENO 2023	BRIAN REBERRY	
49	N21JD	BLUE MAX; WHIPPERSNAPPER	SNJ-5	90996	RENO 1977–78, 1981 (DNQ-DMG), 1982; MOJAVE 1979	JOHN KIRKLAND (MV-1979), JOHN ALLCORN, JOHN HUNT (R-1981), PHILLIP GIST (R-1982)	
49	N2864D		T-6D	42-85696	RENO 1994 (ENT-DNQ)	JOHN MEYER	#64
49	N29931	SMOKIN SUE	T-6G	49-3449	RENO 2000	JOHN JOHNSON	#51
49	N2983	PLAYTIME	T-6D	42-86272*	RENO 2013	JOHN JOHNSON	#48
49	N7296C	MISS ELLANEOUS	SNJ-5	84979	RENO 2017–19, 2021–23	BILL MUSZALA	
50	N17400		HRV IV	20461	RENO 1969	GEORGE SANDERS	
50	N502		SNJ-5	43689	RENO 1968 (ENT-QUL-DNR) NOTE RACE # WAS SHORTENED FROM SIDE #502	WALT OHLRICH	

50	N8539L	BIG WIND	HRV III	EZ200	RENO 1996–2001 (DNQ-RACED)	CARL PENNER	
50	N4763	AFTER MIDNIGHT; ABRACADABRA	HRV II	2832* (AJ731)	RENO 2007–13, 2015–19, 2021–23	JOHN KRAWCZYK, ROB SANDBERG (2015), VITALY PECHERSKYY (2017–23)	#2
51	N7404C	BIG RED	SNJ-4	51542	MOJAVE 1978–79	JIMMY GIST, JERRY McDONALD	#5, #25
51	N8540P	KILLER UNIT	T-6D	44-81646 (1)	RENO 1983 (ENT-DNQ-DNR), 1990 (QUL-DNR), 1993 (ENT-DNQ-DNR), 1995	RALPH RINA, JERRY MILES (1969)	#1
51	N29931	YABA DABA DO	T-6G	49-3449	RENO (QUL-DNR-DMG)	JIM MOTT	#49
51	N2676P	YABA DABA DO TWO	SNJ-5	85066	RENO 1992 (ENT-DNQ-DNR)	JOHN MARLIN (1992), JERRY MILES	
54	N1364J	MIDLIFE MADNESS	T-6G	MM53655	RENO 2011–17	MICHAEL PFLEGER	
54	N620AJ	MISS INFORMED	HRV III	EX811 SAAF 7463	RENO 2018	MICHAEL PFLEGER	#21
55	N2864G		SNJ-6	112169	CLEVELAND 1969; ST. LOUIS 1969–70; WILSON 1970	LEN TANNER (CL-1969; StL-1969), ART CARLSON (StL-1970), JACK LOWERS (WL-1970)	
55	N3203G	LIL MARIA	SNJ-5	90691	RENO 1976 (ENT-DNQ-DNR, ENGINE)	BOB DODSON	
55	N8540Z	SLO THUNDER	SNJ-4	27849	RENO 1991	DAVID BRUCE	#4, #41
55	N3931S	MISS APPROPRIATION	SNJ-5	51811*	RENO 1993–94; PHOENIX 1994	FRED JOHNSON	#17, #55
55	N5FJ	MISS APPROPRIATGN OF FUNDS	SNJ-5	51811*	RENO 1995–96, 1998 (ENT-DNQ)	FRED JOHNSON	#17, #55
55	N7648E	TROPHY HUNTER; BIG DADDY	SNJ-3	01882	RENO 2005–06	GARY MILLER	
56	N101GB		T-6G	49-3137	RENO 2008	SCOTT DOCKTER	#57
56	N73RR	MARGARITA; BLUE TWO	SNJ-6	112131	RENO 2009–10	SCOTT DOCKTER (2009), DUANE WOODS (2010)	#22, #56, #73
57	N3257G	COMSTOCK AIRLINES; SNEAKY PETE	SNJ-5	85087	RENO 1969, 1971, 1973 (QUL-DNR)	WALT OHLRICH (1969) MARVIN QUAID (1971), JAMES WIRTZ (1973)	
57	N2831D		T-6G	53-4577	RENO 1981	EDMOND COLBERT	NOTE: A/C CARRIED SIDE #577
57	N997RD	LUCKY DUCK	HRV IV	20373	RENO 1997 (ENT-DNQ), 1998	CHERYL BLOOM (1997), GARY HUBLER	
57	N101GB	DEUCE of HEARTS	T-6G	49-3137	RENO 2009–10	SCOTT DOCKTER	#56

Race #	Registration #	A/C Name	Model	Mil S/N.	Race	Pilot(s)	Other Race #
58	N7058C	Ole 58	SNJ-4	27352	RENO 2016–17	THOM VAUGHN	
59	N73RR	BLUE BAYOU	SNJ-6	112131	RENO 1990–92	JIMMY GIST	#22, #59, #73
59	N651SH	DULCINEA	T-6G	49-3305	RENO 2012	NATHAN HARNAGEL	
62	N6427D		SNJ-4	51629	RACE # ASSIGNED 1969 NO PROOF OF EVER RACING	JACK WIMER	#8
64	N2864D		T-6D	42-85696	MOJAVE 1976 (DNQ-DNR); RENO 1977	BEN HARRISON	#49
64	CF-WLO	THINKING, RED KNIGHT	HRV IV	20264	RENO 1993–94, 2000–2010 (DNQ-RACED 2001), 2012–13	KEITH McMANN	
65	N7657C	YURAS	T-6G	49-2988	RENO 1972 (ENT-QUL-DNR)	DON WEINBERGER	
66	N7078C		SNJ-4	26755	RENO 1969 (ENT-DNQ-DNR)	ROBERT DREWS	#8
66	N66IL		SNJ-5	90800	WILSON 1971–72; CAPE MAY 1971; RENO 1973	JACK LOWERS, ELMER PAYNE (R-1973)	
66	N1666T	LUSTY LADY	SNJ-5	43725	RENO 1984 (ENT-DNQ-DNR)	LEONARD STONICH	
66	N1466	THE TIME MACHINE	HRV IV	20333	RENO 1986 (ENT-DNQ-DNR); RICHLAND 1986	LEE DONHAM, BRUCE LOCKWOOD (RW-1986)	
66	N7520U		HRV IV	20385	RENO 1995 (ENT-DNQ-DNR)	DENNIS DILL	
66	N8993	MISSTRESS; MISS OPERTUNITY	HRV IIB	2976	RENO 1996–2000, 2001 (DNQ-RACED), 2002–04 (NOTE: B-66 SIDE NUMBER)	THOMAS MARTIN	#89
66	N4802E	GUNSLINGER	HRV II	AJ968	RENO 2008–2013, 2015, 2017, 2018 (DNQ),2019, 2021–23	VIC McMANN	
68	N8048J	TEXAS RED	T-6G	51-15063	RENO 1981–86	JIMMY GIST	#99
68	N4983N	BIG EASY	T-6D	44-81453	RENO 2001–02, 2004, 2006; TUNICA 2005	MICHAEL GILLIAN	#8, #69, #74
69	N9649C		T-6D	42-85456	ST. LOUIS 1969	RICHARD MINGES	#96
69	N3646G	MISS JANICE LEE	HARV II	AJ688	RENO 1969 (QUL-DNR), 1971–74; MOJAVE 1973–75	ROBERT SUACCI	
69	N6424D	TAYLOR MAID	SNJ-4	51360	RICHLAND 1986; RENO 1988	LEE OMAN, JOE TAYLOR (RW-1986)	#19, #41, #94
69	N4983N		T-6D	44-81453	RENO 2000	MICHAEL GILLIAN	#8, #68, #74
69	N3173L	EROS	T-6D	42-85344	RENO 2005–19, 2021–23	LEE OMAN, WAYNE CARTWRIGHT (2010), OTT CLERMONT (2011 ONE HEAT RACE)	

70	N7463C		T-6F	44-81893	RENO 1969	WILLIAM TURNBULL	#70
70	N706F	OLE BETSY	T-6F	44-81893	FT. LAUDERDALE 1970; RENO 1971–74	CHARLES SAUNDERS, CALVIN EARLY (R-1972–73)	#70
70	N10597	SHOW ME	SNJ-4	27748	RENO 1986 (QUL-DNR)	JOE CHIODO/C. J. SCHMIDT	
70	N2269T	MIRAGE	SNJ-4	27505	RENO 2001 (DNQ-RACED), 2002–08	JIM THOMAS	
70	N6414D		SNJ-4	27060	CLEVELAND 1969	DICK FOOTE	
71	N6972C	MISS FOXY LADY	SNJ-5	90680	RENO 1978, MOJAVE 1979	JIM FOX	#72, #77
71	N7011C		SNJ-4	51423	RENO 1983 (ENT-QUL-DNR)	JACK TODOVERTO	
71	N16730	THE COMPANY STORE	HRV II	3198	RENO 1993; PHOENIX 1994	JOHN KRAWCZYK	#11
72	N3666F	CAF BLUNDERBIRDS OLD IRONSIDES; ACE IN THE HOLE	SNJ-5	52031	FT. LAUDERDALE 1970; RENO 1971–75; MIAMI 1973, GRAHAM 1973; MOJAVE 1974	BILL TURNBULL, CALVIN EARLY (MV-1974)	#37
72	N6972C	GITMO; TERRIBLE TEXAN	SNJ-5	90680	RENO 1981–83 (ENT-DNR), 1984–87	JIM FOX	#71, #77
73	N73RR	MISS EVERYTHING	SNJ-6	112131	MOJAVE 1973–76, 1978–79; GRAHAM 1973; RENO 1973–78, 1981–86	RALPH RINA	#22, #56, #59
73	N7765C	JUTTA	T-6G	50-1288	RENO 1991	FRANK ELLIOTT	#74
73	N51KT	STRIP-TEEZE	T-6G	49-3266	RENO 2011 (ENT-DNQ-DNR), 2012–14	RALPH RINA	
73	N158JZ	MISS HUMBOLT HUNNY	T-6G	49-3158	RENO 2017–19, 2021–23	RALPH RINA, LOREN MARBURG (2021–23)	
74	N6900G		T-6G	49-3384	RENO 1968 (ENT-QUL-DNR)	LEROY PENHALL	
74	N4983N		T-6D	44-81453	CLEVELAND 1969 (DNQ-DNR)	FRED EDISON	#8, #68, #69
74	N7765C	HOT KNOTT'S; THE EXORCIST	T-6G	50-1288	RENO 1972–74; MIAMI 1973; MOJAVE 1973–74	DON DEWALT	#73
74	N74DW	EXORCIST	T-6G	49-3386	MOJAVE 1976; RENO 1976–78 NOTE: W/O DURING RENO 1978	DON DEWALT	
75	N832N		HRV II	AJ832	RENO 1973 (QUL-DNR), 1974–75	BARRIE SIMONSON	
75	N7985C	WARLOCK	SNJ-6	112237	RENO 1981–91; RICHLAND 1985	AL GOSS	#75
75	N75AG	WARLOCK	SNJ-6	112237	WENDOVER 1988; RENO 1992–2009; REDMOND 1992; PHOENIX 1994; SHAFTER 1995–96	AL GOSS	#75
76	N30JF	DON'T TREAD ON ME	SNJ-5	44009	RENO 1975–76; MOJAVE 1976; LINCOLN 1976	JOHN GERBER, WALT NITOWSKI (ENT BUT KIRK McKEE RACED, R-1976)	#18
77	N6972C		SNJ-5	90680	RENO 1968 (QUL-DNR)	DAROLD JOLLIFF	#71, #72

Race #	Registration #	A/C Name	Model	Mil S/N.	Race	Pilot(s)	Other Race #
77	N41BT	WILDCATTER; WYOMING WILDCAT	SNJ-5	90789	MOJAVE 1978, 1979 (ENT-DNR); RENO 1978, 1981–1990, 1992–2009; CASPER 1990; REDMOND 1992; PHOENIX 1994; BILLINGS 1994	JACK FRANCIS (MV-1978; R-1978), MIKE WRIGHT (R-1981–85), DICK WRIGHT (R-1986), JAMES GOOD (R-1987–2009; CY-1990; RD-1992; PX-1994)	#41
78	N3579	PATCHES	SNJ-5	51678	RENO 2013	THOMAS BABER	
79	N51979	BOOG; TIGGER II	SNJ-5	51979	RENO 1984–87 (1986–87 QUL-DNR)	JOHN MARTIN, C. J. STEPHENS (1987)	
80	N60380	SAMPSON	SNJ-4	27119	RENO 1971 (QUL-DNR)	ROMAINE "BUD" COLLINS	
80	N4RC	GYPSY; SAMPSON	SNJ-6	111957	RENO 1972 (DNQ), 1973, 1974 (DNQ)	BUD COLLINS	#8
81	N7804B		SNJ-5	51819	RACE # ASSIGNED 1969 DNR UNDER THIS #	WILLIAM LUMLEY RICHARD JENSEN	#8
85	N85JR	BLUE SIX	T-6G	49-3402	RENO 1985	JOHN ROARK	
86	N611F	BAD COMPANY	SNJ-6	112323	RENO 1991–97 (ENT-DNQ); PHOENIX 1994; SHAFTER 1996	SHERMAN SMOOT	#7, #47
87	N87H	BANDERSNATCH; STOCKER	T-6D	41-34571	RENO 1971, 2000–02, 2014, 2023; MOJAVE 1974 (DMG); TUNICA 2005	FRED KOHLER (R-1971; MV-1974), RICHARD SIEGFRIED (R-2023 PP), ROB SANDBERG (R-2023 PP)	#736
88	N13631	SUPER SLUG	HRV IV	20286	RENO 1968–74; MOJAVE 1973; GRAHAM 1973	BOB METCALFE	
88	N88RT (2)	AFTER YOU; MISS MYRAH; BUMPIN DUNKIN IV	HRV II	2780	RENO 1986–87, 1988 (ENT-DNQ)	BRUCE REDDING	#11
88	N3169G	DARING DIANE	SNJ-6	111974	RENO 1992 (QUL-DNR)	CARTER CLARK	#1, #11
88	N86WW	DOUBLE TROUBLE	SNJ-4	27255	RENO 2007	DOUG DOTTER	#2, #42
88	N3272G	RADIAL VELOCITY	SNJ-5	84826	RENO 2010–19, 2021–23	JOHN LOHMAR	#20, #26, #28

#	N-number	Name	Model	Serial	Races	Pilots	Notes
89	N8993		HRV IIB	2976	WILSON 1971	JOHN SILBERMAN	#66
89	N604R	*BOOMER; BABY BOOMER*	T-6H	MM54135	RENO 1989–90, 1992–95, 2001–05, 2007–08, 2011–19; REDMOND 1992	JOE HARTUNG (R-1889–95; CY-1990; RD-1992), FRED TELLING (R-2002–05, 2007–08), LEE OMAN (R-2011–12), JERRY BORCHIN (R-2007 ONE HEAT), GENE McNEELY (R-2013–19)	
89	N817NP		SNJ-5	43928	CASPER 1990	JOE HARTUNG	MAY HAVE USED #2
90	N90629	*OLE BLUE*	T-6A	41-16997	MOJAVE 1978; RENO 1978	LARRY HAVENS	CARRIED #31 DNR WITH THIS NUMBER
90	N991GM	*UNDECIDED*	T-6D	42-85794	RENO 1990–95, 1998–2004; CASPER 1990; REDMOND 1992; PHOENIX 1994	GENE McNEELY	
90	N4269Q	*UNDECIDED II*	T-6G	53-4558	RENO 2005–19, 2021–23; TUNICA 2005	GENE McNEELY (TU-2005), LEE OMAN (R-2010), GREG McNEELY (R-2019–23)	
92	N8FU		T-6G	51-14842	RENO 1994 (ENT-DNQ)	ELLOT CROSS	
92	N94SC	*MISS TRESS*	T-6G	49-3356	RENO 1995 (ENT-DNQ), 1996, 1997–98 (ENT-DNQ)	STEVE CLEGG	
94	N194A	*LITTLE HUMMER; MISS COLORADO*	HRV II	2914	RENO 1969, 1971; CLEVELAND 1969; ST. LOUIS 1969–70; CAPE MAY 1971	BOB MITCHEM	#44
94	N90650	*NUTHIN FANCY*	SNJ-4	10206	RENO 1983–84	GEORGE CATALANO	
94	N694US	*MIDNIGHT EXPRESS; FAST COMPANY*	SNJ-4	51360	RENO 2008–11, 2014–16	OTT CLERMONT (2008), NICK MACY (2009), RICK SIEGFRIED (2010), MICHAEL GILLIAN (2011) CHRIS LeFEVE (2014–16)	#19, #41, #69
96	N9649C		T-6D	42-85456	FT. LAUDERDALE 1969	RICHARD MINGES	#69
96	N1974M	*BIG DADDYS "Special"*	T-6D	44-81252	ST. LOUIS 1970; CLEVELAND 1969; RENO 1969; WILSON 1970; FT. LAUDERDALE 1970	RICHARD MINGES	#33
96	N3188G	*KOLBASA; DOOZIE*	SNJ-5	84839	MOJAVE 1975–76, 1978; RENO 1976–78; LINCOLN 1976	MIKE SUKOSKY, DENNIS BUEHN (R-1977)	

Roaring Texans

Race #	Registration #	A/C Name	Model	Mil S/N.	Race	Pilot(s)	Other Race #
97	N9799Z	PROP-ER LADY	HRV II	2970	RENO 1969 (ENT-DNR), 1973 (QUL-DNR), 1974–75; MOJAVE 1973–75	JACK BRIGGS (R-1969) GORDON RICHARDSON (MV-1973, R-1973) GARY MEERMANS (MV-1974, R-1974–75)	#7, #37, #97
97	N97GM	WILEY E. COYOTE; AFTER YOU II	HRV II	2970	MOJAVE 1976, 1979 (ENT-DNR); RENO 1977, 1986; RICHLAND 1986	GARY MEERMANS, BRUCE REDDING/DENNIS BUEHN (R-1986, NOTE REDDING QUL, BUEHN RACED), BRUCE REDDING (RW-1986)	#7, #37, #97
97	N97AW	TINKER TOY	HRV II	2970	RENO 1987	TOM DWELLE	#7, #37, #97
98	N9831C	MUKELTEO EXPRESS; HRUDUDU!	SNJ-6	112180	RENO 1975–76	BEN HALL (1975), JIM LANDRY (1976)	#41
98	N5500V	COLORADO GOLD	SNJ-6	112023	RENO 1983 (QUL-DNR)	JAMES CUSEO	
98	N101FT	ALMOST PERFECT	T-6G	49-3380	RENO 2019 (DNQ-RACED)	GREG McNEELY	
99	N3626F	MONGOOSE; GIN SPECIAL	SNJ-5	51904	RENO 1969; ST. LOUIS 1969–70; CLEVELAND 1969; FT. LAUDERDALE 1969–70; WILSON 1970–71; JACKSONVILLE 1971; CAPE MAY 1971 (W/O DURING RACE)	ED SNYDER	
99	N83H		T-6D	42-44675	MIAMI 1973	JOHN CARD	
99	N999JP	GOTCHA #2	T-6F	44-81889	MOJAVE 1975, 1976, 1978–1979 (ENT-DNQ-DNR); RENO 1975–78	PAT PALMER	
99	N8048J	TEXAS RED	T-6G	51-15063	RENO 1988–91, 1992 (QUL-DNR), 1993–95; PHOENIX 1994	JOHN LUTHER	#68
302	N666SS		T-6G	49-3302	PHOENIX 1994	BILL EBERHARDT	#30
388	N49388	EZ-SIX	T-6G	49-3066	RENO 2023	AARON SINGER	
444	N7522U	MY T-6	HRV IV	20423	RENO 2000, 2002–06	JIM BOOTH	#44
512	N9035Z		T-6G	49-2990	RENO 1997	KEN/TJ DWELLE	
577	N2831D		T-6G	53-4577	RENO 1981 (NOTE: CARRIED SIDE #577, RACED AS #57)	EDMOND COLBERT	#57
736	N87H	CIRCUS WAGEN	T-6D	41-34571	RENO 2004 (DNQ-DNR)	RICHARD SIEGFRIED	#87
999	N3931R	999	SNJ-5	84923	RENO 2023	JOB SAVAGE	

--	WILDFIRE	BECK-STATLER SPECIAL	C/N. 001	NONE	CHARLES BECK	
N3941Y						
Pace Planes						
N9785Z		HRV II	2780	CAPE MAY 1971	ERNEST OPP	#11
NX72375		HRV IV	20280	RENO 1983–88		
N1038A		SNJ-5	90917	RENO 1991–	LAIRD DOCTOR	
N7520U		HRV IV	20385	RENO 1993–95	LARRY KLASSEN/LAIRD DOCTOR	#66
N39403		SNJ-5	43794	RENO 1997–98	LAIRD DOCTOR	
N3261G		SNJ-5	90612	RENO 1999–2004	STEVE DILDA	#21
N7522U		HRV IV	20423	RENO 2007, 2010, 2013	JIM BOOTH	#44, #444
N717UP		T-6G	49-3529	RENO 2016, 2018–19, 2022	ROB SANDBERG	
N87H		T-6D	41-34571	RENO 2023	ROB SANDBERG/RICHARD SIEGFRIED	#87

Table 3: Assigned Civil Registration Numbers

Each Texan was/is assigned a civil registration number by US and Canadian Aviation Authorities and these numbers, a combination of letters and numbers, must be applied to all aircraft. Assigned numbers are in numerical order for US registered aircraft and in alphabetic order for Canadian registered aircraft. Some racers have had multiple registration numbers. Races are chronological.

Registration Number	Model	Mil S/N.	Race Number(s)	Races
N4RC	SNJ-6	111957	8, 80	RENO 1972–74, 1981–2000, 2006–11; RICHLAND 1985–86; WENDOVER 1988; REDMOND 1992; PHOENIX 1994
N8FU	T-6G	51-14842		RENO 1994
N5FJ	SNJ-5	51811	17, 55	RENO 1995–96
N12KY	SNJ-5	90995	12	RENO 2000–06; TUNICA 2005
N21JD	SNJ-5	90996	49	RENO 1977–78, 1981–82; MOJAVE 1979
N22KD	SNJ-4	27616	22	RENO 1991–92
N25RM	SNJ-4	51542	25	SEE UNDER RACE NUMBER #25
N30HA	T-6B	41-17034	30	WILSON 1970–72; CAPE MAY 1971; RENO 1971
N30JF	SNJ-5	44009	18, 76	CAPE MAY 1971; RENO 1971–72, 1975–76; GRAHAM 1972–73; MIAMI 1973; MOJAVE 1976; LINCOLN 1976
N41BT	SNJ-5	90789	41, 77	RENO 1971–76, 1978, 1981–90,1992–09; CAPE MAY 1971; MOJAVE 1973–75, 1978–79; JACKSONVILLE 1971; WILSON 1971–72; MIAMI 1973; GRAHAM 1973; CASPER 1990; REDMAN 1992; PHOENIX 1994; BILLINGS 1994; TUNICA 2005
N42BA	HRV IIb	EX287	1	RENO 1984–89
N42DQ	T-6C	41-16320	42	RENO 1989
N42JM	T-6G	51-15048	3, 48, 048	RENO 1991–97, 1999–2000
N44ZZ	HRV II	2914	44, 94	RENO 1987–89; CASPER 1990
N48BC	T-6A	41-558	48	RENO 1985–86; RICHLAND 1986
N51KT	T-6G	49-3266	73	RENO 2011–2014
N66JL	SNJ-5	90800	66	WILSON 1971–72; CAPE MAY 1971; RENO 1973
N73RR	SNJ-6	112131	22, 56, 59, 73	RENO 1973–79, 1990–92, 1996–2005, 2007, 2011, 2013, 2015; MOJAVE 1973–76, 1978–79; GRAHAM 1973; TUNICA 2005
N74DW	T-6G	49-3386	74	MOJAVE 1976; RENO 1976–78
N75AG	SNJ-6	112237	75	WENDOVER 1988; RENO 1992–2009; REDMOND 1992; PHOENIX 1994; SHAFTER 1995–96
N77TX	T-6C	41-16320	42	PHOENIX 1994
N83H	T-6D	42-44675	99	MIAMI 1973
N85JR	T-6G	49-3402	85	RENO 1985
N86WW	SNJ-4	27255	2, 42, 88	RENO 1977–78, 1981–93, 2005–15; MOJAVE 1978–79
N87H	T-6D	41-34571	87, 736, PP	RENO 1971, 2000–02, 2014, 2023
N88RT (2)	HRV II	2780	11, 88	RENO 1986–88
N91AM	HRV IV	20218	12	RENO 1992; SHAFTER 1995
N94SC	T-6G	49-3356	92	RENO 1995–96, 1998–99
N97AW	HRV II	2970	7, 37, 97	RENO 1987–90, 1994–2000, 2007–08
N97GM	HRV II	2970	7, 37, 97	RENO 1973, 1986; MOJAVE 1976, 1979; RICHLAND 1986
N101FT	T-6G	49-3380	98	RENO 2019
N101GB	T-6G	49-3137	56, 57	RENO 2008–10
N116SE	T-6G	49-3302	30, 302	RENO 2000–11; TUNICA 2005

Registration Number	Model	Mil S/N.	Race Number(s)	Races
N125JD	SNJ-5	90946*	21	RENO 1990–97; REDMOND 1992; PHOENIX 1994
N127VF	SNJ-4	27491	27	RENO 1984–94, 2016–18, 2022; WENDOVER 1988; CASPER 1990; REDMOND 1992; PHOENIX 1994; PASO ROBLES 1994
N144KM	T-6A	41-16066	4	RENO 1977
N158JZ	T-6G	49-3158	73	RENO 2017–19, 2021–23
N194A	HRV II	2914	44, 94	RENO 1969, 1971–73, 1975–78, 1981–82, 1984–86; ST. LOUIS 1969–70; CLEVELAND 1969; CAPE MAY 1971; WILSON 1971; MOJAVE 1975–78; RICHLAND 1986
N203V	HRV II	2784	7	RENO 1968–69, 1971–72; FT. LAUDERDALE 1970; MIAMI 1973; GRAHAM 1973
N302V	T-6G	49-3221	4, 47	RENO 1971
N212TC	SNJ-5	90946*	21	RENO 1998, 2003, 2005–06, 2008; TUNICA 2005
N260CF	T-6G	49-3536	19	RENO 2023
N447CL	SNJ-5	85056	2	RENO 1969
N502	SNJ-5	43689	50	RENO 1968
N555Q	T-6G	52-8238	22	FT. LAUDERDALE 1970
N604R	T-6H	MM54135	89	RENO 1989–90, 1992–95, 2001–05, 2007–08, 2011–19; CASPER 1990; REDMOND 1992
N611F	SNJ-6	112323	7, 47, 86	MOJAVE 1974–76, 1978–79; RENO 1974–77, 1986, 1991–99; PHOENIX 1994; SHAFTER 1996
N612MD	SNJ-5	43771	12	MOJAVE 1974–75; RENO 1974–75
N620AJ	HRV III	EX811, SAAF7463	54, 21	RENO 2018, 2022–23
N651SH	T-6G	49-3305	59	RENO 2012
N666SS	T-6G	49-3302	30, 302, 030	RENO 1994–99; PHOENIX 1994; SHAFTER 1995
N694US	SNJ-4	51360	94, 19	RENO 2008–11, 2014–16
N706F	T-6F	44-81893	70	FT. LAUDERDALE 1970; RENO 1971–74
N711AP	T-6G	52-8211	2, 2A, 17	MOJAVE 1973; MIAMI 1973; RENO 1973
N717UP	T-6G	49-3529	PP	RENO 2016, 2018–19, 2022
N726KM	T-6G	SAAF 7726	26	RENO 2009
N733L	SNJ-4	26954	33	FT. LAUDERDALE 1969–70; ST. LOUIS 1969; RENO 1969
N777AP	SNJ-5	43924	2, 2A	MOJAVE 1973
N817NP	SNJ-5	43928	(89)	CASPER 1990
N832N	HRV II	AJ832	75	RENO 1973–75
N991GM	T-6D	42-85794	90	RENO 1990–95, 1998–2004; CASPER 1990; REDMOND 1992; PHOENIX 1994
N997RD	HRV IV	20373	57	RENO 1997–98
N999JP	T-6F	44-81889	99	MOJAVE 1975–79; RENO 1975–78
N1038A	SNJ-5	90917	PP	RENO 1991–23
N1040C	SNJ-5	84969	40	RENO 1969, 1971–73, 1977
N1046C	SNJ-5	85080	10	CLEVELAND 1969; ST. LOUIS 1969–70; RENO 1969, 1971–74; FT. LAUDERDALE 1970; CAPE MAY 1971; GRAHAM 1973
N1363R	T-6G	MM53833	6	RENO 1985
N1364J	T-6G	MM53655	54	RENO 2011–17
N1395N	SNJ-4	51584	44	RENO 1969, 1971; ST. LOUIS 1969; CLEVELAND 1969; FT. LAUDERDALE 1969–70; CAPE MAY 1971; WILSON 1971

Registration Number	Model	Mil S/N.	Race Number(s)	Races
N1465	HRV IV	20248	2, 12	RENO 2013–23
N1466	HRV IV	20333	66	RENO 1986; RICHLAND 1986
N1666T	SNJ-5	43725	66	RENO 1984
N1974M	T-6D	44-81252	33, 96	RENO 1969; CLEVELAND 1969; WILSON 1970–71; FT. LAUDERDALE 1970; ST. LOUIS 1970; CAPE MAY 1971
N2269T	SNJ-4	27505	70	RENO 2001–08
N2269U	SNJ-4	27514	19	RENO 2014
N2676P	SNJ-5	85066	51	RENO 1992
N2757	HRV IIa	2757	33	RENO 2007, 2010–12
N2821G	T-6G	52-8211	2, 2A	RENO 1972
N2831D	T-6G	53-4577	57, 577	RENO 1981
N2860G	SNJ-6	112130	3, 46	RENO 1967, 1973–76; MOJAVE 1973–76
N2861G	SNJ-6	112157	2, 5	RENO 1967–68
N2863G	SNJ-6	112168	2, 7	RENO 1967, 1994
N2864D	T-6D	42-85696	64, 49	MOJAVE 1976; RENO 1977, 1994
N2864G	SNJ-6	112169	55	CLEVELAND 1969; ST. LOUIS 1969–70; WILSON 1970
N2885G	T-6G	49-2965	6	RENO 1972–73; WILSON 1972; MIAMI 1973; GRAHAM 1973
N2886G	T-6G	49-2928	14	RENO 1969
N2897G	T-6G	49-3492	6	RENO 1986–94, 1997–2019, 2022–23; WENDOVER 1988; PHOENIX 1994
N2983	T-6D	42-86272*	49, 48	RENO 2013, 2018
N2996Q	T-6G	49-3071	7	RENO 2017
N3169G	SNJ-6	111974	1, 11, 88	RENO 1992, 1999–2000, 2007–08, 2010
N3171P	T-6	SAAF 7320	4, 43	RENO 1996–97, 2000–02, 2005–23
N3173L	T-6D	42-85344	69	RENO 2005–19, 2021–23
N3188G	SNJ-5	84839	96	MOJAVE 1975–76, 1978; RENO 1976–78; LINCOLN 1976
N3194G	SNJ-5	91089	48	RENO 1971; GRAHAM 1972
N3203G	SNJ-5	90691	55	RENO 1976
N3254G	SNJ-5	112034	0	RENO 1968–69, 1971; FT. LAUDERDALE 1970
N3257G	SNJ-5	85087	57	RENO 1969, 1971, 1973
N3258G	SNJ-5	43839	39	RENO 1993; PHOENIX 1994
N3261G	SNJ-5	90612	21, PP	RENO 1969, 1999–04; FT. LAUDERDALE 1969–70; ST. LOUIS 1969–70; CAPE MAY 1971; JACKSONVILLE 1971; GRAHAM 1973
N3272G	SNJ-5	84826	20, 26, 28, 88	RENO 1987–92, 2007–19, 2021–23
N3274G	SNJ-5B	43647	42	RENO 1971–78, 1981, 1983–88; GRAHAM 1972–73; MOJAVE 1973–76, 1978; LINCOLN 1976
N3518G	T-6G	50-1291	22	FT. LAUDERDALE 1969; ST. LOUIS 1969; CLEVELAND 1969; RENO 1969
N3579	SNJ-5	51678	78	RENO 2013
N3626F	SNJ-5	51904	99	RENO 1969; ST. LOUIS 1969–70; CLEVELAND 1969; FT. LAUDERDALE 1969–70; WILSON 1970–71; JACKSONVILLE 1971; CAPE MAY 1971
N3646G	HRV II	AJ688	69	RENO 1969, 1971–74; MOJAVE 1973–75
N3653G	SNJ-4	27280	5, 14	MOJAVE 1973, 1978–79; RENO 1973, 1978
N3653G *	HRV IIb	3324	35	MOJAVE 1974

Registration Number	Model	Mil S/N.	Race Number(s)	Races
N3666F	SNJ-5	52031	37, 72	FT. LAUDERDALE 1970; RENO 1971–75, 2006–13, 2015; GRAHAM 1973; MOJAVE 1974
N3680F	SNJ-5	84843	25	RENO 2021–23
N3682F	SNJ-5	90664	24	RENO 1972–74; GRAHAM 1973
N3931R	SNJ-5	84923	999	RENO 2023
N3931S	SNJ-5	51811	17, 55	RENO 1986–88, 1993–94; PHOENIX 1994
N4269E	T-6G	53-4601	4, 13, 44	RENO 1994–97, 2000–07, 2021–22; PHOENIX 1994
N4269Q	T-6G	53-4558	90	RENO 2003–23; TUNICA 2005
N4434N	HRV IIa	EX600	33	RENO 2019
N4485	T-6	44-81646 (2)*	2, 7	RENO 2003–04, 2007
N4763	HRV II	2832* (AJ731)	2, 43, 50	RENO 2007–13, 2015–23
N4802E	HRV II	AJ968	66	RENO 2008–13, 2015, 2017–19, 2021–23
N4983N	T-6D	44-81453	8, 68, 69, 74	CLEVELAND 1969; FT. LAUDERDALE 1970; RENO 2000–02, 2004, 2006; TUNICA 2005
N5198V	SNJ-5	51952	17	FT. LAUDERDALE 1969
N5199V	SNJ-5	43875	9	RENO 1968–69, 1971–77, 1983–92, 1996–2000, 2002–06, 2016–18; MOJAVE 1973–76, 1979; LINCOLN 1976; RICHLAND 1985–86; REDMOND 1992
N5208V	SNJ-4	27768	5	RENO 1968–69
N5489V	SNJ-5	90646	6	RENO 1967–69; ST. LOUIS 1969–70; FT. LAUDERDALE 1970; CAPE MAY 1971
N5500V	SNJ-6	112023	98	RENO 1983
N5632V	T-6G	52-8218	7	RENO 1982
N6414D	SNJ-4	27060	71	CLEVELAND 1969
N6424D	SNJ-4	51360	19, 41, 69	RENO 1986, 1988–90; RICHLAND 1986
N6427D	SNJ-4	51629	8, 62	TUNICA 2005; SEE NOTE FOR #62
N6601C	T-6F	44-81757	8, 33	MOJAVE 1974–76; RENO 1974–76; LINCOLN 1976
N6625C	T-6G	49-3100	48	RENO 2023
N6900G	T-6G	49-3384	74	RENO 1968
N6972C	SNJ-5	90680	71, 72, 77	RENO 1968, 1978, 1981–87
N6975C	SNJ-5	51677	4, 37	RENO 1967–69, 1972–73; ST. LOUIS 1969
N6979C	T-6D	42-85408	4	RENO 1976
N7011C	SNJ-4	51423	71	RENO 1983
N7038C	SNJ-4	27536	8, 38, 43	RENO 1968–69, 1972–75, 1978; MOJAVE 1973–76
N7055H	T-6D	42-4071	64	RENO 1993–94
N7058C	SNJ-4	27352	58	RENO 2016–17
N7061C	SNJ-4	27386	1	MOJAVE 1978–79
N7065C	SNJ-4	27616	22	RENO 1990; CASPER 1990
N7078C	SNJ-4	26755	66	RENO 1969
N7090C	SNJ-4	27754	38	RENO 1971–72
N7295C	SNJ-5	90735	1	RENO 1968
N7296C	SNJ-5	84979	49	RENO 2017–19, 2021–23
N7404C	SNJ-4	51542	5, 25, 51	WILSON 1970–72; ST. LOUIS 1970; FT. LAUDERDALE 1970; MOJAVE 1972–76, 1978–79; RENO 1972–75, 1981–2016, 2018–23; JACKSONVILLE 1971; GRAHAM 1972–73; MIAMI 1973; REDMOND 1992; TUNICA 2005

Registration Number	Model	Mil S/N.	Race Number(s)	Races
N7412C	SNJ-4	27404	8, 13	RENO 1968–69, 1977
N7437C	SNJ-4	27611	030	RENO 1993
N7446C	T-6D	44-81819	6, 43	MOJAVE 1976; RENO 1978
N7448C	T-6D	44-81494	35	RENO 1969
N7463C	T-6F	44-81893	70	RENO 1969
N7471C	T-6D	42-85550	16	SEE NOTE FOR #16
N7471S	T-6C	41-33790	20	RENO 2004, 2006
N7520U	HRV IV	20385	66, PP	RENO 1993–95
N7522U	HRV IV	20423	44, 444, PP	RENO 1998–2000, 2002–07, 2010, 2013
N7613E	T-6G	49-3243	24	RENO 1994; SHAFTER 1995
N7648E	SNJ-3	01882	55	RENO 2005–06
N7657C	T-6G	49-2988	65	RENO 1972
N7679C	T-6G	49-3310	45	RENO 1994
N7765C	T-6G	50-1288	73, 74	RENO 1972–74, 1991; MOJAVE 1973–74; MIAMI 1973
N7804B	SNJ-5	51819	7, 81	FT. LAUDERDALE 1969; SEE NOTE FOR #81
N7839B	SNJ-4	27687	15	SEE NOTE FOR #15
N7976C	SNJ-5	90649	24	ST. LOUIS 1969; RENO 1969; FT. LAUDERDALE 1970
N7979C	SNJ-5	84827	7	RICHLAND 1986
N7985C	SNJ-6	112237	75	RENO 1981–91; RICHLAND 1985
N8044H	T-6G	51-14791	2, 42	RENO 1999, 2001
N8048E	T-6G	51-14343	25	RENO 1994, 2014–15
N8048J	T-6G	51-15063	68, 99	RENO 1981–86, 1988–95; PHOENIX 1994
N8158H	SNJ-5	90918	4, 43	RENO 1968–69, 1971–72, 1976; ST. LOUIS 1969–70
N8204H	T-6G	49-3284	7	CASPER 1990; RENO 1991–97; REDMOND 1992; PHOENIX 1994; BILLINGS 1994
N8206E	SNJ-5	90789	41	CLEVELAND 1969; FT. LAUDERDALE 1970; ST. LOUIS 1970; WILSON 1970
N8212E	SNJ-5	43968	17	WILSON 1971–72
N8539L	HRV III	EZ200	50	RENO 1996–2001
N8540P	T-6D	44-81646 (1)*	1, 51	RENO 1983, 1990, 1993, 1995, 2005–06
N8540Z	SNJ-4	27849	4, 41, 55	RENO 1986–89, 1992–94, 1997; RICHLAND 1986; REDMOND 1992; PHOENIX 1994
N8993	HRV IIb	2976	66, 89	WILSON 1971; RENO 1996–2004
N9035Z	T-6G	49-2990	512	RENO 1997
N9060Z	SNJ-5	43835	11	RENO 1968; FT. LAUDERDALE 1970
N9525C	SNJ-4	27307	1, 3	RENO 1967–69, 1971 73, 1975–78, 1981–83; MOJAVE 1973–76, 1978–79
N9649C	T-6D	42-85456	69, 96	ST. LOUIS 1969; FT. LAUDERDALE 1969
N9735Z	SNJ-4	51506	35	CAPE MAY 1971
N9785Z	HRV II	2780	11, PP	WILSON 1971; CAPE MAY 1971
N9789Z	HRV II	AJ731	2, 43	GRAHAM 1972; MOJAVE 1975
N9799Z	HRV II	2970	97	RENO 1969, 1973–75; MOJAVE 1973–75
N9800C	SNJ-6	112227	33	RENO 1996
N9801C	SNJ-6	90669	15	MOJAVE 1975–76; RENO 1975
N9831C	SNJ-6	112180	41, 98	RENO 1975–78; MOJAVE 1978–79

Registration Number	Model	Mil S/N.	Race Number(s)	Races
N10597	SNJ-4	27748	70	RENO 1986
N13631	HRV IV	20286	88	RENO 1968–74; MOJAVE 1973; GRAHAM 1973
N16730	HRV II	3198	11, 71	CLEVELAND 1969; ST. LOUIS 1969; RENO 1969, 1971–78, 1982–89, 1991–93; FT. LAUDERDALE 1970; MIAMI 1973; MOJAVE 1973–76, 1978–79; PHOENIX 1994
N17400	HRV IV	20461	50	RENO 1969
N17498 (1)	T-6G	49-3221*	4	RENO 1981
N29931	T-6G	49-3449	49, 51	RENO 1991, 2000
N29939	T-6G	49-3034	7	RENO 1986
N39403	SNJ-4	43794	10, PP	RENO 1990, 1997–98
N49388	T-6G	49-3066	388	RENO 2023
NC51497	T-6A	41-16280	81	CLEVELAND 1946
NX51499	T-6	40-2113	65	CLEVELAND 1947–48
N51979	SNJ-5	51979	79	RENO 1984–87
NX55941	SNJ-4	9985	91	CLEVELAND 1948–49
N57318	T-6A	41-16302	18, 39, 45	CAPE MAY 1971; RENO 1978, 1982–94; MOJAVE 1979; CASPER 1990; REDMOND 1992; PHOENIX 1994; BILLINGS 1994
N57418	T-6B	41-17370	14	RENO 1983, 1986, 1997, 2012–16, 2018–19, 2021–23
N57493	T-6A	41-242	4	RENO 2022
N57584	SNJ-3	5575	35	CLEVELAND 1946–47
NX57799	T-6A	41-15915	83	CLEVELAND 1947–48
NX57805	T-6A	41-15872	23, 72	CLEVELAND 1946–48
N60380	SNJ-4	27119	80	RENO 1971
NX61269	T-6A	41-234	49	CLEVELAND 1947–48
NX62382	SNJ-2	2039	42	CLEVELAND 1947
N62510	T-6B	41-17034	30	RENO 1969; FT. LAUDERDALE 1970; ST. LOUIS 1970
NX63760	SNJ-2	2019	36	CLEVELAND 1947
NX63770	T-6A	41-16743	75, 41*	CLEVELAND 1946–49
NX63829	T-6A	41-784	96	CLEVELAND 1947
NX64448	T-6A	41-277	54	CLEVELAND 1946–47
NX65560	SNJ-3	5519	45	CLEVELAND 1949
NX65619	SNJ-3	6827	79	CLEVELAND 1947
NX66134	SNJ-3	6927	31	CLEVELAND 1948–49
NX72375	HRV IV	20280	PP	RENO 1983–88
NX74108	XAT-6E	42-84241	61	CLEVELAND 1947
N75964	SNJ-4	10116	44	SHAFTER 1996
N86116	SNJ-5	90599	16	RENO 2004
N89013	SNJ-5	90623	23	MOJAVE 1979; RENO 1983; SEE NOTE FOR #23
N90629	T-6A	41-16997	31, 50	MOJAVE 1978; RENO 1978; SEE NOTE ON #31
NX90641	T-6A	41-461	44	CLEVELAND 1947–49
N90650	SNJ-4	10206	94	RENO 1983–84
N98474	HRV IV	20257*	6	RENO 1982, 1984
CF-RZO	HRV IV	20410	12	FT. LAUDERDALE 1970; ST. LOUIS 1970; WILSON 1970–71; CAPE MAY 1971; JACKSONVILLE 1971
CF-WLO	HRV IV	20264	64	RENO 1993–94, 2000–10, 2012–13

Table 4: Military Serial Numbers to Civil Registration Numbers 1946–2019

This list comprises information compiled by Malcolm Gougon and William T. Larkins (unpublished manuscript), from FAA record cards and AOPA records documenting those Texans that have been civil-registered. Serial numbers that are followed by an (*) have queries regarding the authenticity of that particular airframe. Registration numbers or military numbers that are followed by a number represent the number of times that the civil or military number has been used on a Texan as in N88RT (2), which would be the second time it was assigned to a different Texan. Texans with multiple registration numbers are shown with the first assigned registration number followed by the next assigned, as in N42DQ to N77TX. This list only applies to each Texan's racing career as some Texans have had as many as four or five registrations applied before and after racing. Assigned race number are shown in numerical order.

Military Serial Number	Registration Number(s)	Race Number(s)
United States Army Air Corps and United States Air Force		
40-2113	NX51499	65
41-234	NX61269	49
41-242	N57493	4
41-277	NX64448	54
41-461	NX90641	44
41-558	N48BC	48
41-784	NX63829	96
41-15872	NX57805	23, 72
41-15915	NX57799	83
41-16066	N144KM	4
41-16280	NC51497	81
41-16302	N57318	18, 39, 45
41-16320	N42DQ, N77TX	42
41-16743	NX63770	75
41-16997	N90629	31, 90
41-17034	N62510, N30HA	30
41-17370	N57418	14
41-33790	N7471S	20
41-34571	N87H	87, 736, PP
42-4071	N7055H	46
42-44675	N83H	99
42-84241	NX74108	61
42-85344	N3173L	69
42-85408	N6979C	4
42-85456	N9649C	69, 96
42-85550	N7471C	16
42-85696	N2864D	64, 49
42-85794	N991GM	90
42-86272*	N2983	49, 48
44-81252	N1974M	33, 96
44-81453	N4983N	8, 68, 69, 74
44-81494	N7448C	35
44-81646 (1)	N8540P	1, 51
44-81646 (2)	N4485	2, 7
44-81757	N6601C	8, 33
44-81819	N7446C	6, 43

Military Serial Number	Registration Number(s)	Race Number(s)
44-81889	N999JP	99
44-81893	N7463C, N706F	70
49-2928	N2886G	14
49-2965	N2885G	6
49-2988	N7657C	65
49-2990	N9035Z	512
49-3034	N29939	7
49-3066	N49388	388
49-3071	N2996Q	7
49-3100	N6625C	48
49-3137	N101GB	56, 57
49-3158	N158JZ	73
49-3221	N302V	47
49-3221*	N17498 (1)	4, 47
49-3243	N7613C	24
49-3266	N51KT	73
49-3284	N8204H	7, 512
49-3302	N666SS, N116SE	30, 302
49-3305	N651SH	59
49-3310	N7679C	45
49-3356	N94SC	92
49-3380	N101FT	98
49-3384	N6900G	74
49-3386	N74DW	74
49-3402	N85JR	85
49-3449	N29931	49, 51
49-3492	N2897G	6
49-3529	N717UP	PP
49-3536	N260CF	19
50-1288	N7765C	73, 74
50-1291	N3518G	22
51-14791	N8044H	2, 42
51-14842	N8FU	92
51-15048	N42JM	3, 48, 048
51-15063	N8048J	68, 99
51-14343	N8048E	25
52-8211	N2821G, N711AP	2, 2A, 17
52-8218	N5632V	7
52-8238	N555Q	22
53-4558	N4269Q	90
53-4577	N2831D	57, 577
53-4601	N4269E	4, 13, 44
US NAVY BuNo.		
2019	NX63760	36
2039	NX62382	42
01882	N7648E	55

Military Serial Number	Registration Number(s)	Race Number(s)
5519	NX65560	45
5575	NC57584	35
6827	NX65619	79
6927	NX66134	31
9985	NX55941	91
10116	N75964	44
10206	N90650	94
26755	N7078C	66
26954	N733L	33
27060	N6414D	71
27119	N60380	80
27255	N86WW	2, 42, 88
27280	N3653G	5, 14
27307	N9525C	1, 3
27352	N7058C	58
27386	N7061C	1
27404	N7412C	8, 13
27491	N127VF	27
27505	N2269T	70
27514	N2269U	19
27536	N7038C	8, 38, 43
27611	N7437C	030
27616	N7065C, N22KD	22
27687	N7839B	15
27748	N10597	70
27754	N7090C	38
27768	N5208V	5
27849	N8540Z	4, 41, 55
43647	N3274G	12
42689	N502	50
43725	N1666T	66
43771	N612MD	12
43794	N39403	10
43835	N9060Z	11
43839	N3258G	39
43875	N5199V	9
43924	N777AP	2A
43928	N817NP	(89)
43968	N8212E	17
44009	N30JF	18, 76
51360	N6424D, N694US	19, 41, 69, 94
51423	N7011C	71
51506	N9735Z	35
51542	N7404C, (N25RM)	5, 25, 51
51584	N1395N	44
51629	N6427D	8, 62

Military Serial Number	Registration Number(s)	Race Number(s)
51677	N6975C	4, 7
51678	N3579	78
51811	N3931S, N5JF	17, 55
51819	N7804B	8, 81
51904	N3626F	99
51952	N5198V	17
51979	N51979	79
52031	N3666F	37, 72
84826	N3272G	20, 26, 28, 88
84827	N7979C	7
84839	N3188G	96
84843	N3680F	25
84923	N3931R	999
84969	N1040C	40
84979	N7296C	49
85056	N447CL	2
85066	N2676P	51
85080	N1046C	10
85087	N3257G	57
90599	N86116	16
90612	N3261G	21, PP
90623	N89013	23
90646	N5489V	6
90649	N7976C	24
90664	N3682F	24
90669	N9801C	15
90680	N6972C	71, 72, 77
90691	N3203G	55
90735	N7295C	1
90789	N8206E, N41BT	41, 77
90800	N66JL	66
90917	N1038A	PP
90918	N8158H	4, 43
90946*	N125JD, N212TC	21
90995	N12KY	12
90996	N21JD	49
91089	N3194G	48
111957	N4RC	8, 80
111974	N3169G	1, 11, 88
112023	N5500V	98
112034	N3254G	0
112130	N2860G	3, 46
112131	N73RR	22, 56, 59, 73
112157	N2861G	2, 5
112168	N2863G	2, 7
112169	N2864G	55

Military Serial Number	Registration Number(s)	Race Number(s)
112180	N9831C	41, 98
112227	N9800C	33
112237	N7985C, N75AG	75
112323	N611F	7, 47, 86
Royal Air Force and Royal Canadian Air Force		
AJ688	N3646G	69
AJ731 (2832*)	N9789Z, N4763	43, 2, 50
AJ832	N832N	75
AJ968	N4802E	66
EX287	N42BA	1
EX600	N4434N	33
EX811 (SAAF7463)	N620AJ	21, 54
EZ200	N8539L	50
2757	N2757	33
2780	N9785Z, N88RT (2)	11, 88, PP
2784	N203V	7
2914	N194A, N44ZZ	44, 94
2970	N9799Z, N97AW, N97GM	7, 37, 97
2976	N8993	66, 89
3198	N16730	11, 71
3324	N3653G	35
20218	N91AM	12
20248	N1465	2, 12
20257*	N98474	6
20264	CF-WLO	64
20280	NX72375	66, PP
20286	N13631	88
20333	N1466	66
20373	N997RD	57
20385	N7520U	66, PP
20410	CF-RZO	12
20423	N7522U	44, 444, PP
20461	N17400	50
Italian Air Force		
MM53655	N1364J	54
MM53833	N1363R	6
MM54135	N604R	89
South African Air Force		
SAAF7320 (17320*) (133660*)	N3171P	4, 43
SAAF7463	N620AJ	54
SAAF7726	N726KM	26

Table 5: Race Pilots

Pilots are listed in alphabetical order by last name, along with the race number of the aircraft they flew and the locations and years they raced. Included are all pilots that have Entered, Qualified and Raced. It should be noted that some pilots raced multiple aircraft over the years, including aircraft that carried the same race number(s) but had/have different civil registration numbers assigned and military serial numbers. Also, they may have raced the same aircraft with a different assigned race number. As an example: Al Goss used #75 on N7985C when he first started racing, and later used #75 on N75AG, which was the same aircraft with a new civil registration number. Ralph Twombly used #41 on three different aircraft – one of which, BuNo. 90789, used two different civil registrations. Date order is chronological.

Name	Aircraft Race Number(s)	Location and Year(s) Raced
ADAMS, TERRY	12, 25, 33	RENO 2012–14
ALEXANDER, HUGH	30, 30	RENO 1969, 1971; FT. LAUDERDALE 1970; ST. LOUIS 1970; CAPE MAY 1971; WILSON 1970–72
ALLCORN, JOHN	49	RENO 1977–78; MOJAVE 1979
ANDRADE, JOSEPH	13	RENO 1968–69
BAKER, VICTOR	6	RENO 1967–69; FT. LAUDERDALE 1970; ST. LOUIS 1969–70; CAPE MAY 1971
BABER, THOMAS	2, 19, 78	RENO 2013–14
BARRETT, DON	10	CLEVELAND 1969; FT. LAUDERDALE 1970; ST. LOUIS 1969–70; CAPE MAY 1971; RENO 1969, 1971–72
BEAL, HAROLD	15	SEE NOTE ON RACE #15
BECK, CHARLES	2, 2, 46	MOJAVE 1973–74, 1978–79; RENO 1973–74, 1977–78, 1981–94
BENNETT, JAMES	37	RENO 1994–2000
BLOOM, CHERYL	57	RENO 1997
BOOTH, JIM	44, 444, PP	RENO 1998–2000, 2002–07, 2010, 2013
BORCHIN, JERRY	33, 89	RENO 1996, 2007
BOWLES, ART	6	RENO 1972–73; WILSON 1972; MIAMI 1973; GRAHAM 1973
BRANCH, CLIFF	5,	MOJAVE 1978–79; RENO 1978, 1984
BRENNAN, JAMES	6	RENO 1982
BRIGGS, JACK	97	RENO 1969
BRUCE, DAVID	4, 55	RENO 1986–89, 1991–92; RICHLAND 1986; REDMOND 1992
BUEHN, DENNIS	2, 3, 4, 6, 7, 18, 19, 23, 33, 33, 39, 43, 43, 43, 96, 97	RENO 1973–77, 1982–86, 2005–19; MOJAVE 1973–76, 1979; GRAHAM 1972
BURDICK, GEORGE	48	RENO 1971
CAMPAU, TOM	21	TUNICA 2005; RENO 1999, 2000–03, 2005
CARD, JOHN	99	MIAMI 1973
CARLSON, ART	44, 55	CLEVELAND 1969; CAPE MAY 1971; ST. LOUIS 1970
CARTWRIGHT, WAYNE	44, 69	RENO 2000–07, 2010
CATAALANO, GEORGE	94	RENO 1983–84
CHIODO, JOE	70	RENO 1986; SEE NOTE #70
CLARK, BETTY	49, 54	CLEVELAND 1947–48
CLARK, CARTER	1, 11, 33, 88	RENO 1992, 1999–2000, 2007–08, 2010
CLEGG, STEVE	92	RENO 1996, 1999
CLERMONT, OTT	94, 69	RENO 2008, 2011
COLBERT, ED	39, 57, 577	RENO 1981, 1983
COLLINS, ROMAINE (BUD)	80, 80	RENO 1971–74
CONROY, CALVIN	2A, 11	MOJAVE 1973, 1975; RENO 1972, 1974, 1976, 1978

Name	Aircraft Race Number(s)	Location and Year(s) Raced
CORRIGAN, NANCY	83	CLEVELAND 1948
CRANDALL, ROBIN	8	TUNICA 2005
CROSS, ELLOT	92	RENO 1994
CUSEO, JAMES	98	RENO 1983
DAVIS, ARLENE	35	CLEVELAND 1946–47
DAY, KENNY	21, 22, 22	RENO 1990–92; CASPER 1990; REDMOND 1992
DEWALT, DON	74,	MOJAVE 1973–74, 1976; MIAMI 1973; RENO 1972–74, 1976–78
DIECKMAN, RAY	39	RENO 1993; PHOENIX 1994
DIFANI, RANDY	18	RENO 1985–94; CASPER 1990; REDMOND 1992; PHOENIX 1994
DILDA, MARY	21, 22,	RENO 1996–2000, 2002–05, 2007; TUNICA 2005
DILDA, STEVE	22, PP	RENO 1997, 1999–2004
DILL, DENNIS	66	RENO 1995
DOCKTER, SCOTT	56, 56, 57	RENO 2008–10
DOCTOR, LAIRD	PP	RENO 1991, 1993–95, 1997–98
DODSON, BOB	55	RENO 1976
DONHAM, LEE	66	RENO 1986
DOTTER, DOUG	88	RENO 2007
DRAKE, RICK	57	RENO 1998
DOUGHERTY, DORA	96	CLEVELAND 1947
DREWS, ROBERT	66	RENO 1968–69
DWELLE, KEN	2, 7, 7, 512	RENO 1994, 1997, 2003, 2007–08
DWELLE, TOM, Sr.	7, 7, 30, 97	RENO 1987–92, 1995, 2007; CASPER 1990; REDMOND 1992; PHOENIX 1994
DWELLE, TOM, Jr.	7, 7, 7, 512	RENO 1993–97, 2004; BILLINGS 1994; SHAFTER 1994–96
EARLY, CALVIN	70, 72	RENO 1972–73; MOJAVE 1974
EBERHARDT, BILL	30, 302	RENO 1994, 1996–97, 1999; PHOENIX 1994
EBERHARDT, JIM	30, 30	RENO 1998, 2000–11; TUNICA 2005
EBERHARDT, STU	12	RENO 1992
EDISON, FRED	8, 74	CLEVELAND 1969; FT. LAUDERDALE 1970
ELLER, GARY	45	RENO 1994
ELLIOTT, FRANK	73	RENO 1991
ELLIS, BILL	7	RENO 1986
FIELDS, RICHARD	46	RENO 1993–94
FINCH, LINDA	20, 26	RENO 1987, 1988, 1990–92
FLANAGAN, JIM	18	CAPE MAY 1971; RENO 1971–72; GRAHAM 1972–73; MIAMI 1973
FOLEY, GILFORD	44	RENO 1989
FOOTE, DICK	71	CLEVELAND 1969
FOX, JIM	71, 72	RENO 1978, 1981–87; MOJAVE 1979
FRANCIS, JACK	77	MOJAVE 1978–79; RENO 1978
FROST, JACK	47	RENO 1997–99
FURLONG, JIM	1	MOJAVE 1978–79
GAYLAN, DON	38	RENO 1972
GERBER, JOHN	76	RENO 1975; MOJAVE 1976; LINCOLN 1976
GIGLIO, COLENE	7	MOJAVE 1974–76, 1978–79; RENO 1974–77

Name	Aircraft Race Number(s)	Location and Year(s) Raced
GILBERT, CHARLES	6	RENO 1978
GILLIAN, MICHAEL	68, 69, 94	RENO 2000–02, 2004, 2006, 2011; TUNICA 2005
GIST, JIMMY	5, 25, 59, 68	MOJAVE 1979; RENO 1981–86, 1990–92, 1994
GIST, PHIL	11, 49	RENO 1982, 1987
GLASSBURN, HUGH	0	RENO 1968–69, 1971; FT. LAUDERDALE 1970
GNESA, STAN	10	RENO 1969, 1971–73, 1977
GOOD, JIM	77	RENO 1987–2009; CASPER 1990; REDMOND 1992; PHOENIX 1994; TUNICA 2005
GOSS, AL	75, 75	RENO 1981–2009; RICHLAND 1985; WENDOVER 1988; REDMOND 1992; PHOENIX 1994
GOTTSCHALL, KEN	8	RENO 2006–11
GRANLEY, BUD	4, 9, 66	RENO 1988– 2006, 2009; PHOENIX 1994
GRAVES, DOREL	3, 48, 048	RENO 1987, 1990–97, 1999–2000
GREENAMYER, DARRYL	7	RENO 1967
GREGORY, DICK	4, 37	RENO 1967–69; ST. LOUIS 1969
GRIGGS, DAVID	17	RENO 1988
GULOTTA, DON	5	RENO 1967
HACKETT, DON	38	RENO 1971
HALFHILL, W. S.	2	RENO 1968
HALL, BEN	7, 98	RENO 1968–69, 1971–72, 1975; FT. LAUDERDALE 1970
HARNAGEL. NATHAN	59	RENO 2012
HARRIS, GRACE	44	CLEVELAND 1947–49
HARRISON, BEN	64	MOJAVE 1976, RENO 1977
HARTUNG, JOE	89	RENO 1989–95; CASPER 1990; REDMOND 1992
HAVENS, LARRY	90	MOJAVE 1978; RENO 1978
HEALE, ROBERT	7, 9, 19	RENO 1983–87, 1989–90; RICHLAND 1985–86; REDMOND 1992
HEINEMAN, BELLA	36	CLEVELAND 1947
HELVE, RON	8	RENO 1977
HENLEY, MARK	2	RENO 1999
HUBLER, GARY	57	RENO 1998
HUNT, JOHN	49	RENO 1981
HURLBURT, MARGE	81	CLEVELAND 1946
HUTCHINS, CHARLES	1, 21	RENO 1985–95, 1997; PHOENIX 1994
HUYSMAN, JOZEF	17	WILSON 1971–72
JOHNSON, FRED	17, 55, 55	RENO 1987, 1993–96; PHOENIX 1994
JOHNSON, JOHN	49, 49, 48	RENO 2000, 2013, 2018
JOHNSON, RUTH	75 (41)*	CLEVELAND 1946–49
JOLLIFF, DAROLD	77	RENO 1968
JONES, ROBERT	8	RENO 1981–2000; RICHLAND 1985–86; WENDOVER 1988; REDMOND 1992; PHOENIX 1994
KARLIN, JASON	25	RENO 2021–23
KEEFE, HOWIE	11, 11, 44	RENO 1968–69; FT. LAUDERDALE 1969, 1970; CLEVELAND 1969; ST. LOUIS 1969
KIRKLAND, JOHN	49	MOJAVE 1979
KLASSEN, LARRY	PP	RENO 1993–95

Name	Aircraft Race Number(s)	Location and Year(s) Raced
KOHLER, FRED	87	MOJAVE 1974; RENO 1971
KOSTELNIK, ROD	47	RENO 1971
KRAWCZYK, JOHN	1, 14, 21, 50, 71	RENO 1993, 1996–97, 2007–13, 2016; PHOENIX 1994
LAFAVE, CHRIS	2, 2, 4, 43, 94	RENO 2014–19, 2021–23
LANDRY, JAMES	98	RENO 1976
LANDRY, KATHERINE (KADDY)	31	CLEVELAND 1948–49
LEMON, DOROTHY (DOT)	23, 72	CLEVELAND 1946–47
LIVINGSTON, PHILLIP	9	RENO 1968–69
LOCKWOOD, BRUCE	66	RICHLAND 1986
LOGAN, ANNA	65	CLEVELAND 1947–48
LOHMAR, JOHN	28, 88	RENO 2007–19, 2021–23
LOWERS, JACK	7, 44, 55, 66	WILSON 1970–72; CAPE MAY 1971; MIAMI 1973; GRAHAM 1973; RENO 1973
LUMLEY, WILLIAM	8, 81	FT. LAUDERDALE 1969; SEE NOTE #81
LUTHER, JOHN	20, 99	RENO 1988–95; PHOENIX 1994
MacKAY, JAMIE	7	RENO 1986
MACY, NICK	6, 94	RENO 1986–94, 1997–2019, 2022–23; WENDOVER 1988; PHOENIX 1994
MALASPINA, RUDY	14	RENO 1969
MARBURG, LOREN	73	RENO 2021–23
MARLAND, DORI	49	CLEVELAND 1947
MARLIN, JOHN	51	RENO 1992
MARTIN, JOHN	79	RENO 1984–86
MARTIN, TOM	12, 66	RENO 1996–2000, 2001–04, 2006; TUNICA 2005
MAYES, BRUCE	16	RENO 2004
MCBRIDE, HELEN	91	CLEVELAND 1948–49
MCCLAIN, ROY	5, 25	MOJAVE 1972–76; RENO 1972–75; WILSON 1972; MIAMI 1973; GRAHAM 1972–73
MCDONALD, JERRY	5, 51	RENO 1981–86, 1989–95, 1998–2000, 2002–03; MOJAVE 1978–79; REDMOND 1992; PHOENIX 1994
MCGRATH, MARGE	61	CLEVELAND 1947
MCKEE, KIRK	4, 4, 76	RENO 1976–77; SEE NOTE #76
MCKINNEY, B.F.	22, 22	RENO 1969; FT. LAUDERDALE 1969–70; ST. LOUIS 1969; CLEVELAND 1969
MCMANN, KEITH	64	RENO 1993–94, 2000–10, 2012–13
MXMANN, VIC	66	RENO 2008–2013, 2015, 2017–19, 2021–23
MCNEELY, GENE	4, 17, 89, 90, 90	RENO 1986, 1990–2009, 2011–19; CASPER 1990; REDMOND 1992; PHOENIX 1994; TUNICA 2005
MCNEELY, GREG	90, 98	RENO 2019, 2021–23
MEERMANS, GARY	97, 97	MOJAVE 1974, 1976, 1979; RENO 1974–75, 1977
MEIER, WILLIAM	7	RENO 1982
METCALFE, BOB	37, 88	RENO 1968–74; MOJAVE 1973; GRAHAM 1973
MEYER, GRAIG	4	RENO 2022
MEYER, JOHN	49	RENO 1994
MILLER, GARY	21, 55	RENO 2005–06, 2008

Name	Aircraft Race Number(s)	Location and Year(s) Raced
MINGES, RICHARD	33, 69, 96	ST. LOUIS 1969; FT. LAUDERDALE 1969; WILSON 1971; CAPE MAY 1971
MITCHEM, BOB	94	RENO 1969, 1971, CLEVELAND 1969, ST. LOUIS 1969–70, CAPE MAY 1971, WILSON 1972
MODES, JIM	11	RENO 1971, 1973, 1975, 1977; MOJAVE 1974
MOODIE, MARK	24	RENO 1994; SHAFTER 1995
MORGAN, CHAD	22	RENO 2015
MORIARTY, JOHN	17, 33, 96	FT. LAUDERDALE 1969–70; CLEVELAND 1969; RENO 1969; ST. LOUIS 1970; WILSON 1970
MORRISON, WALTER	1, 2	RENO 1967, 1969
MORSE, GREG	10	RENO 1990
MOSBY, JOHN	44, 44, 45, 94	ST. LOUIS 1969; RENO 1969, 1971–72, 1975; WILSON 1971; CAPE MAY 1971; MIAMI 1973; MOJAVE 1975, 1978–79
MOTT, JIM	42, 51	RENO 1971–78, 1983–88, 1991; GRAHAM 1972–73; MOJAVE 1973–76, 1978; LINCOLN 1976
MURGIA, TONY	25	FT. LAUDERDALE 1970; JACKSONVILLE 1971; WILSON 1970–71; MOJAVE 1972–73
MUSZALA, BILL	49	RENO 2017–19, 2021–23
NEELEY, CHARLES	4	RENO 1981
NIGHTINGALE, TOM	44	SHAFTER 1996
NITOWSKI, WALT	76	RENO 1976; SEE NOTE #76
NOTTKE, ROBERT	39	RENO 1978; MOJAVE 1979
OHLRICH, WALT	50, 57	RENO 1968–69
OMAN, LEE	4, 21, 44, 69, 69, 90	RENO 1988, 1996–98, 2000–02, 2005–19, 2021–23
OPP, ERNEST	11, PP	CAPE MAY 1971; WILSON 1971
OTZEN, HENDRIK	1, 3	RENO 1967–68
PAGE, JANE	54, 83, 28	CLEVELAND 1946–47, 1949
PALMER, PAT	9, 99	RENO 1971–78; MOJAVE 1973–76, 1978–79; LINCOLN 1976
PAYNE, BRUCE	2, 2A, 2A	RENO 1972–73; MOJAVE 1973; MIAMI 1973
PAYNE, ELMER	66	RENO 1973
PECHERSKYY, VITALY	50	RENO 2017–19, 2021–23
PEELER, DAVID	030	RENO 1993
PENHALL, LEROY	74	RENO 1968
PFLEGER, MICHAEL	2, 54, 54	RENO 2011–19
PHILLIPPI, DON	4	RENO 1968–69, 1971–72; WILSON 1972
PONKE, FRANK	38	RENO 1969
PRESTON, ALAN	44	RENO 1984–86; RICHLAND 1986
PRIAN, DIMITRY	8	RENO 1978
PUTMAN, CLIFF	48	GRAHAM 1972
QUAID, MARVIN	57	RENO 1971
QUINN, JOSEPH	35, 35	RENO 1969; CAPE MAY 1971
RAYMOND, JAMES	17	RENO
REBERRY, BRIAN	13, 48	RENO 2022–23
REDDING, BRUCE	48, 88, 97	RENO 1985–88; RICHLAND 1986
REDLICH, PAUL	20	RENO 2004, 2006
REYNOLDS, DON	4	ST. LOUIS 1970

Name	Aircraft Race Number(s)	Location and Year(s) Raced
RICHARDSON, GORDON	97	MOJAVE 1973; RENO 1973
RINA, RALPH	2, 51, 73, 73	RENO 1973–78, 1983–86, 1990, 1995, 2011–12, 2014, 2016–19; MOJAVE 1973–76, 1978–79; GRAHAM 1973
ROARK, JOHN	85	RENO 1985
RUSHING, CHRIS	14, 14, 42	RENO 2005–06, 2008–23
SANDBERG, ROB	42, 50, PP	RENO 2012–13, 2015–16, 2018–19, 2022–23
SANDERS, GEORGE	50	RENO 1969
SANDERS, JOEY	5	RENO 2004–16, 2021–22; TUNICA 2005
SAUNDERS, CHARLES	70	FT. LAUDERDALE 1970; RENO 1971
SAVAGE, JOB	999	RENO 2023
SCHUTTE, RAY	11	RENO 1982–1986, 1988–92
SCHMIDT, C.J.	70	RENO 1986; SEE NOTE ON #70
SCOTT, MIKE	7	RENO 2017
SEBBY, FRED	14, 15, 21, 35	MOJAVE 1973–76; RENO 1973, 1975, 2006
SHELTON, GREG	42	PHOENIX 1994
SIEGFRIED, RICHARD	87, 736	RENO 2000–02, 2004, 2014; TUNICA 2005
SIEGFRIED, RICK	5, 21, 33, 94, PP	RENO 2006, 2010–11, 2019, 2023
SILBERMAN, JOHN	89	WILSON 1971
SIMONSON, BARRIE	75,	RENO 1973–75
SINGER, AARON	388	RENO 2023
SISK, MICHAEL	19	RENO 2023
SKELTON, BETTY	45, 79	CLEVELAND 1947, 1949
SMOOT, SHERMAN	86	RENO 1991–97; PHOENIX 1994; SHAFTER 1996
SOMES, JASON	1	RENO 2005–06
SNYDER, ED	99	RENO 1969; ST. LOUIS 1969–70; CLEVELAND 1969; FT. LAUDERDALE 1969–70; WILSON 1970–71; JACKSONVILLE 1971; CAPE MAY 1971
STAVRIDES, PETE	9	RENO 2016–18
STEPHENS, C.J.	79	RENO 1987
STINNETT, JOEL	43	RENO 2021–23
STIRWALT, JIM	46	RENO 1975; MOJAVE 1976
STOKES, CHAN	8	MOJAVE 1975–76; RENO 1975–76; LINCOLN 1976
STONICH, LEONARD	66	RENO 1984
STOVER, EUGENE	37	RENO 1972
STRANG, JAMES	12	FT. LAUDERDALE 1970; ST. LOUIS 1970; WILSON 1970–71; CAPE MAY 1971; JACKSONVILLE 1971
SUACCI, ROBERT	69	RENO 1969, 1971–74; MOJAVE 1973–75
SUKOSKY, MIKE	96	MOJAVE 1975–76, 1978; LINCOLN 1976; RENO 1976, 1978
SUTTERFIELD, KEVIN	42	RENO 2014–15
SWAYZE, GERALD	24, 24	RENO 1969, 1972–74; ST. LOUIS 1969; FT. LAUDERDALE 1970; GRAHAM 1973
SYKES, RICHARD	3, 14	RENO 1968–69, 1971–73, 1975–76, 1981–84, 1986; MOJAVE 1973–76, 1978–79
TANNER, LEN	55	CLEVELAND 1969; ST. LOUIS 1969
TAYLOR, JOE	41, 69	RENO 1986; RICHLAND 1986
TELLING, FRED	89	RENO 2002–05, 2007–08; TUNICA 2005

Name	Aircraft Race Number(s)	Location and Year(s) Raced
THEIS, SHANE	48	RENO 1986; RICHLAND 1986
THOMAS, JIM	26, 70	RENO 2001–09
TODOVERTO, JACK	71	RENO 1983
TOLLE, WES	31	SEE NOTE #31
TRAINOR, JOHN	21	RENO 1969; FT. LAUDERDALE 1969–70; ST. LOUIS 1969–70; CAPE MAY 1971; JACKSONVILLE 1971; GRAHAM 1973
TURNBULL, WILLIAM	70, 72	RENO 1969, 1971–75; FT. LAUDERDALE 1970; MIAMI 1973; GRAHAM 1973
TWOMBLY, RALPH	4, 41, 41, 41, 41, 42, 44	CLEVELAND 1969; FT. LAUDERDALE 1970, ST. LOUIS 1970; WILSON 1970–72; RENO 1971–78, 1981–83, 1987–88, 1993–94; CAPE MAY 1971; JACKSONVILLE 1971; MIAMI 1973; MOJAVE 1973–76, 1979; GRAHAM 1973; RICHLAND 1986; CASPER 1990; PHOENIX 1994
VAN FOSSEN, EDDIE	27	RENO 1984–94; WENDOVER 1988; CASPER 1990; REDMOND 1992; PHOENIX 1994; PASO ROBLES 1994
VAUGHN, THOM	58	RENO 2016–17
VOLKMER, LEO	33	RENO 1969; FT. LAUDERDALE 1969; ST. LOUIS 1969
WALKER III, WILLIAM	5	RENO 2018, 2023
WASHBURN, MARLIN	12	MOJAVE 1974–75; RENO 1974–75
WEINBERGER, DON	65	RENO 1972
WELLS, MARSHALL	9, 33	RENO 1974–79
WELLS, MIKE	42	RENO 1989
WHYTE, EDNA	42	CLEVELAND 1947
WILLIAMS, JAMES	5	RENO 1968–69
WILSON, JIM	10	GRAHAM 1973; RENO 1973–74; MIAMI 1973
WIMER, JACK	64	SEE NOTE ON #64
WIRTZ, FRANK	38, 57	RENO 1968–69, 1973
WOELBING, ERIC	2, 27	RENO 2015–18
WOODS, DUANE "CHIP"	22, 25, 56	RENO 2010–11, 2013, 2015
WRIGHT, DICK	77	RENO 1986
WRIGHT, MIKE	77	RENO 1981–85
YERSAK, RICHARD	23	RENO 1983
YORK III, BEN	21	RENO 2022–23
ZAYAC, JOHN	12, 37	RENO 2000–13, 2015; TUNICA 2005

Further Reading

Periodicals
Pacific Flyer, The
Southland Pilot, The
Western Flyer, The

Magazines
Aero News Photo
Air Progress
EAA Sport Aviation Magazine
Flight Journal
In Flight USA
Ninety-Nines Magazine, The
Plane & Pilot Magazine
Sport Aviation
Sport Flying

Newsletters and Reports
Air Racing
American Air Racing Society newsletter
Aviation newsletter
Golden Pylons, Society of Air Racing Historians
NARA PYLON+ newsletter
National Air-racing Group (NAG)
PRPA
W.A.S.P
Western Air Racing Quarterly

Federal Aviation Administration, aircraft record cards
National Transport Safety Board (NTSB) accident reports

Newspapers
Plain Dealer, The, Cleveland, Ohio
General Aviation News
Jacksonville Journal-Courier
Los Angeles Times
Miami Herald
Mojave Desert News
Nevada State Journal (online archive)
Reno Evening Gazette
Reno Gazette-Journal
Wilson Times, The

Official race programs and press kits
California National Air Races 1972–79
National Air Races 1946-49
National Championship Air Races 1964–2023
St. Louis National Air Races 1969
Phoenix 500 Air Races 1994

Books
American Aviation Historical Society, journals
"Gentlemen, You Have A Race", 1984, Wings Publishing Co, John Tegler
History's Most Important Racing Aircraft, 2013, Pen & Sword Aviation, Don Berliner
North American NA-16/AT-6/SNJ, Warbird Tech, Vol 11, 1997, Specialty Press, Dan Hagedorn
Racing Planes Guide, 1963, Sports Car Press, Joe Christy
Racing Planes and Air Races, Volumes 1–13, Aero Publishers Inc, Reed Kinert and Dusty Carter
T-6 Texan, The Immortal Pilot Trainer, 1991 Osprey Classic Aircraft, William Jesse
U.S. Military Aircraft Designations and Serials From 1909, 1979, Midland Publishing, John M Andrade
Warbirds Directory, various editions, Warbirds Worldwide in Britain, Geoff Goodall
Wet Wings & Drop Tanks, Recollections of American Transcontinental Air Racing 1928–1970, 1997, Schiffer Publishing Ltd, Birch Matthews

Unpublished work
Texan, North American Texan Series Civil Registration Numbers, unpublished manuscript, Malcom L. Gougon

Personal notes
Personal correspondence, Dustin "Dusty" Carter
Personal correspondence, Dan Hagedorn
Personal correspondence, Al Hansen
Personal correspondence, William T. Larkins

Personal observation notes, Robert Kennedy
Personal observation notes, Jerry Liang
Personal observation notes, Emil Strasser